# CONSTRAINTS ON STRATEGY

# Pergamon Titles of Related Interest

**Art, Davis & Huntington** REORGANIZING AMERICA'S DEFENSE
**Close** EUROPE WITHOUT DEFENSE
**Close** TIME FOR ACTION
**Dougherty & Pfaltzgraff** SHATTERING EUROPE'S DEFENSE CONSENSUS: The Antinuclear Protest Movement And The Future Of NATO
**Record** REVISING U.S. MILITARY STRATEGY
RUSI/BRASSEY'S DEFENCE YEARBOOK 1984
RUSI/BRASSEY'S DEFENCE YEARBOOK 1985
**Yost** NATO'S STRATEGIC OPTIONS

# Related Journals
(Free specimen copies available upon request.)

DEFENSE ANALYSIS

# CONSTRAINTS ON STRATEGY
## THE ECONOMICS OF WESTERN SECURITY

Edited by
# David B. H. Denoon

**PERGAMON-BRASSEY'S**
International Defense Publishers, Inc.

Washington  New York  London  Oxford
Beijing  Frankfurt  São Paulo  Sydney  Tokyo  Toronto

Pergamon Press Offices:

**U.S.A.** (Editorial)  Pergamon-Brassey's International Defense Publishers, 1340 Old Chain Bridge Road, McLean, Virginia 22101

(Orders & Inquiries)  Pergamon Press, Maxwell House, Fairview Park, Elmsford, New York 10523, U.S.A.

**U.K.** (Editorial)  Brassey's Defence Publishers, Maxwell House, 74 Worship Street, London EC2A 2EN

(Orders & Enquiries)  Brassey's Defence Publishers, Headington Hill Hall, Oxford OX3 0BW, England

**PEOPLE'S REPUBLIC OF CHINA**  Pergamon Press, Qianmen Hotel, Beijing, People's Republic of China

**FEDERAL REPUBLIC OF GERMANY**  Pergamon Press, Hammerweg 6, D-6242 Kronberg, Federal Republic of Germany

**BRAZIL**  Pergamon Editora, Rua Eça de Queiros, 346, CEP 04011, São Paulo, Brazil

**AUSTRALIA**  Pergamon Press (Aust.) Pty., P.O. Box 544, Potts Point, NSW 2011, Australia

**JAPAN**  Pergamon Press, 8th Floor, Matsuoka Central Building, 1-7-1 Nishishinjuku, Shinjuku-ku, Tokyo 160, Japan

**CANADA**  Pergamon Press Canada, Suite 104, 150 Consumers Road, Willowdale, Ontario M2J 1P9, Canada

---

**Copyright © 1986 Pergamon-Brassey's International Defense Publishers, Inc.**

*All rights reserved. No part of this publication may be reproduced, stored in a retrieval system or transmitted in any form or by any means: electronic, electrostatic, magnetic tape, mechanical, photocopying, recording or otherwise, without permission in writing from the publishers.*

First printing 1986

Library of Congress Cataloging in Publication Data
Main entry under title:

Constraints on strategy.

    Bibliography: p.
    1. North Atlantic Treaty Organization--Armed Forces--Appropriations and expenditures--Addresses, essays, lectures. I. Denoon, David.
UA646.3.C64   1986   355'.031'091821   85-28356
ISBN 0-08-033139-4

***Printed in the United States of America***

# Contents

| | | |
|---|---|---|
| Preface | | vii |
| Chapter | | |
| 1. | The Context<br>*David B. H. Denoon* | 1 |
| 2. | Increase in Defense Expenditure and Its Impact on the U.S. Economy<br>*M. Ishaq Nadiri* | 27 |
| 3. | Defense Burdens and Prospects for the Northern European Allies<br>*Todd Sandler and James C. Murdoch* | 59 |
| 4. | Defense, Growth, and Allocation Behavior in the Alliance: The Southern Tier of NATO<br>*Kevin Forbes, George Korsun, and Martin McGuire* | 114 |
| 5. | Japan and South Korea<br>*Walter Galenson and David W. Galenson* | 152 |
| 6. | Conclusions: Economic Constraints and U.S. Defense Policy in the 1980s<br>*David B. H. Denoon* | 195 |
| Bibliography | | 222 |
| Index | | 245 |
| About the Editor and Contributors | | 253 |

# Preface

This book is designed to address three broad issues:

1. What will be the likely economic performance for the United States and its principal allies in the next 3 – 5 years?
2. What useful generalizations can be made about the relationship between economic performance and defense spending in these countries?
3. How will these economic factors shape defense options in the remainder of this decade?

To approach these questions we have divided the analysis into four country groupings: (a) the United States, (b) Britain, France, and West Germany, (c) Portugal, Spain, Greece, and Turkey, and (d) Japan and South Korea.

The questions above are clearly very broad and complex, and any forecasting will involve considerable uncertainty as well. Nevertheless, we have tried to organize the data and analysis in a manner that will help the reader draw his own conclusions even if he disagrees with our assumptions. We have also tried to make the analysis as systematic as possible so that one can do a comparative review of the basic factors shaping performance in each of the ten countries studied.

It is worth commenting on why we grouped the countries as we did. In the past few years, there has been a growing literature assessing the European versus Pacific interests of the United States. If one counts all of U.S. defense expenditures as part of NATO, then the United States is providing about 60 percent of NATO's total military spending.* Britain, France, and West Germany *each* contribute about 10% of NATO's total, while all the other members of NATO *combined* account for the remaining 10 percent of NATO's total defense spending.

Thus, the future of NATO depends primarily on what the United States, Britain, France, and West Germany decide to do. If these three principal European members of NATO have poor economic performance and are not able to agree on a vi-

---

*Obviously, counting all of U.S. defense expenditures as part of NATO overstates the forces directly committed to the European theatres. Nevertheless, Western Europe certainly benefits from U.S. defense spending in such areas as the South Atlantic, the Persian Gulf region and even the Pacific. Moreover, Soviet military expenditures in South Asia and the Far East are counted as part of Warsaw Pact spending. This means that most NATO – Warsaw Pact spending ratios represent global rather than European theatre comparisons.

able defense program, then even rapid growth on the periphery of NATO cannot compensate for stagnation at its core. Nevertheless, Portugal, Spain, Greece, and Turkey are each critical to NATO because of their geographic location; and, fortunately, their military requirements can be met with far smaller expenditures than are necessary for Britain, France, and West Germany.

If Western European economic performance is poor during the next decade, the United States will face difficult choices. There are strong indications that U.S. trade and investment in the Pacific will grow rapidly and the conventional force balance in the Pacific is still favorable to the United States and its allies. If Western Europe stagnates, it will be hard to resist a shift of U.S. attention to the Pacific.

The intent of this book is to provide a balanced, quantitative evaluation of what future U.S. options actually are. We have not estimated the cost of specific military strategies but do demonstrate that the United States, Japan, and South Korea can all continue to spend modestly increasing amounts for defense without any serious negative effects on their economies. However, the West Europeans have substantially slower growth rates, have far greater structural rigidities in their economies, and seem to be making fewer of the adjustments (development of new industries, increasing labor productivity, and rewarding technical innovation) necessary to regain high levels of economic growth.

One major problem we faced was in evaluating the potential positive spin-off effects (like stimulating research and development) that can come from defense spending. Although M. I. Nadiri was able to draw on some studies about this for the United States and K. Forbes, G. Korsun, and M. McGuire did some estimates of these effects for Portugal, Spain, Greece, and Turkey, we have not found enough quantitative material to make systematic generalizations across all the countries studied. Thus, to the extent that we have focused on the "burden of funding national security," we have almost certainly overestimated the net costs of defense because most of the positive spin-offs have been excluded.

An additional objective of this volume is to focus greater attention on the macroeconomic factors shaping defense choices. Most of the defense economics literature is applied micro work, often looking at comparisons of specific weapons systems. This research highlights why economic constraints will be increasingly prominent in shaping alliance strategy and military doctrine in the next decade.

There have been four major developments since the final drafting of these chapters (June 1985) which could have significant effects on the conclusions of this volume: (1) the Reagan – Gorbachev Summit and the possibility of tangible results in U.S. – Soviet arms control efforts, (2) the precipitous drop in the world price of oil, (3) the growth of trade restrictions and increasing protectionist sentiment among the industrial democracies, and (4) the passage of the Gramm – Rudman legislation which certainly heralds the end of the Reagan administration's dramatic expansion of defense expenditures. Although none of these developments vitiate the basic themes of this volume, it is worth sketching out how they may affect our results.

# PREFACE

The *Reagan – Gorbachev Summit* has unquestionably changed the climate of U.S. – Soviet relations. Developing a model of Soviet motivations and Warsaw Pact actions was beyond the scope of this book. We thus assumed that the Soviet Union would continue its pattern of the past three decades and steadily expand its military outlays by 2 to 4 percent in real terms each year and that it would attempt to expand its influence wherever practical in the developing countries. If the Reagan – Gorbachev dialogue actually produces concrete results (such as significant reductions in strategic arms, force reductions in Europe, and reduced U.S. – Soviet competition in the developing countries), then clearly Western Europe could be less concerned about the NATO – Warsaw Pact military balance and the strains resulting from defense spending could be mitigated. Since we don't know what the results of the Reagan – Gorbachev talks will be and since the Soviet Union steadily expanded its defense capabilities during the period of "detente" in the 1970s, it is clearly premature to say what NATO's strategy should be.

The *drop in the spot oil price* from about $25 per barrel in November 1985 to approximately $15 per barrel in February 1986 (due predominantly to an increase in Saudi Arabian production of 2 million barrels per day) is a major boon to all the U.S allies discussed in this volume except Britain. As long as the oil price stays in its present range, economic growth rates of the major oil importers should increase. Most of the major macro-economic modelers have increased their forecasts of European GNP growth rates by about .5% per year, and it might have even more positive effects on Japan and South Korea. Increasing growth rates should make defense easier to fund, but it is worth noting that, because Japan and South Korea will grow relatively faster than Western Europe, the United States will still face the dilemma of how to balance European versus Pacific interests.

The *growing protectionist sentiment* could have both political and economic reverberations relevant to security policy. Since most of the pro-Western Pacific nations are also export-oriented, attempts by the United States and Western Europe to restrict imports will not only slow the growth rates of the exporters, but reduce the attractiveness of alliance relationships as well. If Western Europe and U.S. GNP growth rates improve, protectionist pressures are likely to abate, but this issue merits attention nonetheless.

The *Gramm – Rudman legislation* is critical to the themes of this volume because it is yet another sign that the U.S. defense build-up in the 1980s is coming to an end. It is too early to know if the Congress will permit small increases in defense spending or whether defense allocations will actually be frozen or cut. Yet, from the standpoint of allied planning, it is obvious that future improvements in allied military capability will need to come from better strategy and tactics or increases in spending by Western Europe and the Pacific nations. The U.S. force structure and readiness levels in 1986 are probably very close to what they will be in the 1990s.

In doing a large, multinational study of this type, many people provided helpful assistance and I want to express my appreciation to them. Early discussions with

Andrew Marshall, William Kaufman, David Chu, and Richard Kugler were vital in helping to shape this research. Financial support from New York University and the Office of Net Assessment in the U.S. Department of Defense was also most helpful. As the work proceeded, Richard Armitage, David Epstein, David Abshire, Dennis Kloske, Arthur Burns, Michel Albert, and Keith Hartley all had useful suggestions. Thanks also go to Elizabeth Rosenthal, Christos Thomas, Anthea Parkinson, Karen Garner-Lipman, and Dolores Scott who provided research assistance and administrative support. Special thanks go to Catherine Labio who not only provided excellent multilingual research assistance but considerable help in the editing process as well. Also, as the editor and director of the initial project which led to this book, I want to express my regards to the country authors for the very cooperative fashion in which the effort developed. Finally, I want to thank Dr. Franklin Margiotta, Director of Publishing at Pergamon-Brassey's, for his encouragement and numerous suggestions as the final drafting and editing proceeded.

*David B. H. Denoon*
February, 1986

# Chapter 1
# The Context

David B. H. Denoon

## THE AMERICAN DILEMMA

On December 26, 1979, the Soviet Union began its invasion of Afghanistan. This move shocked both foreign policy specialists and the general public in the Western democracies because it was so massive, brazen, and unanticipated. The long saga of the American hostages in Iran and the failure in April 1980 of the "Desert 1" rescue mission raised further doubts about U.S. resolve and military capabilities.

These two dramatic and much publicized events, however, had actually followed a sizable series of Western reversals in the developing countries. During the 1970s, the U.S. withdrawal from South Vietnam ultimately led to North Vietnamese control of all of Indochina; India signed a Friendship Treaty with the U.S.S.R.; Iran had become virulently anti-American; South Yemen and Ethiopia became active bases for Soviet operations; Mozambique and Angola and subsequently Nicaragua and Grenada all became Marxist regimes.

What most of the American public did not know was that, in the decade between 1969 and 1978, real U.S. defense spending declined[1] and this had significantly affected the readiness and sustainability of U.S. forces. The 1980 presidential campaign highlighted some of these issues and both candidates made commitments to major increases in defense spending.[2]

This sequence of external and internal events made the American public more aware of the fundamental debates on U.S. and alliance defense policy that had been going on among specialists since the mid-1970s when the Soviet Union had achieved rough parity in strategic weapons.[3] There has also been a broader public recognition that the Soviet conventional force buildup has been broad-ranging and relentless.[4] Since 1980, as the SS-20s were deployed, there has been additional concern about the Intermediate-range Nuclear Force (INF) balance.[5]

The Western debates on how to deal with the rapidly changing East-West military competition have had several major components:

1. uncertainty about military strategy;

2. growing political concerns about the viability of the Atlantic Alliance; and

3. markedly different views on the economic effects of the increased defense spending needed to respond to the Soviet force expansion.

This book will not be able to deal with all these interrelated issues; instead, it will focus on how economic factors shape defense policy. Also, our intent is to show which economic issues are most likely to affect the U.S. government as its long-run national security strategy evolves. To make the analysis manageable, we have divided the work into four geographic regions: (a) the United States, (b) Britain, France, and West Germany, (c) Portugal, Spain, Greece, and Turkey, and (d) Japan and South Korea. These are the principal contributing nations to the North Atlantic Treaty Organization (NATO) and the U.S. security alliances in the Pacific.[6] Thus, the performance of these countries will be key determinants of future U.S. alliance relationships and strategy.

## MILITARY DEBATES

The military debates in the West have developed from the unsettling recognition that there is an imbalance between the West's strategy and its capabilities. Put in highly simplified fashion, the United States and its allies can no longer be confident in the efficacy of threats to escalate to the use of nuclear weapons should a conventional conflict be going badly. Some analysts have emphasized the problems of military tactics,[7] others have stressed the issue of alliance cohesion.[8] The question of appropriate technology has also gotten considerable attention,[9] and there are grave worries about how the evolving military balance will affect the internal politics of the NATO countries.[10]

In the 1950s and 1960s, the United States had such a predominance over the Soviet Union in strategic delivery systems, that the U.S. nuclear guarantee was credible. In fact, there is reasonable evidence that Khrushchev backed down during the Cuban missile crisis precisely because the Soviet Union had insufficient conventional forces in the region or strategic forces to credibly threaten to escalate.[11] At that time, the United States could clearly dominate any escalation process.[12]

With the SALT I accords, the United States agreed to limit its strategic systems and accept a process enabling the U.S.S.R. to move up to rough parity.[13] Although this was originally seen as a stabilizing measure because it reduced the chance of either side risking nuclear escalation, the attention of specialists soon turned to the conventional force balance in Europe. As the Warsaw Pact countries have maintained a predominance of conventional forces for three decades, the basic issue has become: if the NATO threat to escalate using nuclear weapons is no longer credible, will the outcome of a conflict be determined by conventional forces?

General Bernard Rogers, the present NATO Commander in Europe, has claimed that, if a major conflict develops in Europe, NATO forces are adequate to last only approximately one week, and that he would have to request authority to use nuclear weapons early in the fighting.[14] The NATO member governments would thus face a dilemma: since a strategic interchange between the United States and the U.S.S.R. is almost certainly unwinnable, should they risk escalating to the INF level where the Soviet SS-4s, SS-5s, and SS-20s would be daunting?[15] Or should they continue to fight at the conventional level where it might be months before the NATO forces could reverse the Warsaw Pact momentum?[16] The danger of deciding to fight a conventional war in Western Europe for many months is that it is likely to be conducted in the highly urbanized areas of the North German plain and the Low Countries. Even if NATO could ultimately be successful at driving back the Warsaw Pact forces, the devastation wrought in the intervening period would be extensive. Therefore, there would be considerable pressure on the NATO governments to compromise rather than adhere to a prolonged conventional war strategy.

Obviously, the principal goal of NATO is to have an adequate deterrent so that a major conflict never breaks out. Although there is an extensive literature on the problems involved in the making of force comparisons,[17] there is a heated debate about the precise current NATO/Warsaw Pact balance,[18] this leading to a broad and growing consensus among Western defense specialists that steps must be taken to redress the military balance in the European theater.[19]

Why is there so much less concern about developments in the Pacific? Although the Soviet Union has deployed SS-20s in the Far East and now has access to air and naval bases in Vietnam, the conventional military balance in the Pacific still favors the United States and its allies. A combination of political and geographic factors is vital in evaluating the Pacific balance. The current relaxed relations between the United States, Japan, and China pose a formidable obstacle for Soviet planners. Continued tension between China and the Soviet Union has led the latter to devote substantial assets to its eastern military districts.[20] Moreover, Soviet naval access to the Pacific Ocean via the Sea of Japan and Sea of Okhotsk is easily monitored from the Japanese home islands and the Kurile islands.

The principal concerns about Soviet military power in Asia stem from the growth of Soviet INF (SS-20s and Backfire bombers), frontal aviation, and submarines. However, if China and Japan pursue their current course and the South Koreans maintain their level of preparedness against North Korea, Soviet options in Northeast Asia are limited.

In Southeast Asia, the Soviet alliance with Vietnam is a major military asset and Soviet aid has been critical in supporting Vietnam's domination of Laos and Kampuchea. Yet, the cohesiveness of the other countries of Southeast Asia[21] has constrained opportunities for the expansion of Soviet influence.

Thus, if there were to be a global conventional conflict, the Soviet Union would find itself in a far better relative position in Europe than in Asia. The question for the United States and its allies is how to maintain this advantage in the Pacific theater if the U.S.S.R. continues its rapid and steady growth in military spending. The South Koreans already carry a very significant military burden and the principal attention has therefore focused on how Japan will modernize and improve its self-defense capabilities.

The Japanese National Defense Program Outline in 1976 set explicit (though inadequate)[22] standards for air and naval capabilities and these were expanded in the 1981 Mid-Term Defense Program Estimate. However, there is still major controversy inside Japan about which military strategies are both effective and unprovocative.[23] Debates about the character of U.S.–Japanese relations are incessant[24] but substantially less emotional than in the 1960s.

From a global perspective, U.S. policy planning needs to design steps that will preserve the favorable balance in the Pacific, avoid any further erosion of influence in the Middle East, and reverse the unfavorable conventional balance in Europe. The U.S./NATO relationship has thus received a veritable torrent of proposals for improvement. The suggestions for enhancing Western European military security can be divided into four broad categories:

1. arms control agreements with the U.S.S.R. and the Warsaw Pact;

2. expanding NATO conventional forces;

3. modifying and improving Western INF;

4. changing NATO strategy.

Many *advocates of arms control* believe not only that arms limitation helps stabilize military competition but that it also can be a means of reducing military spending. After the Soviet withdrawal from the Intermediate Nuclear Force (INF) talks and the discontinuation of Soviet participation in the Strategic Arms Reduction Talks (START) in November 1983, there was little optimism in the West about arms talks having any substantive effect on NATO or Warsaw Pact behavior. Yet, after a long period of mutual public recriminations during 1984, the United States and the Soviet Union agreed to reconvene arms talks in Geneva in three separate but related forums dealing respectively with space weapons, strategic arms, and intermediate nuclear forces. Supporters of the arms control process have been somewhat encouraged during 1985 and continue to urge that the security of both East and West can be improved through stable arms agreements.[25] The November 1985 Geneva Summit and subsequent Gorbachev proposal for a phased elimination of all nuclear weapons has created further public optimism about arms control.

There is a sizable number of skeptics, however, who think that the Soviet Union used the period after the SALT I accords and the initiation of détente to further strengthen its dominant military position in Europe.[26] The more pragmatic members of the arms control community have thus focused their attention on proposals that might increase stability without requiring comprehensive agreements.[27] In strategic weapons, the concept of having the United States and Soviet Union destroy two old warheads for every new one deployed[28] has gained key adherents, and there is a growing literature on nonmilitary means to reduce incentives for aggression.[29]

The West German Social Democratic Party has taken a slightly different track. In reformulating the Party's position on security matters, the SPD has urged that West Germany should unilaterally give up all its systems which can be used for offensive operations and try to limit arms competition by having just a defensive conventional capability.[30] Clearly, none of these arms control strategies would satisfy those who think that the Soviet Union will only respect greater military capability on the part of the West.

Proposals to *expand NATO's conventional forces* have a long history. Since the late 1950s, when dissatisfaction with the doctrine of "massive retaliation" became widespread, there have been numerous suggestions to develop a doctrine for dealing with limited war[31] and to create sufficient conventional forces to "flexibly respond"[32] and avoid quick escalation to nuclear weapons. Although Western defense analysts have long been able to agree on the advantages of expanding NATO's conventional forces, few of the member countries have been willing to spend the extra resources necessary to field more manpower and maintain higher levels of readiness. The Carter administration made a major effort in this regard, however, and in 1978 prevailed upon the NATO member countries to agree to the "long-term defense program" which called for an expanded force structure and an average annual 3 percent real growth in members' defense expenditures.[33] The United States is the only country to consistently meet this pledge. General Rogers has, therefore, urged a new commitment for all members to pledge a 4 percent real growth in defense allocations.[34] Should these resources be available, they would give the NATO commander a stronger defense in the forward areas (along the East German border) and more confidence that a Warsaw Pact conventional thrust could be contained without nuclear weapons. The question is whether the financing will be provided.

*Improving the Intermediate Nuclear Forces (INF)* has also been given considerable attention. As the Soviet Union began its deployment of SS-20s, the Western European governments began to look for an adequate response. In 1979, at the request of Chancellor Helmut Schmidt of West Germany, the United States and other members of Nato agreed to a "two track approach" on modernizing INF. The approach was: (a) to proceed with U.S.–Soviet negotiations on limiting INF, but (b) to be prepared to deploy U.S. controlled Pershing II and Ground Launched Cruise Missiles (GLCM) in four years if the negotiations failed. By November 1983, the INF negotiations with the Soviet Union had still not produced any tangible results, and the Pershing II and GLCM deployments began.

Many Western strategists have seen theater nuclear and INF weapons as a cost-effective middle range of options[35] but ones that could lead to higher levels of escalation. French defense analysts, on the other hand, have consistently argued that the threat of nuclear devastation is the most effective deterrent,[36] and, not suprisingly, that French independence (within a broad Western defense framework) creates further uncertainties for the Soviets should a conflict develop. Although there was some hope in the 1979–1983 period that both NATO and the Warsaw Pact might agree to substantially reduce INF, it now appears that INF will be a key part of the European military balance for the indefinite future.

*Making basic changes in NATO strategy and tactics* is an alternative means for coping with the Warsaw Pact buildup. The most widely discussed tactical initiative was the effort launched by the Carter administration to achieve "rationalization, standardization, and interoperability" (RSI). This program was designed to permit greater flexibility and maneuver in battlefield situations by ensuring that the different national forces that comprise NATO would have interchangeable equipment and ammunition. As an incentive to encourage RSI, the United States offered its NATO partners attractive terms on the coproduction and codevelopment of new weapons systems.[37]

A more dramatic change in strategy is the concept of "deep interdiction." The essence of this approach is to deny the Warsaw Pact the freedom to choose both the timing and character of its attack.[38] By planning to fly over the main battle areas and attack the second and third echelons of the Warsaw Pact forces as they gather in East Germany and Poland, NATO would not only be extending the battlefield and causing disarray but limiting the number of reserves that could get to the front as well.[39]

Others have proposed a different "division of labor" among the NATO countries. As the United States is well-stocked with fighter and attack aircraft, and planes can be moved more quickly than large numbers of troops, it is conceivable that the Western European countries might be willing to spend less on their air forces and more on their armies if they knew that the United States would provide adequate air cover.[40]

Another approach is to rely on the West's comparative advantage and use some of the latest developments in remote sensing, signal processing, and real-time target identification to increase the efficiency of NATO conventional systems. The United States has offered NATO a number of newly developed systems, referred to as the "emerging technologies," as a further inducement to adopt integrated equipment, communications, and intelligence systems.[41]

There are also some advocates of reorienting NATO's goals away from defense so that it would actually be possible to attack into Czechoslovakia and East Germany.[42] Like the concept of "deep interdiction," this might create greater uncertainty among Warsaw Pact planners about NATO's actions – thus forcing the Pact to keep more divisions in reserve and reducing their strength in the forward battle areas.

The most dramatic change in strategy could come from the eventual deployment of space-based defensive systems. If the Reagan administrations's proposed Strategic Defense Initiative (SDI) proves workable and is funded, it would reduce the potential effectiveness of Soviet offensive missiles.[43] A host of questions would then certainly arise: Would this reduce U.S. concerns about defending Western Europe? Would blunting the effectiveness of strategic missiles increase the salience of conventional forces? Are the funds required for the SDI to be in addition to planned conventional force budgets or would they lead to reduced Western conventional capabilities? At present, there is insufficient information to judge the likely effects of the SDI, but if it were deployed in any of the large-scale configurations proposed, its impact would overwhelm the more limited suggestions for changes in tactics like RSI and the "new division of labor" between the United States and Western Europe.

Each of these options requires decisions on funding and burden-sharing among the allies. Thus, the choice of direction not only includes questions of military strategy but domestic political and economic constraints as well. Our objective in this research has been to determine how economic performance will define one set of constraints. In the concluding chapter of this volume, we will return to the military options and discuss the relationship between these European options and the global issues facing the United States. However, all the plausible options – other than the arms control proposals – require a sizable increase in NATO military expenditures.

## U.S. ALLIANCE PROBLEMS

The debates about U.S. alliances are intertwined with choices about military options but are even broader as they encompass the entire set of issues about how to organize security and what U.S. obligations are to countries unwilling or unable to adequately defend themselves. A legitimate question for Americans to ask is: How did the United States get itself into the current alliance relationships?

In fact, in the last decade there has been a growing chorus of complaints about U.S. alliances. During the 1976 presidential campaign, candidate Carter proposed to cut U.S. troops in South Korea;[44] Defense Secretaries Schlesinger and Brown have been critical of Japan's small contribution to its own defense; the Congress has shown dissatisfaction with developments through the Culver/Nunn,[45] Stevens,[46] and Nunn Amendments;[47] and Henry Kissinger has recently said, "The present controversies in NATO are both unprecedented and unsettling."[48]

There is, of course, a distinguished tradition in American history of skepticism about alliances. The Monroe Doctrine of 1823 was designed to avoid European involvement in the Americas, and the bitter senatorial debate over ratifications of the Treaty of Versailles in 1919 reaffirmed a position of U.S. isolation that was not overcome until the Lend-Lease bill in December 1940. The Vietnam War also led to a crescendo of criticism of U.S. overseas involvement, with some arguing that U.S. bungling was the danger[49] and others asserting that the United States was trying to impose an unsustainable, imperial design on the world.[50]

All the principal U.S. alliances, however, were created between 1949 and 1954.[51] It was during this period that the hopes for a post-World War II rapprochement with the Soviet Union were shattered. The intellectual basis for these alliances was pragmatism. Observers like Walter Lippmann stressed that the United States should strive to protect democracy and Western values, but that predictability and self-interest, not moralism, should motivate alliances.[52]

George Kennan was the principal architect of the approach that has been the centerpiece of U.S. foreign policy since 1947. Though some U.S. presidents lost sight of the limited nature of his recommendations, Kennan diagnosed the historical and cultural factors likely to make the Soviet Union an expansionist power, and urged that the United States take the necessary economic, political, and military steps to ensure that Western Europe and Japan were not drawn under Soviet influence.[53] Kennan's construct deftly incorporated both Mackinder's focus on the importance of the Eurasian landmass[54] and Mahan's emphasis on controlling sea lines of communication.[55] The initial, narrow concept of "containment" thus concentrated on keeping the major centers of industrial strength with the West while preserving U.S. and British dominance of the seas.

The Marshall Plan, the NATO alliance, and the bilateral treaties with Spain, Japan, and South Korea were all a logical outgrowth of the desire to limit long-run Soviet economic and military capabilities. Subsequent commitments by the United States to the SEATO and CENTO treaties and to large aid programs in the Middle East, Africa, and Latin America expanded "containment" to regions of less immediate geopolitical significance.

Interestingly, many of the concerns expressed today about the viability of the Atlantic Alliance were also the subject of controversy in the late 1940s as NATO took shape. For example, the Europeans pressed for joint consultations to avoid unilateral U.S. actions, and were reluctant to show confidence in U.S. policy partly because "of their embarrassing degree of dependence on the U.S."[56]

The initial military goals for NATO also sound remarkably close to current objectives. The four principal needs identified in 1949 were: (a) developing sufficient ground forces to hold off a Soviet attack, (b) maintaining adequate air power to control the air space over Western Europe, (c) having effective strategic air power to retaliate inside the U.S.S.R., and (d) controlling of the air and sea lanes between North America and Europe.[57]

There was also an intense debate over strategy. Advocates of "strategic bombing" argued that the United States should rely on its clear technological lead in destructiveness (atomic weapons), range of aircraft (B-36), and future strengths (rocket development).[58] There was, nevertheless, uncertainty about the optimal deterrent, and a recognition that there was a trade-off between funds used for defensive ground forces versus retaliatory strategic air capability.[59]

The links between political and military objectives were also explored. Many analysts thought that the most serious Soviet threat was subversion rather than overt aggression,[60] leading to an early emphasis on the interaction between economic recovery and political stability in Western Europe. The establishment of the World Bank, the International Monetary Fund, and the Marshall Plan provided a framework for economic expansion; then, as now, economic expansion was viewed as a prerequisite for creating a cohesive alliance.[61]

From the 1940s on, however, there appears to have been a fundamental difference between European and American perspectives on the function of NATO. Although, clearly, there are exceptions to these generalizations, the Europeans have usually stressed the need for political cohesion and minimal military deterrence. In simplified terms, the European view is that direct Warsaw Pact attack is unlikely and the West must demonstrate that it has the ability to eventually repel an invasion by making use of its resources, technology, and economic strength once its forces are fully mobilized.

The American perspective does not disregard the benefits of political unity but focuses more on military assets. In essence, many American analysts of NATO have argued that what has deterred the Warsaw Pact is the knowledge that the West could respond with sufficient punitive strength so that an attack involved exceptional risk.

During the period 1949–1972 when the United States had a clear advantage over the U.S.S.R. in strategic weapons, the differences between the U.S. and European views on NATO could be smoothed over by saying that they were designed to pursue distinct but complementary goals. However, after the United States gave up its strategic lead, the threat to retaliate in the Soviet homeland lost much of its plausibility as a NATO option because that would almost certainly lead to a Soviet response on U.S. soil. Given the presumed superpower preference for avoiding strategic interchanges, the actual military balance and war-fighting capability in Central Europe has thus become critical for determining the credibility of NATO's deterrent.

Because it has been forty years since there was war in Europe, many nonspecialists have discounted problems in the Atlantic Alliance. At the other extreme, there are commentators who have claimed to identify a crisis in NATO in each of the last four decades.[62] Thus, there are several good reasons to believe that the Alliance warrants intense scrutiny now:

1. unfavorable changes in the Warsaw Pact – NATO military balance during the last decade are widely acknowledged;[63]

2. uncertainty about appropriate strategy produces suspicion among the NATO partners;[64]

3. because fundamental issues of strategy are undetermined, long-run plans for manpower and equipment procurement are unsettled.[65]

These alliance debates lead inevitably to questions of how economic factors are shaping defense policy. Obviously in an era when West European per capita incomes are roughly comparable to income in the United States, there are questions in the minds of Americans about why they should allocate extra resources to shore up NATO. This situation is particularly galling when it is clear that the Europeans spend substantially less on defense.[66] Much of the writing on the economics of NATO has therefore been on this burden-sharing issue.[67] This book will deal with burden-sharing but will attempt to go beyond that debate and explain the setting in which economic policy will be made for the United States and its principal allies. We will then try to show how economic factors will affect the defense policy options available to the Western governments.

## THE ECONOMIC ISSUES

The military and alliance discussion above demonstrates that NATO faces fundamental problems of credibility. Now that the NATO members cannot rely on nuclear weapons as their ultimate threat, there is growing pressure to find alternative arrangements. For the United States, there is also the added problem of how to rank the relative importance of Europe, the Middle East, and the Pacific, and how to make a pragmatic assessment of which alliances will prove sustainable.

There are several basic themes that recur throughout this volume:

1. The NATO alliance is being undermined by indecision and lack of commitment to an adequate conventional defense capability.

2. The tendency of U.S. allies to rely on American guarantees is economically rational and will not change substantially unless the United States is willing to risk tension and fundamental alterations in its relations with allies.

3. In the 1970s and early 1980s, Western European economic performance lagged significantly behind that of the Pacific nations and the United States. Without major changes in policy, European economic performance will remain desultory.

4. To know how far the United States should go in pressing for greater equality in military burden-sharing, it is essential to identify what the economic costs of defense spending actually are and what the effects would be of varying levels of defense spending by the allies.

5. Military options must be tailored to economic reality. Although U.S. Secretaries of Defense and allied Defense Ministers have frequently agreed on targets for increases in defense spending, commitments have repeatedly not been lived up to. It could well be that the best long-run path for developing an adequate Western defense is through increasing economic growth. Therefore analysts need to look for the optimal blend of economic and military policies that are mutually reinforcing.

## Why Have Economic Issues Moved to Center Stage in Defense Policy?

There is no single explanation for the prominence of economic issues because the entire context in which defense policy is made has changed so drastically since 1949 when NATO was formed and since 1951 when the U.S.–Japan Security Treaty was signed. In the early 1950s, the economic, political, and military parts to these alliances were all mutually reinforcing. The United States was preeminent in the supply of both agricultural and manufactured goods, producing massive trade surpluses and the era of the "dollar shortage." The Marshall Plan and recovery loans to Japan helped raise living standards and facilitate rudimentary defense efforts, but they were pragmatic commercial policy as well.

By the 1960s the recovery efforts were complete, the United States no longer had assured trade surpluses,[68] and renewed nationalism in Europe caused France's withdrawal from the integrated military command of NATO and the initial blocking of British entry into the Common Market. The stresses on NATO were therefore predominantly political.

In the 1970s the entire constellation of U.S. alliances was subject to challenge. European distaste for the American involvement in Vietnam exacerbated political tension, the U.S. decisions to abandon the gold exchange standard and devalue the dollar were tangible signs of economic weakness, and, though the Europeans applauded the defense initiatives in the early 1970s, by the end of the decade there was growing concern about Warsaw Pact military advances.

Thus, in a period of three decades the key supporting elements of the Atlantic alliance all moved from favorable to adverse conditions. U.S. relations in the Pacific reached their nadir in 1975 as Americans ignominiously withdrew from Vietnam and there was anxiety over whether the United States would drop all its Pacific commitments. Yet, despite dire predictions, the presence of China as a military restraint on the U.S.S.R., the U.S. reaffirmation of its links to the region, and vibrant economic growth have all made Pacific relations less troubling than Atlantic ones.[69]

Making an overall judgment about alliance viability also requires an assessment of likely future trends. Here, Western European indexes are very disturbing. None of the principal econometric forecasting groups sees GNP growth as likely to be more than 2 – 3 percent for the remainder of the 1980s, unemployment will stay high because of the low economic growth rates,[70] and none of the Western European members of NATO has met the 1978 pledge for a 3 percent real growth in defense spending, calling into question the validity of future commitments.[71] It is also important to note that U.S. trade with Europe has consistently declined as a percentage of total U.S. trade, while Asian and Middle Eastern trade has increased in importance. For the United States, trans-Pacific trade surpassed trans-Atlantic trade in 1982.

There are also a host of European indicators, like low productivity growth, low investment rates, small amounts of venture capital, and short work weeks, that cast doubt on whether growth and innovation rates are likely to improve.[72] These quantitative indexes combined with extensive documentation of inefficient work rules, lack of mobility between jobs and locations, and concentration in older, slower-growing industries portend a stagnant European economic scene. Moreover, if social security and transfer payments are not curbed, it will be even harder to find capital available for investment and growth.[73]

These European patterns are critical for defense policy precisely because slow-growing countries face fractious political choices if they want to increase the quantity of resources devoted to a public good. There are already signs that French and West German proposals for changes in strategy are designed to appeal to their domestic arms industries rather than maximizing the effectiveness of NATO.[74]

Thus, even if one is prone to optimism, it is important to ask where the resources, capital, and innovation will come from to reverse the current European economic malaise. Although American emotional and political bonds to Europe are strong, it is essential that the U.S. government be pragmatic in deciding on its long-term military and political alliances. If Western European does not make significant policy changes, the disarray of the 1970s could continue and put insurmountable obstacles into the Atlantic alliance.

## How Have These Economic Issues Been Addressed Before?

The dominant assumption has been that decisions about defense expenditures should be seen as a choice between "guns and butter."[75] In fact, choices are vastly more complex than such a direct trade-off assumption implies. Often it is simply not the case, either politically or economically, that more defense spending means less of other goods[76] – or most especially less social spending.

*Guns versus Butter.* Advocates of the "guns versus butter" view argue that there are finite limits to the resources available to any society; funds devoted to defense cannot be used for consumption; and, therefore, societies face a choice between defense expenditures and social programs.

Although this reasoning is useful for macroeconomic discussions, there are several problems with it. First, it aggregates all defense expenditures and fails to distinguish the differential impact of spending for manpower from funds for research and development which frequently have major spin-off effects. Second, in the industrial democracies, during the past three decades, budgeting for defense and social services has generally been handled in separate arenas with limited direct competition.[77] Moreover, social spending has grown exponentially while defense expenditures have risen more modestly in real terms.[78]

Most importantly, though, the "guns versus butter" view has led many observers to assume that policy-makers should automatically try to minimize defense expenditures. Although there are certainly many examples of wasteful defense spending,[79] there is generally some definable level of defense capability which is necessary to protect national sovereignty. Numerous countries have underspent and ultimately suffered for it.[80] A current example where cost minimization has produced a risky and potentially destabilizing situation is the NATO decision to rely on nuclear weapons to redress the imbalance in conventional forces between Western Europe and the Warsaw Pact. As discussed above, had Western European governments been willing to spend more for conventional forces, a far broader range of non-nuclear options would be available should a conflict start.

What policy-makers should do is select an overall strategy which has an acceptable likelihood of protecting essential national interests. This answers the question: How much is enough?[81] Then, once the basic strategy has been selected, the choice turns to the least cost mix of political, economic, and military measures for implementing the strategy. Only last should there be decisions on the specific military force structure. Focusing at the outset on minimizing military expenditures may well lead to reduced options and even more costly political and economic substitutes.

Therefore, the basic approach of this book is to be skeptical of the "guns versus butter" trade-off as an organizing principle, and, instead, ask the question: What is the most efficient and least disruptive way of obtaining essential military capability? To respond to that question, we clearly need to evaluate the effects of alternative levels of defense spending on the economies of the United States and its key allies.

It is reasonable to divide the cluster of economic issues that concern us into three broad areas: (a) burden-sharing, (b) the effect of defense spending on macroeconomic variables such as GNP growth, inflation, employment, and trade balances, and (c) the microeffects of defense spending on specific sectors.

*Burden-Sharing.* Each of the chapters in this volume deals with this issue. Chapter 2 analyzes the effects on the U.S. economy of proceeding with the Reagan administration's defense buildup despite low defense spending and slow economic growth by the principal U.S. allies. Chapter 3 does extensive econometric estimation of the interactive relationship among the NATO allies as various members have increased or decreased their rates of defense spending. Chapter 4 explicitly deals with the question of whether defense spending impedes or accelerates growth and how the Southern European members of NATO have responded to varying levels of defense spending by their allies. Chapter 5 notes the very large differences between South Korea and Japan in levels of defense burden and estimates the macroeconomic effects of various future levels of defense spending.

The first major article to combine sophisticated economic theory with empirical work on U.S. alliance problems in the postwar period was by Olson and Zeckhauser.[82] By drawing on public goods theory[83] and rational behavior in coalitions,[84] they demonstrated that there is an inherent tendency for the smaller members of any alliance to underspend because the benefits are usually indivisible and it is difficult to apportion costs. It was hardly a new problem[85] and was followed by more precise theory[86] but it did explain the natural inclination of some members of the alliance to become "free riders" on the largesse provided by others.

The focus of more recent work on burden-sharing has been on improving the sensitivity of measures,[87] identifying non-quantitative means by which members can strengthen alliances,[88] noting some anomalies where small countries spend more than expected,[89] and analyzing the spill-over effects[90] when alliance members increase or decrease their defense spending. For our purposes, it is important to note that no single measure of expenditure is an adequate test of "bearing a fair burden" because per capita incomes vary. Also, it is often difficult to ascertain what part of defense expenditures can realistically be attributed to the alliance, and it is hard to quantify the military significance of steps like reducing dependence on imported raw materials.

It is also worth commenting that the "public perception" of a country's contribution may be quite different from the military judgment made. For example, the Mitterand government has taken a strongly anti-Soviet stance on several key foreign policy matters and has gotten favorable notices for the development of a "rapid action force,"[91] but the public is not generally aware that French spending on conventional forces has actually been cut significantly in real terms.[92]

*Macroeffects of Defense Spending.* One of the central concerns of this book is how defense spending affects macroeconomic performance. In terms of available resources, it is also critical to know the converse: how varying economic performance affects funds that governments are willing to allocate for defense. These questions cannot be answered precisely without a fully developed interactive model that shows the feedback relationships and articulates the budgeting process. Building models of that kind is beyond the scope of this book. Nevertheless, what we have done is to draw on extant models and make assumptions that we think are appropriate. It is fortunate that considerable quantitative modeling has been done on this subject for the United States and a modest amount for Britain, France, and West Germany. For Southern Europe, Japan, and South Korea, we have had to define our own specifications for the defense/economic performance interaction. Yet it is useful to review the work on which we drew.

*Growth* related to defense spending has long been a heated topic. The conventional approach among economists, strengthened by the "guns versus butter" analogy, has been to view defense budgets as serving a Keynesian demand-creating function but as limiting growth because expenditures were not investment and did not yield a future stream of income. Emile Benoit challenged this view and showed, in a quantitative study of 44 less developed countries (LDC) for the 1950 – 1965 period, that defense spending and growth were actually positively correlated.[93] Benoit gave several reasons he felt might explain this result: (a) the creation of infrastructure which could be used for both civilian and military purposes; (b) useful training that soldiers received with high defense spending frequently attracted large amounts of foreign aid; and (c) more secure countries provided a better environment for investment.

Attacking Benoit's findings has been a burgeoning industry among researchers.[94] What is important for our purposes is to define precisely those aspects of defense spending that have positive or negative effects on growth. Clearly, money spent for ammunition fired in target practice has no more stimulative effect on the economy than giving the same funds to an unemployed hunter so he can practice in his backyard. Making a balanced judgement on this topic requires assessing: (a) how fully resources are being utilized in the economy; (b) which resources (land, labor, or capital) the military is using; (c) what the spin-off effects are from military research and development;[95] and (d) whether the military expenditure succeeded in providing security so that other economic activities can proceed with assurance.

*Inflation* as a result of defense spending is also a topic that arouses emotion. In a flamboyant and unquantitative article, Lester Thurow has claimed that the Reagan administration's defense plans will wreck the U.S. economy.[96] More careful analysts have noted that inflationary effects depend upon capacity utilization,[97] the stage of the business cycle, and the means by which the spending is financed.[98] The U.S. Congressional Budget Office has done some detailed quantitative modeling on this subject and has distinguished between the general demand creating effects and the "cost-push" effects that may result in specific industries where there are sharp increases in procurement.[99]

*Employment* as related to defense spending is an issue that has been explored quantitatively over a considerable period of time.[100] Much of the work has been carried out by disarmament advocates, but it has formed a useful base for current studies. The thrust of the more recent work is to link country macromodels with input–output models that provide extensive detail on specific subsectors. The U.S. Department of Defense has developed its own Domestic Economic Impact Model Simulator (DEIMS),[101] efforts have been made to look at labor responses during expansions and contractions of defense spending,[102] and defense employment has been addressed as a global issue.[103]

*Trade* and defense spending have also received growing attention as exports of armaments have increased. The arms trade has been analyzed as a source of employment,[104] for its effects on growth,[105] and for its effects on the type of industry which governments favor.[106] There is little evidence that arms differ significantly from other capital goods exports in their economic effects. Yet, a decision to approve arms exports is a highly political one,[107] so that estimates of future magnitudes need to be made with reference to the political setting for the specific countries involved.

*Microeconomic Effects.* Each of the chapters deals with these effects in a slightly different fashion. The most quantitative sectoral material is available for the United

States. In Britain and France, it appears that the governments believe there are significant spin-off effects from nuclear technology, and it is clear that the Japanese and South Koreans are trying to maximize the technological gains from their armaments production. For the Turks, the military has both an employment-creating and job-training objective.

*Defense industry studies* have attracted considerable interest in the past decade both here and abroad. During the 1969 – 1978 period when U.S. defense expenditures actually declined in real terms, the focus was on the relationship between the prime contractors and their suppliers,[108] and how capable the industry would be to respond in a crisis.[109] More recent writing has continued to assess the health of the industry but has concentrated more on potential sectoral bottlenecks,[110] the problems of contracting in an oligopolistic industry,[111] and dependence on foreign suppliers.[112] A new and important issue is the debate over whether defense spending supplements or detracts from industrial competitiveness. Some observers have argued that Japan will gain a lead in consumer technology if the United States spends too heavily on military research and development[113] while others are convinced that military financing of communications, signal processing, and sensing technology will have as much beneficial effect on the economy as did the support provided in the 1950s for development of wide-bodied aircraft and large-scale computers.

Neo-Marxist writing on defense is rarely quantitative, usually hostile to Western defense efforts, and least persuasive when it focuses on military spending as a means to avoid a capitalist underconsumption crisis.[114] Where it has been interesting is in discussing the long-run structural effects on an economy of a large defense sector,[115] noting the cyclical nature of defense investment,[116] and analyzing how political strength affects government procurement.[117]

*Technological change* and defense spending do not make a well-developed subfield. There is ample evidence that technological change is a major explanatory factor in economic growth,[118] and there have been numerous attempts to explain the decline in growth and productivity in the United States in the 1970s.[119] As United States growth and productivity have now begun to increase again in the 1980s, there should ultimately be some interesting studies of the role (positive and negative) that increased defense spending played in that turnaround. A major concern of the present authors is the low rate of technological innovation and growth in Western Europe. Lacking clear, quantitative guidelines for evaluating the role of defense in technological change, we will try to explore the subject on a case-by-case basis where concrete evidence is available.

## THE APPROACH TAKEN IN THIS BOOK

As discussed above, the ideal way to choose a force structure is to decide on the optimal mix of economic, political, and military capabilities required and then to procure the military manpower and hardware in the most efficient manner. Knowing the likely purchase pattern, the economic effects could then be estimated. Although this is a useful exercise and a growing number of organizations carry out some variant of this, it remains essentially a theoretical approach. Not only are military manpower and equipment similar to civilian capital stock which typically changes very gradually, but, in parliamentary democracies, political constraints often determine both the type of systems and quantities that are purchased.

Both our NATO allies and the Japanese have successfully manipulated the U.S. policy-making process. The Europeans are indeed able to reduce their vulnerability to conventional attack, but it would require a substantial allocation of resources and it has been easier to find excuses for their predicament than to commit funds. Moreover, for 35 years the West Europeans have enjoyed much flexibility by being allowed to assume that the United States would make up the difference when they under-invest in defense.

The Japanese have chosen a slightly different variant of the Western European "free rider" strategy. In the post-World War II era, the Liberal Democratic Party and the civilian technocrats have stressed economic performance as the major national goal. This focus has been reassuring to Japan's neighbors and has reinforced the domestic constituency of the LDP. Having lost a fierce political struggle in the 1930s, the civilian technocrats and their business allies are strongly opposed to a strengthened military sector. Also, knowing that the United States did not favor Japanese rearmament in the 1950s and 1960s has provided the Japanese government with a convenient rationale for making only modest increases in defense expenditures in the 1970s and 1980s. The Japanese have thus correctly anticipated that the United States would make up the gap between what Japan feels comfortable with paying and what is adequate to defend the Japanese homeland.

In the United States there appears to be a more cyclical pattern in support of defense. Although the perception of American irresolution during the Iranian hostage crisis and during the early stages of the Soviet invasion of Afghanistan unquestionably created support for greater defense spending in the 1980–1983 period, it is reasonable to assume that the U.S. defense budget will face greater challenges in the future. Yet, there is little indication that our European allies are planning to relieve us of the obligation to defend them.

The situation poses some fundamental questions for U.S. policy: Is Western Europe still the most vital non-American area of U.S. strategic interest? What should the United States do if our allies continue to resist spending adequate amounts to defend themselves? If we ultimately modify our defense commitments to either Western Europe or Japan, how will this affect U.S. global strategy?

Responding to these questions clearly requires information from a number of perspectives. Economic factors are only one element. Nevertheless, it is important to know how significant a constraint economic performance will be. To know this requires a detailed, comparative assessment of likely economic performances by the United States and its allies during the remainder of this decade.

There are three central issues to be addressed in the book:

1. What will be the economic performance of the United States and its major allies in the next 3 – 5 years?
2. What is the relationship between alternative levels of defense spending and economic performance in these countries? How will they respond to the economic conditions they face now?
3. How should the United States respond to varying levels of economic performance and defense expenditures by our allies? What steps can the United States take to make it possible for the allies to more effectively defend themselves?

These questions clearly involve a complex set of issues and there will be considerable feedback as U.S. and allied actions affect one another, as do NATO and Warsaw Pact choices. As indicated earlier, to reduce this complexity to manageable proportions, we have divided the country studies into clusters of nations that have similar characteristics and will permit generalizations about their alliance relationships.

We have adjusted our research methods to the information obtainable for the specific countries. *For the United States* we are fortunate that there is a substantial literature and extensive modeling has been done on the interaction between defense spending and economic performance. M.I. Nadiri was thus able to draw on modeling done by DRI, Chase Econometrics, and Wharton School in addition to the Defense DEIMS model. The United States is also the most autonomous of the economies studied, so it is reasonable for the U.S. analysis to stand alone as a distinct case.

*Britain, France, and West Germany* clearly hold the key to NATO'S effectiveness and their contributions to the alliance are roughly comparable. Todd Sandler and James Murdoch have been able to use results from country macromodels but have also devoted considerable effort to exploring why these economies are foundering and what the spillover effects are from variations in levels of spending.

*Spain, Portugal, Greece, and Turkey* pose far more difficult data collection and modeling problems. Kevin Forbes, Martin McGuire, and George Korsun have thus developed their own model, particularly for testing the effects of defense spending on investment and growth.

*Japan and South Korea* are both rapidly growing, innovative economies. Walter and David Galenson have highlighted how different their defense burdens are and the advantages that both governments face in making defense choices in an environment where public resources can be expected to grow at a fast pace.

The responses to the questions posed above are clearly highly dependent upon the particular contingencies that develop. Yet, it is worthwhile analyzing options open to the United States, including: (a) means for accelerating economic growth among the allies; (b) methods for redistributing the indirect burdens of defense if there is an impasse over increasing direct expenditures; and (c) joint efforts at dealing with those allies who appear to face chronic economic difficulties.

The book will also bring a review of means for integrating military and economic programs so that they best complement each other. For example, if the Japanese are unwilling to move up to levels of military expenditure comparable to the West Europeans, what levels of foreign aid or other economic concessions should her allies expect? Should U.S. concessions under the General System of Preferences (GSP) limit tariff reductions to those countries that cooperate with the United States? If the Japanese choose an economic rather than a military focus for their security programs, how could this be used to buttress the Western position in the Persian Gulf?

In sum, the book will start by estimating the likely economic performance of the United States and its allies in future years, then look at the extent to which economic conditions will constrain defense expenditures, and conclude with a discussion of options which would enhance Allied security while redistributing defense burdens.

# APPENDIX: Chronology of Key Events Leading to U.S. Alliances in Europe and Asia

| | |
|---|---|
| July 1945 | Potsdam Declaration, establishing the Council of Foreign Ministers to deal with the peace transition and creation of the four occupation zones of Germany. |
| 1945 – 1947 | Unraveling of Potsdam agreements: excessive Soviet reparations from Germany and Soviet prevention of elections in Eastern Europe. Communist insurgency in Greece. |
| March 12, 1947 | President Truman requests $400 million for aid to Greece and Turkey. |
| June 1947 | Secretary of State Marshall proposes a general economic recovery program for Europe. |
| 1948 | President Beneš of Czechoslovakia assassinated; the Soviet blockade of Berlin. |
| March 17, 1948 | Brussels Pact between the United Kingdom, France, and Benelux countries on social, cultural, and military cooperation. |
| April 4, 1949 | NATO Treaty signed. Original signatories: United Kingdom, United States, Canada, Belgium, Luxembourg, The Netherlands, Denmark, Iceland, Norway, Portugal, Italy, and France. |
| June 25, 1950 | South Korea (Republic of Korea) attacked by North Korea. |
| September 8, 1951 | U.S. – Japanese Security Treaty signed. |
| April 29, 1952 | Australia – New Zealand – U.S. (ANZUS) Treaty signed. |
| July 27, 1953 | Korean Armistice Agreement signed. |
| October 1, 1953 | United States and Republic of Korea sign Mutual Security Pact. |

August 20, 1954   France rejects the proposal for forming a militarily integrated European Defense Community.

## NOTES

1. U.S. Secretary of Defense, *Annual Report to the Congress,* Fiscal year 1983 (Washington, DC: U.S. Government Printing Office, 1984), p. 67.
2. This was a major change for President Carter who had originally run in 1976 pledging to cut the defense budget by 5 percent in nominal terms which would have meant an 11 percent real cut in 1977 had he kept his pledge.
3. For an early and interesting discussion of this issue, see J.J. Holst and Uwe Nehrlich, eds., *Beyond Nuclear Deterrence: New Aims, New Arms* (New York: Crane, Russak & Co., 1977).
4. David Yost, ed., *NATO's Strategic Options: Arms Control and Defense* (New York: Pergamon Press, 1981), p. xvi.
5. H. Schmidt, "Saving the Western Alliance," *New York Review of Books,* May 31, 1984, pp. 25 – 27.
6. For this study, it would have been desirable to include both Italy and the Philippines in the Southern Europe and Asian groupings, respectively. Because of limited resources for the research, we chose to concentrate on the countries that make the largest financial contributions to defense or have the most critical geographic location.
7. D. Middleton, "Crisis Brings to the Fore Problems Facing NATO," *New York Times,* May 1, 1982, p. 7.
8. M. Bundy, G. Kennan, R. McNamara, and G. Smith, "Nuclear Weapons and the Atlantic Alliance," *Foreign Affairs* 60 (1984): 753 – 768.
9. F. Hampson, "Groping for Technical Panaceas: The European Conventional Balance and Nuclear Stability," *International Security* 8, No. 3 (1983 – 84): 57 – 82.
10. M. Wörner, "Das wertlose Ja zur Nato," *Der Spiegel,* June 4, 1984, pp. 42 – 43.
11. G. Allison, *Essence of Decision* (Boston: Little, Brown, 1971).
12. For a discussion of deterrence and escalation dominance, see C. Gray, "Nuclear Strategy: A Case for a Theory of Victory," *International Security* 4, No. 1 (1979): 54 – 87.
13. H. Brown and L. Davis, "Nuclear Arms Control: Where Do We Stand?" *Foreign Affairs* 65 (1984): 1145 – 1160.
14. B. Rogers, "Greater Flexibility for NATO'S Flexible Response," *Atlantic Community Quarterly* 21, No. 3 (1983): 233 – 243.
15. P. Lellouche, "Does NATO Have a Future? A European View," *The Washington Quarterly* 5, No. 3 (1982): 40 – 52.
16. D. Andelman, "Over Western Europe," *Foreign Policy,* No. 49 (1982 – 83): 37 – 51.
17. J. Blaker and A. Hamilton, "Assessing the NATO – Warsaw Pact Military Balance" (Washington, D.C.: Congressional Budget Office, December 1977).
18. Reuters, "NATO Cuts Soviet Bloc Estimate," *New York Times,* June 22, 1984, p. A4.
19. See, for example, R.L. Kugler's "Warsaw Pact Forces and the Conventional Military Balance in Central Europe" (George Washington University, May 1983) and the 1982 NATO White Paper, *NATO and the Warsaw Pact: Force Comparisons* (Brussels: NATO, 1982).
20. The Soviet approach in dealing with China since the Ussuri River incident in March 1969 has oscillated between calculated shows of force and attempts at negotiating differences. At present, the U.S.S.R. is pursuing a conciliatory stance and recently sent a Deputy Prime Minister, Ivan V. Arkhipov, to Beijing for discussions (*New York Times,* May 5, 1985, p. 3). The People's Republic of China has taken the position that

the Soviet Union must (a) withdraw from Afghanistan, (b) end support for the Vietnamese occupation of Cambodia, and (c) settle the disputed territorial claims on the Sino-Soviet border before overall Chinese-Soviet relations can be eased.
21. The Association of Southeast Asian Nations (ASEAN) – which now includes Brunei as well as Thailand, Singapore, Malaysia, Indonesia, and the Philippines – has been an effective forum and grown increasingly important since the U.S. withdrawal from Vietnam in 1975.
22. The 1976 National Defense Program Outline was an important step forward in developing a credible Japanese self-defense capability because it specified standards of performance needed. It was inadequate because the force structure recommended could not have successfully defended Japan (without extensive assistance from the United States) and because it did not sufficiently take into account the growing Soviet military strength in the Pacific.
23. H. Okazaki, "Japanese Security Policy: A Time for Strategy," *International Security* 7, No. 2 (1982): 188 – 197.
24. O. Miyoshi, "Toward a New U.S.-Japanese Alliance: The Crucial Choices for the Eighties," *Comparative Strategy* 2 (1980): 279 – 301.
25. For an overview of the development of U.S. – Soviet arms talks, see Edward C. Luck's "The Reagan Administration's Nuclear Strategy," *Current History* 82 (May 1983): 193, 232 – 233.
26. A. Neidle, ed., *Nuclear Negotiations: Reassessing Arms Control Goals in U.S.-Soviet Relations* (Austin: University of Texas Press, 1982).
27. C. Bertram, "Europe and America in 1983," *Foreign Affairs: America and the World in 1983* 62 (1984): 616 – 631.
28. A. Frye, "Strategic Build Down: A Context for Restraint," *Foreign Affairs* 62 (1983 – 84): 293 – 317.
29. D. Fischer, "Nonmilitary Defense Strategies," *C.V. Starr Center for Applied Economics Paper #32* (New York: New York University, March 1984).
30. SPD Party Convention Policy Statement, Essen, West Germany, May 1984.
31. R. Osgood, *Limited War: The Challenge to American Strategy* (Chicago: University of Chicago Press, 1957).
32. H. Kissinger, *Nuclear Weapons and Foreign Policy* (New York: Harper, 1957).
33. H. Brown, U.S. Secretary of Defense, *Annual Report to the Congress,* Fiscal Year 1982 (Washington, DC: U.S. Government Printing Office, 1981), p. 78.
34. B. Rogers, "The Atlantic Alliance: Prescriptions for a Difficult Decade," *Foreign Affairs* 60 (1982): 1145 – 1156.
35. J. Thomson, "Nuclear Weapons in Europe: Planning for NATO's Nuclear Deterrent in the 1980s and 1990s," *Survival* 25, No. 3 (1983): 98 – 109.
36. François de Rose, "Alternative Strategy for the West," *NATO's Fifteen Nations* (August/September 1982), pp. 56 ff.
37. R. Komer, "The Trick Is How To Get It," *Armed Forces Journal International* 119, No. 2 (1981): 70 – 74.
38. E. Luttwak, "How to Think About Nuclear War," *Commentary* 74, No. 2 (1982): 21 – 28.
39. B. Schemmer, "NATO's New Strategy: Defend Forward, But Strike Deep," *Armed Forces Journal International* 120, No. 3 (1982): 50 – 68.
40. S. Canby and I. Dörfer, "More Troops, Fewer Missiles," *Foreign Policy,* No. 53 (1983 – 84): 3 – 17.
41. R. DeLauer, "Remarks on Arms Collaboration and the Emerging Technologies," Paper given at a conference sponsored by *The Economist* (London: February 9, 1984).

42. S. Huntington, "Conventional Deterrence and Conventional Retaliation in Europe," *International Security* 8, No. 3 (1983 – 84): 32 – 56.
43. For a survey of the unclassified material about the SDI, see "The U.S. Made 'Star Wars' More Than a Fantasy," *New York Times,* March 5, 1985, p. A16, and "What Moscow Might Do in Replying to U.S. 'Star Wars' Plan," *New York Times,* March 6, 1985, p. B8.
44. Once President Carter was in office, U.S. allies voiced strong opposition to reducing U.S. troop strength in South Korea, and he then quietly dropped the proposal.
45. The Culver/Nunn Amendment of 1974 would make future troop deployments in Europe conditioned on efforts by both the United States and its European allies to achieve greater rationalization and standardization of equipment.
46. The Stevens Amendment to the Fiscal Year 1982 Defense Appropriation Bill limits U.S. troops in Europe to 315,000 and requires the Secretary of Defense to show why U.S. troops should not be withdrawn if the European members of NATO do not meet their 3 percent real growth targets for defense spending.
47. The proposed Nunn Amendment of 1984 did not pass but it would have mandated withdrawals of U.S. troops from Europe beginning in 1986 if the Europeans did not meet agreed force improvements.
48. H. Kissinger, "A Plan to Reshape NATO," *Time,* March 5, 1984, pp. 20 – 24.
49. S. Hoffman, *Gulliver's Troubles or the Setting of American Foreign Policy* (New York: McGraw-Hill, 1968).
50. R. Steel, *Pax Americana* (New York: Viking Press, 1967).
51. See Appendix I for a chronology of the major post-World War II alliances of the United States.
52. W. Lippman, "The Undiplomatic Department," from *Today and Tomorrow,* 13 January 1954, as reprinted in C. Rossiter and J. Lare, eds., *The Essential Lippman* (New York: Random House, 1963).
53. George Kennan expanded his ideas originally presented in the anonymous "X" article in *Foreign Affairs* (Spring 1947) with his *American Diplomacy* (Chicago: University of Chicago Press, 1951).
54. H. Mackinder, "The Geographical Pivot of History," *Geographical Journal* 23 (1904).
55. A. Mahan, *The Influence of Sea Power Upon History, 1660 – 1783* (Boston: Little, Brown & Co., 1890).
56. "A Question of Confidence," *The Economist,* February 19, 1949, pp. 313 – 314.
57. G. Eliot, "Organizing the Atlantic Community: The Strategic Problem," *Proceedings of the Academy of Political Science* 23 (1949): 302 – 309.
58. D. Mitchell, "Strategy and the Atlantic Pact," *Current History* 17, No. 98 (1949): 213 – 215.
59. B. Brodie, "Strategic Implications of the North Atlantic Pact," *Yale Review* 39, No. 2 (1950): 193 – 208.
60. G. Kirk, "The Atlantic Pact and International Security," *International Organization* 3, No. 2 (1949): 239 – 251.
61. C. Kindelberger, "Germany and the Economic Recovery of Europe," *Proceedings of the Academy of Political Science* 23 (1948 – 50): 288 – 301.
62. For example, Henry Kissinger wrote his *Nuclear Weapons and Foreign Policy* in 1957; he did an analysis of the political schisms in NATO in *The Troubled Partnership* (New York: McGraw-Hill) in 1965; declared the "Year of Europe" while he was Secretary of State, stressing the need for a basic reassessment of the alliance (*Department of State Bulletin,* December 24, 1973, Vol. 59, No. 1700); and startled the Europeans with his 1984 *Time* essay.

63. International Institute for Strategic Studies, *The Military Balance: 1983 – 84* (London: IISS, 1983).
64. Two examples of European concerns about NATO's strategy and the unity of the alliance under pressure are Lothar Ruehl's "La Défense de l'Europe," *Politique Etrangère* 48, No. 1 (1983): 27 – 38, and Christopher Coker and Heinz Schulte's "Strategiekritik und Pazifismus. Zwei Haupttendenzen in den Westeuropäischen Friedensbewegungen," *Europa-Archiv* 38, No. 14 (1983): 413 – 420.
65. C. Robinson, "NATO: Reshaping the Alliance – Economics, Politics Portend Shifts," *Aviation Week and Space Technology* 120 (May 1984): 50 – 63.
66. See Tables 2.14, 2.16, 2.17 in Chapter 2 for different quantitative measures of burden-sharing. Many Europeans claim that the U.S. and British "contributions to defense" are overstated because the American and British armies do not have conscription. Clearly, conscription allows countries to recruit entry-level troops, and in some cases reserves, without paying them competitive wages. Market-oriented economists argue that conscription is essentially a disguised tax – so that a government can obtain resources at less than their market value. There is no easy resolution to this problem because once the debate moves to estimating "shadow-prices" of what resources are "really worth" further analytical difficulties ensue. Even if one did make adjustments for higher salaries in the U.S. military (and therefore raised the imputed European contributions) the adjustments would not fully compensate for the fact that the United States spends more than twice as large a percentage of its GDP on defense as do most of the European members of NATO.
67. For several examples of the burden-sharing debate, see R. Rupp, "Sharing the Defence Burden," *NATO Review* 30, No. 5 (1982): 24 – 28; S. Lunn, *Burden-Sharing in NATO* (London: Routledge & Kegan Paul, 1983); G. Kennedy, *Burden-Sharing in NATO* (New York: Holmes and Meier, 1979).
68. For an interesting discussion about the evolution of the Bretton Woods System, the emergence of balance of payments problems for the United States and the role of the dollar, see *Economic Report of the President – 1964* (Washington, DC: U.S. Government Printing Office, January 1964, pp. 133 – 148).
69. T. Oka, "Stability in Asia," *America and the World –1984, Foreign Affairs* 63 (1984): 653 – 671.
70. In June 1984, respective European unemployment rates were Britain: 12.6 percent, France: 9.8 percent, Italy: 13.3 percent, W. Germany: 9.1 percent. Average unemployment rates increased in Europe between 1983 and 1984, while the U.S. rate dropped from 10.1 percent to 7.4 percent in the same period. *New York Times,* June 17, 1984, p. F25.
71. For a skeptical view of the likely cohesiveness of NATO during a crisis, see I. Kristol, "Does NATO Exist?" in K. Myers, ed., *NATO – The Next Thirty Years* (Boulder, CO.: Westview Press, 1980).
72. B. Scott, "Can Industry Survive the Welfare State? *Harvard Business Review* 60, No. 5 (1982): 70 – 84.
73. M. Albert and R. Ball, *Towards European Economic Recovery in the 1980s*, Report presented to the European Parliament, 1983.
74. W. Gregory, "NATO's Newest Crisis," *Aviation Week and Space Technology,* May 21, 1984, p. 13.
75. P. Samuelson, *Economics* (New York: McGraw-Hill, 1961), p. 22.
76. One of the earliest and most committed advocates of the "guns versus butter" view was Bruce Russett, *What Price Vigilance?* (New Haven: Yale University Press, 1970). Russett has since modified his position slightly in "Defense Expenditures and National Well-Being," *American Political Science Review* 76 (1982): 767 –777.

77. For a discussion of budgeting in the United States, see O. Davis, M. Dempster, and A. Wildavsky, *On the Process of Budgeting*, reprint #252 (Pittsburgh: Carnegie-Mellon University, 1966). For Britain, see K. Peroff and M. Podolak-Warren, "Does Spending on Defense Cut Spending on Health?" *British Journal of Political Science* 9, No. 1 (1979): 21 – 39.
78. W. Domke, R. Eichenberg, and C. Kelleher, "The Illusion of Choice: Defense and Welfare in Advanced Industrial Democracies, 1948 – 78," *American Political Science Review* 77, No. 1 (1983): 19 – 35.
79. Council on Economic Priorities, *Military Expansion, Economic Decline: The Impact of Military Spending on U.S. Economic Performance* (New York: M.E. Sharpe, 1983).
80. A.J.P. Taylor, *The Origins of the Second World War* (New York: Premier Books, 1961).
81. For a detailed discussion of how this question was answered in the McNamara years at the Pentagon (1961 – 1968), see A. Enthoven and W. Smith, *How Much is Enough?* (New York: Harper & Row, 1969).
82. M. Olson and R. Zeckhauser, "An Economic Theory of Alliances," *Review of Economics and Statistics* 48, No. 3 (1966): 266 – 279.
83. P. Samuelson, "The Pure Theory of Public Expenditure," *Review of Economics and Statistics* 36 (1954): 387 – 389.
84. W. Riker, *The Theory of Political Coalitions* (New Haven: Yale University Press, 1970).
85. F. Knight, "Some Fallacies in Interpretation of Social Cost," *Quarterly Journal of Economics* 38 (1924): 582 – 606.
86. See M. McGuire, "Group Size, Group Homogeneity, and the Aggregate Provision of a Pure Public Good Under Current Behavior," *Public Choice* 18 (1974): 107 – 126.
87. J. Golden, *NATO Burden Sharing: Risks and Opportunities* (New York: Praeger Press, 1983).
88. H. Brown, *Seventh Report to the U.S. Congress on Rationalization, Standardization Within NATO* (Washington, DC: U.S. Department of Defense, January 1981).
89. R. Eichenberg, "The Myth of Hollanditis," *International Security* 8, No. 2 (1983): 143 – 159.
90. J. Murdoch and T. Sandler, "A Theoretical and Empirical Analysis of NATO," *Journal of Conflict Resolution* 26 (1982): 237 – 263.
91. D. Middleton, "French Army's New Look Draws Praise," *New York Times*, July 31, 1984, p. A3.
92. Ministère de la Défense, *Programme de la Défense, 1984 – 1988* (Paris: Service d'Information et de Relations Publiques des Armées, 1983).
93. E. Benoit, *Defense and Economic Growth in Developing Countries* (Lexington, MA: Lexington Books, Heath, 1973).
94. See, for example, R. Smith, "Military Expenditure and Investment in OECD Countries," *Journal of Comparative Economics* 4, No. 1 (1980): 19 – 32; S. Deger and S. Smith, "Military Expenditure and Growth in Less Developed Countries," *Journal of Conflict Resolution* 27 (1983): 335 – 353; N. Ball, "Defense and Development; A Critique of the Benoit Study," *Economic Development and Cultural Change* 31 (1983): 507 – 524; D. Lim, "Another Look at Growth and Defense in Less Developed Countries," *Economic Development and Cultural Change* 31 (1983): 378 – 384.
95. S. Deger and S. Sen, "Military Expenditure, Spin-Off, and Economic Development," *Journal of Development Economics* 13 (1983): 67 – 83.
96. L. Thurow, "How to Wreck the Economy," *New York Review of Books*, May 14, 1981, pp. 3 – 8.
97. H. Stein, "The Economics of American Defense: Q & A," *The Wall Street Journal*, July 7, 1981, p. 28.

98. C. Schultze, "Do More Dollars Mean Better Defense?" *Challenge* 24, No. 6 (1982): 30 – 35.
99. Congressional Budget Office, *Defense Spending and the Economy* (Washington, DC: Congressional Budget Office, February 1983).
100. See, for example, W. Leontief and M. Hoffenberg, "The Economic Effects of Disarmament," *Scientific American* 204, No. 4 (1961): 47 – 55; R. Bolton, ed., *Defense and Disarmament: The Economics of Transition* (Englewood Cliffs, NJ: Prentice-Hall, 1966); S. Dresch, *Disarmament: Economic Consequences and Development Potential* (New Haven: Yale University Press, 1972).
101. D. Blond, *The Domestic Economic Impact Model Simulator* (DEIMS) (Washington, DC: U.S. Department of Defense, 1983).
102. R. Oliver, "Employment Effects of Reduced Spending," *Monthly Labor Review* 94, No. 12 (1971): 3 – 11.
103. W. Leontief and F. Duchin, *Military Spending: Facts and Figures, Worldwide Implications, and Future Outlook* (New York: Oxford University Press, 1983).
104. Congressional Budget Office, *The Effect of Foreign Military Sales on the U.S. Economy* (Washington, DC: Congressional Budget Office, July 1976).
105. K. Rothschild, "Military Expenditures, Exports and Growth," *Kyklos* 26 (1973): 804 – 814.
106. R. Reich, *The Next American Frontier* (New York: Times Books, 1983).
107. E. Frost and A. Stent, "NATO's Troubles with East – West Trade," *International Security* 8, No. 1 (1983): 179 – 200.
108. J. Fox, *Arming America* (Cambridge, MA: Harvard University Press, 1974).
109. L. Olvey, H. Leonard, and B. Arlinghaus, eds., *Industrial Capacity and Defense Planning; Sustained Conflict and Surge Capability in the 1980s* (Lexington, MA: Lexington Books, Heath, 1983).
110. U.S. Department of Commerce, "Sectoral Implications of Defense Expenditures" (Washington, DC: Bureau of Industrial Economics, 1982). Mimeo.
111. J. Gansler, *The Defense Industry* (Cambridge, MA: MIT Press, 1982).
112. M. Weidenbaum, "Let's Examine National Defense Spending," *Challenge* 25, No. 6 (1983): 50 – 53.
113. "Rearming Japan," *Business Week,* March 14, 1983, pp. 106 – 116.
114. L. Griffin, M. Wallace, and J. Devine, "The Political Economy of Military Spending: Evidence from the U.S.," *Cambridge Journal of Economics* 6 (1982): 1 – 14.
115. S. Melman, ed., *The War Economy of the U.S.* (New York: St. Martin's Press, 1971).
116. M. Reich, "Military Spending and Production for Profit," in R. Edwards, ed., *The Capitalist System,* 2nd ed. (Englewood Cliffs, NJ: Prentice-Hall, 1978), pp. 409 – 418.
117. J. Kurth, "Why We Buy the Weapons We Do," *Foreign Policy,* No. 11 (1973): pp. 33 – 56.
118. R. Solow, "Technological Change and the Aggregate Production Function," *The Review of Economics and Statistics* 39 (1957): 312 – 320.
119. E. Denison, *Accounting for Slower Economic Growth* (Washington, DC: Brookings Institution, 1979).

# Chapter 2

# Increase in Defense Expenditure and Its Impact on the U.S. Economy

M. Ishaq Nadiri*

## INTRODUCTION

Both political and military considerations usually determine the level and pace of military spending. To assess the magnitude and types of resources that should be devoted to national defense purposes, the political leadership of a country must evaluate the nature and scope of the threat the nation faces at a particular period. The relevant economic questions are how the increased expenditure should be financed, and what impact a given level of spending and a sustained rate of growth of defense spending have on the U.S. economy. To assess this properly, it is necessary to consider the future development of the economy, and to evaluate what impact defense spending may have on economic growth and on the sectoral distribution of output, employment, and investment. Such an evaluation may help answer the question of whether a given national defense program is affordable.

The Reagan administration's defense program that was announced in 1981 constituted a major undertaking to increase the U.S. defense expenditures over the 1980s. The assessment of the need for a substantial increase in military spending had been based, as will be noted, on the evaluation of the perceived threat facing the United States and its allies and of the state of defense preparedness of the U.S. military forces. The economic issues were, first, whether the U.S. economy could accommodate the planned increase in defense spending in the short run as part of

---

*I would like to thank David Denoon, David McNicol, and David Blond for their help and comments, and Catherine Labio for her excellent assistance.

the aggregate demand, and second, whether a sustained increase in defense spending could lead to structural distortion of the economy in the long run. The administration's plans to expand defense spending in the context of its overall economic design were assumed to produce neither short-term aggregate demand management problems such as serious inflationary bottlenecks, rising prices, and deficits, nor any structural distortion of the economy in the long run.

In this chapter we will briefly examine the economy-wide and industry-level effects of the planned increase in defense expenditure, and try to answer the question of the affordability of the defense program in today's economy. We shall note the salient features of defense spending and of its catalytic role in the U.S. economy and discuss briefly some of the factors that determine defense spending, focusing particularly on the reason why the Reagan administration argued for substantial increases in defense expenditure over the 1981 – 1985 period. Alternative military spending programs put forward by the Reagan administration critics will be briefly noted. We shall also discuss the outlook of the U.S. economy in the next few years, and analyze the macroeconomic consequences of defense spending in the context of the evolution of the federal budget. Finally, the sectoral and regional effects of the increasing defense spending will be examined.

## THE CONTROVERSIAL NATURE OF DEFENSE SPENDING

The study of the effect of increased military expenditure on the U.S. economy has a long and controversial history.[1] Controversies arise at various levels of discourse and for a variety of reasons. Since it is not possible to discuss all the issues that separate proponents and opponents of a large defense buildup, we shall only briefly mention some of their arguments.

Some critics argue that in the context of the present international situation, increased defense spending may not necessarily lead to national security. According to them, larger defense expenditure by the United States stimulates higher defense expenditure by the U.S.S.R., while the resulting weapon sophistication leads to national insecurity for both countries, and the rest of the world. Another group opposes increased defense expenditure because resources are then diverted from meeting social needs such as health, education, assistance to urban areas, etc. Also, it is often but nevertheless mistakenly argued that expenditures on defense programs are wasteful because no useful products or services are created. This argument ignores the fact that "security" is a service with special characteristics and value, and that without it the performance of the civilian economy would definitely be severely hampered. Moreover, the defense program is often criticized for its waste and lack of efficiency. (Cases of excessive cost overruns on major defense systems and of enormous overpayments for simple tools are often pointed out as examples of a mismanaged defense buildup). Finally, there are those who do not question the need for further defense buildup but question the composition of the defense expenditure program and the need for some of the military procurement systems suggested by the administration, claiming that alternative but more efficient programs are available to meet the national security needs.

The controversy on the economics of defense looks somewhat suprising at first when we examine aggregate economic data. Military expenditure accounts for only one fifteenth of the Gross National Product (GNP) and for a much smaller portion of the labor force. In general, few of the major industries take part in provisioning the military goods and services while even the biggest defense contractors sell the bulk of their products in the civilian markets.[2] Also, even though a few states and localities are significantly affected by changes in military expenditures, the majority of the states and metropolitan areas are only slightly concerned about the defense programs.[3] However, despite the fact that at the aggregate level the defense expenditure appears to be of marginal importance, it nevertheless often plays an important catalytic role in the U.S. economy. This is partly due to the unusual nature of the resources devoted to defense programs, and also to the decision process involved in implementing the defense programs. A number of these special features can be identified:[4]

1. In the United States, a major share of the scientific and engineering talent is used in the provisioning of the United States defense program. Increased defense expenditure may also lead to substantial increases in supply of these resources as well.

2. Defense expenditure constitutes the bulk of federal government purchase of goods and services. Thus, defense programs have been a major vehicle for the increased role of the federal government as a purchaser of goods and services.

3. U.S. defense spending has been and is likely to be in the forseeable future the major component of total NATO defense expenditure. Currently U.S. defense spending constitutes over 50 percent of the NATO total expenditure. Because of the weak economic performance of the U.S. allies, and/or the political and social constraints, it is unlikely that major efforts will be made to reduce the U.S. share.

4. Because of the specialized nature of the defense purchase, a small number of durable goods and high technology industries supply the bulk of the goods directly purchased by the Department of Defense (DoD). The indirect defense purchases are, on the other hand, not highly concentrated and are, to a much lesser extent, very specialized goods.

5. Increased defense expenditure, because of its autonomous nature, means that increasing shares of the national economy are independent of the fluctuations in the private sector.

6. Because of its size and rate of buildup, as well as the method used to finance defense programs, the impact of defense spending has taken on a new dimension since 1981. A serious examination of the effects of defense spending must there-

fore take place within the context of the evolution of the federal budget and the national economy.

Three central economic questions arise from a large defense buildup. First, is there an optimal transfer of resources from the civilian into the defense production sector, i.e., one which disrupts the civilian economy the least? Second, given the method used in the transfer of resources, what are the likely effects on the civilian economy in the near future and on the long-term growth of the economy? Third, can the U.S. economy afford a sustained increase in defense spending over a long period of time?

Critics argue that the transfer mechanism imposed on the economy by the Reagan administration is not optimal – rather it is disruptive.[5] They point to the Korean and Vietnam wars as examples of the right and wrong ways of achieving this transfer. During the Korean War taxes were raised dramatically at the beginning of the war, and a full range of wartime controls on wages and prices, investment, labor, and materials were imposed. Taxes were used to lower consumption, provide resources for military production, and curb excess demand inflation. Controls were used to shift materials, labor, and capital to military production, severely damaging the civilian economy and preventing bottleneck inflation from breaking out. In the Vietnam War taxes and controls were avoided, and the excess demand generated by the military buildup led to the substantial inflationary pressure of the early 1970s. It is argued that, as included in the federal bugetary process, the new military expenditure buildup is deficit-financed, and that as part of the federal budget deficit, it is responsible for the high interest rates in the United States and the rest of the world. The high interest rate has had, in turn, a major retarding effect in most European and developing economies.

Since it takes several years to significantly increase the supply of engineers and scientists, the argument goes that the military buildup will necessarily take a significant amount of manpower away from existing civilian industries. This shift may jeopardize the U.S. high technology firms that compete with businesses from allied nations since the United States alone, among the Western allies, is carrying out a military buildup. The policy option facing the United States is either to pressure the allies to engage in similar military buildups so that their firms face the same conditions as the American firms, or to slow down the acceleration in U.S. military procurement.[6]

It is also argued that a rapid increase in defense expenditure may produce shortages of materials, equipment, and skilled labor which in some sectors would create bottleneck inflation and could lead to general excess demand inflation in the rest of the economy. Bottleneck inflation may arise from two sources. First, as resources flow out of civilian industries, civilian production drops, which in turn leads to price increases. Secondly, in the absence of controls, the military industries have to compete by paying high wages for labor and high prices for materials and equipment. Because of the need to move these resources rapidly and the risk associated with boom-and-bust cycles in military procurement, the economic benefits from moving these resources are likely to be small, wages and material costs will increase, and the price of capital goods for both military and civilian use will rise. The administration's defense buildup focuses heavily on the procurement of advanced hardware where bottlenecks and shortages can develop very rapidly and spread to the rest of the economy. Particularly since the Vietnam War the economy has become more inflation-prone; wages are highly indexed today, and businesses now pass cost increases through to their customers much faster than before.

## DETERMINANTS OF THE DEFENSE EFFORT AND THE RATIONALE FOR INCREASED DEFENSE SPENDING

Defense spending is primarily determined by strategic and noneconomic factors. Perception of threat and security needs are critical in determining military budgets but the allocation between defense and nondefense also has to be solved in the most efficient and optimal way, i.e., the least disruptive to the current and future growth of the civilian economy.

There are a number of welfare optimizing models which can explain the stylized facts of the military expenditure;[7] they assume that a country maximizes its intertemporal welfare function subject to constraints. The preference function depends on a society's preference between expenditure on civilian goods and services (consumption and investment), security, and the level of threat. According to these models the U.S. military expenditure is a function of the U.S. level of income, relative prices of military goods and services compared with their counterparts in the civilian sector, military expenditure by the U.S. allies, and an index of "threat" often measured by the Soviet Union's or the Warsaw Pact's military expenditure. Other factors such as population size, extent of the country's borders to be defended, and economic shocks such as the increase in oil prices in the 1970s are also mentioned as influencing U.S. military expenditure.[8] The purpose of these types of econometric models is to establish a *stable* demand function for military expenditure in terms of the variables mentioned. This line of research is promising and could lead to significant insights about the determinants of the level and timing of the military expenditure. However, further work is required to establish that these demand functions are stable over time; also, these functions should be embedded in larger econometric models to capture the interplay between the variations in the level and composition of the defense expenditure, and other types of public and private spending and trace their impacts on the various sectors of the civilian economy.

Nonetheless, these types of economic models particularly emphasize three factors which seem to have received specific attention in the administration's defense program initiatives. First, there is the index of threat which, however measured, is a critical factor in analyzing the defense burden. The level of threat is assumed to be given exogenously and is measured either by the defense burden of the belligerent power or by the difference between the defense burdens of the rival countries. This defense burden is often measured by the military expenditures/GNP ratio to indicate the opportunity cost of defense in terms of civilian goods and services. The second factor is that decision-makers are influenced by subjective evaluations of security needs. Third, even though military expenditure may be caused by strategic considerations, there is the need for balancing the military and nonmilitary needs and taking account of the financial and economic resource constraints facing the nation.

The overall thrust of the Reagan administration's defense program has been to restore U.S. defense capabilities that had eroded over the preceding decade. The rationale behind the allocation of more resources for national defense than President Carter had proposed, was based on an examination of U.S. resource allocation which showed that the share of the federal budget devoted to national security had remained substantially below the 1964 percentage throughout the last decade, while the share of the federal budget devoted to nondefense spending had greatly increased.[9] But these trends alone do not necessarily prove that defense was being underfunded during the 1970s. Such a judgment must be based upon a careful assessment of Soviet military capabilities and the state of readiness of the U.S. forces. In this respect, several observations helped the administration to decide to substantially increase the defense budget. First, the slowdown of the U.S. defense effort occurred at a time of uprecedented Soviet buildup. During the 1970s, the Soviet Union embarked on the greatest military buildup in history. When the dollar estimate of Soviet expenditures for defense investment (procurement, research and development, and military construction) is compared to U.S. levels, the Soviet Union out-spent the United States by almost $.05 trillion during the 1970 to 1981 period. Moreover, during that same period, the Warsaw Pact countries out-invested NATO and Japan by a net of $185 billion (1984 dollars).[10]

The administration's review of the state of preparedness of U.S. military forces also revealed some important shortcomings. First, the readiness of the forces was found inadequate. Army divisions were not combat ready, Navy ships with major combat deficiencies were being deployed, and combat aircraft could not fly for lack of spare parts. In particular, personnel readiness in the Army and Navy was unacceptably low. Another indicator of the problem facing the military planners was the fact that in most cases, the age of the U.S. General Purpose forces had increased over the 1970s – a consequence of inadequate force modernization. The average age of Air Force tactical combat aircraft had increased from about seven years in 1979 to about ten years in 1981. The average age of Navy combat aircraft had increased from approximately five years to about 10.5 years. The average age of naval ships was more or less the same as in 1970, i.e., about sixteen years.[11]

Based on these arguments, the administration developed a major defense expansion program. Under this program, defense spending as a percentage of GNP was to rise steadily from 5.6 percent in 1981 to slightly less than 8 percent by 1989. This represented a gradual increase back to the 1964 claim of 8.3 percent of GNP which was considered affordable prior to the Vietnam War. The administration plan called for a gradual decrease in nondefense spending as a percentage of GNP, to a level of more than 12 percent by 1989 – still well above the claim of 9.5 percent in 1964.[12]

## THE BUILDUP PROGRAM IN THE CONTEXT OF THE PROPOSED ECONOMIC PLAN

The administration's 1981 economic program gave a precise description of how the structure of federal expenditure and tax receipts was to be shifted so as to accommodate the proposed dramatic jump in defense spending while also ensuring a reduction in the inflation rate and increased economic growth. It is useful to look at the general outlines of this program in order to assess the impact of the increased defense expenditure on the U.S. economy.

The economic program proposed by the administration in 1981 essentially redrew economic policies along lines which differed from those of preceding U.S. administrations in their political roots and theoretical foundations. Major tax relief was linked to a restructuring of federal expenditure, thereby sharply altering the impact of taxation on the economy. With a view to combat stagflation, the "Program for Economic Recovery" included a variety of measures: tax reductions, a slowdown in federal spending with the hope of leading to a balanced budget, regulatory relief, and monetary restraint. The latter measure was expected to curb inflation, while the others were to pave the way for a stronger and more sustained economic growth. The tax cuts were to play a crucial role, providing a supply-side boost to the economy by promoting savings, investment, work effort, and productivity. By historical standards, the budgetary shifts implied by these policies and the administration's economic forecast were truly enormous. The expected economic recovery, along with the planned reductions in federal domestic spending, were to bring revenues into balance with total outlays by 1986, despite the large tax cuts and the defense buildup (Table 2.1).

The result was predicted to be an annual real growth of GNP in excess of 4 percent during calendar years 1982 – 1986, with annual inflation declining to below 5 percent by 1986. In essence, the president embraced a set of tax and defense policies that could be reconciled with his balanced budget objective only through extremely optimistic economic projections and large reductions in domestic spending.

In the context of this economic program, a substantial increase in the level and a dramatic change in the composition of the defense spending were proposed. In the first three years of the Reagan administration total defense budget authorization grew by about 52 percent (about 31 percent in real terms). The original budget and the five-year defense plan submitted to Congress called for $305 billion in budget authorization in fiscal year 1985 and increases of up to 446 billion by fiscal year

Table 2.1. The Original Budget Projections for Fiscal Years 1981 – 1986
Submitted by the Administration

|  | FY 1981 | FY 1982 | FY 1983 | FY 1984 | FY 1985 | FY 1986 |
|---|---|---|---|---|---|---|
| *Percentage of GNP* | | | | | | |
| Revenues | 21.1 | 20.4 | 19.7 | 19.3 | 19.3 | 19.5 |
| Outlays (including off-budget) | 23.9 | 22.3 | 20.6 | 19.5 | 19.4 | 19.1 |
| National defense | 5.7 | 5.9 | 6.3 | 6.4 | 6.9 | 7.1 |
| Nondefense programs | 15.9 | 14.3 | 12.5 | 11.4 | 11.0 | 10.6 |
| Net interest | 2.3 | 2.1 | 1.9 | 1.7 | 1.5 | 1.3 |
| Total deficit (surplus) | 2.8 | 1.9 | 0.9 | 0.2 | 0.0 | (0.4) |
| *Billions of Constant (FY 1972) Dollars* | | | | | | |
| Outlays | | | | | | |
| National defense | 77.8 | 83.0 | 92.6 | 98.4 | 110.8 | 118.9 |
| Nondefense programs | 213.9 | 197.0 | 180.1 | 172.6 | 173.6 | 176.6 |

*Source:* Office of Management and Budget, "Federal Government Finances," March 1981.

1989, a 22 percent increase in real terms over the fiscal year 1984 budget. These figures, though to some extent adjusted downward by Congress, showed that the administration had undertaken a large and sustained increase in the defense expenditure.[13] Another feature of the new defense program was its dramatic shift toward investment accounts: procurement, research and development, and military construction. The rate of increase (in real terms) of these accounts over the 1981 to 1984 period was quite high as shown in Table 2.2. Procurement of technologically advanced equipment takes a substantial lead time, which results in increasing backlog of orders which in turn may complicate control of the defense budget in the future and could lead to sectoral or general inflation if the private sector experiences rapid growth in the near future. Furthermore, the emphasis on new and technologically advanced weapon systems may entail substantial maintenance and replacement costs. Technological advance may lead to substantial obsolescence of highly capital intensive weapon systems. Finally, the changed composition of the defense expenditure may have a differential effect on the different firms and sectors of the economy that provision the defense sector's demand for goods and services. If the rate of increase and the compositional mix of the defense expenditure are sustained through the 1980s, a substantial shift of resources toward durable goods industries – and particularly defense-related industries – could occur, which may have important economic consequences. Moreover, the compositional shift in the defense budget may also have a regional impact, as will be noted subsequently.

Table 2.2. The Reagan Defense Budget, Fiscal Years 1985 – 1989

| Item | FY 1985 | FY 1986 | FY 1987 | FY 1988 | FY 1989 | Total |
|---|---|---|---|---|---|---|
| *Budget authorization* | | | | | | |
| Billions of dollars | 305.0 | 349.6 | 379.2 | 411.5 | 446.1 | 1,891.4 |
| Percent real increase | 13.0 | 9.2 | 3.5 | 3.8 | 3.9 | 21.9 |
| *Outlays* | | | | | | |
| Billions of dollars | 264.4 | 301.8 | 339.2 | 369.8 | 398.8 | 1,674.0 |
| Percent real increase | 9.3 | 8.4 | 7.0 | 4.1 | 3.3 | 24.9 |
| *Pay and price deflators* | 100.0 | 105.3 | 110.6 | 115.8 | 120.9 | – |

*Source:* Department of Defense *Annual Report,* Fiscal Year 1985, p. 71.

The critics of the administration's defense buildup have argued that the defense program is both misguided and costly. They have proposed alternative plans which, they argue, provide the appropriate level of national security and are economically efficient.[14] It is argued that the administration had overestimated the pace and level of Soviet modernization of both nuclear and nonnuclear forces. According to CIA estimates, Soviet defense spending had slowed down to 4 percent real growth per year in 1964 – 1975 and to about 2 percent per year in 1976 – 1981.[15] Critics have also pointed out that the surge of investment has concentrated almost entirely on weapon modernization while major changes in force structure have yet to occur. Moreover, some have recently maintained that after several years of substantial expenditure, the level of preparedness of the U.S. forces has remained fairly inadequate. Finally, it has also been pointed out that undisciplined planning and programming in the Defense Department has led to substantial duplication of defense systems by the Army, the Navy, and the Air Force.

Researchers at the Brookings Institution have proposed an alternative program which incorporates three major modifications of the administration's defense plan:[16] canceling those programs aimed at modernizing those nuclear and general purpose forces that are deemed to be duplicative; slowing down the pace of procurement and other investment expenditures; and, more importantly, abandoning several questionable objectives incorporated in the administration plan. The savings from these changes are estimated to amount to about $45 billion in the fiscal year 1985 budget authority. Additionally, the Grace Commission has also suggested that savings of about $7.3 billion could be achieved, mainly by modifying the defense retirement program.[17] The main thrust of the changes suggested in the Brookings report is not only to lower the level of expenditure (by $45 billion in 1985) but also to change its composition by reducing the procurement account by 32 percent ($34 billion), and the research and development and military construction accounts by about 17 percent each.

We cannot resolve here whether the administration's critics are correct about the level and composition of the planned defense buildup. Obviously, the total resource needs for a defense program, as well as the skewed demand toward capital goods industries would be reduced under the critics' plan. As a consequence, the problems of adjustment and affordability of the defense buildup would also be less. The savings thus generated could be used to increase other needed public sector infrastructure investments in roads, bridges, education, health, etc., or to reduce the federal deficit. Any such economies are clearly desirable and need to be pursued, particularly if there is a clear military justification for them. However, for the purpose of this study, we take the administration's planned expenditure as the upper limit for defense expenditure and trace its impact on the economy. Should actual expenditures be similar to the alternative defense plans suggested by the critics, some of these consequences could be mitigated or modified.

## THE ECONOMIC OUTLOOK

Forecasting the evolution of the U.S. economy for the rest of this decade and beyond is a hazardous task. Year to year estimates can vary substantially; the long-run outlook of the economy can be significantly affected by drastic shifts in economic policy, autonomous changes due to technical change, and unforeseen events such as the OPEC price increases in the 1970s and decreases in the 1980s. The available estimates also differ greatly depending on the nature and quality of the forecasting models used.[18] Most of these models are generally demand-oriented and do not fully account for the changes in quantity and quality of the supply of factors of production and types of output. Also, they do not explicitly take technical progress (which may alter the basic structure of the economy or particular sectors in it) into account. These uncertainties are very real and the results presented below should be interpreted with a great degree of care.

There are several well known large-scale econometric models that attempt to forecast the behavior of aggregate economic variables, such as GNP, employment, prices, balance of payments, wage rate, investment in plant and equipment, etc. Although on particular issues the models' estimates may differ considerably, there is a rough consistency among the forecasts. Some highlights of these forecasts are instructive.[19] Nominal GNP was forecasted to grow by 8.6 percent in the 1981 – 1985 period and by about 9.2 percent for the remainder of this decade. Real GNP grew by about 6.8 percent in 1984 and is estimated to grow about 2.8 percent in 1985 and by about 3 percent until 1990. Government purchase was to grow about 6 percent in 1984 and 1985 and then slow down to about 1.1 percent over the 1987 – 1990 period. This is partly attributed to a major reduction in growth of government defense expenditure, which is to grow by about 6 percent in the 1981 – 1985 period, and then decline after 1986, averaging a growth rate of less than one percent in 1986 – 1990. The rate of growth of investment in the first period is dominated by the effect of the 1982 recession, which depressed investment, particularly in residential construction. In 1984, the growth of investment was almost 20 percent and is projected to grow at a rate above 5 percent for 1985 – 1988. This is substantially above the growth rate of investment in 1971 – 1975 but similar to the growth rate of 5.7 percent during 1976 – 1980. The growth rate of investment in fixed assets is forecasted to be about 5 percent in 1986 – 1990.

The rate of inflation, measured by either the consumer price index or the implicit GNP deflator, is generally projected to be around 4 percent for the period 1984 – 1988. According to the models, capacity utilization rate would increase from a low of 71 percent in 1982 to about 82 percent in 1985 and then rise gradually to about 85 percent in 1990. The unemployment rate is forecasted to fall from 7.5 percent to 6.8 percent during the period 1985 to 1988 and reach about 6.6 percent in 1990. Net exports of goods and services are also projected to decline in the 1986 – 1990 period. However, the interest rates on long-term bonds are forecasted to remain high, above 11.5 percent. Similarly, the government deficit, which has increased from $62 billion in 1981, is projected to rise substantially at first (about $200 billion in 1985) and then decline to about $145 billion in 1988. There is considerable uncertainty regarding the size and rate of increase of the federal deficit among the various models.

The period covered in these projections is too long, and the predictions from the econometric models are often too unreliable, to take these estimates as firm forecasts. However, barring basic changes in policy or structure of the economy, the estimates may indicate the trend of the economic activity for at least the next six to seven years. It shows that if there is a small real growth of defense expenditure for the period 1986 – 1990, and the assumptions of the models hold, the economy as a whole can perform satisfactorily, at least as indicated by the aggregated economic series. However, potential crises generated by the international indebtedness, a burst of inflationary forces similar to those of the 1970s, a rapid increase in international commodity prices, the reemergence of inflationary expectations, and a host of other factors could change these forecasts substantially. Therefore, a close monitoring of the economic activities and policies will be essential to keep the economy on a reasonable course.

In evaluating the potential growth and performance of the U.S. economy, it is important to note, aside from the quantitative projections, some of the major changes which have occurred in the last few years in economic policy, technology, institutions, and the political and economic environment. These changes will certainly affect the course of the economy in the next few years. Some of these can be summarized as follows: (a) the Federal Reserve has abandoned interest rate targeting, permitting demand pressure to affect interest rates directly; (b) a huge fiscal stimulus has stimulated consumer and investment expenditures in the private sector; (c) the business cycle has become more volatile, which has had significant effects on the decisions of U.S. firms; (d) information-based technology is spreading very rapidly throughout the economy; (e) deregulations in the trucking, airlines, and financial sectors, changes in wage setting, etc. have changed some of the institutional framework of the economy; (f) the economic and financial markets are now global in nature, with consequences such as high values for U.S. dollars, greater international competition, and larger flow of capital to the United States; (g) finally, there has been a change from public sector solutions to private sector incentives. These changes will probably lead to a scenario of "generally sustained growth in the economy, although not without some interruptions; relatively low inflation rates; low but still high nominal and real interest rates; a strong dollar; frequent ebbs and flows in economic performance; increasing influence of the new technology on the economy and social fabric; continuing tendencies toward deregulation, competition, and increased productivity; and a shift of emphasis to the private from the public sector."[20]

## MACROECONOMIC EFFECTS

We shall discuss three types of macroeconomic effects caused by the increase in defense expenditure: (a) the effect of the defense program as part of the overall federal budgetary deficit of the past four years and the projected future budgetary developments; (b) the impact of defense expenditure on aggregate demand; and (c), the aggregate supply-side or "crowding out" effect of the governmental budgetary deficit.

## The Deficit Problem and Defense Spending

The economic game plan envisaged by the administration faltered in two major respects: the substantial increase in the federal budget deficit and the unanticipated deep recession of 1981 – 1982. There are contending explanations for the recent budgetary history. The administration contends that the actual and projected budget deficits are due primarily to growth of nondefense expenditure which was not cut back sufficiently, and that Congress enacted tax policies that reduced tax burdens beyond the level proposed by the administration. It rejects the claim that the defense buildup is excessive. The opposing view is that both the individual income tax cut and the planned defense buildup were excessive, and should be scaled down substantially. What matters is that the enacted and planned defense buildups are taking place while the U.S. economy is facing a significant structural deficit for the rest of this decade. *Structural deficit* refers to non-business cycle related deficit, for example, a deficit that would prevail if the economy was at full employment. In this type of economic situation, the important issue is what happens to the performance of the economy when military spending is not paid for by taxes. This issue is also closely related to the affordability of the defense program.

There are several causes for the federal budget deficits. The most important one is a $750 billion reduction in personal and business taxes which pushed the budget into a permanently deep deficit. The next important factor, ironically, was the success in sharply lowering the inflation rate, from a 13 percent annual rate in early 1980 to about 4 percent in early 1984. (It is estimated that a one percentage point decline in the rate of inflation will, over a five-year period, cause a rise of $18.2 billion in the federal budget deficit). The net interest paid is also a major expense item, now the third largest source of budget outlays. The fourth factor is the three years of slow growth and recession from 1980 to 1982, which greatly reduced tax receipts and raised government spending.[21] It is probably true that budget problems reflect the government's inability to control spending rather than the impact of tax cuts which left revenues above their historical level as a percentage of GNP. U.S. government revenues represented 18.7 percent of GNP in 1984, which is close to the historical value of this ratio while U.S. government outlays represented 23.5 percent in 1984, which is above its historical level. This has happened despite the administration's success in slowing down the rate of growth in federal spending.[22]

Table 2.3 indicates the size of the projected deficits for the years 1984 to 1989. In Table 2.3, varying estimates, generated by both the administration and Congress, and by private forecasting services, are reported in order to indicate the existing uncertainty about the magnitude of future deficits. There are some important differences in the projected figures and the actual deficits for 1984 and 1985 have substantially exceeded these figures. Also it is unlikely that without a major effort to reduce the size of the deficits in 1986, the decline in absolute size of the deficit in 1988 and 1989 forecasted by some of the models will not come about. It is clear that precise estimates of future deficits will be difficult to obtain; the underlying models that generate these estimates rest on a number of assumptions which, in a dynamic economy, are subject to substantial changes. Nonetheless, the fact that the federal deficit has grown substantially and is likely to be sizable in the future is clearly supported by the available evidence.

To properly assess the problem of the deficit and consequently the affordability of the accelerated defense buildup it is important to interpret the deficit figures properly. Several issues have to be considered. One issue relates to the way the deficit figures are calculated. They refer to the federal budget and do not include the budgetary condition of the state and local governments. For a comprehensive view of how much pressure for resources the public sector puts on the economy, one must look at the net budget situation on all three government levels – federal, state, and local. There are sizable transfers to the states and municipalities as part of the federal government's expenditure that add to budgetary deficits at the federal level but help to balance or contribute to budgetary surpluses at the lower levels of government. The state and local government budgets have been in surplus since the 1960s and are projected to continue to indicate fairly sizable surpluses in the period 1984 – 1989. According to one estimate, if the state and local government budgets' surpluses were combined with the deficit in the federal budget, the overall government

Table 2.3. Projected Federal Budget Deficits 1984 to 1989

|  | 1984 | 1985 | 1986 | 1987 | 1988 | 1989 |
|---|---|---|---|---|---|---|
| Reagan Administration | 174.3 | 172.4 | 174.2 | 184.8 | 176.0 | 161 |
| Congressional Budget Office | 172 | 178 | 195 | 216 | 238 | 263 |
| *DRI* | 176 | 194 | 184 | 193 | 177 | 175 |
| Shearson Lehman[a] | 185 | 205 | 189 | 176 | 145 | – |
| Chase Econometrics | 178 | 183 | 170 | 157 | 126 | 103 |

[a]These estimates assume that most of the spending cuts contained in the Senate Budget Committee-White House compromise in 1985 are enacted after the Senate-House Conference in June 1985.

sector deficit would be substantially reduced and would represent a fairly insignificant percentage of GNP in the next few years.[23]

The frequently drawn comparison between the federal budget and individual family budgets also adds to the confusion. In fact, it would be more appropriate to compare the federal government's budgets with those of the business sector. In government budgets, one does not distinguish between capital and current accounts as is the case for a particular firm. The business sector continuously accumulates debt. It is in fact much larger than that of the federal government. The government debt, like that of the business sector, creates wealth. So, if viewed appropriately, the size of the deficit need not be so alarming. According to one estimate, if the government had a separate capital budget, as is the case with corporate budgets, the expenditures on capital assets (such as public buildings, roads, harbors, trucks, military bases, etc.) would not be part of the yearly deficit; these expenditures are not current expenses.[24] This correction alone would have reduced the recorded deficits of the years 1980 to 1983 by $20, $27, $43, and $31 billion dollars respectively,[25] Another appropriate correction would be to take into account the increase in valuation of government-accumulated assets and financial assets such as the federal debt (held by the Federal Reserve System, Social Security, and government pensions) and gold reserves. If all these adjustments were made, the real burden of the government budgetary deficit would be substantially reduced, and for some years, even reversed.[26]

Finally, some recent evidence suggests that the magnitude of the structural deficit may have been overstated. Most of the available estimates of the potential growth rate of the U.S. economy rest on the assumption that the natural rate of unemployment is 6 – 7 percent, the rate consistent with noninflationary situations.

However, some economists have argued that because of demographic changes and changes in the work force (such as the slower growth rate in the number of working women and the drop in the number of teenagers in the labor force, two groups with traditionally high unemployment rates) the natural rate of unemployment has declined below 6 percent to possibly 5 percent. Using the latter figure for the natural unemployment rate would, according to one estimate, reduce the deficit by $36 billion in 1985 and would result in still higher reductions in subsequent years.[27]

There are other aspects of the deficit problem, such as its impact on interest rates and consequently on investment decisions, capital flow from other industrial countries to the United States, the exchange rate, and finally the debt repayment of the developing countries, all of which require close attention. To be sure, the interest-sensitive sectors, such as housing and the automobile industry, are likely to be adversely affected by the high interest rates. The sharp rise in value of the dollar in recent years is also considered to be partly due to the large projected federal deficits. This, in turn, may have led to a sharp increase in the merchandise trade deficit, which recently exceeded the annual rate of $100 billion. It is true that increased imports have slowed the increase in the rate of inflation and have raised the standard of living of the consumers but the negative impact of high dollar values on the export industries has been considerable.[28] The high interest rate has stimulated a large outflow of capital from Europe and other areas of the world, and has helped to finance the U.S. government's deficit and meet the capital needs of U.S. firms. This year, the capital inflow from the rest of the world will probably add $100 billion to the U.S. savings pool, which is enough to finance one-half of the deficit or 40 percent of all net investments in the United States.[29] The outflow of capital from foreign nations – and the high interest rates existing in other countries – may have contributed to the slow growth of these economies. The high interest rates in the United States have increased the debt burden of several developing countries and created severe adjustment problems in these countries, which may still threaten the stability of the world's financial structure and may further retard the growth of world trade and development. These issues require considerable attention but exceed the scope of this study. We nevertheless mention them here so that significant adverse side effects of U.S. budgetary deficits not be ignored.

## Demand Effects of the Defense Spending

The argument that deficits may hurt rather than help economic growth rests on the notion that the deficits are so large and so prolonged that the increase in real interest rates may more than offset their direct expansionary impact. Their "unsustainability" rests on the notion that a country running such deficits will repudiate the debt either explicitly or through inflation depreciation.[30] A prolonged deficit could undermine "business confidence," and even if there were no increase in real rates of interest, the fall in investments might offset the expansionary effects of deficits. But increased deficits can also strengthen business confidence if firms believe that there is a positive fiscal stimulus that would achieve economic recovery and growth. However, prolonged deficits may increase the real rates of interest so much that they offset their positive fiscal stimulus, i.e., though current deficits may be expansionary, anticipation of growing deficits may reduce economic activity. Finally, it is argued that a negative fiscal multiplier is possible if the increased deficit raises the overall price level by increasing the price of consumption goods more than that of investment goods. The increase in the overall price level would, via the reduction in real balances, offset the expansionary effect of deficits.[31] Such an outcome is possible under specific circumstances. However, the recent experience of extremely low inflation rates and the projected rate of price increases for the next five years make this outcome rather implausible.

The effects of defense spending on economic aggregates (such as growth rate of GNP, employment and investment, wages and prices, unemployment rate, capacity utilization rates, deficits, etc.) are often analyzed with the aid of large econometric models. To trace the impact of defense expenditure or any other type of change in economic policy at a disaggregated industry level, these econometric models are often combined with input-output models, and simulation techniques are used to trace the effect of alternative policies on the evolution and structure of the economy and its various sectors. Several available studies have examined the aggregate effects of the increased defense expenditure. In a conference sponsored by the Department of Defense (DoD) in October 1980, five prominent private forecasting companies presented the results of their simulation runs on the impact of accelerated defense spending.[32] Two types of simulations were run: in the first scenario, the planned defense expenditure was held to a 4 percent real growth, and in the second scenario, defense expenditure was increased to 10 percent per year in *real terms* over the period 1980 – 1985. The results are interesting from several viewpoints: (a) a 10 percent increase in defense expenditure is a very large change and much larger than the administration's planned increase in defense spending. It would be interesting to see how the economy would respond to such a large increase; (b) a number of models with different structural features are employed to forecast the behavior of economic variables. It is of interest to note whether they predict similar results; (c) enough time has elapsed to judge whether the forecasts of these models have been validated by actual events.

The forecast results of these models were basically similar and pointed to the same type of developments between 1980 and 1986. Specifically, it was estimated that the increase in real defense expenditure from 4 percent to 10 percent would lead to:

- increased growth of GNP, lower unemployment rate, higher productivity growth, and higher investment (except for the DRI model which forecasted a substantial decline in the rate of growth of investment);
- a modest price inflation and wage rate increase;
- an increase in the size of deficits and a rise in the interest rate.

These models did not take into account the occurrence and impact of the largely unanticipated deep recession of 1982 which, with its high level of unemployment and capacity underutilization, created a climate that accommodated the increased expansion of the defense expenditure without much difficulty. This accommodation is clearly supported by the available evidence. Eckstein's simulation results (using the DRI model) suggest that even if the rate of economic activity were very high, the adverse side effects of the rapid increase in defense expenditure might not occur until 1987.[33] These results suggest that there is enough slack in the economy to accommodate the increased defense expenditure without much difficulty. The models nevertheless do warn against deficit financing of government expenditure of any type because it may have adverse effects on the rate of capital formation of the private sector.

## The Crowding-Out Effect

The argument for the crowding-out of private investment expenditure rests on the notion that a large and growing federal deficit forces the treasury to go to the capital market frequently and raise substantial amounts of funds, which puts pressure on the interest rate. The high rate of interest, in turn, inhibits the rate of capital formation in the private sector, the growth and development of which is thus hindered by defense and other federal expenditures. The high interest rates also lead to growing strength of the dollar and absorption of investable funds from abroad. Therefore, since defense spending represents a large portion of total expenditure of the federal government, it may be responsible for part of the crowding-out effect of the private sector and of the long-term slowdown of the growth of the economy.

There is no conclusive empirical evidence on the causal relationship between budget deficits and high interest rates. Even if the increase in interest rate was caused by the deficit, it is arguable whether the rate of capital formation has been negatively affected to a great extent. The quantitative effects of crowding-out were addressed by Eckstein.[34] His results indicate that, if the defense spending is not paid for by taxation, the level of investment and potential GNP will be lower by almost one percentage point. Interest rates will be driven up by the combination of fiscal stimulus of the defense spending and monetarist policies likely to be pursued by the Federal Reserve. The rise in interest rates substantially affects the interest-sensitive housing and automobile sectors and, to a lesser extent, the fixed investment capital formation. By 1988 the aggregate supply or potential GNP will be reduced by .9 percent and will grow larger in subsequent years. The conclusion arrived at by Eckstein is that the United States can afford the defense spending program laid out by the Reagan administration but unless it is financed through taxation, the future development of the U.S. economy is likely to be adversely affected.

However, these estimates may overstate the effect of the deficit on private investment. Even if it is true that the deficit causes the high interest rates, the issue is how sensitive investment demand is with respect to changes in interest rates. If investment expenditure is not very responsive to interest rate changes, then even a large increase in interest rates will not dampen the pace of private investment. The crowding-out hypothesis assumes high interest elasticity of investment. Eckstein's and other investment models, for example, are based on a Jorgenson type of neoclassical investment model that give equal weight to changes in growth of demand and changes in relative prices.[35] But growth of output and changes in relative prices may not have the same effect on investment expenditure.[36] If firms perceive a continued growth and high return on their investment they will probably undertake investment despite high interest rates.

We should also note that the interest rate is only one element of the rental price of capital; other components of this price are the rate of depreciation, the price of capital goods, and tax rates of various kinds. In 1981 the tax laws governing depreciation allowances and tax credits were substantially revised to stimulate further investment. The reduction in taxes lowered the rental price of capital while the rise in interest rate increased it. The two effects may very well have offset each other and may be one reason why investment demand has not declined in response to the increase in the interest rate.[37] Also, the interest rates, though still high, have declined substantially in the past three years from their 1981 levels.

The deficit also increases aggregate demand. Business firms do consider a sustained shift in aggregate demand as a crucial element of their decision to increase capacity. Because of the deep recession of 1981 – 1982 capacity utilization rates had been low and most firms were waiting for signs of a sustained expansion of the economy to utilize their excess capacity first and then undertake further investment. The buoyancy of the private investment in 1983 – 1984 fits this pattern. (Thus, the stimulative effect of the deficit may have dominated its impact via interest rate on investment expenditure). Such as scenario leads to a hypothesis of "crowding-in" and not "crowding-out" of private investment expenditure.

On balance, what can be said from the available evidence on macroeconomic effects of the increased defense expenditure? The deficit issue, as far as the defense budget is concerned, can be summarized as follows. If the deficit is understood properly (i.e., if we make all the adjustments noted earlier) it is not as big, wasteful, or dangerous as is often claimed. The defense budget need not be reduced on account of the deficit alone if national security needs require the level and rate of defense expenditure suggested by the administration. There is, in fact, a reasonable chance that the economy could accommodate the planned increase in the defense expenditures.

The arguments for, the crowding-out of private investment are not self-evident when the economy's resources are underutilized. However, a prolonged deficit may become a serious problem at or near full employment; the government's absorption of savings would outstrip any plausible increases in the savings rate; this situation would worsen if the foreign capital inflow failed to fill the gap. Under these conditions the interest rate would rise and the share of the nation's output devoted to net capital formation would at best remain low.[38] Also, the increase in the interest rates have adverse side effects on the U.S. interest-sensitive sectors, the export industries, and the rest of the world.

Congress has already adjusted some of the tax reductions of the 1981 tax cut, and is at work to cut the deficit further in the next few years. In 1986, the defense budget is likely not to increase in real terms which will slow the potential rise in future deficits. Economic growth could also offset some portion – though not the entirety – of the projected deficit. Also, defense spending could be reduced on the grounds of economic efficiency and military relevance, as noted by the Brookings and other studies. However, it is important to note that the attempts to reduce deficits by curtailing public spending and/or raising revenues by taxes together with tax simplification and reform could generate enough uncertainty to affect the rate of growth of the economy, at least in the short run. This, is turn, may make the closing of the deficit gap more difficult.

## SECTORAL AND REGIONAL EFFECTS

The macroeconomic effect of the increased defense expenditure does not reveal some of the critical influences that a sustained military buildup might have on the structure of the economy. If the growth of the defense sector greatly exceeded that of the private sector, the sectoral and regional distribution of the output, employment, occupation, and investment in the economy could be substantially altered. This is because defense expenditures do not affect all the industries of the economy and all the regions of the nation equally. Some industries may be more closely dependent on defense needs than other industries and some regions and localities may specialize to a large extent in goods and services needed for national defense. Thus the aggregate, sectoral, and regional impacts of the defense program are basically intertwined and must be treated together.

### Sectoral Output Growth

The estimates generated from econometric input-output models indicate that for some industrial products generated by defense spending the growth rates of demand are substantially larger than for those generated by civilian spending, and also that the configurations of industries that respond to a given increase in demand for defense and nondefense expenditures are quite different.[39] Sectors supplying national security needs directly, such as electronics, aircraft, missiles, shipbuilding, and ordnance, have experienced – and are forecasted to experience – substantial growth. Other sectors, such as refined petroleum products, electronic measuring equipment, chemicals, transportation and communications, and hotels and restaurant services meet the defense needs indirectly by providing immediate goods and services for the defense industries. These industries are likely to continue to experience substantial growth in the next few years.[40]

However, the total production indices for defense-sensitive sectors do not indicate rapid increases. This is partly because in the aircraft industry, for example, the civilian demand has fallen while the defense demand has increased. The shipping and electronic component industries have had a sizable excess capacity and the production indices in these industries are not increasing greatly. Data on shipments and new orders in the defense-sensitive industries confirm the same results. Except for communication equipment, there seems to be little evidence of significant tightening in these industries.

However, there is a long-run aspect to changes in the composition of demand between the military and civilian sectors of the economy. If military spending continues to grow at a higher rate than civilian spending, the industrial and sectoral structure of the economy will change, pulling resources such as skilled workers and investments away from the civilian to the military sector of the economy. This in turn will raise the issue of the desirability of such a structural change and also problems of transition associated with the resource transfer among the civilian and military sectors. The transitional problems could become important if military spending slackens after a few years, and the resources released from production of military goods and services have to be absorbed into the civilian sector.

## Capacity Utilization Rates

Whether the various industries can meet the substantial demand generated by military spending without running into capacity constraints depends on the degree of excess capacity available and the willingness of the industries to undertake expenditure on plant and equipment. The recession of 1982 was deep and the defense expenditure, rather than competing with strong demand from the civilian sector of the economy, has been a source of demand growth. The recession thus provided a "grace period" within which the demand from the Department of Defense could be accommodated with ease by the industry. Now that the economy is out of the recession, expanding the planned defense expenditure will put additional pressure on industrial capacity. The estimates of excess capacity in the key defense sectors indicate that the likelihood of industrial capacity constraints and production bottlenecks is relatively minor in the near future. Measures of capacity utilization in total manufacturing, electrical machinery, transportation equipment, and aircraft show that the capacity utilization still reflects the impact of the recession.[41] The capacity constraints will probably be reached in the late 1980s. A recent long-term projection by DRI of capacity utilization rates for 52 sectors of the U.S economy for the period 1983 to 1995 suggests that both potential and actual demand in these sectors will grow at equal rates, indicating no significant pressure on capacity rates. Only in 20 percent of the sectors are there indications of potential pressure on capacity utilization which could lead to increases either in prices or in imports to meet the demand over this period.[42]

However, in future years, the investment decisions of the firms will be critical as to whether the economy can accommodate defense demand beyond 1986 without adverse effects. The planned expansion of plant and equipment in 1983 did not occur, because of several factors such as the presence of substantial overcapacity, low profits, high interest rates, and uncertainty about the future course of demand. The 1984 investment increases were generally quite substantial. Expansion of plant and equipment expenditure was robust in most industries, particularly in sectors such as durables, electrical machinery, aircraft, and transportation equipment where the defense-related demand is very strong. What matters is whether the investment expenditure will continue to grow beyond 1985. As we noted earlier, one factor which may be critical in business investment decisions is the potential impact of the federal deficit on the expected increase in interest rates and on the expansion of aggregate demand, which in turn will affect investment in plant and equipment. Also, if there are uncertainties about future defense budget levels in the context of the debate on the federal deficit, investment in plant and equipment will be discouraged in industries closely related to defense production.

Nevertheless, the likelihood of bottlenecks and capacity constraints retarding the accommodation of defense demand in the near future is fairly small. This is because of excess capacity available in defense-sensitive industries as well as in the rest of the economy and also because of some indications of a fairly robust investment in plant and equipment in 1984 and possibly beyond. However, this precarious situation may be reversed very suddenly: the federal budget uncertainties, the tax reform and simplification efforts, and the cumulative impact of the federal deficit may adversely affect business expectations, which could significantly affect investment expenditures.

## Defense Spending Deflator

There is some evidence that, unlike what happened in the 1970s, the deflator for defense expenditure has, in recent years, been growing at a slower rate than the Consumer Price Index. This improvement is mainly due to the decrease in the rise of energy costs. Also, increases in labor costs, which are an important component of defense producers' cost structures, significantly affect weapon procurement programs, which are generally labor intensive. The moderate pace of escalation in wage rates experienced in recent years has therefore also contributed to the slow rise in the deflator for the defense expenditures. Additionally, the slowing down in prices of materials purchased by the Department of Defense has made a similar contribution. The same basic slowdown in energy price, labor cost, and material prices is also reflected in the defense deflators for particular categories of expenditure, such as military construction, aircraft missiles, shipbuilding, combat and noncombat vehicles, communication and electrical equipment, ammunition, and research and development. It has been estimated that in the period from 1983 to 1988, the pace of the overall defense expenditure deflator and the specific deflators will grow at fairly slow rates.[43] Thus the implication of the projected slow growth of the defense deflators is that the military programs should reach their goal without being forced to seek more funds on account of higher than national rates of inflation. Also, the available indices suggest that there is still excess capacity in most of the industries which directly or indirectly provide the goods and services needed by the Department of Defense.

## Employment Effect and Occupational Impact

Considerable controversy surrounds the employment effect of the increased defense expenditure. Some estimates suggest that each $1 billion in defense expenditure creates approximately 35,000 incremental jobs and that by 1987 this employment multiplier will drop to 31,000 jobs for $1 billion defense spending.[44] This is an outcome of the industrial distribution of defense requirements for goods and services. Most direct defense requirements are met by the durable goods industries, particularly by the electrical machinery and transportation equipment sector. However, the overall defense multiplier is probably somewhat smaller than that for the civilian economy. Production runs are often short and some defense goods, because of their specialized nature, are labor intensive; as noted below, the final demand and the composition of defense production is similar to that of nondefense production.

The planned increase in defense expenditure will have a major impact in terms of the industry distribution of the U.S. labor force. In Table 2.4, a summary of employment projections (in growth terms) for several sectors and manufacturing industries are shown for the years 1982 and 1987. Some of the results are quite significant. The growth rate of defense employment of 8.2 percent is over five times greater than the 1.6 percent growth rate projected for the U.S. nonagricultural sectors. The same type of differential exists in almost all of the industries shown in the table. If this pattern persists, the defense share of employment growth will be quite high. About 16 percent of all new jobs will be devoted to the production of defense output and over half of the new jobs in the durable goods industries will be related to defense production. In some specific industries, such as petroleum products, primary metals, and electrical machinery, almost the entire employment growth is projected to be due to increased demand for defense production.

A sustained growth in defense spending will also affect the occupational distribution in the labor market. The average annual growth and the share of defense in the growth rate of a number of critical skilled jobs are shown in Table 2.5. Most of the additional employment in the different industries mentioned earlier will be drawn from these occupational groupings. The average annual percentage of employment growth in defense industries is greater than that for the entire economy in each occupational category. The last two columns illustrate the significant role of the increase in defense spending. The overall defense share of employment exceeds 15 percent only in a few narrowly defined occupational specialties, but the defense

Table 2.4. Employment Forecast for 1982 – 1987 Period (Millions of People)

|  | Average Annual % Growth | | Defense Share of Growth (%) |
| --- | --- | --- | --- |
|  | Defense | Total |  |
| Total nonagricultural employment | 8.20 | 1.59 | 15.7 |
| Construction | 8.78 | 1.14 | 29.0 |
| Finance, insurance, and real estate | 8.94 | 1.79 | 5.7 |
| Mining | 7.46 | 1.36 | 22.1 |
| Transportation and utilities | 5.28 | 1.23 | 16.6 |
| Services | 8.23 | 2.19 | 9.2 |
| Wholesale and retail trade | 9.47 | 1.45 | 5.4 |
| Federal government | — | 2.89 | — |
| State and local government | — | 1.22 | — |
| Manufacturing | 8.34 | 1.12 | 62.1 |
| Nondurable goods | 7.16 | −0.12 | — |
|   Food and products | 5.13 | −0.12 | — |
|   Tobacco and products | 7.24 | −0.08 | — |
|   Textiles and products | 5.39 | 1.00 | 7.5 |
|   Apparel and products | 5.36 | −2.92 | — |
|   Paper and products | 7.45 | 0.75 | 21.8 |
|   Chemicals and products | 7.64 | 1.15 | 20.9 |
|   Printing and publishing | 6.01 | 0.18 | 58.4 |
|   Petroleum products | 5.28 | 0.16 | 145.1 |
|   Rubber and plastic products | 10.33 | 1.66 | 20.9 |
|   Leather and products | 5.51 | −0.99 | — |
| Durable goods | 8.44 | 1.91 | 55.5 |
|   Lumber and wood products | 9.17 | 2.56 | 8.0 |
|   Furniture and fixtures | 4.28 | 1.41 | 3.1 |
|   Stone, clay and glass | 8.91 | 0.77 | 38.2 |
|   Primary metal industries | 8.39 | 0.63 | 105.5 |
|   Fabricated metal products | 8.33 | 1.28 | 61.4 |
|   Nonelectrical machinery | 8.33 | 1.75 | 22.33 |
|   Electrical machinery | 9.02 | 2.92 | 64.9 |
|   Transportation equipment | 8.08 | 2.45 | 102.0 |
|   Instruments and parts | 8.37 | 2.52 | 33.5 |
|   Miscellaneous manufacturing | 6.07 | 1.27 | 5.2 |

*Source:* Data Resources, Inc. "Industry/Occupational Outlook," *Defense Economics Research Report,* December 1982.

share of the 1982 – 1987 net growth exceeds 15 percent in all but a few of the occupational groups.

An analysis of occupational developments in a number of key defense-supplying industries, including both prime contracting industries and various indirect supply

Table 2.5. Employment Forecasts for Selected Occupations, 1982 to 1987 (Thousands of Persons)

|  | Average Annual % Growth | | 1987 Defense Shares (%) | |
| --- | --- | --- | --- | --- |
|  | Defense | Total | Total | Net Growth |
| Engineers | 8.8 | 3.0 | 14.5 | 35.9 |
| aero-astronautic engineers | 10.7 | 6.0 | 51.5 | 81.7 |
| electrical engineers | 8.9 | 3.9 | 15.7 | 31.4 |
| Scientists, NEC | 7.1 | 1.9 | 3.6 | 11.6 |
| Engineering and science technicians | 8.0 | 2.5 | 7.1 | 19.4 |
| Electrical and electronic technicians | 8.6 | 3.2 | 10.0 | 23.2 |
| Technicians, NEC | 6.2 | 1.6 | 4.6 | 15.7 |
| Computer specialists | 10.9 | 4.9 | 5.4 | 10.2 |
| Social scientists and other professionals | 5.9 | 1.2 | 2.0 | 8.4 |
| Business professionals and staff | 6.7 | 1.6 | 2.5 | 9.0 |
| Craft and related workers | 6.4 | 1.3 | 4.7 | 20.2 |
| Construction crafts workers | 6.3 | 1.1 | 4.1 | 19.6 |
| Mechanics, repairers and installers | 6.6 | 1.7 | 3.1 | 10.6 |
| Metalworking craft workers excluding mechanics | 6.6 | 1.1 | 9.2 | 47.3 |
| Operatives | 6.7 | 1.0 | 5.7 | 32.6 |
| assemblers | 7.5 | 2.3 | 14.4 | 40.3 |
| metalworking operatives | 6.9 | 1.5 | 10.7 | 42.5 |
| Service workers | 7.3 | 1.7 | 1.9 | 6.8 |
| Laborers, except farm | 5.9 | 1.1 | 3.2 | 15.4 |

*Source:* Data Resources, Inc., "Industry/Occupational Outlook," *Defense Economics Research Report,* December 1982.

industries, is also instructive. The results strongly support the notion that the impact of defense expenditure on occupation distribution is quite skewed. The employment growth requirements in four key prime defense contracting industries – ordnance and accessories, communications equipment, aircraft and parts, and other transportation equipment – show that in each of these key industries, the growth rate of jobs for the period 1982 – 1987 is substantially higher in each occupation because of increased defense expenditures.[45]

These observations and forecasts suggest that labor force planning, as well as the expansion of plant and equipment, can become important constraints in fulfilling the national security needs at reasonable costs. These constraints will become particularly tight if the economy keeps growing, and particularly after 1985 when the current level of unemployment and the relatively slack level of capital utilization will have decreased substantially. There is no solid evidence on how much the supply of labor with critical skills will be expanding in the next few years. Nor is there any reliable evidence on how much the defense expenditure will stimulate the supply of engineers and skilled workers. If the supply of skilled workers and the expansion of capacity proceed smoothly, it is not very likely that serious sectoral and economy-wide bottlenecks would emerge. Serious attention must therefore be given to training and educational policies to expand the supply of skills and workers that are projected for the next few years.

## Regional Impacts

There are regional dimensions to the changing composition of output, employment, and capacity expansion caused by a vigorous increase in demand for military goods and services. These effects arise because of the existing distribution in different regions of the country – or localities within each region – of industries specializing in goods and services needed for national defense. Since the administration's defense plan emphasizes procurement accounts in the defense budget, the states where large procurement suppliers are situated are likely to show rapid growth. With the shift in defense spending toward procurement in the past three years, the eastern and northern regions (where defense expenditure is relatively more purchase-oriented) have experienced more growth than the southern and western regions. States with key indirect supplying industries for national security needs will also benefit from a rapid growth of defense spending. There are wide variations among the states in terms of the level of spending and share of defense output in the total output of a state.[46] In some states, both the direct and indirect production of defense-related goods and services is high, while in other states the impact of defense spending is skewed toward one or the other of the two categories.[47] Also, the projected impact of defense spending for the period 1981 – 1988 for different states shows that the growth in defense share of output varies considerably, from low rates of about 7 percent to 9 percent to high rates of 18 percent to 44 percent. Some of the high growth rates such as Vermont's (27 percent) or Alaska's (44 percent) apply to a very small industrial base, while the medium rate applies to states like California (18 percent) and Illinois (16 percent), states with a very large industrial base. It is also important to note that in every state, the growth in the defense share is much higher than the growth in the share of nondefense sectors in its economy.[48]

The impact of defense expenditure on an individual state can be substantial if there is a change in the composition of the defense spending even when its level remains unchanged. Thus, the shift toward procurement in the administration's defense program mentioned earlier will have an important impact on geographical patterns of production, employment, and investment. Some of these changes arise from uncertainties inherent in the decision process related to defense spending: competition among suppliers forces particular programs such as aircraft procurement to shift fairly often from one state to another. Particular changes in military objectives, or congressional decisions to curtail one set of programs and initiate another, can affect a few states more than others. Also, firms may decide to locate their plants in different states in response to defense contracts, which may affect the pattern of defense contracts, which may affect the pattern of development and growth in different states and regions.

## SUMMARY AND CONCLUSIONS

The relationship between defense expenditure and the economy is complex and inherently controversial. A discussion of all the relevant issues and controversies lies outside the scope of our analysis. Instead, we have focused on two important questions. The first was whether the resource transfer from the civilian to the defense sector of the U.S. economy – in response to the sizable military buildup program of the past four years – has been smooth or disruptive; that is, has military spending generated any sectoral bottleneck, generalized inflation, or distortions in patterns of economic activity? The second question was whether the U.S. economy can afford to finance the administration's defense buildup program.

To answer these questions, we briefly examined the determinants of the defense expenditure and the rationale for the Reagan administration's military buildup. We also discussed the alternative defense buildup advocated by the administration's critics. Moreover, we analyzed the defense program in the context of the administration's overall economic plan, and briefly examined the performance of the U.S. economy in the past four years as well as its outlook for the next few years, as projected by various econometric models. Additionally, we considered several macroeconomic consequences of military spending: the defense buildup as part of the overall federal budgetary deficit, the impact of defense expenditure on aggregate demand, and finally the aggregate supply-side or "crowding-out" effect of the government's budgetary deficit. Finally, we assessed the sectoral and regional effects of defense spending in order to examine the possibility that sectoral bottlenecks and regional distortions might have developed as substantial changes in the composition and method of financing of the federal spending were taking place.

The main findings of our analysis can be briefly summarized as follows:

1. We find no evidence of any major disruptive effect of defense expenditure on the U.S. economy, such as had been predicted by the Reagan administration critics. No major bottlenecks or tendency toward general inflationary pressure has been evident. The industry rates of utilization have not reached their critical levels; the inflation rate has actually declined and is predicted to remain low for some time in the future. Even the deflator for defense expenditure has not increased substantially. In fact, the defense expenditure has served to stimulate demand, directly in defense-related industries, and indirectly in other industries, thus countering the effect of the recent recession.

2. The outlook of the U.S. economy remains fairly optimistic, except for the uncertainty due to the federal budgetary deficit. The econometric projections point to a sustained growth in the economy (with some likely interruptions), low inflation rates, lower – but still high – nominal and real rates of interest, a relatively strong dollar, increasing competition in international markets, and inflow of capital.

3. The deficit issue has been, and is likely to remain, a major policy challenge. We have noted that if proper adjustments were made, the size of the deficits and their economic impact might not be as threatening as has been claimed. When proper economic accounting methods are used, the size of the deficit as percentage of GNP is likely to be small.

4. The defense expenditure has had a definite expansion effect on many sectors of the economy. Simulation results have indicated that the administration's military expenditure could be accommodated without much difficulty. In fact, defense spending served as an important, though unplanned, counter-recessionary force in the recent economic downturn.

5. There is no strong empirical evidence on the relationship between interest rates and deficits. Even though there may be a strong and positive relationship between the nominal interest rate and the federal deficit, it is not clear from the evidence that a "crowding-out" of private investment has taken place at least in the past several years. If investment decisions were highly interest-elastic, the recent investment boom could not be accounted for. In fact, it is the expansionary effect of the deficit and the interest in elasticity of private investment that explain the robust expansion of business investment. However, if the economy were near or at full employment, continued federal deficits and increased government absorption could easily outstrip the plausible increases in the savings rate, and as a result the share of output devoted to net capital formation would remain low. This would particularly be the case if foreign inflow of capital slowed down.

6. There are other effects of the deficit, however, which should not be ignored; the large capital inflow from other countries in response to the high U.S. interest rates, the high U.S. exchange rate, and the increasing U.S. merchandise trade deficit, the high interest rate burden on the developing countries with the potential consequence of disrupting the world financial markets, and the retardation of the world trade are important issues that cannot be ignored. Also, the deficit issue has become an important topic of debate in both political and economic circles in the United States. This continuous debate does generate uncertainties about the future course of economic policy and performance. Such an uncertainty may very well lead to slowed economic growth and even another recession.

7. Examination of the sectoral and regional impact of the defense expenditure suggests that, in many defense-related industries and regions with high concentrations of defense industries, there has been a substantial growth of demand for labor, and a shift of employment – especially highly skilled labor – toward the defense industries. But these shifts have not lead to any bottlenecks as yet, mainly because of overall excess capacity in many industries. However, if the defense program continues to grow, and the civilian sector resumes its vigorous pace of the 1983 – 1984 period, the likelihood of such bottlenecks is high. Also, in long run, if a large portion of highly skilled labor is absorbed by the defense sector, it may become difficult for the civilian sector of the economy to command such resources at reasonable cost.

These observations suggest that, on the whole, the defense buildup has not yet had the harmful effects predicted by its critics, and that the U.S. economy has been able to finance such a sizable effort. However, a large and rapidly growing military expenditure may not be so easily accommodated in the future if the growth rate of the economy slows down, the size of the deficit remains large or increases, or substantial inflationary pressures develop. Also, there may be important military reasons why the size and composition of the military buildup program should be changed. If this is so, the reduction in military spending could be used to lower the deficit or to finance many other public investments in education, environment, urban redevelopment, etc. It is likely that in the next few years, a combination of expenditure reduction (including military spending), tax increase, and tax reform will be undertaken by the administration and Congress to reduce the projected future deficits. Such adjustments will affect the growth rate of the economy. Thus the rate of growth of the economy, the expenditure for national security, and other types of public spending and methods of financing them are part of a simultaneous process which will require very close monitoring.

## NOTES

1. The literature on the subject is voluminous. As an example see the articles and references contained in James L. Clayton, ed., *The Economic Impact of the Cold War: Sources and Readings* (New York: Harcourt, Brace and World, Inc., 1970).
2. There are a few four-digit SIC industries where defense production accounts for at least half of total output. These industries usually contain segments that specialize in producing for the military.
3. See, for further details, *The Geographic Distribution of Potential Defense Expenditure*, Department of Defense, July 1984.
4. Murray Weidenbaum, "Defense Expenditure and the Domestic Economy," in Edwin Mansfield, ed., *Defense, Science and Public Policy* (New York: W.W. Norton & Co., 1968).
5. Lester Thurow, "How to Wreck the Economy," *The New York Review of Books*, May 14, 1981, pp. 3 – 8.
6. Ibid.
7. For an example of such models, see Saadet Deger and Somnath Sen, "Military Expenditure, Spin-Off and Economic Development," *Journal of Development Economics* 13 (1983): 67 – 83; and Leonard Dudley and Claude Montmarquette, "The Demand for Military Expenditures: An International Comparison," *Public Choice* 37, No. 1 (1981): 5 – 21, and Chapters 3 and 4 of this volume together with the appropriate references given at the end of these chapters.
8. See James Murdoch and Todd Sandler, "A Theoretical and Empirical Analysis of NATO," *Journal of Conflict Resolution* 26 (1982): 237 – 263. Also see chapter by the same authors and chapter by K. Forbes and M. McGuire in this volume for further discussion and references.
9. Or in terms of percentage of the GNP, throughout the decade, defense resources were below the 1964 (pre-Vietnam) level of 8.3 percent, with a low of 5 percent in 1978/79. By 1981, the defense claim was still only 5.6 percent. On the other hand, nondefense spending as a percentage of GNP increased sharply over the decade rising from its 1964

level of 9.5 percent. By 1981 nondefense spending was about 15 percent of GNP – an increase of over 40 percent for the decade – and 57 percent from the pre-Vietnam benchmark. See for further detail Alton G. Keel Jr., "The FY 1984 Defense Budget: The View from OMB," presented to the Southern Economics Association, November 21, 1983, mimeo, and the *1984 Annual Report of the Council of Economic Advisors*, 1984, Table 1, mimeo.
10. For an explicit account of Soviet weapons production compared to that of the U.S. over the 1974 – 1981 period, see Alton G. Keel Jr., op. cit.
11. For a detailed analysis of these shortages and shortfalls in U.S. combat readiness see Alton G. Keel, Jr., op. cit.
12. See *Economic Report of the President, 1984*, pp. 18 – 22.
13. Estimates by the Council of Economic Advisors projects the following figures for defense spending as a percent of GNP:

| 1984 | 1985 | 1986 | 1987 | 1988 | 1989 |
|---|---|---|---|---|---|
| 6.7 | 7.3 | 7.7 | 7.7 | 7.7 | 7.8 |

*Source:* 1984 *Annual Report of the Council of Economic Advisors*, Table 1.

14. See "Paying for National Security," in Alice Rivilan, ed., *Economic Choices 1984* (Washington, DC: The Brookings Institution, 1984), Chapter 4.
15. *The Allocation of Resources in the Soviet Union and China – 1983*. Hearing before the Subcommittee on International Trade, Finance and Security Economics of the Joint Economic Committee, 98 Congress, cited in A. Rivilan, op. cit. p. 72.
16. See for further detail W.W. Kaufman, *The 1985 Defense Budget* (Washington, DC: The Brookings Institution, 1984), and *Economic Choices 1984*, Chapter 4.
17. *Economic Choices 1984*.
18. For an interesting discussion of the substantial forecasting of several econometric models, see Robert D. Hershey Jr., "Frustrations of Forecasters," *The New York Times*, July 2, 1984, pp. D1 & 11, and R.J. Gordon, "Do Economists Deserve a Failing Grade?" *The Gordon Update*, Fall 1984.
19. Most of the specific estimates are taken from Allen Sinai, *Economic Outlook and Issues*, Shearson Lehman Brothers, May 28, 1985, Table 2, page 6.
20. Allen Sinai. *Aftermath of the First Four Years*. Shearson Lehman, Bulletin Series, September 28, 1984, p. 3.
21. Some estimates indicate a 5-point reduction in real economic growth would depress tax receipts by an average of $34.4 billion a year over five years and raise federal government spending by $11.8 billion over the same period.
22. *See Economic Report of the President, 1984*, p. 29.
23. That is:

| Year | 1985 | 1986 | 1987 | 1988 | 1989 |
|---|---|---|---|---|---|
| Total Deficit | 94 | 85 | 77 | 45 | 11 |
| as % of GNP* | 2.3% | 1.9% | 1.6% | .8% | .2% |

*Source: Wall Street Journal*, July 23, 1984, p. 16.

24. Robert Eisner, "Deficit Madness," *The New York Times*, July 14, 1984, p. 23, and Robert Heilbroner, "Reflections: The Deficit," *The New Yorker*, July 30, 1984, pp. 47 – 55.

25. The Eisner estimates are as follows:

|  | 1980 | 1981 | 1982 | 1983 |
|---|---|---|---|---|
| *Actual budget deficits* | 61 | 62 | 112 | 186 |
| *Capital account correction* | 20 | 27 | 43 | 31 |
| *Total* | 41 | 35 | 69 | 155 |

26. For example, according to Eisner's calculation, instead of having a deficit of $61 billion in 1980 the budget would indicate a surplus of $7 billion in that year.
27. See Ashok Chandrasekhar, "Some Economists Call for Lowering Natural Jobless Rate to Cut Deficit," *Wall Street Journal,* September 11, 1984, p. 37.
28. Martin Feldstein, "Depressing the Dollar, Gently," *Wall Street Journal,* November 9, 1984, p. 30.
29. Ibid.
30. J. Oliver Blanchard, "Current and Anticipated Deficits, Interest Rates and Economic Activity." NBER Working Paper No. 1265, January 1984.
31. Martin Feldstein, "Can an Increased Budget Deficit Be Contractionary?" NBER Working Paper No. 1434, August 1984.
32. David Blond, "Measuring the Impact of the Defense Budget 1983–1988: The Industrial and Labor Composition of Defense Demand." Office of the Secretary of Defense, 1983, mimeo.
33. See Otto Eckstein, "Measuring of the Defense Budget, 1983–1988." Prepared statement before the U.S. Joint Economic Committee of Congress on Impact of Defense on U.S. Economy, 1983.
34. Three simulation scenarios were performed; the only assumption that differed across these scenarios was the rate of increase in real consumption expenditure (2.6 percent in the ROBUST scenario, 2.2 percent in the BASE scenario, and 1.9 percent in the SLUGGISH scenario). Defense spending levels and other fiscal and monetary policy variables were held constant across the various scenarios.
35. Dale Jorgenson, "Capital Theory and Investment Behavior," *American Economic Review* 53 (1963): 247–259.
36. R. Eisner and M.I. Nadiri, "Investment Behavior and the Neoclassical Theory," *Review of Economic Statistics* 50 (1968): 369–381, and M. Ishaq Nadiri, "An Alternative Model of Investment Spending." *Brookings Economic Paper,* 1971, pp. 547–578.
37. See Allen Sinai, Andrew Lint, and Russell Robbins, "Taxes, Saving and Investment: Some Empirical Evidence," *National Tax Journal* 36 (1983): 321–345.
38. For a clear discussion of this issue, see Benjamin M. Friedman, "Managing the U.S. Government Deficit in 1980," in Michael L. Wachter and Susan M. Wachter, eds., *Removing Obstacles to Economic Growth* (Philadelphia: The University of Pennsylvania Press, 1984), pp. 265–301.
39. The estimates of the sectoral impact of defense expenditures are obtained from models which combine macroeconometric models with a fairly detailed input-output model. The procedure involves projections of not only the conventional aggregates (such as GNP and its components, general prices, etc.) but also the sources of final demand for the output of each of over 400 industries; the translation of projected DoD outlays by program and by service into constant dollar purchases from each producing industry, and the use of an adjusted I-O matrix to translate these projected final demands into total requirements (direct and indirect) for the output of the various industries and the development of selected industry capacity utilization and projected capacity growth. See for further description, "Sectoral Implications of Defense Expenditures," U.S. Department of Commerce, Bureau of Industrial Economics, August 1982, mimeo, and David Blond,

*Defense Economic Impact Modelling System (DEIMS)*, Office of the Secretary of Defense, July 1983.

40. The impact of indirect or intermediate demand of the national defense spending is strongest in the energy sector; demand for crude and refined products and those of electrical and gas utilities rank among the top intermediate products. Consulting services represent another important intermediate product; after that comes the demand for steel mill products, electronic components, and aluminum products, nonferrous products, iron and steel foundries, and some chemical products. Electronic components as intermediate input are forecasted to grow rapidly due to the emphasis of the defense program on sophisticated hardware. Wholesale trade, real estate, and sales of eating and drinking establishments, as well as hauling and insurance services, communication and transportation services are also significant areas servicing the intermediate demand generated by defense spending. See Blond, op. cit., for further analysis and methodology. Also see David Blond, "Defense Analysis – Guns versus Butter in Today's Economy," Data Resources, Inc., *Inter-Industry Review*, Fall (1981): 1.55 – 1.64.
41. "Sectoral Implications of Defense Expenditure." U.S. Department of Commerce, Bureau of Industrial Economics, 1982, mimeo.
42. Estimates of capacity utilization for a period of twelve years are risky and subject to substantial measurement errors. However, the DRI estimates indicate the direction of changes in capacity utilization but may not predict its actual values precisely. For detail and methodology, see Data Resources, Inc., *An Approach to Evaluating Industry Bottleneck Potential: The Industrial Capacity Monitoring System*, March 1984, mimeo.
43. Data Resources, Inc., "Defense Inflation Prospects," *Defense Economics Research Report*, Vol. 3, No. 5, May 1983.
44. The relative decline of the multiplier in 1987 is mainly due to changes in the composition of defense spending planned for the period and the fact that 1987 is likely to be a near full-employment economy.
45. Data Resources, Inc., "Industry/Occupational Outlook," *Defense Economics Research Report*, Vol. 2, No. 12, December 1982.
46. In absolute terms, South Dakota, Idaho, Wyoming, and Alaska received in 1981 less or just slightly more than a billion dollars while the large states received very large sums: California, $42 billion; Texas, $26 billion; New York, $18 billion; Pennsylvania, $13 billion; and Florida, $12 billion. See for details, "Regional Impacts of Defense Spending," Data Resources, Inc., *Defense Economics Research Report*, Vol. 3, No. 2, February 1983, and *The Geographic Distribution of Potential Defense Expenditure*, Department of Defense, July 1984.
47. Virginia, Connecticut, Washington, Missouri, and Massachusetts were high direct suppliers while Illinois, Ohio, Michigan, New Jersey, and Indiana were among the top ten indirect suppliers. "Regional Impacts of Defense Spending," Data Resources, Inc., *Defense Economics Research Report*, Vol. 3, No. 2, February 1983.
48. A study of the average annual growth rate for direct, indirect, and total defense production for ten sectors of economic activities indicates some interesting results. Some states like California are key supplying states in several of these sectors while other states account for large shares of national defense output only in a few sectors. In all, the ten sectors contributed a substantial portion of the growth projected for the state for the period 1981 – 1988. In some sectors, such as construction and petroleum, defense production is concentrated in a few states. Also, production for defense within the indirect supplying industries has a different geographical distribution in comparison to industries pro-

visioning the defense needs directly. For further discussion, see "Regional Impacts of Defense Spending," Data Resources, Inc., *Defense Economics Research Report,* Vol. 3, No. 2, February 1983 and "Regional Prospects for Key Defense Supplying Industries," Data Resources, Inc., *Defense Economics Research Report,* Vol. 3, No. 3, March 1983.

# Chapter 3

# Defense Burdens and Prospects for the Northern European Allies

Todd Sandler and James C. Murdoch

## INTRODUCTION

Since the oil price shocks of the 1970s, the French and the West German (hereafter called German) economies have not duplicated their miraculous post-1945 economic performances, performances characterized by low rates of unemployment and high rates of savings, investment, and labor productivity. During the 1945 – 1973 period, the British economy had much more modest economic growth, and in keeping with this lower growth, British savings rates, investment rates, and labor productivity were typically much smaller than those of either France or Germany. This difference in economic performance is highlighted by the growth rates in Gross Domestic Product (GDP) recorded in the post-1945 period. For most years during the 1945 – 1973 period, including the whole of the 1959 – 1973 period, the French economy grew at an annual rate of 6.5 percent.[1] The German economy grew on average at an 8 percent rate during 1951 – 1960 and at a 4.5 percent rate during 1961 – 1973.[2] In contrast, British GDP grew at a 2.6 percent rate during 1953 – 1963 and at a 3.2 percent rate during 1964 – 1973.[3] On average, the French and German economies grew at twice the rate of the British economy until 1974. The French and German economies showed more modest growth, growing at an average rate of 2.4 percent and 2.1 percent per year, respectively, during the 1974 – 1982 period.[4] The British growth performance was also worse than its pre-1974 record, with GDP growth measured at an average rate of 0.8 percent per year from 1974 to 1982.[5]

In assessing the future of NATO in the 1980s, the outlook for these three economies is crucial, since these allies represent the major European contributors to the alliance. Past burden-sharing behaviors of these allies are depicted in Tables 3.1

Table 3.1. Military Expenditures as a Percentage of Gross Domestic Product by Country for Various Years

| Year | U.S. | France | Germany | U.K. | Belgium | Netherlands | Denmark | Norway | Italy |
|---|---|---|---|---|---|---|---|---|---|
| 1961 | 9.2 | 6.3 | 4.0 | 6.3 | 3.2 | 4.6 | 2.6 | 3.0 | 2.9 |
| 1963 | 8.8 | 5.6 | 5.2 | 6.2 | 3.4 | 4.4 | 3.0 | 3.5 | 3.1 |
| 1965 | 7.6 | 5.2 | 4.3 | 5.9 | 3.2 | 4.0 | 2.8 | 3.8 | 3.1 |
| 1967 | 9.5 | 5.1 | 4.3 | 5.7 | 3.1 | 4.0 | 2.7 | 3.5 | 2.9 |
| 1969 | 8.7 | 4.4 | 3.6 | 4.9 | 2.9 | 3.6 | 2.5 | 3.6 | 2.5 |
| 1971 | 7.0 | 4.0 | 3.3 | 4.9 | 2.8 | 3.4 | 2.4 | 3.4 | 2.7 |
| 1973 | 6.0 | 3.8 | 3.5 | 4.8 | 2.7 | 3.3 | 2.0 | 3.1 | 2.7 |
| 1975 | 5.9 | 3.9 | 3.7 | 4.8 | 3.1 | 3.4 | 2.4 | 3.2 | 2.5 |
| 1977 | 5.3 | 3.9 | 3.3 | 4.7 | 3.1 | 3.3 | 2.3 | 3.1 | 2.4 |
| 1979 | 5.1 | 4.0 | 3.3 | 4.7 | 3.3 | 3.2 | 2.3 | 3.1 | 2.4 |
| 1981 | 5.8 | 4.2 | 3.4 | 4.9 | 3.5 | 3.2 | 2.5 | 2.9 | 2.5 |

*Sources: SIPRI Yearbooks* (various years) and IMF, *International Financial Statistics Yearbook 1983.*

* Military Expenditures and Gross Domestic Product expressed in 1980 prices using the GDP price deflators for each country. Converted into U.S. dollars using 1980 exchange rates.

and 3.2.[6] In Table 3.1, the percentages of GDP devoted to military expenditures for the nine major NATO nations from 1961 to 1981 are shown. France, Germany, and the U.K. are typically among the top four contributors in terms of the shares of their GDP devoted to defense; the sole exception is Germany in 1961 and 1971. Since the 1960s, the major contributors have decreased the percentage of GDP earmarked for defense. In 1981, France, Germany, and the U.K. devoted 4.2 percent, 3.4 percent, and 4.9 percent of GDP to defense, respectively. These figures have been quite stable since 1970. The most current figures available show no significant change in these percentages. In the NATO press release of December 1984, France, Germany, and Britain devoted 4.2 percent, 3.4 percent, and 5.3 percent of GDP to defense in 1983. Only the U.K. has raised its percentage.[7] In Table 3.2, we have computed a different burden-sharing measure, in which a country's share of total NATO military expenditures is calculated (i.e., the nation's military expenditures as a proportion of total NATO military expenditures).[8] For this latter burden-sharing measure, the United States, France, Germany, and Britain again occupy the top four positions, with the United States first. This latter share measure accounts for the relative sizes of the economies and their expenditures by making comparisons with NATO totals. In all years reported (and in the interim years), the three Northern European allies accounted for between 18 and 31 percent of the total NATO military expenditures. This may not seem like a large overall percentage, but it corresponds to at least two-thirds of the entire European share. In 1982, French, German, and British defense expenditures accounted for 11.4 percent, 9.1 percent, and 9.1 percent, respectively, of NATO's total expenditures. These share percentages clearly demonstrate that these three allies' combined military expenditures are

Table 3.2. NATO Defense Burdens by Country for Various Years* (In Percentages)

| Country | 1955 | 1960 | 1965 | 1970 | 1975 | 1980 | 1982 |
|---|---|---|---|---|---|---|---|
| U.S. | 77.1 | 73.2 | 71.2 | 74.5 | 58.3 | 56.2 | 56.7 |
| Canada | 3.0 | 2.6 | 2.2 | 1.9 | 1.7 | 1.8 | 2.1 |
| Belgium | .6 | .6 | .7 | .7 | 1.4 | 1.5 | 1.4 |
| Denmark | .3 | .3 | .4 | .4 | .6 | .6 | .5 |
| France | 5.3 | 6.3 | 6.3 | 5.8 | 9.1 | 10.3 | 11.4 |
| Germany | 2.7 | 5.4 | 7.0 | 5.9 | 10.6 | 10.4 | 9.1 |
| Greece | .2 | .3 | .3 | .5 | 1.0 | .9 | 1.3 |
| Italy | 1.4 | 2.1 | 2.5 | 2.4 | 3.2 | 3.7 | 3.4 |
| Luxembourg | 0 | 0 | 0 | 0 | 0 | 0 | 0 |
| Netherlands | .7 | .9 | 1.1 | 1.1 | 2.0 | 2.1 | 1.8 |
| Norway | .3 | .3 | .4 | .4 | .6 | .7 | .7 |
| Portugal | .1 | .2 | .4 | .4 | .5 | .3 | .4 |
| Turkey | .3 | .5 | .6 | .6 | 1.2 | 1.0 | 2.0 |
| United Kingdom | 7.8 | 7.2 | 7.0 | 5.6 | 9.8 | 10.4 | 9.1 |

*Source: SIPRI Yearbooks* (various years).

*Military expenditures divided by total NATO military expenditures multiplied by 100.

Military Expenditure expressed in 1980 prices using the GDP price deflators for each country. Converted to U.S. dollars using 1980 exchange rates.

(Columns may not sum to 100 due to rounding errors.)

the most important in NATO when analyzing who among the NATO allies *can* and will share military burdens with the United States.

If past burden-sharing behavior is predictive of future behavior (as we feel that it is), and if Western Europe is to assume a larger share of European defense, then the three major Northern European allies' economies must experience strong economic recovery and growth in order to generate the additional resources needed for the defense sector. A strong economy is essential for these three allies to meet their pledged 3 percent increase in *real* defense expenditures (i.e., expenditures adjusted for price level rises). This pledge was given in the 1978 NATO ministerial meeting where a long-term defense program was discussed.

The economic prospects for Germany and France are not optimistic; however, German prospects are better than French ones. These countries' miracle postwar expansions are not expected in the near future to be duplicated in either economy, since the conditions that once led to these expansions no longer hold. In particular, both economies are plagued by aging capital, increased foreign competition in their export sector, high real interest rates, and relatively low savings rates. Labor unrest, high unemployment rates, and large government budget deficits are other difficulties that will limit French and German economic recovery in the 1980s. The U.K. faces somewhat similar problems that should dampen its recovery, keeping growth rates well within the range achieved during the 1960 – 1979 period. These problems include high real interest rates, government budget deficits, and a continuing decline in its manufacturing sector. In 1960, 36 percent of Britain's GDP was in manufacturing; by 1983, this figure had fallen to 23 percent.[9] Such a decline hurts the all-important export sector (which has traditionally depended on manufacturing) and underlies some of British balance of trade difficulties. These difficulties might be partially overcome by augmenting service-sector exports.

Using both current growth projections and our own insights, we will make short-range and medium-range growth predictions for these three countries. The reader is reminded that this chapter was written during 1984 – 1985, hence, forecasts here will be history when the book is published. All in all, the immediate and medium-range outlooks are not encouraging. Average growth rates in the 1 to 3 percent range are predicted to be the most likely scenario over the next five years. Of the three nations, Germany has the best chance to exceed the 3 percent level in some years; but we seriously doubt whether the German growth rate will exceed 3 percent on average during the next five years.

These growth predictions are crucial in allowing us to comment on whether official rhetoric and pledges to increase real defense expenditures by 3 percent are realistic for the Northern European allies. To examine this question, we develop a projection device that predicts future real defense percentage increments, based upon GDP growth *and* changes in one's allies' defense expenditures. This device is a novel feature of our study since it includes interactive spending patterns between allies; thus, a past tendency for one ally to get a *free ride,* or rely on another ally's expenditures, is accounted for. According to our estimates, France would have to grow by 7.5 percent, Germany by 11.0 percent, and the U.K. by 10.0 percent if the 3 percent target rate of defense increase is to be achieved under a best-case scenario. "Best-case" refers to a situation where these nations do not cut back on their defense expenditures as their allies, especially the United States, increase their military expenditures. When this so-called free-riding tendency (which exists for these three allies) is also adjusted for, even higher growth rates must be achieved if the target is to be reached. The conclusion that we must draw is obvious: If past burden-sharing behavior is predictive of future behavior, then the promised increases in real defense expenditures will not be met by the three major Northern European allies.

## Other Issues Examined in the Chapter

In addition to examining the likely economic performance and burden-sharing behavior of the Northern European allies, we intend to address the following issues and questions:

- We want to determine whether the medium-sized nuclear allies' (i.e., France and Britain) demand equations for military expenditures are identical with respect to the effects that GDP and spillins (i.e., the expenditures of one's allies) have on defense expenditures.

- We want to ascertain whether the Soviet threat, as measured by Soviet military expenditures, has been a significant influence on British, French, and German military expenditures. Furthermore, we intend to examine whether population levels are important in determining a country's military expenditures.

- A look at either Table 3.1 or 3.2 suggests that a significant shift in defense burdens between the United States and its allies occurred in the early 1970s. We intend to determine whether this shift is statistically significant by testing for structural changes in each of the three allies' demand for military expenditures during the early 1970s. If such structural changes show up, we intend to argue that the doctrine of flexible response, effectively instituted in the early 1970s, is responsible.[10]

- We plan to quantify the free-rider hypothesis for the four major NATO allies. Using our demand equations, we will show that when the U.S. spends a dollar more on defense, the Northern European allies in total spend about 18 cents less. Furthermore, we will show that the United States also relies on its allies' military expenditures; each time our allies spend a dollar less, the United States typically spends 87 cents more.

- We intend to estimate income elasticity and spillin elasticity measures for France, Germany, and the U.K. These measures show how responsive an ally's defense expenditures are to percentage changes in either GDP or other allies' defense expenditures. Each measure indicates the ratio of the marginal to the average response, thereby eliminating units of measurement.

- We plan to examine whether oil prices are a significant influence on military expenditures. A comparison of the British defense expenditure equation with those of the French and the German should allow us to answer this question, since the former is a net oil exporter (as of 1980) and the latter two countries are sizable importers.

- We want to ascertain whether it is realistic to ask allies to meet real growth in defense expenditure targets, when interactive effects between allies' expenditures are present, as they are in NATO. Quite simply, we want to determine whether a fixed-percent target rate is a workable policy.

- We want to study the welfare-military expenditures trade-off for Northern Europe.

## The Importance of France, West Germany, and the U.K. to NATO's Future

Any serious study of the future of the NATO alliance must pay particular attention to the major Northern European allies. There are a number of factors that make the study of these allies especially important for predicting NATO's future strength, and that distinguish these allies from other European allies. First, the Northern European countries include two allies, France and Britain, with strategic capabilities. These two nations possess strategic, tactical nuclear, and conventional weaponry in their arsenals. With the exception of the United States, they are the only NATO allies with strategic forces. Since these forces add to the overall deterrence capabilities of NATO, the strategic buildup currently underway in the United States must take French and British forces into account.[11] More importantly, the ability of these allies *to augment* and *to modernize* their strategic forces, at a time when the United States is doing the same, should influence current U.S. expenditure choices. That is, greater military expenditures on strategic forces by these medium-sized nuclear powers could take pressure off the United States, since their strategic weaponry can partially substitute for U.S. strategic forces. In fact, both France and the U.K. are currently modernizing their strategic and tactical nuclear forces.[12] In 1983, France authorized a 9 percent increase in the procurement budget for strategic forces and a 379 percent increase in the procurement budget for tactical nuclear forces.[13] These increases are quite dramatic. The Stockholm International Peace Research Institute (SIPRI) reports that France is currently augmenting its nuclear triad of submarine-launched, air-launched, and land-based missiles at the expense of conventional forces. The U.K. is also planning to replace its aging Polaris submarines, first deployed in 1967, with 4 to 5 Trident submarines in the 1990s. The English parliament has made commitments for 4 Tridents and holds out an option for a fifth. These replacement submarines will have significantly greater deterrence capabilities than the Polaris; the Polaris submarines carry 16 missiles, each with 3 warheads, while the Trident carries 24 missiles, each with between 8 and 14 warheads. When these new British and French strategic forces are accounted for, the United States may not require as many new strategic forces as currently planned.

Second, the major Northern European nations are among the most industrialized in the NATO alliance. Germany, the U.K., and France rank second, third, and fourth in NATO in terms of their GDP. If military strength is related to economic strength, as we intend to argue throughout this report, then the future prospects for the military strength of NATO in the 1980s is crucially dependent on the economic outlook of these three economies as well as that of the U.S. economy. This concept of economic strength goes beyond the "guns versus butter" argument,[14] which is concerned with trade-offs, by focusing on a nation's overall supply capabilities for contributing to governmental expenditures in general.

A third factor that highlights the importance of these three allies concerns these nations' past burden-sharing behavior as shown above in Tables 3.1 and 3.2. If these burden-sharing patterns continue, as their apparent stability suggests, then any help that the United States expects to receive in sharing NATO burdens must come from these countries.

A fourth consideration that distinguishes these three allies from other European allies concerns their arms industries. All three countries, and especially France and Britain, have sizable arms industries and are significant arms exporters. France, the United Kingdom, and West Germany ranked third, fourth, and fifth among the world's arms exporters in 1980 with 11.1 percent, 6.9 percent, and 5 percent of total arms exports, respectively.[15] The Soviet Union and the United States were first and second, respectively. Both France and Britain have sophisticated aerospace industries, which produce combat aircraft.[16] The French Mirage and the British Harriers are well-known export items. In Germany, Leopard tanks have been produced and exported; they are currently supplied to eight NATO allies. The well-being of these countries' economies is certainly reflected in their arms industries, since each country's customers include, to some extent, all the others. Furthermore, if these industries are to grow, then these countries' economies must have the necessary environments in terms of savings rates, interest rates, and investment incentives. A deterioration of these arms industries would mean that smaller NATO nations would have to look elsewhere for arms suppliers. The ability of NATO to support a conventional war of any duration depends, among other things, on its allies' arms industries.

A final consideration, distinguishing these three allies, involves their strategic locations. Germany is an important flanking nation, bordering on Warsaw Pact states. Many strategic experts predict that any conventional exchange would initially be fought on German soil.[17] Both the U.K. and France are strategically important owing to their position on either side of the English Channel. The strength of the British navy is important in any consideration of the protection of the English Channel, the North Sea oil fields, and the North Atlantic shipping lanes.

## The Plan of the Chapter

The body of the chapter is organized into four major sections. First, the descriptive economic analyses of the French, German, and British economies are presented. Each country's economic record and key indicators are briefly examined, with the focus on the post-1972 period. This examination is followed by a description of these countries' recent economic policies. We also examine some economic forecasts, given at the time when this chapter was initially written, and use our insights to predict a likely range of growth for each of the three countries. These growth scenarios are later used to predict future defense expenditures for the Northern European allies. The next section includes the descriptive analysis of defense spending and its effects. In particular, past burden-sharing behavior is analyzed to suggest the likely path of defense expenditures for each of the Northern European allies. Different measures of defense burdens are given for the allies in order to determine consistent trends. Our analytical analysis is contained in the following section, where burden-sharing behavior is analyzed both theoretically and empirically. In particular, we estimate a demand for military expenditures equation for each of nine allies. These demand equations isolate the significant determinants of defense expenditures and are used to forecast future defense spending. The last section contains our conclusions.

## DESCRIPTIVE ANALYSES OF THE NORTHERN EUROPEAN ALLIES' ECONOMIES

Before providing a description of the three economies, their current status, and prospects, we briefly indicate the essential ingredients for good economic growth. The foremost ingredient is a high net investment rate. Gross investment rates in the mid-twenty percent range are considered good. If high investment rates are to be achieved, then economic conditions must be supportive. In particular, real interest rates must not be too high if enough profitable investment opportunities (those that can meet the cost of borrowing funds and still have something left over) are to be available. Since savings finance investment, savings rates must also be high. For *net* investment rates to remain high once capital depreciation is deducted from gross investment, depreciation levels must be reasonable. Another important consideration concerning a country's capital is the size of its accumulated capital stock, as measured by the country's gross fixed capital stock. In particular, the age structure or the "vintage" of the capital stock is important. Economies with an aging capital stock will be less competitive than countries with newer stocks, which embody more advanced technologies.

A second important ingredient for high growth is high increases in labor productivity, as measured by increases in the output per man-hour. Labor productivity depends on schooling, training, job experience, and the type of capital employed, i.e., more technologically advanced capital helps labor productivity.

Another supportive condition for growth includes structural balance in international trade, so that the exchange rate is not experiencing wide fluctuations that may inhibit trade. This factor is especially important for Britain, France, and Germany, whose export sectors are large. A high trade deficit may lead to capital outflows due to speculative fears of devaluation, unless offset by interest rates high enough to attract capital. Capital outflows eliminate financing sources for new investment.

Structural balance in the government budget is also important for growth. High budget deficits can crowd out private investment, when government bonds (debt) compete with the private sector for scarce funds.

## The Past Performances of the Northern European Allies' Economies

*France.* After World War II, France faced an economy in ruin: 91,000 factories were destroyed, 2 million buildings were damaged, railway networks were inoperative, and many lives were lost.[18] From this devastation, France built a diversified economy whose largest industrial sectors included chemicals, energy, automobiles, building and civil engineering, transport, iron and steel, and electrical engineering. The French postwar economic miracle is well known. From 1945 to 1973, its rate of growth averaged 6.5 percent per year. Labor productivity increased on average 5.5 percent per year during the 1959 – 1973 period.[19]

Many factors led to the French miracle. These included high savings rates, high investment rates, and high labor productivity. In spite of energy imports at around 80 percent of energy consumed, France prospered since energy imports were relatively inexpensive until the 1973 oil shock. These cheap energy imports added to French growth.

The new industries built after the war could employ the latest capital and technology and this made French exports quite competitive. A high tariff structure helped to protect French products from foreign competition. This strong competitive situation greatly assisted the French economy, since, as in Germany, French growth was export-led. Another factor that supported the French miracle was the movement of labor from the agricultural sector to the industrial sector.[20] This movement provided the expanding French industry with a fairly cheap source of labor.

The end of the miracle, and the beginning of more modest French economic performance, can be traced to the mid-1970s. The high rise in the price of energy hurt the French economy greatly owing to its foreign dependency. The lifting of trade barriers by Raymond Barre in the mid-1970s also damaged the industrial sector in the short run by making foreign products relatively cheaper for the French consumer. In the mid 1970s, France's major industries faced intense competition in the international markets, partly due to an aging French capital stock. This aging stock contributed to smaller increases in labor productivity. Moreover, the exodus from the agricultural sector had ended.

A picture of the recent French experience can be seen from Table 3.4, which lists the key macroeconomic variables for the 1973 – 1983 period. Table 3.3 defines the variables reported and the abbreviations used in Table 3.4. The figures reported in Table 3.4 are in terms of billions of U.S. dollars, expressed in 1980 prices, except where noted in Table 3.3. For example, GDP per capita (GDPCAP) is in thousands of 1980 U.S. dollars. Other indices, such as unemployment rates (URATE) and the government bond rate (IRATE), are in percentage terms. Table 3.4 contains two measures for increases in capital stocks. Increases in inventories (i.e., raw material input stocks, finished goods, and work in progress) are measured by NEWCAP. Gross fixed capital formation (GFCF), which includes NEWCAP, indicates

68    CONSTRAINTS ON STRATEGY

Table 3.3. Definitions of the Measures of Economic Performance*

| Measure | Definition |
|---|---|
| GDP | Gross Domestic Product (billions of U.S. dollars). Conforms to the United Nations System of National Accounts (SNA). |
| GDPCAP | Gross Domestic Product per person. |
| GEXP | Government expenditures (billions of U.S. dollars). |
| GSGDP | Government's share of Gross Domestic Product GEXP ÷ by GDP × 100. |
| DEF | Government deficit ($-$) or surplus ($+$) (billions of U.S. dollars). Defined as government revenues minus government expenditures. |
| GFCF | Gross Fixed Capital Formation (billions of U.S. dollars). SNA definition is the sum of increases in stocks and Gross Capital Formation. |
| NEWCAP | Increase in stocks (billions of U.S. dollars). SNA definiton. |
| URATE | Unemployment rate (percentage). |
| CPI | Index of consumer prices (1980 = 100). |
| INFLATE | Percentage change in the CPI. |
| IRATE | Government bond yield (long term). |
| CURBAL | Current account balance (billions of U.S. dollars). |

*All values are expressed in 1980 prices using each country's Gross Domestic Product price deflator and converted into U.S. dollars using 1980 exchange rates.

*Sources: Yearbook of Labor Statistics 1983, 1984. International Financial Statistics Yearbook 1983, 1984.*

changes to the capital stock in value terms. Both NEWCAP and GFCF are standard United Nations measures of investment.

A number of features of Table 3.4 are noteworthy. The overall rise in GDP averages out to be 2.35 percent per year, much less than earlier periods. The initial impact of the oil shock is seen by the zero growth recorded in 1975 and the high rate of inflation (INFLATE) that characterized the post-1972 era in France. The consumer price index (CPI) increased by upwards of 9 percent per year throughout the 1973–1983 period. This high inflation rate has affected the competitiveness of French products as can be seen by the poor performance of the current account balance (CURBAL), which measures the trade balance. Seven of the eleven years reported indicate current account deficits. These deficits are due to the high(er) cost of imported energy and the erosion of the competitiveness of French industry. The unemployment rate was relatively low throughout the 1970s; however, it has crept upwards during the period, and this trend is predicted to continue for the next couple of years as the French continue to scrap aging capital. In 1984, unemployment surpassed the ten percent mark. Another important feature of the 1970s is the trend in the government budget deficit (DEF), which has characterized the French economy since 1975. Except for 1975, this deficit has been relatively modest, running at about 1 percent of GDP. After 1981, the deficit has grown as shown in Table 3.5, which gives the ratio of the budget deficit to gross private savings. France's deficit

Table 3.4. Descriptive Measures of Economic Performance for France, 1973 – 1983*

| Measure | 1973 | 1974 | 1975 | 1976 | 1977 | 1978 | 1979 | 1980 | 1981 | 1982 | 1983 |
|---|---|---|---|---|---|---|---|---|---|---|---|
| GDP | 536.42 | 554.49 | 554.66 | 584.19 | 602.01 | 624.84 | 645.07 | 652.08 | 654.04 | 667.56 | 675.10 |
| GDPCAP | 10290.00 | 10560.00 | 10510.00 | 11050.00 | 11340.00 | 11730.00 | 12060.00 | 12140.00 | 12120.00 | 12310.00 | 12353.00 |
| GEXP | 107.23 | 119.62 | 129.30 | 126.52 | 130.43 | 133.81 | 136.88 | 142.09 | 151.70 | 168.47 | 174.76 |
| GSGDP | 19.99 | 21.57 | 23.31 | 21.66 | 21.67 | 21.41 | 21.22 | 21.79 | 23.20 | 25.24 | 25.87 |
| DEF | 3.53 | 1.87 | −16.43 | −4.40 | −4.58 | −5.00 | −0.67 | −0.09 | −6.93 | −15.82 | −27.32 |
| GFCF | 127.59 | 134.86 | 129.05 | 136.03 | 134.14 | 133.93 | 137.77 | 141.16 | 137.59 | 139.69 | 133.12 |
| NEWCAP | 12.95 | 13.27 | −1.37 | 6.89 | 6.64 | 3.85 | 9.10 | 10.59 | −1.33 | 5.10 | −.55 |
| URATE | 2.60 | 2.60 | 4.10 | 4.40 | 4.70 | 5.20 | 5.90 | 6.30 | 7.30 | 8.0 | 8.0 |
| CPI | 47.90 | 54.50 | 60.90 | 66.80 | 73.00 | 79.70 | 88.20 | 100.00 | 113.30 | 127.10 | 139.00 |
| INFLATE | 13.78 | 11.74 | 9.69 | 9.28 | 9.18 | 10.66 | 13.38 | 13.30 | 12.18 | 9.36 | na |
| IRATE | 8.25 | 10.49 | 9.49 | 9.16 | 9.61 | 8.96 | 9.48 | 12.99 | 15.66 | 15.56 | 13.61 |
| CURBAL | 3.11 | −8.03 | 4.51 | −5.61 | −0.64 | 9.31 | 5.78 | −4.21 | −5.53 | −12.08 | 6.41 |

* Definitions given in Table 3.3.

Table 3.5. Ratio of Budget Deficit to Gross Private Savings:
Germany, France, and the United Kingdom (Percentage Ratios)

| Country | 1976 | 1977 | 1978 | 1979 | 1980 | 1981 | 1982 | 1983[b] | 1984[b] |
|---|---|---|---|---|---|---|---|---|---|
| Germany | 17.0 | 12.9 | 12.5 | 13.2 | 15.9 | 19.5 | 17.1 | 15.0 | 10.1 |
| France | 2.5 | 4.2 | 8.8 | 5.3 | −1.4 | 10.1 | 14.6 | 19.2 | 21.3 |
| United Kingdom | 28.7 | 17.0 | 20.5 | 16.4 | 18.3 | 15.3 | 11.9 | 17.6 | 14.7 |

*Source: OECD Economic Outlook*, December 1983, Table 13, pg. 43.

[a] General government financial deficit as a percentage of private savings. A minus sign indicates a financial surplus. Gross private savings = households + business gross savings, net of stock appreciation but before allowance for capital consumption.

[b] OECD estimates and forecasts.

has been increasing as a proportion of private savings since 1981. Government expenditures (GEXP) have risen throughout the 1973 – 1983 period; however, the government's share of GDP has remained relatively constant in the 21 – 23 percent range until 1982 (see Table 3.4).

Table 3.4 also shows that long-term interest (IRATE) was near or below the inflation rate before 1981. This means that the real interest rate (i.e., money interest rate minus the inflation rate) was low or negative until recently! These low rates should stimulate investment, but might also stimulate wasteful consumption. The inventory and gross fixed capital formation figures bear out this prediction with respect to investment.

In summary, the 1973 – 1983 period marked the beginning of France's problems. The signs of economic decay, in terms of higher unemployment rates, trade balance deficits, persistent government deficits and inflation, are very evident. Table 3.6 also shows the disturbing trend of falling savings and investment rates since 1970.[21] In Table 3.7, French labor productivity increases are seen to fall below usual levels in both 1980 and 1981, but show significant improvement in 1982.

*West Germany.* [22] In many ways, the German miracle followed the same path as the French. Germany was in ruins after World War II. Rebuilding its industries meant incorporating the latest technologies, thus giving Germany a competitive edge over industrial countries not devastated by war. German growth during the 1951 – 1970 period was an export-led growth. By 1952, 50 percent of German exports were in the capital goods sector. Iron, steel, and chemicals accounted for another 17.8 percent of exports.[23] Throughout her recovery, Germany's strong industrial sectors included motor vehicles, energy, iron and steel, capital goods, and chemicals.

Many factors contributed to the German miracle. Like the French, the German industries drew cheap labor from agriculture. Foreign workers provided yet another inexpensive source of labor. Foreign aid also contributed significantly to German

Table 3.6. Comparison of Savings and Investment Trends in France, Germany, and the United Kingdom (as a Percentage of GDP at Current Prices)

| Average over the Period | France | Germany | United Kingdom |
|---|---|---|---|
| Gross Savings | | | |
| 1970 – 73 | 26.0 | 27.3 | 20.6 |
| 1974 – 78 | 23.3 | 23.1 | 17.5 |
| 1979 – 81 | 21.3 | 22.6 | 18.9 |
| Net Savings | | | |
| 1970 – 73 | 16.3 | 16.9 | 11.4 |
| 1974 – 78 | 12.1 | 11.9 | 8.3 |
| 1979 – 81 | 9.9 | 10.8 | 7.0 |
| Gross Fixed Investment | | | |
| 1970 – 73 | 23.6 | 25.6 | 18.7 |
| 1974 – 78 | 22.9 | 21.0 | 19.0 |
| 1979 – 81 | 21.4 | 22.2 | 17.1 |
| Gross Investment (including inventories) | | | |
| 1970 – 73 | 25.7 | 26.6 | 19.5 |
| 1974 – 78 | 23.9 | 21.8 | 19.5 |
| 1979 – 81 | 22.3 | 23.7 | 16.5 |

*Source:* OECD, National Accounts, also see Table 19 in OECD, *OECD: Economic Surveys 1982 – 1983*, Paris: OECD, 1983.

Table 3.7. Labor Productivity for Germany, France and the United Kingdom (Annual Percentage Rate of Change)

| | 1976 | 1977 | 1978 | 1979 | 1980 | 1981 | 1982 |
|---|---|---|---|---|---|---|---|
| Germany | | | | | | | |
| Total economy | 6.7 | 3.0 | 2.8 | 2.6 | 0.8 | 0.5 | 0.7 |
| Manufacturing | 8.7 | 3.6 | 2.2 | 5.0 | −0.5 | 0.8 | 0.6 |
| France | | | | | | | |
| Total economy | 3.4[a] | 3.4[a] | 3.4[a] | 3.5 | 1.6 | 1.4 | 4.4 |
| Manufacturing | 4.7[a] | 4.7[a] | 4.7[a] | 5.9 | 2.2 | 3.0 | 5.1 |
| United Kingdom | | | | | | | |
| Total economy | 2.0 | 1.3 | 1.7 | 0.0 | −1.3 | 1.6 | 3.1 |
| Manufacturing | 5.3 | 1.6 | 1.1 | 1.3 | −3.7 | 3.9 | 6.2 |

*Source: OECD Economic Surveys*, France, Germany, the United Kingdom, various years.

[a] These are average values for the 1976 – 1978 period.

recovery, as did capital inflows which were generated by favorable trade balances. German public policy was very conducive to industrial expansion, allowing for favorable tax write-offs for profits plowed back into investment. Moreover, the German government permitted large business concentrations to form, thus allowing industries to take advantage of economies of scale. The German government also had an active involvement in both economic and social affairs so as to foster rapid industrial expansion. High savings rates were encouraged, and the currency was kept undervalued to encourage the export-led growth. The government gave many sizable research and development grants to large companies to foster their competitive position.[24]

The era of the 1960s, though strong, already marked the moderation of the miracle. GNP grew at 8 percent per year throughout the 1950s and at 4.7 percent per year throughout the 1960s.[25] Industrial production increased by 9.6 percent each year in the 1950s, while it increased by 5.4 percent each year in the 1960s. Labor productivity increased by 5.8 percent per year in the 1950s, and by 4.5 percent in the 1960s. In the 1970s, GNP grew by 2.9 percent per year, industrial production rose by 2.2 percent per year, and labor productivity increased by 3.2 percent per year.

What, then, ended the miracle? The answer is similar to that provided for France. Increased foreign competition in steel and iron, chemicals, and capital goods hurt the German export sector. An aging capital structure added to this deterioration in competitiveness. Strong labor unions had also bid up labor costs, thus eroding the German competitive edge. Cheap sources of labor had already been utilized. Moreover, foreign aid had ended by the 1960s. Starting in 1955, some German resources had to be earmarked for the defense sector. Government social programs and pension plans had grown, and drew savings away from the private sector. Scale economies had been fully exploited through industrial concentration. Finally, the oil shock of 1973 severely affected the German economy, which imported 70 percent of its energy.

Table 3.8 gives the key economic indicators for Germany for the 1973–1983 period, and uses the same symbols listed in Table 3.3. The table shows that the government budget has had deficits since 1975 and that this problem has continued into the 1980s. Some improvements in deficits have been registered in 1982 and 1983. These deficits are attributable to myriad social programs financed by government.[26] The table also indicates that current trade balances experienced deficits during the 1979–1981 period and are only now beginning to recover. This is in keeping with Germany's lost competitive position. The table shows, too, that the unemployment rate has been slowly rising from extremely low levels since 1973. Most analysts see this unemployment rate (which is 9.2 percent as of April 1985) worsening over the next year or so in spite of an otherwise improving economy. This is due to the difficulty in Germany of firing a worker once hired. Hence, as recovery occurs, employers would rather pay overtime wages than hire new workers, until employers are

Table 3.8. Descriptive Measures of Economic Performance for Germany, 1973 – 1983*

| Measure | 1973 | 1974 | 1975 | 1976 | 1977 | 1978 | 1979 | 1980 | 1981 | 1982 | 1983 |
|---|---|---|---|---|---|---|---|---|---|---|---|
| GDP | 692.32 | 696.25 | 684.48 | 722.09 | 744.28 | 767.50 | 799.49 | 813.79 | 814.10 | 807.05 | 813.36 |
| GDPCAP | 11170.00 | 11220.00 | 11070.00 | 11740.00 | 12120.00 | 12520.00 | 13010.00 | 13220.00 | 13200.00 | 13090.00 | 13243.00 |
| GEXP | 93.32 | 97.73 | 109.46 | 110.70 | 111.54 | 117.52 | 122.19 | 125.42 | 130.60 | 130.34 | 142.96 |
| DEF | −2.03 | −7.15 | −22.70 | −19.45 | −13.84 | −15.30 | −15.00 | −15.80 | −21.02 | −18.22 | −16.74 |
| GFCF | 165.59 | 150.41 | 139.70 | 145.75 | 151.15 | 159.34 | 175.00 | 185.66 | 178.97 | 165.24 | 184.76 |
| NEWCAP | 5.43 | 3.89 | −0.87 | 8.84 | 8.21 | 5.61 | 14.70 | 10.38 | −0.42 | 4.28 | 10.58 |
| URATE | 1.20 | 2.60 | 4.70 | 4.60 | 4.50 | 4.30 | 3.80 | 3.80 | 5.50 | 7.50 | 9.10 |
| CPI | 72.30 | 77.40 | 82.00 | 85.50 | 88.60 | 91.00 | 94.80 | 100.00 | 106.30 | 111.90 | 115.60 |
| INFLATE | 7.05 | 5.94 | 4.27 | 3.63 | 2.71 | 4.18 | 5.49 | 5.90 | 5.29 | 3.30 | 2.40 |
| IRATE | 9.30 | 10.40 | 8.50 | 7.80 | 6.20 | 5.80 | 7.40 | 8.50 | 10.40 | 9.00 | 7.90 |
| CURBAL | 9.41 | 18.96 | 6.69 | 6.40 | 5.95 | 11.08 | −6.60 | −15.92 | −7.64 | 3.93 | 2.11 |

* Definitions given in Table 3.3.

positive that the recovery is real. Similar problems characterize Britain and France; thus, high unemployment and recovery can coexist in these three economies.

Table 3.8 shows a medium level of inflation, but a level that is clearly lower than most other European countries. Inventories and new investments display a cyclical pattern, with moderate levels as compared to previous periods. Unlike France, a comparison of inflation and interest rates shows that the real interest rate was positive throughout the period. Returning to Table 3.6, we see that savings rates dropped in the 1970s and that investment rates dropped until 1979. Though investment is recovering, its level is still smaller than those of earlier periods. Finally, Table 3.7 depicts the dramatic decline in labor productivity since 1976.

In summary, Germany is in a much weaker position than in the 1950s and 1960s; however, the economic deterioration does not appear to be as severe as that of France. Government deficits, high unemployment, and reduced labor productivity seem to be the major difficulties.

*The United Kingdom.* Unlike the French and German economies, the British economy never experienced a miracle performance in the 1950s and 1960s. The conditions that produced the miracle in France and Germany simply did not exist in Britain. The British economy depended on trade, with exports and imports each equal to approximately 25 percent of GNP.[27] This large dependency on foreign trade meant that the British government had to worry about supporting the pound in spite of the possible adverse impacts on the domestic economy. Throughout the 1950 – 1980 period, Britain often had to keep interest rates high to attract currency, even though the policy discouraged investment and growth.

Much has been written on what kept Britain from rapid postwar growth. Factors usually mentioned include: (a) low research and development budgets; (b) excessively large numbers of small-scale producing units; (c) antiquated capital; (d) old-fashioned management techniques; (e) restrictive shop and union practices; (f) an entrepreneurial gap; (g) an education system that ignored technical training; and (h) low labor productivity.[28] Other factors hurt Britain, not the least of which were union pressures that increased hourly wages in the 1953 – 1963 period at twice the average rise of labor productivity.[29] Such increases hurt the competitiveness of British products by starting a wage-push inflation. The U.K.'s flip-flop program of nationalizing industries under the Labour party and denationalizing them under the Conservative party led to wasteful transaction costs.[30] Another factor in the U.K.'s poor economic performance concerned its declining share of the total world exports of manufacturing goods: this share fell from 16.5 percent in 1960 to 8.8 percent in 1974.[31]

Despite the North Sea oil discovery, British economic performance in the 1973 – 1983 period was not dramatic or different from earlier periods. Without North Sea oil, which greatly helped Britain's trade balance and which ended its dependency on imported energy, Britain's economic growth would have been much smaller. As shown in Table 3.9, Britain's economy grew at an annual rate of 1.1 percent during the 1973 – 1983 period. In Table 3.9, the key indicators depict a weak economy. Government expenditures increased both in nominal terms and as a share of GDP. By 1982, approximately 41 percent of GDP was accounted for by public spending; this share fell slightly in 1983. The budget deficit had also risen until 1979, and had been declining under the Thatcher government until 1983; high levels of unemployment should keep deficits from declining further. Gross fixed capital formation is relatively low as compared with either France or Germany. On the positive side, inflation has also started to fall significantly since 1979. In earlier years, Britain was inflating at an extremely high level, causing her products to become less competitive. The latter effect is seen in the current account deficits. The trade balance improvement after 1976 is primarily due to North Sea oil revenues and a depreciating pound.

Table 3.6 documents the drop in both savings and investment rates that characterized Britain during the 1970 – 1981 period. In Table 3.7, labor productivity is seen to be relatively low until 1981. Since 1981, some improvement has been recorded.

Though the British economy showed a weak performance throughout the decade, some hopeful signs of improvement have materialized since 1979. These signs include reduced budget deficits, higher labor productivity, lower inflation, and improved trade balances.

## Recent Policy Measures, Developments, and Prospects

*France.* Though the socialist government of France is committed to a strong defense policy, the recent performance of the French economy makes us doubt whether they will achieve their 1983 – 1988 defense targets calling for an 11 percent real growth in defense spending.[32] In examining recent French fiscal policy, we see a policy without direction and favoring short-term results. The main fiscal policies introduced in mid-1981 sought to stimulate the economy and to curb unemployment. During the 1981 – 1982 period, the minimum wage was raised, social benefits were increased, and employees' social insurance contributions were reduced. These policies stimulated consumer demand and temporarily kept France from experiencing the recession which had hit Europe. The current account balance went into the red as demands of imports increased dramatically owing to this consumer demand increase. Moreover, the government deficit increased as expenditures were increased and revenue sources were cut. These fiscal policies also had a detrimental effect on investment, leading to a lack of confidence among investors.

In 1982, the French also pursued a significant policy of nationalization, bringing more private industries into the public sector. After nationalization, the labor force in the nationalized sector doubled.[33] Sales in the public sector increased from 17.2 percent to 29.4 percent of all industrial activities because of nationalization. Huge switchovers to the public sector of this magnitude are usually disruptive. Moreover,

Table 3.9. Descriptive Measures of Economic Performance for the United Kingdom, 1973 – 1983.*

| Measure | 1973 | 1974 | 1975 | 1976 | 1977 | 1978 | 1979 | 1980 | 1981 | 1982 | 1983 |
|---|---|---|---|---|---|---|---|---|---|---|---|
| GDP | 493.08 | 488.83 | 485.27 | 502.95 | 509.90 | 528.52 | 536.98 | 527.00 | 515.66 | 523.32 | 554.26 |
| GDPCAP | 8820.00 | 8740.00 | 8680.00 | 9000.00 | 9130.00 | 9460.00 | 9610.00 | 9420.00 | 9240.00 | 9382.00 | 9831.00 |
| GEXP | 156.28 | 173.81 | 184.22 | 192.82 | 186.79 | 193.75 | 195.79 | 200.71 | 207.99 | 214.13 | 205.11 |
| GSGDP | 31.69 | 35.56 | 37.96 | 38.34 | 36.63 | 36.66 | 36.46 | 38.08 | 40.34 | 40.92 | 37.00 |
| DEF | −15.80 | −20.53 | −38.82 | −27.42 | −15.85 | −26.75 | −28.97 | −26.00 | −21.11 | −14.96 | −26.73 |
| GFCF | 96.17 | 99.03 | 94.54 | 95.14 | 91.25 | 95.02 | 95.64 | 91.66 | 81.44 | 80.62 | 84.03 |
| NEWCAP | 9.79 | 7.53 | −6.67 | 3.55 | 6.67 | 5.11 | 8.36 | −6.38 | −8.75 | −3.77 | 1.59 |
| URATE | 2.70 | 2.70 | 4.10 | 5.70 | 6.20 | 6.10 | 5.70 | 7.40 | 11.10 | 12.10 | 12.90 |
| CPI | 35.50 | 41.10 | 51.10 | 59.60 | 69.00 | 74.70 | 84.80 | 100.00 | 111.90 | 121.50 | 127.10 |
| INFLATE | 15.77 | 24.33 | 16.63 | 15.77 | 8.26 | 13.52 | 17.92 | 11.90 | 8.58 | 4.61 | na |
| IRATE | 10.72 | 14.77 | 14.39 | 14.43 | 12.73 | 12.47 | 12.99 | 13.79 | 14.74 | 12.88 | 10.81 |
| CURBAL | −6.56 | −19.24 | −7.22 | −3.48 | 0.04 | 3.28 | −2.19 | 7.06 | 12.98 | 7.74 | 5.62 |

*Definitions given in Table 3.3.

during this same period, capital outflows were significant owing to fear of nationalization. The French entrepreneurial class was clearly shaken.

In late 1982 and in 1983, the French government began reversing some of its fiscal policies. In particular, the employees' social security contributions were set to increase from 8.5 to 10.8 percent in real terms, while social security benefits were set to fall from 6.5 to 4.3 percent between 1982 and 1983.[34] Fiscal policy was tightened, as was monetary policy, to bring down inflation and to reduce the government deficit. This flip-flop in policy leads us to conclude that French policy lacks direction. The March 1983 devaluation of the franc reduced consumption, but added to inflation. Household saving ratios fell from 15.5 in 1982 to 14.5 in 1983 as a partial means to offset losses in real income owing to governmental policies.[35] Reduced savings will also hurt investment through a lack of funds.

There are a number of important French long-term policies that may begin to reverse the deindustrialization process that has occurred since 1974. The OECD reports that legislation was enacted in 1982 to improve technological developments in France.[36] In 1985, the share of GDP allocated to research and development has been increased to 2.5 percent, compared with 1.8 percent in 1981. In the Ninth Plan, priority has been given to developing the French electronics industry. Modernization is also planned for the traditional French industries of leather products, chemicals, furniture, toys, machine tools, textiles, and clothing. The big push is toward new technologies to improve the French competitive position. To show that he means business, President Mitterrand recently appointed Laurent Fabius, a young technocrat, to be prime minister. Unfortunately, by modernizing the traditional French industries, the Mitterrand government is investing in many industries, such as chemicals, textiles and clothing, that have *low growth potential and intense foreign competition.* The policy does not appear to be sound.

Since 1973, France has had a long-term policy of decreasing its dependency on foreign oil imports, turning instead to nuclear energy. Table 3.10 indicates the tremendous progress made thus far. In 1973, oil accounted for 67.2 percent of French primary energy requirements; by 1982, oil accounted for only 46.7 percent of French energy requirements. Table 3.10 also documents the huge percentage increase in nuclear energy. Overall French import dependency on primary energy sources fell from 78 to 64 percent during the 1973 – 1982 period.

Though the French have made great progress in curbing their dependency on foreign oil, their current account has not reflected this progress, because oil sales are denominated in dollars and the French franc has depreciated significantly in terms of the dollar in the last couple of years. Only in 1982 has the French policy shown up as an actual reduction in its net value of imported oil.[37] A fall in the price of the dollar would, of course, help the French greatly in realizing the full gains from its oil substitution policy. Such a fall is not likely in the near future, unless France can curb its high rate of inflation and increase labor productivity.

Table 3.10. France: Breakdown of Total Primary Energy Requirement (in %)

|  | 1973 | 1980 | 1981 | 1982 |
|---|---|---|---|---|
| Coal | 16.9 | 17.0 | 17.0 | 18.1 |
| Oil | 67.2 | 56.7 | 48.0 | 46.7 |
| Natural gas | 7.6 | 10.2 | 13.1 | 13.2 |
| Hydro-electric power and new sources | 6.4 | 8.7 | 10.2 | 9.7 |
| Other sources (including nuclear) | 1.9 | 7.4 | 11.7 | 12.3 |
| Import-dependence (net imports as a percentage of total primary energy requirement) | 78 | 72 | 65 | 64 |

*Source*: International Energy Agency and, for 1982, provisional data in "Industrie et energie françaises."
Also see p. 52 of *OECD: Economic Surveys 1982 – 1983, France*, Paris: OECD, 1983.

These long-term strategies of industrial development and imported-oil substitution should make for a more prosperous France in the late 1980s and the 1990s; however, the near-term outlook is less optimistic. The French government appears committed to increase defense expenditures and to improve strategic forces. We believe that they will succeed in the latter goal but at the expense of conventional forces, owing to poor economic performance.

On March 25, 1983,[38] the French government embarked on an austerity program aimed at cutting inflation rates (which are currently twice those of Britain and Germany) and at reducing record-high trade deficits. The results have been mixed; inflation has dropped one half percent from 9.8 percent to 9.3 percent, and the trade deficit has been cut in half.[39] However, unemployment rates have risen to 9.9 percent in 1984. More recent figures put unemployment at 10.9 percent.[40] It is interesting to note how out-of-step the Mitterrand government is with the rest of the industrial world. This government deflated during the world economic recovery of 1983 – 1984 and reflated during the world slump of 1981 – 1982. Such contrary policies, if continued, will keep French trade balances and competitive positions in imbalance with the rest of the world. For example, France's Renault and Peugeot automakers recorded huge losses in 1984, while most European automakers were reporting profits and are now making inroads into the French domestic market.[41] Investment confidence has not returned to France in spite of some small increases in industrial production. *The Economist* reports that the volume of industrial investment was down by 20 percent as compared with the 1970 investment figures.[42]

All things considered, the prospects of the French economy are not hopeful in the near term or in the medium run. Investment confidence has not returned. Government deficits, trade deficits, and high inflation rates will require continued austerity, an austerity that labor does not appear willing to accept as they continue their push for shorter work weeks, longer holiday periods, and earlier retirements. Even the French plan to decrease its dependency on imported energy by switching to nuclear energy may backfire, since, as U.S. experience has shown, nuclear energy technology is not fully developed. In addition, the Mitterrand government has unwisely chosen to boost investment in many industries characterized by low growth potential and intense foreign competition. Alas, the French miracle appears to have ended for good. Growth rates approaching 2 percent are the best that can be hoped for. Near-term growth in the − 1 to 1 percent range is the most likely scenario.

*West Germany.* [43] The recession in Germany began in early 1980 and has continued through 1982. Some signs of recovery have been noted in 1983. Though unemployment was 7.1 percent in December 1983, real economic growth ran between 2.5 and 3 percent for 1983.[44] Currently, the German recovery continues with real GNP growth running at 2.5 percent in 1984,[45] but with unemployment rates near 9 percent. As mentioned before, restrictive labor-firing rules keep employers from hiring new workers in spite of the recovery, relying instead on overtime. Such practices strain the German government budgets as payments to unemployed individuals must continue. A primary concern of the German government has been to institute measures to reduce the structural public sector deficit, measures first taken in 1982. Table 3.11 shows the trend in public sector spending since 1970. The size of the public sector, as a percent of GNP, has more than doubled since 1970, with significant increases registered at all levels of government. The increasing interest on the public debt is of special concern; it now comprises some 2.8 percent of GNP with 12.9 percent of the debt held by foreigners. The federal budget for 1984 is extremely tight, as was the 1983 budget. The 1984 budget includes the following specific measures: (a) postponement of civil servant pay raises to 1985; (b) pension reductions; (c) unemployment benefits reductions; (d) increases in social security contributions; (e) increases in tax exemptions for corporations, and (f) special depreciation allowances.[46]

There are many black clouds over the German economic horizon which will curb economic recovery, keeping it within the 1 to 3 percent growth range. Budget deficits may well persist into the medium run. In Germany, the retiree-to-worker ratio has reached 45 percent and is *not* expected to change until 1995.[47] This means that the government social security outlays will remain high and must be generated from a relatively small base of workers. Such large social security burdens, perhaps the largest in the world, make it difficult to bring the large German budget deficits down and to reallocate funds toward defense as promised. Moreover, this large social security commitment uses savings needed to support increased investment.

Another adverse sign concerns the industrial structure of the German economy and recent investments in the traditional sectors of petrochemicals, chemicals, iron, and steel. Many analysts see bad times ahead for the petrochemical industry, in terms of new recessionary fears and increased competition from the Saudis.[48] *The Economist* reports that industry insiders feel that Western Europe needs to reduce its petrochemical capacity by 10 – 20 percent.[49] In both the chemical and iron

Table 3.11. Public Debt in Germany in Billions of German Marks

| End of Year | 1970 | 1975 | 1980 | 1981 | 1982 |
|---|---|---|---|---|---|
| Public Sector[a] | 125.9 | 256.4 | 468.6 | 545.6 | 614.9 |
| Percent of GNP | 18.6 | 24.9 | 31.6 | 35.4 | 38.4 |
| Central government | 47.3 | 108.5 | 232.3 | 273.1 | 309.1 |
| State authorities | 27.8 | 67.0 | 137.8 | 165.2 | 190.6 |
| Municipalities | 40.3 | 74.4 | 95.2 | 102.6 | 110.0 |
| Foreign creditors | 1.5 | 6.8 | 41.6 | 66.8 | 79.3 |
| Percent of total | 1.2 | 2.6 | 8.9 | 12.2 | 12.9 |
| *Memorandum item* | | | | | |
| Interest on public debt | 6.6 | 25.3 | 38.8 | 35.4 | 44.2 |
| Percent of GNP | 1.0 | 1.4 | 1.9 | 2.3 | 2.8 |
| Percent of public expenditure | 2.7 | 2.9 | 4.0 | 4.6 | 5.5 |

*Source:* Statisches Bundesamt. This table is Table 9 in *OECD Economic Surveys 1982 – 1983, Germany,* Paris: OECD, 1983.
[a]Excluding social security.

and steel industries, Germany faces the prospect of tough foreign competition from third-world countries.

Labor unrest adds to German economic woes. The settlement of the IG METALL metalworkers strike in June 1984 for a 38.5-hour work week has paved the way towards a 35-hour workweek.[50] This 35-hour week is the primary target of the strong German labor unions. Such a policy will raise labor costs (which already are relatively high) and will further reduce the competitiveness of German exports. In a country with a high labor productivity in the past, recent years have seen poor performance of German labor, partly due to aging capital. In 1980, labor productivity actually fell by 0.5 percent. Labor productivity rose by less than 1 percent in 1981 and 1982.

Recovery is also held back by tight fiscal and monetary policy, needed to bring down runaway government spending. Moreover, higher interest rates might be needed to help curb short-term capital outflows to the United States. Capital outflows have plagued the German and other major European economies in 1984 and at the start of 1985. Such capital inflows into the United States have strengthened the U.S. dollar until recently despite record U.S. trade deficits. Obviously, these capital outflows are needed for German investment.

If Germany is to show sustained recovery, the following conditions must prevail: (a) real interest rates must fall; (b) investment must increase and must favor nontraditional "high-growth" sectors; (c) savings must increase to finance investment; (d) government spending must be brought into line with revenue; and (e) labor productivity must increase. Recent developments reported above do not allow us to be confident that the German economy will rebound significantly in the short or medium run. German recovery will be modest, within the 2 to 4 percent range. The German miracle, like the French, is a thing of the past.

*The United Kingdom.* [51] The recent recession in Britain has been worse than in most OECD countries. Tight economic policies and a substantial loss in competitiveness have contributed to the deepness of this recession. Though the U.K. showed signs of recovery in 1983 with growth estimates in the 3 percent range, unemployment was 12 percent and has been rising further. It stood at 13 percent in April 1985. Inflation has fallen dramatically over the last five years in response to tight monetary policy and now stands at about 5 percent. Monetary and fiscal restraint still rules Britain, and these policies will, of course, limit recovery. As recently as March 1985, the prime interest rate was increased, in the hopes of stemming capital outflows and speculative pressures on the pound. Even the improving trend in the government budget deficits is now predicted by the London Business School[52] and others to reverse itself owing to a rising unemployed work force, now standing above 3 million.

A significant recent development in the U.K. is the end to the coal strike, which started in mid-March 1984 and which ended nearly 12 months later in early March 1985. The coal strike disrupted steel production and general industrial activity in Britain. Estimates for the cost of the coal miners' strike vary, with some analysts estimating a cost of $3 billion.[53] These costs include, among others, police cost ($200 million), lost coal output ($1.15 billion), and higher fuel costs ($1.25 billion). Whatever the true costs, one impact of the strike is clear: the strike significantly cut British growth in 1984. The actual cut in growth is mere speculation; a one percent reduction in GDP is often mentioned.[54] Of course, the coal miners' union defeat will hurt union power in Britain for many years to come. Hence, some favorable long-term effects from the strike might be realized.

Has Thatcherism put the British economy onto the right track? We would have to argue that it has not, despite its recent successes noted previously. Inflation has indeed fallen, but every indication is that it will rise as labor's wage demands in the public sector and elsewhere rise above the 4.5 percent rate target. Pay settlements have been recently running at 5.5 percent.[55] The deteriorating pound also adds to inflation by making imported materials and goods more expensive. Inflation expectations do not appear to be cured, even with unemployment rates at 13.0 percent. Despite the rhetoric, Thatcher has not cut public spending, nor has she restructured the economy. The manufacturing sector is still declining. The deindustrialization process in Britain has been well documented by the *OECD Economic Surveys*, which have noted that the manufacturing sector accounted for 31 percent of GNP in 1970–1974. By 1981, this share had fallen to less than 25 percent with the service sector gaining much of the difference. If Britain is to recapture its industrial base, public expenditures and policies must stimulate investment in manufacturing. Even the Nigel Lawson budget of March 1985, which has helped the pound, should do little to augment the British economy. The latest budget features only £¾ billion of tax cuts; most of the budget involves tax redistributions.[56]

The sole reason why the British economy is not worse is because of North Sea oil, which has given the government 7 to 11 percent of its needed revenues.[57] Since 1980, Britain has become a net exporter of oil.[58] Oil revenues also give Britain foreign exchange, needed to import new technologies for modernizing industries. Oil production peaked in 1985; however, reserves will not be exhausted until 2010.[59]

Taking all the evidence together, we see no future British miracle; rather, we predict that Britain will perform as it always has, with growth rates in the 0 to 3 percent range. The most-likely growth scenario for the near term is 2 percent, judging from current trends.

## Short-Run and Medium-Run Growth Estimates and Forecasts

In this subsection, some short-run and medium-run growth estimates and forecasts are presented and compared with our intuitive predictions, given in the previous subsection. Table 3.12 presents the short-run growth estimates for Chase

Table 3.12. Short-term Growth Estimates for France, Germany, and the United Kingdom

| Survey Source and Countries | 1984 | 1985 |
|---|---|---|
| *Chase Manhattan* | | |
| (September 1983) | | |
| France[1] | 0.3 | 2.0 |
| Germany[2] | 2.7 | 2.7 |
| United Kingdom[3] | 0.8 | 1.2 |
| *OECD Outlook, December, 1983* | | |
| France[4] | 0 | 1.5 |
| Germany[5] | 2.0 | 2.25 |
| United Kingdom[4] | 2.25 | 2.0 |
| *IMF World Economic Outlook* | | |
| France[6] | 1.25 | 0.5 |
| Germany[7] | 2.5 | 2.5 |
| United Kingdom[6] | 1.5 | 2.5 |

[1]Real GDP growth in 1970 francs.

[2]Real GNP growth in 1976 German marks.

[3]Real GDP growth in 1975 pounds.

[4]Real GDP, expressed in 1982 U.S. dollars, annual percentage change from previous period.

[5]Real GNP, expressed in 1982 U.S. dollars, annual percentage change from previous period.

[6]Real GDP growth for France and the United Kingdom.

[7]Real GNP growth for Germany.

Manhattan, OECD, and IMF. Though the actual numbers differ somewhat, the overall picture is similar for the three estimates. In particular, all three view French performance as poor in 1984 with near-zero growth. Moderate performance, however, is expected for France in 1985. These estimates see the German economy as showing the best near-term growth in the 2 to 2.7 percent range. More moderate growth in the 0.8 to 2.25 percent range is predicted for the United Kingdom.

In Table 3.13, we report the Chase Manhattan and the Data Resources Inc. (DRI) medium-run (1984 – 1987) projections for real GDP growth. The ordering of the economies agrees in the two forecasts, with France, the U.K., and Germany ranked from lowest to highest in terms of future growth. As in its short-term estimates, Chase Manhattan predicts an improvement in the French economy from 1985 onwards. This prediction agrees with that of DRI. Both forecasts expect French growth to be in the 1.9 to 2.6 percent range. The two forecasts see better times ahead for Germany; however, DRI is more pessimistic than Chase Manhattan. DRI predicts growth in the 2.3 to 3.2 percent range, while Chase forecasts growth in the 3.0 to 4.6 range for Germany. Both forecasts for the U.K. are in close agreement. Growth rates in the 1.3 to 2.0 range are predicted by Chase. A somewhat higher range of 1.6 to 2.4 percent is forecast by DRI.

These forecasts are in close agreement with our previous predictions. Obviously, no one sees either the German or French miracle being repeated in the near future. Further on we will use the following ranges of growth to forecast defense expenditures increases: −1 to 2 percent for France, 1 to 4 percent for Germany, and 0 to 3 percent for the United Kingdom.

Table 3.13. Medium-Range Real Growth Projections for France, Germany, and the United Kingdom

| Survey Source and Countries | 1984 | 1985 | 1986 | 1987 |
|---|---|---|---|---|
| *Chase Manhattan* | | | | |
| (October 1983) | | | | |
| France[1] | 0.3 | 1.9 | 2.4 | 2.6 |
| Germany[2] | 3.0 | 3.9 | 4.3 | 4.6 |
| United Kingdom[3] | 1.3 | 1.3 | 1.8 | 2.0 |
| *Data Resources, Inc.*[4] | | | | |
| (June 1984) | | | | |
| France | 0.7 | 1.9 | 2.6 | |
| Germany | 3.2 | 2.3 | 2.4 | |
| United Kingdom | 2.4 | 1.6 | 2.0 | |

[1] Real GDP growth in 1970 francs.

[2] Real GNP growth in 1976 German marks.

[3] Real GDP growth in 1975 pounds.

[4] Real GDP growth seasonally adjusted and in terms of dollars.

## Other Considerations

This subsection is meant to tie up some loose ends in our description of these allies. In particular, we examine the impact of accumulating budget deficits, the peace movement, and the so-called defense – welfare trade-off.

*Impact of Budget Deficits.* Our previous discussion and tables have shown that all three countries have experienced accumulating deficits in recent years. Both Britain and Germany have taken decisive measures to halt this trend and to turn things around; tight fiscal policy has been the result. The French are yet to deal successfully with this problem. Owing to automatic stabilizers, such as unemployment benefits, social security payments, and welfare payments, budgets are expected to go into deficit in recessionary periods. However, since the 1960s, economists have noted a trend toward deficit spending even in good years. Public choice theorists attribute this tendency to officeholders trying to please too many special interest groups so as to remain in office; thus, they spend beyond government revenue sources.

This deficit-spending tendency has a number of important implications for our analysis of military expenditures. First, it gives rise to *crowding-out* when governments go to the financial markets to finance their deficits, thus drying up sources of funds for private investment. Without adequate financing, investment and therefore growth are limited. Table 3.5 is suggestive of the crowding-out effect.[60] In Table 3.5, the budget deficit is expressed as a ratio of gross private savings. For France, this ratio was small until recent years. The German and British experiences show that a high proportion of private savings go in government debt financing, and may be a contributing factor toward the deindustrialization of these economies.

Second, deficit spending can lead to inflation which, in turn, may reduce a country's competitive position. If this occurs, the current-account balance will decline.

Third, accumulating budget deficits force a nation's government to look more carefully at its expenditures. This may lead to cuts in defense as a means of balancing the budget. Clearly, the welfare – defense trade-off is more important during deficit years.

*The Peace Movement.* The peace movement has reemerged in strength in the 1980s with over one million Europeans demonstrating in 1982. The 1983 *SIPRI Yearbook* has devoted an entire chapter to the growth of the movement.[61] In Germany, an environmentalist political party, the Greens, has spearheaded the opposition to the deployment of Pershing II intermediate-range missiles and cruise missiles on German soil. By 1984, the Greens held 27 seats in the Bundestag,[62] giving them a political means for voicing their opposition to military spending. Nonetheless, they were unsuccessful in blocking the West German parliament's approval to deploy intermediate-range nuclear missiles on German soil. The vote on November 22, 1983, was 286 to 226.

In Britain, the Campaign for Nuclear Disarmament (CND) has grown significantly since 1970. CND membership rose from 2,120 in 1970 to 41,000 in 1982.[63] The U.K. has also experienced many antinuclear demonstrations. Even the Labour party has embraced the nuclear disarmament issue in their national platform. In an April 1981 survey held in Britian SIPRI reports that 50 percent opposed the government's decision to base cruise missiles on British soil.[64]

Except for some demonstrations, there has been less organized opposition in France to nuclear weapons. This is surprising in light of the declared policy of the Mitterrand government to modernize French strategic and tactical weapons.

The future impact of the peace movement is difficult to judge. Currently, it represents a very vocal and visible minority. If, however, current membership trends continue, the movement may become a formidable political force.

*The Welfare – Defense Trade-off.* There have been numerous attempts to establish a defense – welfare trade-off within central government budgetary behavior.[65] Most studies have not found a significant short-term defense – welfare trade-off, meaning that increased defense expenditures need not imply smaller welfare payments. We shall focus our remarks on the Domke, Eichenberg, and Kelleher study, because it represents a careful analysis and because it examines the Northern European allies.

Domke et al. examined the U.S., the German, the French, and the British central government budgets during the 1948 – 1975 period and concluded that no significant short-term trade-off was evident, except in wartime or periods of postwar reconstruction.[66] These researchers used a three-stage least squares model. One equation regresses the percentage change in defense expenditures on the percentage change in central government expenditures, the percentage change in welfare expenditures, war deaths, and tension. A second equation regresses the percentage change in welfare expenditures on the percentage change in central government expenditures, changes in unemployment, and political variables. The third equation regresses the percentage change in central government expenditures on the percentage change in revenue, changes in unemployment, changes in lagged GDP, and budget deficit measures.

While a simultaneous-equations approach is an improvement over the usual single-equation approach, since variables can be better identified, we still feel that the equation system could be better specified. For example, the defense equation never considered the military expenditures of one's allies or adversaries. The lag-structure used in the equations was never clearly justified; for example, why lag tension but not war deaths? Problems of multicollinearity (where independent variables are closely related) were never tested or corrected. Hence, we still do not know whether the absence of a significant trade-off is due to the misspecification of the equations or the absence of such a trade-off.

Table 3.14, which is an upgrade of the Domke et al. table, is suggestive of a long-term trade-off for the United States, France, and the United Kindgom. The table indicates a tendency for welfare expenditures to rise as defense expenditures fall.

Table 3.14. Percentage Shares of Central Government Expenditure for Defense and Welfare, 1950 – 1979: United States, France, Germany, and the United Kingdom

|  | United States % | France % | Germany % | United Kingdom % |
|---|---|---|---|---|
| *Defense* | | | | |
| 1950 | 30.4 | 17.6 | 31.2 | 22.6 |
| 1960 | 49.8 | 27.8 | 25.2 | 25.7 |
| 1970 | 47.3 | 17.7 | 21.9 | 17.8 |
| 1975 | 26.7 | 15.2 | 19.9 | 14.8 |
| 1979 | 21.5 | 7.3 | 9.7 | 14.5 |
| *Welfare* | | | | |
| 1950 | 12.0 | 10.8 | 40.6 | 33.8 |
| 1960 | 21.7 | 16.3 | 32.0 | 39.2 |
| 1970 | 32.9 | 27.0 | 34.8 | 44.7 |
| 1975 | 46.8 | 26.8 | 41.9 | 44.9 |
| 1979 | 47.2 | 35.0 | 41.6 | 29.9 |

*Source:* Domke, Eichenberg, and Kelleher, "The Illusion of Choice," p. 22. For 1979, the data is taken from the IMF, *Government Finance Statistics Yearbook*, Washington, DC: IMF, 1982, p. 25. Percentages are calculated using Domke et al. definitions.

We would want to see more convincing evidence before concluding that even a long-term trade-off exists.

## DESCRIPTIVE ANALYSIS OF DEFENSE SPENDING AND ITS EFFECTS

This section examines defense spending in the northern European allies since 1955. In particular, we will here focus on descriptions, leaving the statistical analysis to the next section. This section contains two subsections. The first subsection contains a breakdown of the military budgets into major spending categories, and the second subsection includes different burden-sharing measures.

### Military Expenditure Breakdowns

In Table 3.15, military expenditures in France, Germany, and the United Kingdom are broken down into five major categories: personnel, operations and maintenance, procurement, construction, and research and development (R&D). We have only given the breakdown for a recent year since these divisions do not appear to vary much from year to year for most countries.[67] In fact, SIPRI notes that personnel costs alone account for over 45 percent of the total in 12 of the 16 major countries analyzed.[68] Moreover, procurement accounted for 20 percent of the total, while operations and maintenance typically included another 20 percent of the total.

Clearly, France, Germany, and the U.K. follow these general patterns. An interesting fact to note for France and the U.K. is the relatively large percentage going

Table 3.15. Military Expenditures Breakdown: France, Germany, and the United Kingdom (Operating Costs as Percentage of Total Military Budget)

| Country | Year | Personnel | Operations and Maintenance | Procurement | Construction | R + D |
|---|---|---|---|---|---|---|
| France | 1980 | 37 | 27 | 19 | 4.3 | 13.0 |
| Germany | 1978 | 41 | 28 | 19 | 7.0 | 4.4 |
| United Kingdom | 1979 – 1980 | 43 | 11 | 25 | 6.5 | 14.0 |

*Source: SIPRI Yearbook 1983,* Table 8.4, p. 203.

to R&D. The French 13 percent and the British 14 percent were many times those of other countries, except for the nuclear nations of the United States and the U.S.S.R. In the United States, 8.4 percent went to R&D in 1977 – 1978.[69] This, however, is a lower-bound estimate since a significant portion of the NASA budget also represents defense R&D and should be included. Thus, we see that nuclear powers tend to have higher R&D percentages than non-nuclear powers.

If the British and French achieve their objectives in modernizing their strategic and tactical nuclear forces in the 1980s and 1990s, the procurement percentage should rise somewhat over the next few years. The British intentions to purchase between 4 and 5 Trident submarines, along with the need to rebuild parts of their navy, should augment their procurement budgets relative to other categories. The French defense budgets for 1983 – 1988 call for large procurement items to modernize their nuclear triad.[70] This, too, should increase the French procurement share.

## Burden Sharing: A Descriptive Analysis

There are numerous military burden-sharing measures available, each with its own virtues and drawbacks. We report four such measures here: (a) military expenditures as a percent of GDP; (b) military expenditures as a percent of government expenditures; (c) military expenditures per capita; and (d) an ally's military expenditures as a percentage of total NATO military expenditures. The first measure is most commonly used and indicates the percentage of current income going to defense. The second measure depicts the share of government expenditures allocated to defense and helps to indicate the trade-off, if any, between defense and welfare. The third measure denotes a per-person burden of defense. The fourth measure differs significantly from the other three, since it indicates the relative burdens between allies by depicting the share of the alliance's total military expenditures picked up by each.[71] The first three measures are within-ally burden-sharing measures, since each is expressed in terms of a country-specific resource measure;

the fourth measure is a between-ally burden-sharing measure, because it is expressed in terms of alliance-wide expenditure.

We here refer the reader to Table 3.2, which gives this between-ally burden-sharing measure for selected years since 1955. There are a few important aspects of Table 3.2 to note. Over time the defense burdens of NATO have been redistributed between the United States and Europe. In the middle 1970s, the Europeans took over a greater portion of NATO military expenditures. This is the time period when flexible response became a workable doctrine owing to technological breakthroughs in counterforce weaponry. Even though this doctrine has been around since 1957, *renewed* official interest has been shown since 1971, as documented in footnote 10. On May 25, 1971, the NATO Nuclear Planning Group discussed how best to pursue this doctrine at a meeting held in Mittenwald, West Germany.[72] Ever since the middle 1970s, the public has been made acutely aware by the press of NATO's "new strategy" for fighting a limited nuclear war.[73] The recent deployment of high-precision Pershing II missiles and cruise missiles on European soil gives NATO the technical ability to fight such a war, a war requiring pinpoint accuracy.

We intend to show in the next section that this renewed interest in flexible response has contributed toward a significant redistribution of NATO defense burdens between the United States and Europe. European allies were motivated to increase their defense expenditures since any initial conflict of a "limited war" would be fought on their soil. Allies who did not build up their forces would make for easier targets. Thus, Table 3.2 depicts a jump in defense burden-sharing in Belgium, Denmark, France, Germany, Greece, Italy, Netherlands, Norway, Portugal, Turkey and the United Kingdom. In total, nearly 18 percent of the burden was shifted to Europe by 1980. Most of this redistribution has been picked up by France, Germany, and the United Kingdom. In 1982, each of these three allies accounted for approximately the same proportion of the total – i.e., between 9 and 11.5 percent. The drop of 1 percent in the German and the British contributions since 1980 has been simply shifted back to France and to the United States, both of which have significantly increased their tactical and strategic nuclear forces in the 1980s. Even with this small redistribution acknowledged, the overall burden-sharing behavior depicted in the Table 3.2 has been extremely stable since 1975. This stability lends support to our forecasting technique in the next section, which uses past behavior patterns (those since 1974) to predict future defense expenditures. This stability, which is established through empirical tests, also suggests that no single political change (e.g., Carter's presidency) could have explained these expenditure patterns. Moreover, the end of the Vietnam War helps explain *some* post-1970 military expenditure changes for the United States, but it does not explain the other allies' expenditure patterns (i.e., other allies spent a smaller portion of their budgets on defense – see Table 3.16).

Table 3.1, presented previously, indicates the percentage of GDP devoted to military expenditures for the nine major NATO allies. For most years since 1961, the United States and the three major Northern European allies occupied the top four

Table 3.16. Military Expenditures as a Percentage of
Government Expenditures by Country for Various Years*

| Year | U.S. | France | Germany | U.K. | Belgium | Netherlands | Denmark | Norway | Italy |
|---|---|---|---|---|---|---|---|---|---|
| 1961 | 48.9 | 27.2 | 28.0 | 22.8 | 14.2 | 18.6 | 14.8 | 18.1 | 18.5 |
| 1963 | 47.0 | 23.6 | 36.5 | 21.1 | 14.5 | 18.3 | 14.9 | 18.8 | 19.3 |
| 1965 | 43.8 | 24.0 | 31.4 | 20.2 | 13.6 | 16.1 | 13.4 | 19.6 | 16.4 |
| 1967 | 47.7 | 22.7 | 28.6 | 18.6 | 12.5 | 14.7 | 11.0 | 17.9 | 16.1 |
| 1969 | 42.8 | 19.6 | 26.7 | 16.0 | 11.5 | 13.2 | 9.9 | 17.0 | 14.2 |
| 1971 | 34.2 | 19.0 | 26.1 | 15.9 | 11.0 | 12.0 | 8.4 | 14.9 | 12.4 |
| 1973 | 30.4 | 19.0 | 25.8 | 15.2 | 10.6 | 12.0 | 6.4+ | 13.6 | 12.0 |
| 1975 | 25.5 | 16.7 | 23.2 | 12.7 | 10.2 | 10.1 | 6.7 | 13.5 | 8.3 |
| 1977 | 24.2 | 18.1 | 22.4 | 12.9 | 9.7 | 9.9 | 6.3 | 6.8+ | 8.4 |
| 1979 | 24.0 | 18.6 | 21.3 | 12.8 | 9.1 | 8.8 | 6.1 | 6.8 | 7.1 |
| 1981 | 24.5 | 18.1 | 21.1 | 12.2 | 8.2 | 8.3 | 5.7 | 7.0 | 6.4 |

*Sources:* SIPRI Yearbooks (various years) and IMF, *International Financial Statistics Yearbook 1983*, Washington DC: IMF. 1983.

*Military expenditures and government expenditures expressed in 1980 prices using each country's GDP price deflator. Converted to U.S. dollars using 1980 exchange rates.

+ The data are taken from *World Military Expenditures and Arms Transfers: 1972 – 1982*, ACDA Publication 117, 1984.

positions. Hence, both within-ally and between-ally burden-sharing measures indicate the importance of France, Germany, and the United Kingdom. The shares of GDP devoted to defense have dropped since 1961 for each of the four major allies. In fact, this drop characterized all nine allies. Since a similar pattern has not characterized the U.S.S.R.,[74] NATO allies do not appear to respond to threat as embodied by Soviet military expenditures. Our statistical analysis in the next section supports this observation.

Table 3.16 gives the percentage of government expenditures devoted to military expenditures. Since 1961, all nine allies have cut back on the share of their governments' expenditures going to defense, giving instead a greater share to welfare. Once again, we see that the defense shares have remained relatively constant for the four major industrial allies since 1975. This is further evidence that burden-sharing behavior has been stable since the mid-1970s.

In the German case, the increasing defense shares from 1961 to 1963, shown in Table 3.16, can be attributed to factors characterizing the 1955 – 1963 period. First, this period marked a time of crisis regarding Berlin. This crisis increased German desires to be armed. Second, the German economy was constantly improving during this period, showing the signs of postwar reconstruction. This improvement allowed the Germans to increase their defense burdens dramatically. Third, Germany only entered NATO in 1955, and consequently it took some time to build up its defenses.

In Table 3.16, the fall in the U.S. burden share between 1961 and 1975 has been much greater than the drop in French, German, and British shares of government expenditures devoted to defense, thus explaining how the Northern European allies have been able to assume a larger between-ally share of NATO military expenditures. Judging from previous trends, we would not expect much change in this burden-sharing measure over the next five years.

In Table 3.17, military expenditures per capita for various years are given for France, Germany, and the United Kingdom. The German per capita burden has increased significantly since 1961, while the French and British figures have fluctuated within the $300 – $500 range; but no apparent trend is obvious.

## ANALYTICAL ANALYSES OF BURDEN-SHARING AND DEFENSE SPENDING

This section contains a comprehensive investigation of the burden-sharing behavior described in the last seciton. Drawing from our previous work,[75] we present a specification of the demand equation for military expenditures. This demand equation permits us to test for the significant determinants of an ally's military expenditures. In particular, the analysis shows that an ally's GDP and the defense expenditures of its allies are the two most important determinants of military expenditures. The demand specification is examined with both cross-sectional data and time-series data. The cross-sectional analysis groups all allies together and examines the hypothesized relationship between defense expenditures and their determinants at a point in time (i.e., for a given year). In contrast, the time-series

Table 3.17. Military Expenditures per Person for Various Years*

| Year | France | Germany | United Kingdom |
|---|---|---|---|
| 1961 | 327 | 133 | 487 |
| 1963 | 318 | 184 | 496 |
| 1965 | 327 | 168 | 505 |
| 1967 | 342 | 170 | 498 |
| 1969 | 305 | 162 | 395 |
| 1971 | 287 | 184 | 414 |
| 1973 | 371 | 265 | 446 |
| 1975 | 403 | 304 | 400 |
| 1977 | 382 | 319 | 325 |
| 1979 | 475 | 422 | 408 |
| 1981 | 397 | 359 | 395 |

*Source: SIPRI Yearbooks* (various years).

*Military expenditure expressed in 1980 prices using each country's GDP price deflator. Converted to U.S. dollars using 1980 exchange rates.

analysis treats each ally separately and estimates a demand equation for each, using data collected from 1955 – 1981. The estimated demand equations for France, Germany, and the United Kingdom are then used to make forecasts for defense spending, based on the growth ranges we settled on in a previous section.

The remainder of this section is organized as follows: The first subsection reviews some important ideas, such as pure public goods, thinning, and free riding. These ideas underlie the demand equation specifications, which is also given in that subsection. The theoretical foundation for the demand equation is found in our previously published work.[76] The second subsection contains the cross-sectional statistical analysis of the demand equation; while the third subsection includes the time-series statistical analysis. Defense expenditure forecasts are given for Britain, France, and Germany in the last subsection.

## Preliminaries and the Defense-Demand Relationship

*Preliminaries.* When analyzing alliance behavior, economists have called attention to the free-rider problem where smaller allies rely on larger allies for defense protection.[77] That is, large allies take on a disproportionately large defense burden. This hypothesis is based on the notion of a *pure public good.*

A pure public good exhibits two crucial characteristics. First, the benefits of the good are nonrival in consumption. This means that more than one nation (or individual) can simultaneously consume the *same unit* of the good without detracting from the benefits available to others. Consider the case of deterrence, which is usually characterized as purely public. The threat of punishment embodied in our strategic triad can protect any number of allies. Taking additional allies under the deterrent umbrella does not necessarily diminish the protection of the original allies, provided that the retaliatory threat is credible.

The second characteristic of a pure public good is that it is prohibitively expensive to exclude nations from using the good once it is provided. This characteristic of nonexcludability leads to the free-rider problem, since *both* contributors and noncontributors receive the good's full benefits. Obviously, in the absence of exclusion, it is in many nations' self-interest to undercontribute to the public good, knowing that the contributions of others will provide enough of the good for their needs. Such selfish behavior allows the free riders to spend their scarce resources on other things, which they cannot get without contributing. Again consider deterrence. Once a strategic triad is deployed and the associated threat is credible, it is not always possible to deny an ally protection. A nuclear attack on Canada would, due to fallout, misses, and wind direction, kill millions in the United States. Clearly, the United States could not deny Canada deterrent protection. Judging from the Canadian defense burdens (see Table 3.2), the Canadians are aware of this and are free riders, relying on the United States for protection. In general, however, the second characteristic of pure publicness is less certain to apply to deterrence. It, however, applies whenever an attack on a nation's allies inflicts unacceptable damage, in terms of fallout or the loss of foreign investment interests and/or military personnel, on the nation(s) providing the deterrence.

In previous studies done in the 1960s (see reference 77), investigators found strong evidence of free riding in NATO. In particular, the wealthy allies shouldered the defense burden of the smaller, poorer allies who free rode. This free-riding behavior is clearly seen in Tables 3.1 and 3.2. Table 3.2 shows that in 1960, over 92 percent of the NATO burden fell on the four largest allies. During the 1950s and 1960s, NATO relied on its strategic arsenal to deter the Soviet Union's use of conventional forces in Western Europe, since NATO's conventional forces were no match against Soviet tanks and ground troops.

In the 1970s and 1980s, there has been a closing of the "share gap" between the defense burdens paid by the rich and the poor allies in NATO[78] that cannot be explained by the public good model. For example, in 1970, the U.S. share of NATO expenditures was 74.5 percent. This figure dropped throughout the 1970s and in 1982 was 56.7 percent (see the data presented in Table 3.2). Why is it that the largest ally, the United States, has been able to decrease its contributions so dramatically? Moreover, why was Norway, a small ally, increasing its share during the same period?[79] This same trend is evidenced when considering the percentage of GDP devoted to military expenditures by country (see Table 3.1). In 1971, the United States allocated 7 percent of GDP to military spending; by 1979, the measure stood at 5.1 percent. Although the percentage of GDP devoted to defense has increased since Reagan took office, the *overall trend* for this percentage in the United States has been declining for the long run. On the other hand, Belgium, The Netherlands, Denmark, Norway, and Italy have maintained a fairly constant rate of military expenditures in terms of GDP.

To explain the closing of the "share gap," we and others have put forth a *joint product* model, which generalizes the pure public good model by allowing an ally's arsenal to produce more than one output. In particular, an arsenal provides deterrence, damage-limiting protection (needed when deterrence fails and conflict begins), and private or country-specific benefits (e.g., protection of coastal waters, relief during national disaster, and thwarting of terrorism). Each of these three types of benefits has varying degrees of publicness. For example, most country-specific benefits must be paid for if the nation is ever to receive the benefit; i.e., free riding is not expected for these excludable benefits. Conventional forces are not purely public, since they are subject to *thinning* as the same size arsenal is spread along a longer perimeter. In other words, the degree of protection provided by a conventional arsenal depends, unlike deterrent missiles, on how much land or border is being defended. The addition of an ally with large areas needing defending would diminish the damage-limiting capabilities of an alliance arsenal, unless sufficient armaments are added. Moreover, conventional forces and their damage-limiting benefits can be withheld at will. This degree of excludability also cuts down on intra-alliance free riding for conventional forces.

The joint product model predicts that the extent of free riding is inversely related to the proportion of excludable defense outputs produced by the arsenal. Alliances whose sole benefit is deterrence would be characterized by many free riders; however, an alliance whose primary purpose were country-specific or damage-limiting protection would have fewer free riders. If the proportion of excludable defense outputs grew in the late 1970s and in the 1980s, then the closing of the share gap can be explained. Any viable alliance will always produce a certain amount of deterrence. Even in the presence of this purely public output, free riding is still reduced whenever the deterrence-producing weapons need to work in conjunction with the conventional weaponry. Benefits or goods that are best consumed together are termed *complements* (e.g., guns and bullets). If deterrent weapons are now complementary to conventional weaponry, then an increase in spillins (e.g., increased deterrence provided by one's allies) may stimulate the ally's demand for its own conventional forces.

During the 1970 – 1974 period, the NATO alliance changed its emphasis from a strategy of Mutual Assured Destruction (MAD) to one of flexible response. The flexible response doctrine is not new, but a great deal of new interest is being shown in it since 1970 (see the evidence in reference 10). This doctrine allows NATO to respond in different ways to a Warsaw Pact challenge; conventional forces or strategic forces may be used and, in the latter case, a missile exchange may be limited or complete. With this doctrine, the European allies must be prepared to defend themselves against conventional aggression in the European theater, since the initial stages of warfare are expected to involve conventional and tactical nuclear weapons exchanges. No longer can these allies rely on nuclear weapons' deterrence for their external security. An ally who does not increase its military activity in response to other allies' increased military activities would invite aggression, since an opposing alliance would have a better chance to gain an advantage in a conventional war fought on that ally's soil. By tying warfare to a sequence of measured responses involving the deployment of all three kinds of weaponry, flexible response enhances the importance of the conventional, non-nuclear arsenals relative to strategic deterrence. The nuclear and non-nuclear arsenals contribute to each other's value; they become complementary and must be used together.

This increased complementarity affects an ally's defense expenditure response as the other members of the alliance increase their expenditures; in particular, increases in one's allies' expenditures (or spillins) could increase an ally's own defense expenditures. This prediction would hold for most non-nuclear allies, but would not apply to the same extent to the nuclear allies. The nuclear allies provide all three classes of weapons and, unlike the non-nuclear allies, can substitute their military expenditures with those of any of the other allies. The doctrine of flexible response may actually enhance the ability of nuclear allies to free ride if, as appears to be the case, strategic weapons budgets are increased as a proportion of these allies' total defense expenditures. This is so because relatively more nonexcludable benefits are then produced.

Two non-nuclear allies who can still free ride even under the doctrine of flexible response are the two flanking nations of Germany and Italy, whose strategic positions require NATO troops to be stationed on their soil. Hence, they receive conventional forces automatically from their allied. To some extent, these allied forces *relieve pressures* for these flanking allies to provide their own forces. In 1984, 330,000 troops from other NATO allies were stationed on German soil; 3,800 foreign troops from NATO were on Italian soil.[80] In the case of Italy, contingency plans exist to airlift NATO troops if needed. Next to Germany, Britain has the greatest number of NATO troops in its country – 27,000 men from the United States. Substituting one's allies' troops for one's own is also free riding. We will return to these substitution and complementary aspects of the new doctrine once the demand equation is specified.

*The Demand for Military Expenditures Equation.* The theory behind the demand for military expenditures equation is given elsewhere (see reference 76). Equation (1) denotes the basic form for the relationship, where environmental factors (i.e., oil prices and foreign threat) have been added:

$$ME = F (PRICE, INCOME, SPILL, OIL, THREAT). \qquad (1)$$

There are five primary influences or variables that determine an ally's military expenditures (ME). As for all demand relationships, military expenditures depend on the relative price of military goods as compared with all other goods. Because countries do not maintain indices of the price of military activity, data on price are not available. Price can be dropped from the equation without biasing our results, provided that the price of military activities has inflated at the same general rate as that of nondefense activities. Evidence to this effect is provided by SIPRI, which conducted an investigation on the relative prices of military activities.[81]

INCOME, as measured by an ally's GDP, is a crucial determinant of military expenditures. As GDP rises, an ally has both more resources to protect and greater means to provide protection. Thus, we hypothesize that military expenditures and income are positively related. This positive relationship means that defense is a "normal good," whose demand rises with income. We expect that a one-dollar increase in GDP will induce less than a one-dollar increase in defense expenditures, since a major portion of any additional dollar goes for private consumption and investment.

Another influence on an ally's military expenditures is the defense expenditures of the other allies, as measured by SPILL. For free riders, military expenditures and spillins should be negatively related; an increase in spillins causes a decrease in defense expenditures. If this relationship has a coefficient of $-1$, then a dollar increase in the military expenditures of the other allies serves to replace a dollar of one's own expenditures. This $-1$ value corresponds to a high degree of free riding. When complementarity exists between allies' arsenals, as might be the case for some non-nuclear allies after the early 1970s, we would predict a positive relationship or a very small negative relationship between ME and SPILL.

In equation (1) we have also included oil prices (OIL). Since oil is a major input into an ally's military activity, we would expect that changes in its price would have a "derived demand" influence on defense expenditures. For an oil importer, the effect of a change in oil prices depends on whether other fuel sources, whose prices have not risen, are easily substituted for oil. If oil is not easily replaced, then the *quantity* of oil purchased will remain unchanged in spite of the price rise; thus, the higher price will increase the ally's military expenditures on oil. In the short run, most allies cannot substitute other fuels for oil, since military equipment runs on oil-based fuels. Hence, we would expect a positive relationship between OIL and ME. This positive relationship should become especially important after 1973.

Equation (1) also includes THREAT, as measured by Soviet military expenditures. If this threat measure is a determinant of military expenditures, then we would expect a positive relationship.

At least two other possible determinants of defense expenditures could be added to equation (1). A country's population size could positively influence defense expenditures, since population is a proxy for what is being protected. Another influence is thinning of conventional forces. An increase in thinning (i.e., less forces per mile of border being guarded or fewer armor divisions per mile) should positively influence an ally's military expenditures, since its conventional strength is falling. The influence of these additional factors, as well as those given in equation (1), are empirically examined in the next two subsections.

## Cross-Sectional Analysis

This subsection gives a cross-sectional analysis of equation (1). In particular, we intend to determine which of the hypothesized influences are highly correlated with military expenditures. We should note that some of the data for 1982 are still only estimates, however, we believe that these estimates represent the best data currently available.

The use of cross-sectional data requires that we somehow scale the data so that relative comparisons between countries can be facilitated.[82] Since the primary focus here is on burden-sharing and defense spending, we have chosen to scale the data by the relevant totals of the NATO alliance. This means that each variable measures the "slice" of the total NATO pie attributed to each ally. By comparing the relative sizes of the various slices, we can analyze the spending patterns of the allies in NATO.

The measures used and their definitions are presented in Table 3.18. DEFBURDEN measures an ally's contributions to the total military spending of the alliance. As this measure grows for a particular ally, that ally is shouldering more of the burden of defense for the alliance. The remaining variables of Table 3.18 represent some of the hypothesized determinants for defense burdens. The variable GDPBE-

Table 3.18. Description of the Variables Used in the Cross-Sectional Analysis of Military Spending*

| Variable | Description |
| --- | --- |
| DEFBURDEN | Defense burden. Calculated as the military spending of the ally divided by the total military spending in NATO (in percentage terms). |
| GDPBENEFIT | An ally's share of GDP. Calculated as the GDP of the ally divided by the total GDP of NATO (in percentage terms). |
| POPBENEFIT | An ally's share of population. Calculated as the population of the ally divided by the total population of NATO (in percentage terms). |
| EXPOSED | An ally's share of NATO's total miles of exposed border (in percentage terms). |
| AREA | An ally's share of NATO'S total landmass (in percentage terms). |

Sources: *SIPRI Yearbook 1983* and *IMF, International Financial Statistics Yearbook 1983*.

*All expenditures values were intially expressed in 1980 prices using each country's GDP price deflator and were converted to U.S. dollars using 1980 exchange rates.

NEFIT measures the size of each ally's GDP in relation to the total income generated by the NATO members. We expect GDPBENEFIT and DEFBURDEN to be positively and significantly correlated to one another.

POPBENEFIT, EXPOSED, and AREA are also hypothesized to have positive influences on DEFBURDEN. Each of these measures represents a benefit to an ally from being in the alliance. POPBENEFIT proxies the benefits of saving citizens as a result of forestalling war with an enemy. Since the larger countries, in terms of population, receive more benefits, they should be willing to pay more for defense.[83]

EXPOSED measures the percentage of NATO's total exposed borders attributable to each ally. Luxembourg, for example, is completely surrounded by friendly nations. Therefore, it has zero miles of exposed borders to protect. Turkey, however, has many miles exposed to direct attack; hence, Turkey has a relatively large percentage of NATO's exposed border to protect.

EXPOSED provides for a unique test of our hypothesis concerning the doctrine of flexible response. In the 1950s and 1960s, the miles of exposed border were relatively unimportant to the NATO allies because deterrence relied primarily on MAD, a doctrine not sensitive to borders needing protection. With the adoption of a flexible response, exposed borders need to be defended. Those allies with more miles to defend are therefore induced to spend more on defense to counter the thinning of their forces. If our hypothesis is correct, then EXPOSED and DEFBURDEN should be positively correlated during the years under the doctrine of flexible response. In fact, the strength of the relationship should grow as the allies become more adapted to the new doctrine. Many of the same arguments apply to AREA, which measures an ally's share of NATO's total land area.

The data for DEFBURDEN, GDPBENEFIT, POPBENEFIT, EXPOSED, and AREA are presented in Table 3.19 for each ally for the years 1978, 1980, and 1982, respectively. Because the miles of exposed borders and the square miles of land area remain constant over time, these measures are only presented once.

The hypothesis concerning DEFBURDEN and GDPBENEFIT cannot be rejected on the basis of the estimated correlation coefficients (Kendall's tau) between these measures.[84] The correlation coefficient was .89 in 1978, .85 in 1980, and .82 in 1982. In each year the measure is positive and statistically significant at the .01 level of significance. Hence, GDP is an important determinant of defense spending as hypothesized.

The correlation coefficients between DEFBURDEN and POPBENEFIT remained fairly constant during the three years examined here. The correlation coefficient was .74 in 1978 and 1980, while increasing somewhat to .76 in 1982. These measures are not inconsistent with the hypothesis that population has a significant influence on defense expenditures.

Positive and significant correlations are also evidenced between DEFBURDEN and EXPOSED. The correlation estimates are .38, .42, and .49 for 1978, 1980, 1982, respectively. In 1965, the same correlation was only .36. The increase in this measure over time is consistent with the hypothesis concerning the doctrine of flexible response. Borders needing protection are now becoming a more important determinant of defense burden sharing.

Similar findings are evidenced by the correlation coefficients with respect to DEFBURDEN and AREA. In 1965, the measure stood at .41; by 1978, it was .49; and in 1982 it was .63. The steady increase in these correlation coefficients agrees with our prediction concerning flexible response.

From these cross-section data, there is some evidence that France, the United Kingdom, and Germany may be overcontributors to NATO'S defense. If GDPBENEFIT, POPBENEFIT, EXPOSED, and AREA are appropriate benefit proxies, then some aggregation of these measures should predict an ally's efficient defense contribution. Unfortunately, there is no way of knowing the appropriate weights to attach to the various benefit proxies. *If each is given equal weight,* the *average benefit shares* for France, the United Kingdom, and Germany are, respectively, 6.9, 7.3, and 7.2 in each of the three years under consideration. Comparing these measures to DEFBURDEN, presented in Table 3.19, we find that each country is an overcontributor. This is, in part, due to Canada's undercontribution. Of the three, these calculations indicate that France is the greatest overcontributor. Thus, even with the increased substitution possibilities as a result of the doctrine of flexible response, the two medium-sized nuclear allies are still major influences in the alliance. Germany has gone from a free rider in 1960 (average benefit share greater than defense share) to a rather large overcontributor by 1982.[85] In the time series analysis, we conclude that France, the United Kingdom, and Germany are free riders (i.e., undercontributors) owing to the negative sign on the spillin coefficient. This result *suggests* that our equal weighting of the benefit proxies above is not ap-

Table 3.19. Relative Defense Burdens and the Benefits in NATO, 1978, 1980, 1982

| Country | DEFBURDEN | | | GDPBENEFIT | | | POPBENEFIT | | | EXPOSED* | AREA* |
|---|---|---|---|---|---|---|---|---|---|---|---|
| | 1978 | 1980 | 1982 | 1978 | 1980 | 1982 | 1978 | 1980 | 1982 | | |
| United States | 54.9 | 56.2 | 56.7 | 45.4 | 44.8 | 45.0 | 39.2 | 39.4 | 39.7 | 27.4 | 42.3 |
| Canada | 2.1 | 1.8 | 2.1 | 4.4 | 4.4 | 4.3 | 4.1 | 4.1 | 4.2 | 20.0 | 45.1 |
| Belgium | 1.6 | 1.5 | 1.4 | 2.0 | 2.1 | 2.0 | 1.7 | 1.7 | 1.7 | 0.1 | 0.1 |
| Denmark | 0.6 | 0.6 | 0.5 | 1.2 | 1.2 | 1.2 | 0.9 | 0.9 | 0.9 | 2.2 | 0.2 |
| France | 10.5 | 10.3 | 11.4 | 11.2 | 11.3 | 11.5 | 9.4 | 9.3 | 9.3 | 4.4 | 2.5 |
| Germany | 10.9 | 10.4 | 9.1 | 13.8 | 14.1 | 13.9 | 10.8 | 10.7 | 10.5 | 2.7 | 1.1 |
| Greece | 1.1 | 0.9 | 1.3 | 0.7 | 0.7 | 0.7 | 1.6 | 1.7 | 1.7 | 5.8 | 0.6 |
| Italy | 3.7 | 3.7 | 3.4 | 6.5 | 6.9 | 6.8 | 10.0 | 9.9 | 9.6 | 9.1 | 1.4 |
| Luxembourg | 0.0 | 0.0 | 0.0 | 0.1 | 0.1 | 0.1 | 0.1 | 0.1 | 0.1 | 0.0 | 0.0 |
| Netherlands | 2.1 | 2.1 | 1.8 | 2.9 | 2.9 | 2.8 | 2.5 | 2.4 | 2.4 | 0.9 | 0.2 |
| Norway | 0.7 | 0.7 | 0.7 | 0.9 | 1.0 | 1.0 | 0.7 | 0.7 | 0.7 | 5.7 | 1.5 |
| Portugal | 0.3 | 0.3 | 0.4 | 0.4 | 0.4 | 0.5 | 1.7 | 1.7 | 1.7 | 1.5 | 0.4 |
| Turkey | 1.2 | 1.0 | 2.0 | 1.0 | 1.0 | 1.1 | 7.5 | 7.7 | 7.9 | 10.7 | 3.5 |
| United Kingdom | 10.3 | 10.4 | 9.1 | 9.5 | 9.1 | 9.0 | 9.8 | 9.7 | 9.5 | 9.3 | 1.1 |

*These measures remain constant over time. Kendall's coefficient of concordance is 0.8 for all three years. The Kendall coefficent of concordance measures the degree of correlation between the variables. The rather high concordance value of 0.8 indicates that, taken together, all of the variables appear to be correlated with one another.

propriate. Clearly, we put more confidence in the time-series analysis than in the cross-section analysis. The variables in the two analyses also vary — e.g., EXPOSED must be dropped from the time-series analysis since borders have not changed over time.

## Time-Series Analysis

In this section statistical estimates of the military expenditures equations are presented for nine NATO allies. Estimating an equation for each ally requires data for a time period sufficiently long to ensure credibility. The nine allies considered here satisfy this requirement, whereas the other allies do not. The allies in the sample include the United States, the three major Northern European allies, Belgium, The Netherlands, Denmark, Norway, and Italy. According to Table 3.2, these nine allies accounted for approximately 94 percent of NATO's total expenditures in 1982; hence, the allies left out of the sample are indeed a minor consideration. Our estimates cover the period 1955 – 1981. The statistical results are discussed in detail for France, Germany, and the United Kingdom; however, the other six equations provide some useful comparisons with those allies.

*Variable Descriptions and Hypotheses.* The variables and their definitions are presented in Table 3.20. All expenditure data are expressed in billions of constant U.S. dollars, making possible direct comparisons of the estimates across countries. By holding prices and exchange rates constant, the variations in the data are isolated to *real* changes, not changes in currency valuations. OIL is the Saudi crude price per barrel. For each ally, the Saudi price has been divided by that country's GDP price deflator before being converted to U.S. dollars. Therefore, OIL measures the *relative price of oil* when compared to all other goods in the country. If the oil prices and other prices change in the same manner year after year, then there will not be any change in OIL. THREAT represents the military expenditures of the Soviet Union. We have used SIPRI's estimates.[86]

The hypothesized relationship between ME and GDP is positive for each ally. Similarly, the hypothesized relationship between ME and THREAT is positive, i.e., increased threat should induce an ally to arm.

In a previous section we argued that an alliance's strategic doctrine and the mix between conventional and strategic forces determine an ally's response to SPILL. In particular, we hypothesized free-riding behavior for all allies up until NATO's new emphasis on flexible response in the early 1970s. Before this new emphasis, the alliance reliance on strategic deterrence (MAD) meant the sharing of a purely public benefit, which, in turn, would lead to free riding. This free riding will show up as a significant *negative* coefficient on the spillin term in the ally's demand for ME. After this new emphasis, three classes of allies must be distinguished: nuclear

Table 3.20. Definitions of the Variables Used in the Time-Series Analyses of Military Spending

| Variable | Definition |
| --- | --- |
| ME | Military expenditures in 1980 prices. Converted to U.S. dollars using 1980 exchange rates (billions of U.S. dollars). |
| GDP | Gross domestic product in 1980 prices. Converted to U.S. dollars using 1980 exchange rates (billions of U.S. dollars). |
| SPILL | Spillins from NATO allies lagged one year. Calculated as total NATO defense spending minus the military expenditures of the country under consideration. Expressed in 1980 prices, converted to U.S. dollars using 1980 exchange rates (billions of U.S. dollars). |
| THREAT | Military expenditure of the Soviet Union lagged one year. Expressed in 1980 prices using SIPRI's conversion to U.S. dollars (billions of U.S. dollars). |
| POP | Population in millions. |
| OIL | Saudi crude oil price per barrel. For each country the Saudi price was divided by its GDP price deflator before converted to U.S. dollars using 1980 exchange rates. |
| D | Dummy variable, equal to zero for the years 1955 – 1973 and equal to one for the years 1974 – 1981. |
| D · SPILL | D times Spill |
| D · OIL | D times OIL. |

*Sources: SIPRI Yearbooks* (various years) and *International Financial Statistics Yearbook 1983*.

allies, non-nuclear flanking allies (Germany and Italy), and all others. For nuclear allies, the doctrine of flexible response allows for greater substitution possibilities, since, for example, the buildup in one ally's strategic stockpile relieves the pressures for another to build up its own stockpile. The flanking allies could also free ride to a greater extent after this new emphasis on flexible response, since they would automatically receive conventional troops from other allies. Under the doctrine, the other non-nuclear allies would find that their conventional forces were complementary to the nuclear nations' strategic and tactical nuclear forces. This complementarity would induce the small non-nuclear allies to free ride *to a smaller extent;* hence, the coefficient on their spillin terms should be positive or less negative after the early 1970s.

The relationship between ME and oil prices is more difficult to predict. An ally's ability to substitute between oil-based fuels and other fuels is clearly the crucial influence on the derived demand for oil within the military expenditures equation. Limited substitution possibilities would mean, *ceteris paribus,* that rises in oil prices would imply greater military expenditures. One determinant of the impact of oil price rises on military activity is the percentage of the military budget earmarked for operations and maintenance, since this portion of an ally's military expenditures uses oil-based fuels. Any increase in this item's share of the budget over time would imply greater oil needs. Currently, we have not been able to find a complete time series on this breakdown for the allies; such a time series would allow us to fine-tune our predictions. Moreover, if the doctrine of flexible response increased the importance of conventional forces, then this would increase oil-based fuel demands through operations requirements. Thus, this doctrine may also decrease the substitution possibilities with respect to oil, thus implying that ME and oil prices would be positively related. One other factor at work with respect to oil prices is the distinction between oil-importing and oil-exporting allies (Britain after 1980 and Norway after 1975). Oil-exporting allies receive additional revenues as oil prices increase. These additional revenues might account for an increase in military expenditures, since budgetary trade-offs become less severe.

*Empirical Results.* Equation (1) was estimated in linear form using various possible formulations, in which some influences such as population, threat, and oil prices have been added or dropped. Most of our remarks focus on the best-case result, reported in Table 3.21. The other cases are available from the authors and are not reported. These other cases indicate that neither population nor threat is a significant influence on most allies' demands for military expenditures. In the case of population, we suspect that the high correlation between GDP and population is causing these results to be poor. The poor result with respect to THREAT may be due to the measure of THREAT that we used. A better measure might be changes in strategic weapon stockpiles.[87] Elsewhere, we tried such a measure without significant success. At this point, we conclude that an arms race between NATO and the Warsaw Pact does not appear to depend on military expenditures.

Equation (2) denotes the military expenditures equation that we estimated for each of the nine allies:

$$ME = \beta_0 + \beta_1 \, GDP + \beta_2 \, SPILL + (\beta)_3 D \cdot SPILL + \beta_4 \, OIL + \beta_5 D \cdot OIL \quad (2)$$

The term D·SPILL is added to equation (2) to test for a structural change in an ally's response to spillins occurring after 1973.[88] If such a change occurred, and if the change is in the direction that we predicted, then this would provide evidence not inconsistent with our predicted impact of the doctrine of flexible response. Similarly, the term D·OIL tests for a structural shift in an ally's response to oil prices after 1973.

Table 3.21 gives the estimated value of the coefficients for each of the independent variables. Out of the 54 coefficients estimated, 33 are significant at the .10 level. Moreover, with the exception of the U.S. equation, the R-squares are high.[89] The addition of the oil measures improves the estimates significantly over previous estimates.

As expected, most of the coefficients on GDP are positive and significant. Interestingly, there is a wide variation between allies with respect to their marginal responses to GDP. For France, a one-dollar increase in GDP induces a 1.6 cent increase in *real* military expenditures. In Germany, a one-dollar increase in GDP induces only a .9 cent increase in military spending. Similar to France, the United Kingdom's marginal response is 1.5 cents. The U.S. response to GDP is also quite close to that of the other two nuclear allies. In Table 3.22, some income elasticity measures are presented for France, Germany, and the United Kingdom. The income elasticity measure shows the *percentage* increase in real defense expenditures resulting from a 1 percent increase in real GDP, holding other factors constant. If, for example, this measure is 1.0, then a 1 percent increase in real GDP translates into a 1 percent increase in real defense expenditures. In 1980, the French income elasticity is .40, which means that a 1 percent increase in GDP causes a 0.4 percent increase in defense. The reported estimates in Table 3.22 indicate that France is the most income-responsive ally of the three. Since 1968, the German measure has been relatively stable with values estimated in the .25 – .28 range. Though both French and British income elasticity measures showed upward trends until 1970 and 1968, respectively, thereafter these measures have been fairly stable in the .38 – .42 and .28 – .33 ranges.

Returning to Table 3.21, the estimated coefficients for SPILL and D·SPILL are given in the second and third rows, respectively. The post-1973 responses are calculated *as the sum* of the two coefficients presented. Therefore, for France, the marginal response in the late 1970s and early 1980s is estimated to be $(-.037 - .038 =) -.075$. In Germany, this response is $(-.043 - .049 =) -0.92$ and for the United Kingdom it is $(-.010 - .005 =) -.015$. Of interest is the United States, whose post-1973 response to spillins is approximately $(.058 - .927 =) -.869$. This indicates that if the U.S allies increase their total military expenditures by one dollar, the United States will respond (holding GDP and OIL constant) by cutting its defense spending by 87 cents. It also implies that the United States will increase its military expenditures by 87 cents for every dollar drop in our allies' expenditures.

Our hypothesis concerning the doctrine of flexible response cannot be rejected on the basis of our estimated coefficients for D·SPILL. For the United Kingdom, France, and the United States, the negative sign provides evidence that is not inconsistent with the hypothesis that the new doctrine has enhanced the substitution possibilities of the nuclear allies, causing their free-riding behavior to worsen. Furthermore, as flanking nations, Germany and Italy were predicted to exhibit free riding. This evidence supports this contention. The positive signs of D·SPILL for Belgium, The Netherlands, and Norway suggest increased complementarity between the public and private defense outputs, and less free riding in the post-1973 period. Denmark's equation yields the only inexplicable sign with respect to D·SPILL.

Table 3.21. Estimated Coefficients for the Military Expenditure Equations by Country, 1955-1981

| Independent Variable | United States | France | Germany | United Kingdom | Belgium | The Netherlands | Denmark | Norway | Italy |
|---|---|---|---|---|---|---|---|---|---|
| GDP | .018 | 0.16* | .009 | .015* | .022* | .022* | .006* | .029* | .022* |
| SPILL | .058 | −.037* | −.043 | −.010 | .002 | .003 | .002* | .003* | −.010* |
| D · SPILL | −.927* | −.038* | −.049* | −.005 | .001 | .002 | −.0005 | .001* | −.008* |
| OIL | −9.187* | −.805* | −1.656* | .380* | .030 | .055* | −.028* | .012 | −.049 |
| D · OIL | 11.025* | 1.061* | 1.820* | −.219 | −.013 | −.056 | .035* | −.027* | .083 |
| Intercept | 137.081* | 23.985* | 34.263* | 15.986 | .027 | .578 | .604* | −.479* | 3.822* |
| R-Square | .61 | .94 | .92 | .77 | .97 | .95 | .95 | .98 | .97 |
| Durbin-Watson | .72 | 1.43 | 1.37 | 1.13 | 1.07 | 1.24 | 1.34 | 1.14 | 1.19 |

*Statistically significant alpha level equals .10.

*Note*: The Dependent Variable is ME. Ordinary Least Squares Estimates.

Table 3.22. Estimated Income Elasticities for Various Years

| Year | France | Germany | United Kingdom |
|---|---|---|---|
| 1961 | .25 | .23 | .24 |
| 1963 | .28 | .17 | .24 |
| 1965 | .31 | .21 | .26 |
| 1967 | .31 | .21 | .26 |
| 1969 | .37 | .25 | .30 |
| 1971 | .40 | .27 | .31 |
| 1973 | .42 | .26 | .31 |
| 1975 | .41 | .24 | .31 |
| 1977 | .41 | .27 | .32 |
| 1979 | .40 | .28 | .32 |
| 1981 | .38 | .27 | .31 |
| 1982 | .39 | .27 | .32 |

The results of Table 3.21 also show that a one dollar increase in spillins results in a 7.5 cents reduction in military expenditures for France, a 9.2 cents reduction in Germany, and a 1.5 cent reduction in the United Kingdom. In total, *an increase in one dollar of U.S. expenditures means a reduction of about 18 cents in the Northern European military expenditures.* These countries appear to be more responsive to spillins than GDP. However, this can be misleading because spillins do not change in the same magnitude as GDP. Thus, even though the allies appear responsive, their opportunities to substitute other allies' military expenditures for their own are limited. Some spillin elasticity measures are presented in Table 3.23 for France, Germany, and the United Kingdom. This elasticity shows the percentage change in an ally's defense expenditures, resulting from a 1 percent change in the other allies' aggregate defense spending. Of the three nations shown in Table 3.23, the U.K. is the least responsive to spillins, while France is less responsive than Germany. Since 1974, both Germany and the U.K. have displayed stable responses to spillins. The French spillin elasticity has been stable since 1977, after showing a downward trend during 1974–1979.

Finally, we consider the estimated coefficients on OIL and D·OIL as presented in the fourth and fifth rows of Table 3.21. To measure the response of the allies to OIL in the post-1973 period, it is necessary to sum the coefficients for OIL and D·OIL in each equation. For France, the response is $(-.805 + 1.061 =)$ .164 and in the United Kingdom it is $(.380 - .219 =)$ .161. The positive response indicates that, as an important input into defense, oil has relatively few substitutes in these countries. Hence, since 1973, increases in oil prices have led to increases in military expenditures for the oil importers as predicted. The D·OIL term is positive and significant for the United States, France, Germany, and Denmark. For the other oil importers, the coefficient has the wrong sign, but is insignificant. The results for the oil exporters are less easy to interpret. Both exporters decreased their defense expenditures as oil prices increased in the post-1973 period. If the operations and maintenance budgets were small and decreasing, then these negative signs could be explained owing to input substitution. Table 3.15 showed that the U.K. operations and maintenance budget amounted to only 11 percent of total defense expenditures.

Table 3.23. Estimated Spillin Elasticities for Various Years

| Year | France | Germany | United Kingdom |
|---|---|---|---|
| 1961 | −.35 | −.50 | −.08 |
| 1963 | −.39 | −.39 | −.08 |
| 1965 | −.37 | −.41 | −.08 |
| 1967 | −.39 | −.45 | −.09 |
| 1969 | −.46 | −.54 | −.11 |
| 1971 | −.40 | −.47 | −.09 |
| 1973 | −.37 | −.41 | −.08 |
| 1975 | −.71 | −.72 | −.13 |
| 1977 | −.70 | −.70 | −.12 |
| 1979 | −.61 | −.70 | −.12 |
| 1981 | −.60 | −.74 | −.13 |
| 1982 | −.60 | −.72 | −.13 |

This figure is unusually low and is consistent with the evidence in Table 3.21. For Norway, operations and maintenance in 1978 accounted for 27 percent of the military budget.[90] This typical share is not supportive of the significant negative response. To be more conclusive in our interpretation, we would need time series on the operations and maintenance budgets for each country. Hence, we view our interpretations as inconclusive, but suggestive of the oil response relationship. The results in Table 3.21 are, nonetheless, very encouraging for future research in the area of resource constraints and defense spending.

A comparison between the two medium-sized nuclear allies' demand equations reveals that the two equations are not identical. Both nations respond similarly to GDP, but their responses to oil prices (as expected) are significantly different. Moreover, France is much more responsive to spillins than is the United Kingdom.

## Defense Growth Forecasts

In 1978, the NATO allies agreed in principle to increase their real defense expenditures by 3 percent per year in response to Soviet increases, which have been running at a rate of 2 to 4 percent per year. Examining the allies' behavior since 1978 shows that, with the exception of the United States and the United Kingdom, no ally has moved to meet these pledges. The recession of 1980 may be part of the problem, but we intend to show that it is not entirely responsible. In this section, we present defense expenditure forecasts, based on the likely performances of the Northern European economies as presented in a previous section. The forecasts predict that 3 percent growth in defense will *not* be achieved by any of the three allies under any reasonable scenario. In fact, each ally will be far from its targeted level, owing to poor growth and a willingness to free ride on U.S. increases.

Tables 3.22 and 3.23 provide estimates of income elasticities and spillin elasticities for France, Germany, and the U.K.; these measures have been extremely stable since around 1975. This stability permits us to forecast future behavior based upon past tendencies. Interestingly, this stability also indicates that past trends have not changed since the pledges were made in 1978.

Using the predicted changes in GDP and our 1981 estimates of income and spillin elasticities, we can forecast the most likely response of an ally in terms of the percentage change in its military expenditures. The current economic climate and the reduced pressures on oil prices have led us to conclude that oil prices will not change appreciably in the near future. We have, therefore, held oil prices constant when computing our forecasts.

The scenario examined and the predicted changes in military expenditures are presented in Table 3.24. For each ally, the percentages along the top row denote the growth ranges projected in both the short-run and long-run periods. Hence, French growth is projected between $-1$ and $+2$ percent, German growth is between $+1$ and $+4$ percent, and British growth is between 0 and $+3$ percent. The long-run growth figures tended to be in the higher range of these projections. Seven different spillin scenarios are indicated in the left-hand column ranging between $-3$ and $+3$ percent change in spillins. Since all three allies respond negatively to spillins and positively to income, defense projections increase by either moving up each column in Table 3.24 (as spillins fall) or moving rightward along each row (as income increases). Insofar as the United States is the major contributor in NATO, the most important determinant of spillins for France, Germany, and the United Kingdom is U.S. spending. Currently, U.S. increases, coupled with other allies' responses, make the bottom row of Table 3.24 the most-likely scenario.[91] Unfortunately, U.S. increased spending is predicted to *keep* our Northern European allies from achieving their pledges owing to free riding. Table 3.24 indicates that both France and Germany *will cut* their defense expenditures by 1 to 2 percent under this scenario. The United Kingdom will increase its expenditures by less than one-half of 1 percent. Other entries in Table 3.24 show that under no reasonable scenario will these three allies meet their pledges, provided that their past behavior can be used to forecast their future actions.

Simple calculations using income elasticities show that France would have to grow at 7.5 percent, Germany at 11 percent, and the United Kingdom at 10 percent if the 3 percent targeted increase were to be met. In fact, these figures are underestimates, since they do not account for the Reagan defense increases. When these are included, the three allies would have to grow beyond these now near-impossible

Table 3.24. Forecasts of Percentage Changes in Military Expenditures for France, Germany, and the United Kingdom. Based on Different Scenarios for GDP and SPILL.*

%ΔGDP

| %ΔSPILL | France | | | | Germany | | | | | United Kingdom | | | |
|---|---|---|---|---|---|---|---|---|---|---|---|---|---|
| | −1 | 0 | +1 | +2 | +1 | +2 | +3 | +4 | 0 | 1 | 2 | 3 |
| −3 | 1.42 | 1.80 | 2.18 | 2.56 | 2.49 | 2.62 | 2.89 | 3.30 | .39 | .70 | 1.01 | 1.32 |
| −2 | .82 | 1.20 | 1.58 | 1.96 | 1.75 | 2.02 | 2.29 | 2.56 | .26 | .57 | .88 | 1.19 |
| −1 | .22 | .6 | .98 | 1.36 | 1.01 | 1.28 | 1.55 | 1.82 | .13 | .44 | .75 | 1.06 |
| 0 | −.38 | 0 | .38 | .76 | .27 | .54 | .81 | 1.08 | 0 | .31 | .62 | .93 |
| +1 | −.98 | −.6 | −.22 | .16 | −.47 | −.20 | .07 | .34 | −.13 | .18 | .49 | .8 |
| +2 | −1.58 | −1.20 | −.82 | −.44 | −1.21 | −.94 | −.67 | −.40 | −.26 | .05 | .36 | .67 |
| +3 | −2.18 | −1.80 | −1.42 | −1.04 | −1.98 | −1.72 | −1.45 | −1.14 | −.39 | −.08 | .23 | .54 |

*Assuming no change in the price of oil and using the estimated income and spillin elasticities for 1981.

rates to meet their promises. We are, therefore, confident that the 3 percent target will not be achieved.

A spending policy that asks each ally to pledge a certain real increase in defense, while ignoring future economic realities and allies' interactive spending behavior (i.e., free riding), is, we believe, an unworkable and foolish policy. Allies' free-riding behavior must be taken into account when soliciting pledges.

## CONCLUSIONS

Based on the analysis contained in this chapter, we have reached the following conclusions:

1. Under current growth scenarios, no Northern European ally is expected to come close to its pledged 3 percent real increase in defense expenditures.

2. A policy that asks allies to meet a targeted real growth in defense expenditures constitutes a near-impossible task. Sensible policy must account for economic realities and free-riding behavior.

3. Every time our allies spend a dollar less on defense, the United States spends 87 cents more. Moreover, every time the United States spends a dollar more, the Northern European allies (i.e., France, Germany, and the United Kingdom) in total spend about 18 cents less.

4. The doctrine of flexible response appears to have had a significant effect on NATO's spending behavior in the 1970s. Conventional weaponry has taken on an increased importance in Western Europe. This is evidenced by the increased influence of the thinning variable as shown by our statistical analysis.

5. The doctrine of flexible response appears to have been an important factor in shifting about 18 percent of the NATO burden onto the Europeans in the mid-1970s. The recent military buildup of the Reagan administration seems to be shifting the burden back onto the United States.

6. Threat, as measured by Soviet military expenditures, is not a significant determinant of NATO allies' defense expenditures.[92] GDP is the best determinant, followed by one's allies' expenditures (i.e., spillins).

7. The medium-sized nuclear allies respond in a similar manner to increases in their GDP, spending about 1.5 cents for every dollar increase in GDP. However, the influence of oil prices makes these nations respond differently to oil shocks and changes in spillins.

8. Oil prices are a crucial determinant of defense spending among the NATO allies. For most allies, increases in oil prices raise military expenditures, owing to an inability to find substitutes for the higher-priced fuels.

9. The smaller European allies have similar demands for military expenditures. This and other results suggest that NATO allies can be grouped into four distinct classes (the United States, medium-sized nuclear powers, small European allies, and flanking nations, i.e., Germany and Italy) for policy purposes. Such a grouping would streamline policy-making.

10. Income and spillin elasticities have been extremely stable since 1974, despite the 1978 pledge to increase real defense expenditures by 3 percent.

11. The growth scenarios for the medium run are as follows: $-1$ to 2 percent for France, 1 to 4 percent for Germany, and 0 to 3 percent for the United Kingdom.

## NOTES

1. These figures are taken from J. R. Hough, *The French Economy* (New York: Holmes and Meier, 1982), pp. 45–46.
2. The West German figures are from Eric Owen Smith, *The West German Economy* (New York: St. Martin's Press, 1983), p. 33.
3. These figures are from Alan G. Gruchy, *Comparative Economic Systems* (Boston: Houghton Mifflin Co., 1977), p. 109, and from OECD, *OECD Economic Outlook* (Paris: OECD, 1983), p. 152.
4. These growth figures are from OECD, *Economic Outlook*, p. 152.
5. OECD, *Economic Outlook*, p. 152.
6. Interim years agree with the observations given in the text and tables. In compiling these tables, we have used the most current data available at the time of writing.
7. NATO Press Release, M-DPC-2 (84) 28, December 4, 1984.
8. This defense burden-sharing measure was developed in Todd Sandler and John F. Forbes, "Burden Sharing, Strategy, and the Design of NATO," *Economic Inquiry* 18 (July 1980): 425–444.
9. *The Economist*, June 9–15, 1984, p. 70.
10. This doctrine has been around since 1957 when Henry Kissinger proposed the possibility of a limited war, where counterforce targets (i.e., military installations) are hit first. The doctrine is also contained in McNamara's Single Integrated Operational Plan, announced in 1961. However, some experts, such as Richard Burt, believe that not until the development of precision-guided munitions in the early 1970s did NATO have the ability to fight the type of war required by flexible response. Such a war requires extremely accurate missiles and munitions to achieve counterforce capabilities, while limiting nuclear fallout. The doctrine was more completely expressed by Secretary of Defense James R. Schlesinger in a speech on January 10, 1974, to the Overseas Writers Association in Washington. It was reiterated by Schlesinger in his February 5, 1974 testimony before the Senate Armed Services Committee and in the *Annual Defense Department Report for Fiscal Year 1975*, released on March 4, 1974. The National Security Decision Memorandum signed by President Nixon in January 1974 and the Nuclear Weapons Employment Policy signed by Schlesinger on April 14, 1974 also expressed the doctrine. On May 26, 1971, the Nuclear Planning Group of NATO met to discuss methods of supporting the doctrine of flexible response by use of nuclear armaments. It is on the basis of this renewed interest that we attribute the doctrine's effective institution to the early 1970s. Our dates and support come from Desmond Ball, "Déjà Vu: The Return to Counterforce in the Nixon Administration," *California Seminar on Arms Control and Foreign Policy* (Los Angeles: UCLA, 1975); Henry A. Kissinger, *Nuclear Weapons and Foreign*

*Policy* (New York: Harper and Row, 1957); Richard Burt, *New Weapons Technologies: Debates and Directions* (London: International Institute for Strategic Studies [IISS], 1976); and NATO Information Service, *NATO: Facts and Figures* (Brussels: NATO Publications, 1976).
11. The importance of these strategic forces is underscored by the Soviet demand that they be counted in any missile reduction agreement.
12. See Stockholm International Peace Research Institute (SIPRI), *World Armaments and Disarmament: SIPRI Yearbook* (New York: Crane, Russak and Co., 1983), Chapter 2.
13. SIPRI, *SIPRI Yearbook 1983*, p. 146.
14. On the "guns versus butter" controversy, see William K. Domke, Richard C. Eichenberg, and Catherine M. Kelleher, "The Illusion of Choice: Defense and Welfare in Advanced Industrial Democracies, 1948 – 1978," *American Political Science Review* 77, No. 1 (1983): 19 – 35; Lloyd J. Dumas, "The Impact of the Military Budget on the Domestic Economy," *Economic Forum* 13, No. 1 (1982): 71 – 86; Kathleen Peroff and Margaret Podalak-Warren, "Does Spending on Defense Cut Spending on Health? A Time Series Analysis of the U.S. Economy 1929 – 74," *British Journal of Political Science* 9, No. 1 (1979): 21 – 39; and Bruce Russett, "Defense Expenditures and National Well-Being," *American Political Science Review* 76 (1982): 767 – 777.
15. See SIPRI, *SIPRI Yearbook,* Chapters 11 – 13, on arms trade. The *Wall Street Journal,* July 20, 1984, p. 1, noted a 25 percent drop in French sales in 1983 owing to recessionary conditions. These sales are picking up significantly in 1984, as reported in *The Economist,* October 20 – 26, 1984, pp. 72 – 73.
16. Keith Hartley, "Estimating Military Aircraft Production Outlays: The British Experience," *Economic Journal* 79 (1969): 861 – 881; John Stanley and Maurice Pearton, *The International Trade in Arms* (London: Chatto and Windus, 1972).
17. Another possibility would be a conventional attack launched from the Kola Peninsula. In this scenario, Norway takes the attack. Terrain and weather considerations make this scenario less likely than a crossing of the Rhine River.
18. J. R. Hough, *The French Economy,* p. 110.
19. Ibid., p. 47.
20. Ibid., Chapters 2 – 4.
21. More current figures using the OECD definitions were not available at the time that this chapter was drafted. Tables 3.4, 3.8, and 3.9 contain 1982 and 1983 gross fixed investment and gross investment figures.
22. Our description of the German economy follows those provided by Eric Owen Smith in his *The West German Economy,* and Allan G. Gruchy in his *Comparative Economic Systems,* Chapter 5.
23. Eric Owen Smith, *The West German Economy,* p. 26.
24. Ibid., p. 52.
25. All the statistics reported in this paragraph are taken from Eric Owen Smith, *The West German Economy,* p. 26.
26. Since 1980, German government deficits have exceeded 2 percent of GNP.
27. Alan G. Gruchy, *Comparative Economic Systems,* Chapter 4.
28. Ibid.
29. Alan G. Gruchy, op. cit., p. 109.
30. Industries were first nationalized by the Labour party during the 1945 – 1951 period.
31. Alan G. Gruchy, op. cit., p. 104.
32. See *Aviation Week and Space Technology* 118 (April 25, 1983): pp. 22 – 23.
33. See OECD, *OECD: Economic Surveys 1982 – 1983, France* (Paris: OECD, 1983), p. 30.
34. OECD, *OECD Economic Survey 1982-1983: France.*

35. OECD, *OECD Economic Outlook*, December 1983.
36. OECD, *OECD Economic Survey 1982 – 1983: France*, p. 51.
37. OECD, *OECD Economic Outlook*, Table 54, p. 127.
38. *The Economist*, March 24 – 30, 1984, p. 65.
39. These figures and other information in this paragraph are taken from *The Economist*, March 24 – 30, 1984, pp. 65-66.
40. *The Economist*, March 30 – April 5, 1985, p. 103.
41. *The Economist*, May 26 – June 1, 1984, p. 67.
42. *The Economist*, June 9 – 15, 1984, p. 77.
43. Our sources for this section include OECD, *OECD Economic Surveys 1982 – 1983: Germany* (Paris: OECD, 1983); IMF, *IMF World Economic Outlook 1983* (Washington, DC: IMF, 1983); Facts on File Inc., *Facts on File* (New York: Facts on File Inc., various years); and magazines such as *The Economist* and *Time*.
44. *Wall Street Journal*, January 9, 1984, p. 1.
45. *London Financial Times*, June 29, 1984, p. 1.
46. OECD, *OECD Economic Outlook*, December 1983, p. 85.
47. *The Economist*, May 19 – 25, 1984, p. 54.
48. *The Economist*, June 16 – 22, 1984, p. 65.
49. Ibid.
50. *London Financial Times*, June 29, 1984, p. 1.
51. Our sources for this section include OECD, *OECD Economic Surveys 1982 – 1983: United Kingdom* (Paris: OECD, 1983); *IMF World Economic Outlook 1983*; Facts on File, *Facts on File;* and magazines such as *The Economist* and *Time*.
52. *London Sunday Times*, June 24, 1984, p. 1.
53. *New York Times*, March 6, 1985. Also see *The Economist*, March 9 – 15, 1985, pp. 52, 57.
54. *London Sunday Times*, June 24, 1984, p. 1. Also see *The Economist*, March 9 – 15, 1985, p. 52.
55. Kent Matthews and Patrick Minford, "Recent Developments and Forecasts," *Quarterly Economic Bulletin: Liverpool Research Group in Macroeconomics* 4, No. 4 (1983): 12.
56. See *The Economist*, March 23 – 29, 1985, pp. 53 – 64, 71 for a detailed description of the Lawson budget.
57. *The Economist*, May 12 – 18, 1984, p. 89
58. OECD, *OECD Economic Outlook*, p. 127.
59. *The Economist*, May 12 – 18, 1984, pp. 88 – 89.
60. The Nadiri chapter raises some debate over the crowding-out effect.
61. SIPRI, *SIPRI Yearbook 1983*, Chapter 6.
62. The Greens won 7 seats in the Hesse elections held in June 1984. *The Economist*, June 16 – 22, 1984, p. 40.
63. SIPRI, *SIPRI Yearbook 1983*, p. 107.
64. SIPRI, *SIPRI Yearbook 1983*, Chapter 6.
65. See references listed in footnote 14.
66. Domke, Eichenberg, and Kelleher, "The Illusion of Choice," p. 19.
67. See SIPRI, *SIPRI Yearbook 1983*, Chapter 8.
68. SIPRI, *SIPRI Yearbook 1983*, p. 203.
69. Ibid.
70. SIPRI, *SIPRI Yearbook 1983*, Chapter 2.
71. Todd Sandler and John F. Forbes, "Burden Sharing, Strategy, and the Design of NATO," *Economic Inquiry* 18 (July 1980): 425 – 444.
72. NATO, *NATO Facts and Figures*, p. 284.

73. This awareness has, we believe, increased the peace movement membership and activities.
74. On Soviet defense expenditures, see Richard F. Kaufman, "Soviet Defense Trends," A Staff Study, Subcommittee on International Trade, Finance, and Security Economics, Joint Economic Committee, Congress of the United States, September 1983; Thomas R. Cusack and Michael D. Ward, "Military Spending in the United States, Soviet Union, and the People's Republic of China," *Journal of Conflict Resolution* 25, No. 3 (1981): 429–469; Franklyn D. Holzman, "Are the Soviets Really Outspending the U.S. on Defense?" *International Security* 4, No. 4 (1980): 86–104; William T. Lee, *The Estimation of Soviet Defense Expenditures, 1955–75: An Unconventional Approach* (New York: Praeger Publishers, 1977); Miroslaw Nincic, "Fluctuations in Soviet Defense Spending: A Research Note," *Journal of Conflict Resolution* 27, No. 4 (1983): 648–660; and William Zimmerman and Glenn Palmer, "Words and Deeds in Soviet Foreign Policy: The Case of Soviet Military Expenditures," *American Political Science Review* 77, No. 2 (1983): 358–367.
75. See James C. Murdoch and Todd Sandler, "Complementarity, Free Riding, and the Military Expenditures of NATO Allies," *Journal of Public Economics* 25, No. 3 (1984): 83–101; James C. Murdoch and Todd Sandler, "A Theoretical and Empirical Analysis of NATO," *Journal of Conflict Resolution* 26, No.2 (1982): 237–263: James C. Murdoch and Todd Sandler, "Australian Demand for Military Expenditures: 1961–1979," *Australian Economic Papers* 24 (June 1985); Todd Sandler, "Impurity of Defense: An Application to the Economics of Alliances," *Kyklos* 30, No. 3 (1977): 443–460; Todd Sandler, "The Economic Theory of Alliances: Realigned," in C. Liske et al., eds., *Comparative Public Policy: Issues, Theories, and Methods* (New York: John Wiley and Sons, 1975), pp. 223–239; Todd Sandler, Jon Cauley, and John F. Forbes, "In Defense of a Collective Goods Theory of Alliances," *Journal of Conflict Resolution* 24, No. 3 (1980): 537–547; Todd Sandler and John F. Forbes, "Burden Sharing, Strategy, and the Design of NATO," *Economic Inquiry* 18, No. 3 (1980): 425–444; and Todd Sandler and Jon Cauley, "On the Economic Theory of Alliance," *Journal of Conflict Resolution* 19, No. 2 (1975): 330–348.
76. See James C. Murdoch and Todd Sandler, "Complementarity, Free Riding and the Military Expenditures of NATO Allies," *Journal of Public Economics*, 25, No. 3 (1984): 83–101.
77. On public goods and free riding, see Francis Beer, "The Political Economy of Alliances: Benefits, Costs, and Institutions in NATO," *Sage Professional Papers in International Studies* (Beverly Hills, California: Sage Publications, 1972); Martin C. McGuire and Carl H. Groth, "A Method for Identifying the Public Good Allocation Process Within a Group," *Quarterly Journal of Economics* 100, forthcoming; Martin C. McGuire, "U.S. Foreign Assistance, Israeli Resource Allocation, and the Arms Race in the Middle East: An Analysis of Three Interdependent Resource Allocation Processes," *Journal of Conflict Resolution* 26, No. 2 (1982): 199–235; Martin C. McGuire, "The Structure of Choice Between Deterrence and Defense," in Roland McKean, ed., *Issues in Defense Economics* (New York: National Bureau of Economic Research, 1967), pp. 129–149; Mancur Olson and Richard Zeckhauser, "Collective Goods, Comparative Advantage, and Alliance Efficiency," in Roland McKean, op. cit., pp. 25–48; Mancur Olson and Richard Zeckhauser, "An Economic Theory of Alliances," *Review of Economics and Statistics* 48, No. 3 (1966): 266–279; Joe Oppenheimer, "Collective Goods and Alliances: A Reassessment," *Journal of Conflict Resolution* 23, No. 3 (1979): 387–407; Stephen M. Shaffer, "The Influence of Threat and Alliance Setting on National Defense Expenditure: NATO, 1950–1969," unpublished Ph.D. dissertation, University of Michigan, 1975; Jacques van Ypersele de Strihou, "Sharing the Defense Burden Among

Western Allies," *Review of Economics and Statistics* 49, No. 4 (1967); 527 – 536; and Raimo Väyrynen, "The Theory of Collective Goods, Military Alliances and International Security," *International Social Science Journal* 38, No. 2 (1976): 288 – 305. Also see all of the references listed in footnote 75.
78. See James C. Murdoch and Todd Sandler, "Complementarity, Free Riding..."
79. "Largest" and "smallest" are determined by GDP.
80. These troop figures come from International Institute for Strategic Studies, *The Military Balance 1984 – 1985* (London: International Institute for Strategic Studies, 1984).
81. SIPRI, *SIPRI Yearbook 1983*, Chapter 8.
82. For this reason, we could not examine the effects of oil prices and spillins until we switched to time series analysis.
83. But, given the public good qualities of deterrence, additional people can be added under the deterrent umbrella at zero cost; thus, an ally may not be very responsive to changes in its population. Moreover, GDP is highly correlated with population for the NATO allies, meaning that GDPBENEFIT and POPBENEFIT are highly correlated as well. Kendall's tau for these two measures was over .71 in each of the three years considered. In the section "Time-Series Analysis" we illustrate, using time-series data, that population is rarely a consideration for an ally when determining its military expenditures.
84. Kendell's tau is used herein, rather than Spearman's rho, because the distribution of the Kendall measure approaches the standard normal distribution for sample sizes greater than 10. It also has the advantage that it can be generalized to be a partial correlation measure, a measure not used in this section.
85. See Sandler and Forbes, "Burden Sharing," Table 4.
86. On Soviet defense expenditures see references in footnote 74.
87. See Michael D. Ward, "Differential Paths to Parity: A Study of the Contemporary Arms Race," *American Political Science Review* 78, No. 2 (1984): 297 – 317.
88. In examining the data for structural change, we noted evidence of structural change throughout the 1969 – 1975 period, with the peak of the change concentrated in 1974. Hence, we settled on the year 1974 as the shift year for our test.
89. Moreover, the Durbin-Watson statistics are within the range of uncertainty.
90. SIPRI, *SIPRI Yearbook 1983*, Table 8.4, p. 203.
91. This row could correspond to the case where the other allies meet their pledges.
92. Other threat variables, such as the number of bombers and missile launchers, were examined in our previous work without success. See Murdoch and Sandler, "Theoretical and Empirical Analysis of NATO."

# Chapter 4

# Defense, Growth, and Allocation Behavior in the Alliance: The Southern Tier of NATO

Kevin Forbes, George Korsun, and Martin McGuire

## INTRODUCTION

This chapter examines the prospects and performances of the four least developed members of the Atlantic Alliance, viz., Portugal, Spain, Greece, and Turkey (PSGT). Politically and economically diverse as they may be, these four share several characteristics which suggest that they all can be usefully grouped together for this analysis. In all, the military has involved or does involve itself intimately with economic development. All have been at one time client states of the United States, providing basing rights and other types of cooperation in exchange for military, economic, or technical assistance. All are fairly small and, by comparison with the other members of the alliance less developed; thus all four of these countries are free rider candidates within NATO and in all four the interaction between defense and development is especially important. At the same time, major differences in geographical location, vulnerability to potential Warsaw Pact aggression, and local animosities (which place a demand on security needs) must make each of the four country's perceptions of the Soviet bloc threat differ widely. Accordingly, the need for forces *independent* of the common defense might be expected to be highly differentiated among the four countries.

Any analysis which hopes to bring systematic economic thinking to bear on the interdependencies between economic well-being and defense in these countries must extrapolate from what they have in common without submerging their differences. Thus the task of generalizing for predictive purposes without losing the particularity of each country is the aim of this study.

What is it we might hope to analyze, understand, predict, and then bring to bear on U.S. policy in the region? Essentially, it is the structure of resource allocation behavior in these four countries. This structure, in reality, is extremely complex. It includes (a) the economic and political factors which determine the resource allocation choices in each country; (b) the manner in which the countries PSGT interact with other members of the alliance and in particular with the United States; and (c) the inter-temporal long-term interactions or interdependencies in the allocation of resources, particularly between development and defense. Our aspiration is to formulate models of these various subsystems and, within the restrictions of data availability, to separate out these effects.

To build up a cohesive picture of resource allocation in these four countries will require that the allocation process be modeled, that data be collected, and the models tested. This approach must necessarily assume that some entity's behavior is being hypothesized, formulated mathematically, and tested. But which entity? Is it the representative consumer, the median voter, the average bureaucrat, or who? This is a recurrent and always troubling question in any economic analysis of aggregate or corporate persons. The most we can hope for is that the set of decisive actors in each country – whether parliaments, consumers, voters, bureaucrats, or markets – is stable and robust enough to allow tentative projections.

Each of these states bears more importance for U.S. security interests than their mere size in population or wealth might suggest; because of geography they provide intelligence outposts for the collection of strategic and tactical information, potential staging areas for extension of U.S. power during war and peace (i.e., U.S. bases in Spain and Greece), and critical parcels of real estate (i.e., Turkey and Greece) which border on the Warsaw Pact. Moreover, not only are these nations important to the West in their own right, but their loss would be a severe blow to the NATO alliance. In this light, an effort to understand the economic forces which mold defense decisions in these countries is surely worthwhile. And insofar as NATO is a lasting institution frequently reflecting lasting U.S. interests in Europe, we must concern ourselves with the long-range economic health of our partners overseas and with the effects that defense has on them. Similarly, as the lead member of the alliance, we have an interest in just how U.S. or other large NATO members' allocations influence those of these four small countries.

To address these questions, this chapter is organized as follows. The next section reports on the economic and political trends in PSGT. The following section provides a broad overview of two topics central to this chapter. First discussed are the determinants of defense spending. A key issue here is the effect of economic performance on defense spending. Another is the question of whether or not PSGT is contributing its fair share to the defense of Europe. In other words, is PSGT a free rider in the sense of sitting back and letting the rest of NATO provide for the common defense? The second topic explored in that section is the effect that defense has on economic growth. Here the central question is whether defense retards or fosters economic development. Subsequent sections construct and test models designed to

Table 4.1. Defense Spending as a Percentage of Total Defense Spending by NATO Members

| Year | Greece | Portugal | Turkey | GPT | U.S. | Belgium |
|---|---|---|---|---|---|---|
| 1960 | .2 | .2 | 1.0 | 1.4 | 74.5 | .6 |
| 1965 | .2 | .4 | .7 | 1.3 | 71.9 | .7 |
| 1970 | .4 | .5 | .6 | 1.5 | 74.3 | .7 |
| 1975 | .7 | .4 | 1.1 | 2.2 | 60.4 | 1.3 |
| 1979 | .6 | .1 | .4 | 1.1 | 58.8 | 1.5 |

help resolve these issues. The last section projects future defense outlays. Also discussed are the implications of the findings for U.S. policy.

As an introduction to these questions, we report aggregate data in Table 4.1 which shows the percentage contributions of Portugal, Greece, and Turkey to the NATO defense total, and Table 4.2 which shows the burden of defense on each country as a proportion of its gross domestic product (GDP). In both tables, Belgium, as a small but developed, industrialized, high income democracy, is included for comparison. Inspection of these tables gives a snapshot of the cycles and trends in defense efforts by these smaller NATO partners. While the U.S. share in NATO shows a secular decline (74.5 percent in 1960 to 58.8 percent in 1979), Belgium has followed the lead of the other Northern Europeans and picked up its share. PGT, however, after a transient proportionate increase in the mid-1970s have reverted to their historical contributions of somewhat more than 1 percent. Table 4.2 gives information on the individual country burdens which correspond to those defense shares. The prime explanation for PGT's reversion to historical NATO shares is seen to be the slightly elevated percentage burden borne by Greece (with relatively high GDP) which is more than offset by reduced proportions in Turkey and Portugal.

# HISTORIC TRENDS AND MID-RANGE FORECASTS FOR NATO'S FRINGE

As an attempt to blend analytical rigour with policy insight, this essay will draw substantially on others' projections of the countries in our sample. Based on the country analyses of two major forecasting sources (Chase Econometrics Europe

Table 4.2. Defense Spending as a Percentage of GDP

| Year | Greece | Portugal | Turkey | U.S. | Belgium |
|---|---|---|---|---|---|
| 1960 | 4.3 | 5.0 | 6.3 | 9.3 | 3.5 |
| 1965 | 3.3 | 7.1 | 6.9 | 8.2 | 3.1 |
| 1970 | 4.7 | 7.3 | 5.1 | 7.8 | 2.9 |
| 1975 | 6.2 | 5.2 | 6.5 | 5.9 | 3.0 |
| 1979 | 5.1 | 1.6 | 2.6 | 5.7 | 3.3 |

Service, and *Wharton World Economic Outlook, 1983*), we summarize the trends (interpolated) and prospects for each country.

## Greece

*Economic Setting.* Domestic output and personal incomes grew much faster in aggregate than the OECD average in the period covering 1960 – 1980 but this fact belies some fundamental problems in the Greek economy which will make it extremely difficult to maintain this level of performance. Due to past persistent slackness in domestic final demand many industrial sectors have never developed, leaving the country with an industrial base heavily concentrated in traditional industries such as textiles, food, chemicals, and furniture. The manufacturing sector, which showed some growth between 1950 and 1973, was largely stagnant in the late 1970s and early 1980s as a result of growing labor costs and attendant uncompetitive pricing. Continued growth in this sector is further complicated by the fact that 93 percent of industrial firms employ 10 people or less, which will limit access to experienced managerial skills or economies of scale. There are few heavy industries and the majority of capital goods must be imported. Capital markets are largely undeveloped since most savers prefer to acquire land or gold; what private investment has been generated has gone primarily to the construction industry. Three sizable sources of income – tourism, shipping, and migrant remittances – are down considerably in the 1980s because of the worldwide recession. Finally, large and consistent increases in nominal wages and hence labor unit costs have generated inflation rates running at 3 to 4 times the OECD average (about 21 percent) while productivity growth rates have been consistently lower than comparable OECD rates (See Table 4.3).

*Political Setting.* Two major recent changes on the Greek political scene should have future impact. The two-year-old socialist government has an expressed policy of reducing inflation and unemployment simultaneously and of stimulating increases in productivity and capital spending but not private consumption. One unfortunate early manifestation of this plan has been an increase in public sector employment leading to a decline in already low sectoral rates of productivity. High public sector investment and lending in certain industries make the entrepreneurial sector very nervous and expectations are widespread that nationalization may follow in these targeted sectors; these expectations may well lead to further declines in private capital formation.

The second major event is Greece's membership in the EEC which dates from January 1981. This should have a mixed impact on GDP since the gradual elimination of tariff barriers will increase competition from more efficient producers and thus increase imports but there will be an influx of EEC money for development projects to strengthen certain manufactured goods export sectors. To preclude fur-

Table 4.3. Selected Historical Data for Greece

|  | 1960 | 1965 | 1970 | 1975 | 1979 | 1982 | 1983 | 1984 |
|---|---|---|---|---|---|---|---|---|
| Pop* | 8.33 | 8.55 | 8.79 | 9.05 | 9.45 | 9.68 | 9.85 | – |
| GDP** | 5.180 | 7.615 | 10.794 | 13.806 | 16.806 | 17.134 | 17.185 | 17.597 |
| Savings** | .639 | 1.247 | 2.240 | 2.497 | 3.040 | 3.001 | 2.921 | – |
| Govt. Consumption** | .711 | .982 | 1.309 | 1.950 | 2.374 | 2.795 | 2.865 | 2.965 |
| Defense Expenditure** | .224 | .254 | .508 | .855 | .856 | .953 | 1.062 | – |
| Inflation % | 2.3 | 1.8 | 3.0 | 13.4 | 19.0 | 21.0 | 20.7 | 18.5 |
| Growth % | – | 9.5 | 7.9 | 6.1 | 3.8 | 0.0 | .3 | 2.4 |

*millions
**In 1972 U.S.$, billions

ther increases in the trade deficit, imports from EEC members have been fixed at 1982 levels for at least one year.

It should be noted that the drachma was devalued twice in 1983 and will probably be devalued again in the near future. Any benefits to exports, however, are likely to be offset by the high relative inflation rates.

*Economic Outlook.* Consumption is expected to rise in line with real income. To the extent that the government goal of income redistribution is successfully reached, there may be a further increase in future consumption due to an increase in the aggregate propensity to consume. The negative trade balance is supposed to suffer further from the removal of tariffs and the trade deficit will rise through 1985 and perhaps later. The investment portion of GDP, which has been depressed in the past few years, will see a decline in real private capital formation because of the fear of nationalization and low short-term domestic demand. This decline will net out to a small but positive growth rate for capital formation after public investment is accounted for. The government is planning a major infusion of funds into seven industries with the aim of substituting domestic goods for imports.[1] There is unfortunately a high probability of failure on these projects since the selected industries are heavy industries which must compete in world markets and the high inflation rate and low productivity rates typical of Greece will make it difficult to price outputs competitively (See Table 4.4).

GDP growth rates should hover around 2 percent until the 1990s when they may increase to about 3.5 percent. Gross capital formation rates should match GDP growth rates until 1990. Wholesale price inflation is predicted to decline from a high of 27 percent in 1984 to 22 percent in 1990 and possibly lower rates thereafter.

Table 4.4. Projected Economic Indices for Greece

|  | 1988 | 1992 |
|---|---|---|
| GDP* | 28.070 | 31.291 |
| Unemployment | 10.0 | 9.6 |
| Inflation** | 21.7 | 20.6 |
| Trade Balance* | −3.896 | −4.333 |

*In 1975 U.S.$, billions
**These inflation rates were forecast by Chase Econometrics in 1983.

## Turkey

*Economic Setting.* The Turkish economy grew faster than the OECD average in the 1970s but this resulted from a risky expansionary response to the first oil shock which seriously distorted domestic relative prices and greatly increased foreign borrowing. By 1977, however, Turkey could obtain no more credit and shortly thereafter GDP growth rates declined radically (negative in 1979) while employment and inflation rose (from 24 percent in 1977 to 64 percent in 1979 for inflation). Although a policy reversal toward more conservative economic plans alleviated many problems there still remain several potentially troublesome factors in the Turkish economy which could affect the government's ability to achieve reasonable growth rates in the long term (See Table 4.5).

As with all other countries in this study, shifting population demographics – primarily the return of emigrants – caused growth in prime-age, employable workers not matched by the rate of job creation. Dependence on oil, while reduced in the near past by more realistic pricing policies, is still high and some effort must be made to increase domestic production and thus reduce vulnerability to foreign shocks. The productive structure is hampered by the existence of State Economic Enterprises (SEEs) which operate in manufacturing as well as traditional markets such as utilities and transportation.[2] The financial sector also suffers because credit allocations are heavily subsidized and not widely available; the private capital market is weak and the unregulated money market has collapsed altogether.

*Political Setting.* Turkish policy behavior of the past decade and a half was marked by two widely different approaches to the same exogenous phenomenon, oil shocks. The 1974 response was aggressively expansionary, a policy put into effect to offset growing unemployment, but worldwide economic difficulties accentuated Turkey's reliance on foreign borrowing. By 1977, when a number of short-term debts were due, Turkey was virtually bankrupt and lost all creditworthiness. By contrast, the 1980 policy reduced government intervention in the market and en-

Table 4.5. Selected Historical Data for Turkey

|  | 1960 | 1965 | 1970 | 1975 | 1979 | 1982 | 1983 | 1984 |
|---|---|---|---|---|---|---|---|---|
| Population | 27.76 | 31.15 | 35.23 | 40.03 | 44.24 | 46.3 | 47.28 | – |
| GDP | 15.042 | 10.252 | 13.879 | 20.241 | 21.468 | 24.288 | 25.065 | 26.544 |
| Savings | .986 | 1.330 | 2.464 | 3.460 | 3.411 | 3.859 | 4.086 | – |
| Govt. Consumption | .808 | 1.179 | 1.694 | 2.327 | 3.974 | 4.496 | 4.577 | 4.756 |
| Defense Expenditure | .951 | .709 | .702 | 1.313 | .548 | .595 | – | – |
| Inflation % | 18.8 | 3.7 | 7.9 | 21.2 | 63.5 | 32.7 | 28.8 | 45.6 |
| Growth % | – | 2.5 | 3.0 | 8.9 | -8.9 | 4.4 | 3.2 | 5.9 |

couraged the development of exports over the medium run. In addition, a more realistic exchange rate policy was adopted along with tight monetary conditions. These new policies were not immediately successful because of extreme political instability; it was not until 1981 after military intervention that the policies took effect. For 1981 and 1982, GDP grew at a 4 percent rate, again higher than the OECD average; concurrently, inflation dropped from a previous high of 100 percent in 1980 to 33 percent in 1982. As desired, exports grew rapidly despite the fall in world trade because Turkey found ready specialty markets for its exports of food and other nondurable goods in North Africa and the Middle East.

The restrictive fiscal and monetary policies of 1980 were further reinforced by centrally imposed income restraints on public and private sector labor; nominal wage rates increased by 45 percent, less than half the extant inflation rate. The election, late in 1983, of Prime Minister Turgut Ozal brought with it the promise of continued restrictive policies consistent with IMF recommendations as inflation reduction became a primary objective of the newly elected government.

*Economic Outlook.* The new administration currently enjoys support from most of the political spectrum, including the military. It is not clear how long this will last but most observers believe that, at a minimum, a two-year grace period is a reasonable expectation. Given the rapidity with which legislation was enacted after the November 1983 election, there is reason to be optimistic that the turnaround experienced by the economy in 1984 will continue (See Table 4.6).

In the short term, GDP growth rates should remain around 4 percent as exports pick up and real private consumption also increases. Public consumption and investment should increase as government capital spending programs go into effect; private sector investment growth should remain around 3 percent and may grow at a faster rate later though there is some concern that high real interest rates may choke off new capital goods orders by firms. Inflation is anticipated to be around 28 percent as falling real incomes and higher food prices offset each other.

The mid- and long-term prognoses depend largely on the success of the government's plans to "privatize" the SEEs and to introduce more competition in all sectors of the economy. They also depend on the government's ability to rely more on

Table 4.6. Projected Economic Indices for Turkey

|  | 1988 | 1992 |
|---|---|---|
| GDP | 59.431 | 71.853 |
| Unemployment | 15.3 | 14.0 |
| Inflation* | 24.5 | 21.3 |
| Trade Balance | .575 | 1.246 |

*These inflation rates were forecast in 1983 by Chase Econometrics.

domestic resources and less on foreign borrowing, and on the continued growth of exports. *The latter goal will require a shift in product mix from the current preponderance of nondurable goods to more durable and capital goods* because of an increase in competition over nondurables from other low-cost exporters and a decline in the number of markets for these goods – a decline caused by a drop in the oil-derived income of the major clients. Assuming mixed success in these objectives, the country should see GDP growth rates approaching 5 percent through the end of the decade, declining inflation rates (but still high at 20 percent), and fairly constant capital formation growth rates pegged around 4.5 percent.

## Spain

*Economic Setting.* Spain has been mired for the last 6 – 7 years in a recession more severe than those suffered by other OECD countries in general with a post-1975 average GDP growth rate of 1.5 percent and an unemployment rate which reached 18 percent by 1983. The explanation for this sub par performance lies in the country's ineffectiveness in dealing with energy costs, growing labor costs, and large growth in the public sector deficit. Dependence on foreign oil was quite high from 1970 to 1980 (35 percent of total imports, 1980) but has since declined as coal and nuclear power have been substituted; unfortunately, the newer energy sources also have a high import component so that total energy imports still accounted for 41 percent of the import bill. Labor costs have increased at twice the rate of price increases for manufactured goods since 1970 but because of an increase in unemployment, average productivity per worker has risen (See Table 4.7).

Rapidly rising wages have led to a surge in domestic demand, the majority of which is for current consumption; capital formation has contributed negatively to GDP growth over the last nine years. They have also led to, along with increases in food prices, private borrowing costs, and indirect taxes, inflation rates which are much higher (often double) than those of other industrial countries. Given the inflationary environment, savings and investment have not done well; gross capital formation as a percentage of GNP has declined from 28 percent in 1974 to less than

Table 4.7. Selected Historical Data for Spain

|  | 1960 | 1965 | 1970 | 1975 | 1979 | 1982 | 1983 | 1984 |
|---|---|---|---|---|---|---|---|---|
| Population | 30.30 | 32.06 | 33.78 | 35.60 | 37.18 | 38.02 | 38.23 | – |
| GDP | 21.026 | 34.747 | 47.063 | 61.523 | 67.806 | 69.997 | 71.607 | 73.182 |
| Savings | 4.294 | 7.040 | 8.991 | 10.846 | 12.951 | 13.439 | 12.603 | – |
| Govt. Consumption | 1.941 | 2.595 | 3.412 | 4.649 | 4.738 | 4.785 | 4.981 | 5.080 |
| Defense Expenditure | .463 | .625 | .753 | 1.046 | – | – | 1.575 | – |
| Inflation % | 8.7 | 8.5 | 5.8 | 16.8 | 15.7 | 14.4 | 12.1 | 11.3 |
| Growth % | – | 6.3 | 4.2 | 1.1 | 0.8 | 1.3 | 2.3 | 2.2 |

19 percent in 1983. Furthermore, corporate profits also showed a severe contraction in real terms over that period.

Spain has been running a deficit in its current account, which in percentage terms, is one of the largest in Europe. Energy prices have played a part but so has a three-year stagnation in exports, a manifestation of exchange rate policies aimed at monetary control rather than economic development. Evidence of these policies can be found in the peseta's recent depreciation (relative to other major currencies) against the U.S. dollar. The reluctance to adjust the currency has led to an attendant buildup of foreign debt and reduction in foreign reserves. The government currently believes that the negative balance of payments is the principal constraint on future economic growth.

*Political Setting.* Spain is still plagued by the transitional problems associated with the move from a dictatorship to a parliamentary democracy, namely, some instability and dissension. The socialist administration of Prime Minister Gonzales has been in office for over a year but appears to be still formulating economic policies for the midterm after a careful assessment of the causes of the drawn-out recession.

Previous governments were plagued with high labor costs and a rapidly expanding public sector over which they had little control. Final budgets often bore little relationship to initial budgets. The social security system has run a deficit for several years even though employer contributions are pegged at 21 percent of payrolls. The trend is likely to continue as more workers are brought into the system and population demographics change, but a major restructuring has been proposed which would lighten employer contributions at the expense of the government. Public expenditures have also grown as subsidies to public enterprises have increased since the institution of an expansionary fiscal policy in 1977. The public sector is burdened by an overdeveloped bureaucratic structure which is likely to enlarge as a program of decentralization is put into effect.

The new administration has an industrial policy aimed at dealing with the problems of adjustments in capacity and employment necessitated by the recession and a special partnership agreement with the EEC. This policy is being applied first to the steel sector and is expected to effect employment most heavily with a possible

Table 4.8. Projected Economic Indices for Spain

|  | 1988 | 1992 |
|---|---|---|
| GDP | 112.798 | 125.478 |
| Unemployment | 18.4 | 17.7 |
| Inflation* | 10.5 | 11.4 |
| Trade Balance | .094 | 1.747 |

*These inflation rates were forecast in 1983 by Chase Econometrics.

total reduction of some 200,000 steel and related jobs, mainly in public enterprises. No attempt to replace declining industries with new ventures has been devised yet. Macro fiscal policy has been largely expansionary with attendant contractionary monetary policies to control inflation but the tight monetary policies and rising public sector deficits have raised financial costs to private enterprises.

*Economic Outlook.* Spain's recovery from its recession and return to acceptable growth rates (around 3.5 percent) depends greatly on its ability to increase export volume by rates approximating 10 percent. Given anticipated rates of increase in world trade, this could only be accomplished by significant increases in market share; there is no *a priori* reason to believe this is likely to occur. Government authorities are aware of this and therefore are aiming at the more modest target of 2.5 percent GDP increases for the next couple of years coupled with ambitious reductions in inflation, balance of trade deficits, and unemployment (See Table 4.8).

It is difficult to see how even the more modest targets can be achieved since the goals are not complementary. Exports can be expected to rise by 5 – 7 percent in 1985 while imports, after a comparable decline in 1983, should decline marginally if at all in the near future. Efforts to reduce the trade and public sector deficits will dampen domestic demand in 1985; GDP growth rates should fluctuate around 2 percent until 1987 when they may approach 3 percent. Recommended cuts in real wages and the increase in unemployment should help drive inflation down to the 10 percent range by 1986 with wholesale price inflation about a point below that. The annual percentage change in total fixed investment is predicted to be 1.5 percent in 1985 and perhaps 2 percent for 1986 and beyond.

# Portugal

*Economic Setting.* Portugal has experienced rapid GDP growth throughout the 1970s and early 1980s relative to other OECD countries. This growth has come primarily through an expansion of domestic demand due to rising public expenditures on consumption and investment financed by borrowing abroad. Inflation rates have

Table 4.9. Selected Historical Data for Portugal

|  | 1960 | 1965 | 1970 | 1975 | 1979 | 1982 | 1983 | 1984 |
|---|---|---|---|---|---|---|---|---|
| Population | 8.83 | 9.20 | 9.21 | 9.43 | 9.84 | 10.00 | 10.10 | – |
| GDP | 4.013 | 5.468 | 7.430 | 9.202 | 11.378 | 12.623 | 12.610 | 12.345 |
| Savings | .503 | .811 | 1.642 | .861 | 2.503 | 1.742 | 2.686 | – |
| Govt. Consumption | .369 | .582 | .913 | 1.227 | 1.637 | 1.907 | 1.983 | 2.042 |
| Defense Expenditure | .202 | .391 | .540 | .478 | .184 | .197 | – | – |
| Inflation% | 2.1 | 2.8 | 6.4 | 15.2 | 23.9 | 22.4 | 25.5 | 29.3 |
| Growth % | – | 7.4 | 9.1 | −4.4 | 6.6 | 3.3 | −.1 | −2.1 |

been high throughout this period but especially so since the 1974 revolution and the first oil shock when they were driven up to 30 percent; they have remained in the 20–30 percent range since then because of high relative import prices, excessive gains in wages, and growing domestic demand. The balance of trade has been negative and rising consistently in the 1970s because of rising debt service payments, weak exports, and reductions in migrant remittances. There has been a concomitant decline in international reserves and Portugal has had to sell or pledge portions of its sizable gold reserves to secure or retire loans.[3] (See Table 4.9.)

Several structural characteristics of the economy will influence potential growth. Labor force demographics portend a shift to older, more experienced workers with an attendant possible productivity rise but the increase in immigrants from former colonies is still problematic. Although per capita consumption of oil is low, dependence on foreign oil is high; in fact, dependence grew between the two oil shocks, in part because of extensive government subsidies. The productive structure is inadequate for the size of demand, particularly in agriculture. In industry, development has been hampered by a policy of nationalization which has been used to rescue troubled firms and to support employment (particularly in heavy industries such as steel and chemicals); there is now, however, some movement toward reprivatization. Private fixed investment has declined since 1971 after several years of expansion, and capital markets are weak to nonexistent.

*Political Setting.* Two events in 1974 caused drastic changes to the Portuguese economy. A revolution brought into power a left-wing government which instituted a policy of nationalization and land expropriation combined with increases in social benefits and real wages (24 percent). Concurrently, Portugal lost its African colonies, thereby losing a captive export market and gaining an influx of refugees for which few jobs were available.

Consequently, public sector outlays grew tremendously (from 19.5 percent of GDP in 1973 to 30.9 percent in 1976 to 36.5 percent in 1981) while taxes were raised only insignificantly. This resulted in government deficits equal to over 10 percent of GDP by 1981. Since 1976, fiscal policy has remained highly expansionary (including an ambitious investment program); this has been due to a rapid succession of short-lived governments concerned primarily with applying extensive subsidies and employment programs to garner votes. Monetary policy has also been expansionary (growing by approximately 200 percent between 1978 and 1982), in part to accommodate the burgeoning borrowing needs of the public sector and in part as a response to private sector needs (themselves encouraged by negative real interest rates). Authorities did not adjust the overvalued currency until 1977; once begun, however, the devaluation continued strongly until 1980 when the slide eased.

Portugal has been negotiating for membership in the EEC for six years but progress has been very slow. A treaty of accession was finally signed in April 1985, with ratification to follow within two years. The treaty provides for a gradual inclusion into the community over a ten-year period but membership will be a mixed blessing since it should bring an infusion of financial and technical assistance but will force exports and domestic products into more competition.

In August of 1983, Portugal became an IMF client and agreed to an austerity program which will govern economic policy in the short term. The various policy aspects of the agreement include further devaluation of the escudo, reduction in the subsidies on staples, petroleum products, and other goods, reduction in the public sector deficit, and a reduction in real wages.

*Economic Outlook.* To the extent that the IMF/domestic stabilization package can be implemented, and this may prove difficult since the trade unions are already balking and threatening a general strike, the Portuguese economy should be ready for improved growth by mid-decade. In the near term, there should be a policy dictated decline in real domestic demand and real disposable income. After a decline in 1984 real GDP should stabilize at a 3 percent average growth rate for the rest of the decade. Wholesale price rate changes are expected to decline from 26 percent in 1984 to an end of the decade average around 17 percent. Unemployment should rise in the short term as a result of both the severe cutbacks in public sector payrolls mandated by the IMF program as well as a depressed demand. Gross capital formation should follow the trend of GDP and stabilize around +3 percent in the late 1980s (See Table 4.10).

To make these projections and historical trends meaningful to policy requires that they be related to the perceptions, behavior, and choices of the countries in which they occur. This in turn requires a set of models to summarize the behavior structure of those countries. Therefore, we now will turn to two central topics in the relation between defense and economic performance.

## DEFENSE AND ECONOMIC PERFORMANCE: ANALYTIC ISSUES

## Determinants of Defense Effort

The determinants of defense spending for any one of our southern tier countries, as well as for the group as a whole, are immensely complex. Many are outside the realm of economics altogether. Completely unanticipated political developments

Table 4.10. Projected Economic Indices for Portugal

|  | 1988 | 1992 |
|---|---|---|
| GNP | 22.252 | 24.905 |
| Unemployment | 11.4 | 10.7 |
| Inflation* | 16.1 | 15.6 |
| Trade Balance | −2.188 | 2.043 |

*These inflation rates were forecast in 1983 by Chase Econometrics.

(external or internal), gross expected changes in the world economy such as the oil embargoes of 1973 – 1979 are examples. Notwithstanding our inability to predict the unpredictable, many structural characteristics of defense effort can be illuminated by careful quantitative and qualitative analyses of several determinants. The foremost candidates for explaining defense resource allocations include:

- *Gross Domestic Product.* For example, if the next five to ten years see economic revival and healthy growth in the southern tier countries of Portugal, Spain, Greece, and Turkey, how might this affect security outlays in these countries? If, on the other hand, overall performance continues to be sluggish, how will this influence defense effort? In part, our answer to these questions follows from the *ceteris paribus* estimates of the marginal propensity to spend on defense.

- *The magnitude of the perceived security threats as seen by each individual country.* To understand the allocative behavior of one or more members of the alliance, the distinction must be made between the reaction to changes in the threat (e.g., changes in defense spending by the Warsaw Pact) and the reaction to increases or decreases in one's own resources. Even if economic conditions deteriorate, defense outlays could increase in response to greater international tensions. Of particular interest in the case of our sample is the effect of Soviet or Warsaw Pact defense spending on Greece (or Turkey) as compared to the impact of Turkey's (Greece's) defense outlays. That is, how much of each country's defense should be regarded as a response to the common external threat, and how much to the *internal* rivalry between the two.

- *The nature of the interaction among the members of the alliance.* Do the members of the alliance cooperate with one another or are they free-riders? In the latter case, nations underallocate resources to the common defense, the result being a level of defense lower than what is thought "optimal." In brief, the outcome of the resource allocation process in an alliance is influenced by the reactive behavior of the member with one another. Understanding a country's probable future allocative behavior can enhance the instruments for United States leadership. For instance, if it is known that a $100 increase in defense spending by the United States results in country $X$ changing its defense expenditures by $Y$ dollars (either positive or negative), then the United States is in a better position to appraise the overall effect of its policy. Moreover, if free-riding is so pervasive that increases in U.S. defense spending result in defense reductions among its allies (i.e., $Y$ is negative), then closer coordination of defense outlays is clearly indicated.

- *Foreign assistance.* The allocative behavior of each of the four countries in our group has been conditioned by unilateral military and economic assistance from the United States. Knowledge of the effect of foreign assistance on defense outlays should assist policy-makers and current event analysts in interpreting PSGTs allocative behavior and in realistically assessing their future contributions to NATO.

Given the inevitable incompleteness of the set of variables used to explain the demand for military expenditures, caution in stating our results will be justified. Thus it seems quite possible that some (perhaps unavailable) measure of threat would be very significant, as would the impact of electoral results or political moods, budgetary stringencies, elite opinions, key world events (e.g., Falklands, Afghanistan), etc. Our method tends to exclude the impact of factors we would broadly label political; this may both limit its accuracy and its usefulness in drawing conclusions about how to improve NATO performance. While there may be no good quantitative approach to political factors, some examination and comparison of, for instance, the public and parliamentary debates in these countries about defense policy would be relevant to an assessment of how their defense spending levels have been and are likely to be determined.[4]

## Effects of Defense Outlays on Economic Growth

A second issue crucial for appraising future expectation of PSGT concerns the effect of defense spending on the economic health of each country in question. That is, what is the effect of defense spending on development? This question has drawn increasing attention from economists since Emile Benoit's intriguing finding that for a wide spectrum of developing nations over the period 1955 – 1970 high growth rates were correlated with high defense outlays.[5] Several other economists have more recently challenged Benoit's conclusion.[6] Lim, for instance, using the Harrod-Domar growth model, examines the cross-section data bearing on the relationship between defense and growth.[7] While it is claimed that the results indicate that defense spending reduces growth, some doubt remains. For in the case of Asia and South Europe (including the Middle East) Lim's results are less than clear-cut; in those two cases, his estimates suggest that defense spending may be growth neutral. In summary, it appears that the issue of the relationship between defense and growth is far from resolved.

Our study reexamines the relationship between defense and growth by employing a country specific time series approach within the framework of the Harrod-Domar growth model. The results should shed light on the sustainability of high defense outlays – whether defense reinforces developmental growth or retards it. The answer to this question should influence whether high defense efforts in PSGT are desirable from the viewpoint of the United States. If it appears that defense fosters growth, then the argument that these countries could increase their defense efforts is more valid then ever. But if higher defense levels lead to impoverishment or stagnation, the argument is less persuasive both to them and us. Any quantitative insight on the effect of defense spending on economic performance should help resolve this potential dilemma.

## EFFECTS OF DEFENSE SPENDING ON GROWTH

## Analytical Models of Resource Allocation

As argued above, one key question for appraising the prospects for defense effort in the southern tier countries concerns the effect of such expenditures on future growth. Does an increased defense burden curtail economic growth by diverting resources away from capital formation? Or does defense spending enhance a nation's stock of human and physical capital, increasing its rate of economic growth? As a point of departure, we will employ the elementary Harrod-Domar macroeconomic growth model to capture these effects, then test that model on data such as those presented in the section on historic trends and mid-range forecasts. This analysis will lay a foundation for extrapolating those historical findings to the future.

To answer the questions raised above we first analyze the relationship between a nation's level of investment and its rate of economic growth; then the impact of defense spending on investment will be examined.

*The Level of Investment and the Economic Growth Rate.* In explaining the relationship between a nation's level of investment and its rate of economic growth, the incremental capital/output ratio (ICOR) is helpful. ICOR is defined as

$$k = I/\Delta Q \tag{1}$$

where

$k$ indicates ICOR
$Q$ indicates total output of goods and services
$\Delta Q$ indicates change in total output
$I$ indicates investment

The growth rate in output ($\Delta Q/Q$) can now be represented as

$$\Delta Q/Q = \frac{I/Q}{I/\Delta Q} = \frac{I/Q}{k} \quad (2)$$

The above expression indicates that the growth rate in output is directly related to investment relative to output and is inversely associated with ICOR. Appendix A reports the values of $k$ and $I/Q$ for PSGT as well as some of the pitfalls associated with this approach to modeling economic growth.

One of the advantages to this approach is that it allows us to explore rather easily the effect of a change in investment on economic growth in our sample countries. Such a change in investment might be caused by an exogenous change in savings behavior or by an increase in defense if it crowded out investment, by both these, or by other factors altogether. The implications of such change are sketched out in Table 4.11. This table reports the change in the growth rate for PSGT resulting from a 1 percent increase in $I/Q$. The results suggest that Turkey and Greece are most sensitive in terms of their growth rates to changes in capital formation. The growth rates of Portugal and Spain are less sensitive to changes in $I/Q$ because of those nations' relatively high ICORs.

While seemingly insignificant, these changes in growth rates, if sustained, can have substantial effects on living standards. For instance, a 1.46 percent difference between West Germany's and Britain's growth rates propelled West Germany's living standard which was 4 percent lower than Britain's in 1955 to 39 percent higher in less than 30 years.[8] Eventually a higher growth rate will permit higher levels of both defense spending and consumption.

## Defense Spending and the Level of Investment

A nation's defense burden may influence its level of capital formation in two ways. First, defense spending may stimulate economic development by augmenting a nation's social and physical infrastructure.

For instance, military training may improve the quality of a nation's labor force. It is well known that employers in a free market economy may not have the incentive

Table 4.11. The Effect of a 1% Increase I/Q

|  | Greece | Portugal | Spain | Turkey |
|---|---|---|---|---|
| Change in the Growth Rate | .233 | .130 | .110 | .313 |

to provide their employees with the optimal amount of training – employers who aid employees in the development of general skills such as literacy and work discipline may be unable to recoup their investment because of employee mobility. As a result, an economy can be disadvantaged by inadequately trained workers and the resulting disencouragement to investment. To avoid such underinvestment in human capital, countries typically mandate government-provided primary, secondary, and vocational education. Benoit's painstaking analyses of lesser developed countries suggested that military training may add to human capital. One likely effect of this is an increase in private nonhuman capital as entrepreneurs take advantage of the improvement in human capital.

In addition to training, military spending may augment physical infrastructure. Military spending may provide for the construction of roads, ports, etc., all of which provide spillover benefits to the private sector. There may even be spillover benefits to the private sector from prosaic items such as military bases. An improved infrastructure can increase the level of private investment by making that investment more profitable. Thus, it is conceivable that defense spending, by its effects on infrastructure, may lead to a higher level of capital formation and, accordingly, a faster rate of economic growth. Benoit's work suggests that the evidence supports this conjecture in the case of LDCs although his methods and data have come under critical attack.[9] Since the four countries comprising our study are the least developed ones in NATO, Benoit's work may be applicable to them.

The second aspect of the relationship between defense and investment, however, is that the two must compete for resources. Resources available to defense are potentially available to alternative uses. The converse also holds; resources not currently devoted to defense are potentially available for defense purposes. To be more specific, consider three uses of a nation's resources: consumption, capital formation, and defense. Given a fixed level of overall economic activity, an increase in the amount of resources devoted to defense diverts resources away from consumption and/or capital formation.

The overall effect of a change in defense spending on capital formation equals the amount of capital formation that defense spending induces via the "Benoit effect" as discussed above minus the amount of resources absorbed by defense that would otherwise be committed to capital formation.

## Empirical Tests of the Diversionary versus Stimulative Effects of Defense Spending

*Empirical Results.* In this section we estimate the effect of defense and foreign assistance on investment. The regression equation of interest is

$$I/Q = B_1 + B_2 D/Q + B_3 AID \tag{3}$$

where *AID* represents the aid received. Our interest is in the sign and magnitude of $B_2$ and $B_3$. If the resource diversion effect of military spending on investment outweighs the Benoit effect, then $B_2$ will be negative. In the limiting case where the Benoit effect is zero, increases in defense will at most divert resources away from investment dollar for dollar ($B_2 = -1$). Thus, if $B_2$ is negative, we would expect it to be greater than or equal to minus one. The coefficient $B_2$ will be positive if the Benoit effect outweighs the resource diversion effect of defense on investment. In this case, defense spending stimulates capital formation and thus fosters economic development. Finally, $B_2$ will be zero when the two influences are equal in absolute value.

The variable *AID* has been included in the equation to be estimated to capture the effect that foreign aid has on capital formation. The sign of the coefficient $B_3$ indicates whether foreign aid stimulates, retards, or leaves unaffected the level of capital formation by PSGT. If economic and military assistance stimulates capital formation, then $B_3$ will be positive. Because *AID* is entered in equation (3) as an absolute amount rather than as a proportion of GDP even a small value for $B_3$ can indicate that *AID* has a relatively important percentage influence on the savings/investment rate.

Regression results are reported in Table 4.12. The results are mixed. Defense spending appears to have a depressing effect on capital formation in the case of Spain and Turkey. The estimated value of $B_2$ for these two countries is negative and statistically significant. It was hypothesized that $B_2$ would exceed minus one. While the estimated value of $B_2$ for Spain, $-4.22$, is less than minus one, this value is not statistically different from minus one at a 95 percent confidence level.

In these two countries, there appears to be a weak if not nonexistent Benoit effect as well as a propensity on the part of policy-makers to finance increases in defense out of funds that would otherwise be devoted to capital formation. In this way, security needs can be provided for without reducing present consumption dollar for dollar. While perhaps attractive in the short run, such an approach has the long-run cost of a lower rate of growth.

The estimated value of $B_2$ for Portugal is positive but is statistically insignificant. One explanation for this is that the Benoit effect is positive but is swamped by the growth-inhibiting effects of investment-financed military spending. Alternatively, there may not be any positive spinoffs from defense while policy-makers have chosen to finance defense out of consumption instead of out of investment.

In the case of Greece, $B_2$ is positive and significant but only at the 90 percent confidence level. Thus, only in the case of Greece is there any clear evidence of a Benoit effect. An explanation for this result is that policy-makers in Greece have had the latitude to finance defense spending out of consumption rather than investment or that any defense-induced resource diversion away from investment was more than offset by the Benoit effect. In the latter case Greek propensity to finance defense out of investment is not lower than in PST but rather there is a stronger Benoit effect in Greece as compared to PST.

Table 4.12. Tests of the Diversionary vs. Stimulative Effects of Defense Spending on Capital Formation

| Estimated coefficients for the Investment Equation: 1960 – 1979[a] Maximum likelihood estimates | Portugal | Spain | Greece | Turkey |
|---|---|---|---|---|
| $B_1$ | .172*** | .295*** | .159*** | .25*** |
| $B_2$ | .168 | −4.22** | 1.81* | −.88** |
| $B_3$[b] | .00 | .00 | −.0005* | −.00008** |

\*Significance at a 90% confidence level.
\*\*Significance at a 95% confidence level.
\*\*\*Significance at a 99% confidence level.
[a]This period was selected because data consistent with national income accounts was only available through 1979.
[b]The coefficient $B_3$ indicates the effect that aid has on the ratio of investment to GDP. In the case of Greece, for instance, a unit increase in aid reduces I/Q by .05%.

Somewhat surprisingly, in no case was the estimated value of $B_3$ positive. In two instances, Greece and Turkey, $B_3$ was actually negative and statistically significant, indicating that aid might serve the purpose of closing an investment *gap* in these countries – the bigger the gap, the more aid.

*Implications.* The above results indicate that higher levels of defense spending will lower the growth rates of Spain and Turkey. For both countries the value of $B_2$ does not statistically differ from − 1. Assuming the estimates in Table 4.11 capture the essentials of the growth process and assuming as well that the ICORs are stable over time (over the business cycle, for instance), then it appears that a 1 percent increase in Spain's defense spending relative to GDP can be expected to lower its growth rate by 0.11 percent. A comparable increase in Turkey's defense spending will lower its growth rate by 0.313 percent. In contrast, it appears that a 1 percent increase in Greece's defense spending (relative to GDP) will *increase* its growth rate by .23 percent. Military spending in the case of Portugal appears to be growth neutral.[10] Somewhat oddly, these figures indicate that of the four countries in our sample the richest, most highly developed (Spain) and the poorest (Turkey) finance defense out of investment. The conclusion challenges the notion that richer countries rightly afford defense the easiest. For the four countries of NATO's southern tier, factors other than stage of economic development are evidently important in the interaction between capital formation and military outlay.[11]

## THE DETERMINANTS OF DEFENSE SPENDING

Having examined the investment effects of defense spending, we now turn to a further investigation of the determinants of such spending with special attention to the question of how each of PSGT's defense effort is influenced by (a) the defense expenditures of the others and (b) the defense expenditures of the remaining NATO countries including the United States. Again, we will construct an explicit model. This model will make a number of crucial assumptions. First, we will assume that the members of the alliance all, whether witting or not, contribute to their common defense. Accordingly, the defense outlays by *each* country influence the expenditures of *every* other country. Second, we will assume that *the entire* defense capability (expenditures) of each country constitutes a contribution to alliance defense. At the level of detail of this study, a more sophisticated assumption does not seem worthwhile. Third, we will assume that the patterns of expenditure in each country are regular enough to be described by a system of demand equations for each alliance member. This is logically equivalent to an assumption that each member of NATO allocates its resources so as to maximze its utility. Demand for defense is derived from the time-tested Stone-Geary functional form as given below.

$$U^i = a_1^i \log(D - \delta_N^i T_N - \delta_L^i T_L^i) + a_2^i \log(C^i - \theta^i) + a_3^i \log I^i \quad (4)$$

$$D = D^i + \overline{D}^i \quad (4a)$$

$D$ represents defense expenditures for the entire alliance,
$D^i$ is country $i$'s defense outlay,
$\overline{D}^i$ All other countries' (other than $i$) defense outlays,
$T_N$ represents total military expenditures by the Warsaw Pact,
$T_L$ "Threatening" defense expenditures by a local, non-Bloc rival (e.g., Greece-Turkey),
$\delta_N^i$ is the rate at which \$1 of Warsaw pact outlays reduces the benefit that nation $i$ receives from NATO's defense expenditures,
$\delta_L^i$ is the rate at which \$1 of a local rival's defense reduces the benefit $i$ enjoys from NATO defense provision,
$C^i$ represents all nondefense consumption expenditures in nation $i$,
$\theta^i$ represents nation $i$'s subsistence level of consumption,
$I^i$ represents nation $i$'s level of investment,
$a_1^i, a_2^i$, and $a_3^i$ are parameters, with $a_1^i + a_2^i + a_3^i = 1$.

The above utility function posits that a nation's level of well-being is dependent on its level of security (where security is a function of NATO's defense spending in relation to the perceived threat), the amount of consumption in excess of the subsistence level, and the level of investment. This utility function when maximized subject to a resource constraint will yield a set of equations for each country representing that country's outlays on defense as depending on $T_L$ and $T_N$, the threats, the expenditures of other countries $\overline{D}^i$, the parameters in the system (i.e., $a, c, \delta$, etc.) *and the form of the resource constraint.*[12]

It has been shown elsewhere that the form which the resource constraint takes depends critically on the character of the resource allocation process occurring among allies.[13] Although there is an infinite variety in the types of resource allocation processes, two "pure" cases of such processes suggest themselves as reference points on a spectrum. The first is commonly called a "Nash-Cournot" process; the second, a "Lindahl" process. The theoretical properties of these two have been extensively studied. It is known, for example, that Nash-Cournot processes are inefficient – producing less than the amount of defense which all countries would collectively demand if they were a single entity or were able to optimally coordinate their defense expenditures. Lindahl processes are collaborative – at least implicitly so – and therefore tend to produce "efficient" allocations to defense. Nash-Cournot processes are *redistributive* from rich countries to poor, in that for these processes the rich tend to pay a disproportionately high share of alliance costs. Lindahl processes on the other hand are less redistributive.

In the case at hand, which process governs alliance allocations can be *represented by the form of the resource constraint* and by the implied form of the system of demand equations. Thus, for the Nash-Cournot case, the form of the resource constraint becomes

$$Q^i = D^i + C^i + I^i \tag{5}$$

where

$Q^i = i$'s GDP
$C^i = i$'s nondefense consumption
$I^i = i$'s investment

and the implied demand equation for defense outlay by country $i$ becomes

$$D^i = -a_I^i \Theta^i + a_I^i Q^i + (b_I^i - 1) \overline{D}^i + (1 - a_I^i) \delta_N^i T_N + (1 - a_I^i) \delta_L^i T_L^i \tag{6}$$

Strictly speaking, $a_I^i$ and $b_I^i$ are identical parameters; however, if $\overline{D}^i$ and $D^i$ are not perfectly interchangeable in $i$'s demands, statistical tests should reveal that $b_I^i \neq a_I^i$.

If rather than a Nash-Cournot process, country allocations are generated by the more collaborative Lindahl type process, then the operative ex ante resource constraint facing country $i$ becomes

$$Q^i = C^i + I^i + \frac{D^i}{D} D \tag{7}$$

and implies demand equation for defense rather than as in (12) now becomes

$$D^i = -a_I^i \Theta^i + a_I^i Q^i + (1 - a_I^i) \delta_N^i T^N \frac{D^i}{D} + (1 - a_I^i) \delta_L^i T^L \tag{8}$$

*Resource Allocation Behavior of Portugal, Greece, and Turkey.* Estimates of the determinants of defense expenditures and tests of alternative resource allocation behavior have been confined to Portugal, Greece, and Turkey because Spain did not join NATO until 1982. The results of this estimation are summarized in the following three tables. The idea is to determine which model best describes the allocation processes of these three countries.

Table 4.13 shows the results from estimating equation (6), i.e., testing the assumption that the Cournot allocation process is in effect. Two results are worth noting. First, the Cournot assumption does not yield a very reliable or meaningful structure for explaining the behavior of these countries. For instance, most of marginal propensities to spend on defense ($a_1$) are either insignificant or implausible. Second, if the Cournot framework is nevertheless accepted, it appears that Greece, Portugal, and Turkey are most decidedly insensitive to changes in defense spending by the other members of NATO. With $b^i$ close to unity, increases in defense outlays elsewhere in NATO (*other things being equal*) evokes no response or leads PGT to

Table 4.13. Portugal, Greece, and Turkey's Resource Allocation Behavior Assuming a Nash-Cournot Structure

|  | $a_1$ Marginal Propensity to Spend GDP on Defense | $b_1$ Substitutability between Allies and Own Defense | $\delta_N$ Effect of Warsaw Pact Threat | $\delta_L$ Effect of Local Rival's Threat |
|---|---|---|---|---|
| **GPT Alone** | .014 | 1.0027*** | .0036 | GR = .317*** <br> TU = 4.5 *** |
| **GPT and U.S.** | | | | |
| GPT | .063* | .993* | −.0017 | GR = .235*** <br> TU = .230 |
| U.S. | .124* | .372 | −.162 | − |
| **GPT, U.S., and WP** | | | | |
| GPT | .053 | .997*** | .0002 | GR = .188* <br> TU = .899 |
| U.S. | .135 | .507 | −.646 | − |
| WP | .062 | − | −.180 | − |

\*\*\* significant at 99% confidence level.

\* significant at 90% confidence level.

decrease their defense expenditures by a slight amount. It is noteworthy also that these estimates of $b^i$ are statistically independent of the systematic interdependence among NATO partners. On a raw correlation basis PGT appear to be completely unresponsive to NATO. As shown, if each equation (6) is estimated *alone* (i.e., not together with the United States) equation values of $b^i$ close to unity emerge. We are driven to the conclusion that Portugal, Greece, and Turkey are *not* free-riders in the sense of sitting back and reducing defense outlays when the major NATO players increase theirs.

Next, Table 4.14 indicates values of the parameters estimated under a Lindahl assumption as in equation (8). These estimates appear to be more plausible than did the Nash-Cournot values. PGT all have relatively modest but positive marginal propensities to spend on defense. Each places a negative value on Warsaw Pact defense outlays $\delta_N^i$ (Turkey having the highest such value), but not so great as to require 1:1 NATO increases. The $\delta_L^i$ estimates show Turkey and Greece to be significantly involved in their local arms race. Moreover, most of the estimated coefficients are highly significant. In short, the Lindahl collaborative model seems to be unexpectedly appealing. What might explain this novel result – small, poor members of a group collaborating with the larger members rather than taking a free ride as economic theory would predict? Several possibilities seem worth explaining. First, the degree to which NATO defense provides a *public good* to these small countries may have been overestimated. If the beneficial spillover of defense protection across national boundaries are slight, and therefore most of each country's defense outlays benefit only the country itself, then similar proportional reactions by diverse countries to the *same* threat (but not a common threat) will produce similar-to-Lindahl

Table 4.14. Portugal, Greece, and Turkey's Resource Allocation Behavior Assuming a Lindahl Structure

|  | $a$<br>Marginal Propensity to Spend GDP on Defense | $\delta_N$<br>Effect of Warsaw Pact Threat | $\delta_L$<br>Effect of Local Rival's Threat |
|---|---|---|---|
| GPT Alone | .039** | .365** | GR = .111<br>TU = −.133 |
| GPT and U.S. | | | |
| GPT | .026* | .872*** | GR = −.012<br>TU = .674 |
| U.S. | .088* | .522 | |
| GPT, U.S. and WP | | | |
| GPT | .027* | .854*** | GR = .036<br>TU = .550 |
| U.S. | .101* | .838 | – |
| WP | .004 | −.257[a] | – |

\* significant at 90%.

\*\* significant at 95%.

\*\*\* significant at 99%.

[a] "wrong sign" but not significant.

looking expenditure patterns. The concept that defense outlays may provide a public good among alliance members along one dimension and private goods between them along another has been recognized and described by Sandler and Forbes.[14] Thus, it may be the case that the above results are explained in part by the need to maintain a military force independent of the common defense. In other words, the enmity between Greece and Turkey, as well as Portugal's former empire, may create the appearance of Lindahl behavior.

A second explanation for our novel result might be that other NATO members have coerced or induced collaborative behavior on the military expenditure front by their use of foreign assistance, diplomatic pressure, or moral suasion. Third, it could be that these individual small countries simply prefer to shoulder their share of the burden. There is in fact a substantial literature on the behavior of individuals in small groups indicating that unconstrained free riding is a rarity, even when individuals are anonymous and allocations are to occur only once.[15] NATO surely qualifies as a small group, and the suggestion that individual members feel a necessity to live up to some standards of cooperation for long-run survival is not untenable. Obviously, this is one area which requires more study at a "micro" level.

*A Test to Discriminate between Nash-Cournot and Cooperative Processes.* Given the mixed results reported above, it would be desirable to find a way of discriminating between Nash-Cournot and more (or less) cooperative processes. One way of doing this is to introduce directly into equation (6) an adjustment for the possibility that when a country allocates \$X to defense it *anticipates* that *others* will change their allocation. (The standard economic terminology for such anticipation is "conjectural variation"). Using $\lambda^i$ to denote country $i$'s anticipation as to how its defense outlay influences others' defense outlays we can write

$$\lambda^i = (\partial \overline{D}^i / \partial D^i) c \qquad (9)$$

where $c$ indicates that the term is a conjecture. When this adjustment is made to equation (6), the resulting coefficients in (6′) can be reinterpreted as follows:

$$D^i = B_o^i \theta^i + B_1^i Q^i + B_2^i \overline{D}^i + B_3^i T_N \qquad (6')$$

where: $i = P, G, T$

$$B_o^i = \frac{-a_I^i (1 + \lambda^i)}{1 + a_1^i \lambda^i}$$

$$B_I^i = \frac{a_I^i (1 + \lambda^i)}{1 + a_1^i \lambda^i}$$

$$B_2^i = \frac{-(1-a_I^i)}{1+a_1^i\lambda^i}$$

$$B_3^i = \frac{(1-a_I^i)\delta_N^i}{1+a_1^i\lambda^i}$$

The parameter $\lambda^i$ represents $i$'s estimate about how other countries in the alliance will respond to changes in its level of defense expenditures. Previous work has assumed that each country takes the military spending of its allies as given.[16] This assumption produces the familiar Nash-Cournot equilibrium since spending by allies is taken to be fixed and $\lambda^i$ is implicitly zero. However, as argued by Cornes and Sandler as well as by Borcherding, this assumption is highly questionable when the number of members of the group is small as in military alliances such as NATO.[17] For in the small number case the amount of the common good provided by one member is likely to be obviously seen and understood to depend on the contributions made by others. In other words, the *actual response* of $i$'s allies to a change in $i$'s defense expenditures is likely to be nonzero. If nation $i$ is not myopic but instead exercises accurate foresight, then the response it expects (i.e., $\lambda^i$) will equal the actual response. In this case, the conjectural variation is said to be consistent in the sense that $\lambda^i$ is an accurate estimate about how other countries in the alliance will respond to changes in its level of defense expenditures.

It follows that estimation of $\lambda^i$ should shed some light on the resource allocation process within the alliance. If our estimate of $\lambda^i = 0$, then the interaction between $i$ and its allies can be categorized as being Nash-Cournot. If $\lambda^i$ is negative then $i$ expects its allies to reduce their expenditures in response to an increase in its military outlays; consequently, $i$'s equilibrium level of expenditures would be less than otherwise – it is less willing to contribute to the common defense since it perceives that increases in the amount it provides lead to a reduction in the amount contributed by others. The end result is an outcome in which there is a lower level of defense than that associated with the Nash-Cournot solution.

If $\lambda^i$ is positive, then $i$ expects its allies to increase their defense expenditures in response to an increase in $i$'s level of expenditures. From equation (6') it can be shown that $\lambda^i > 0$ results in a level of $D_i$ that is higher than that associated with nonpositive values of $\lambda^i$. Nation $i$ in this case is interacting with its allies in a cooperative fashion. The resulting level of defense expenditures exceeds the Nash-Cournot level and approaches the Lindahl outcome.

A further modification of equation (6') is in order before we proceed with the estimation of $\lambda^i$. Each of the countries in our sample has been a recipient of military and economic assistance. To account for the effect of this aid on defense expenditures we rewrite (6') as (6") with a variable representing the amount of aid received. "Aid" for these purposes has been defined as all U.S. government to government grants and loans for military and economic support. Other countries' foreign assistance (e.g., German assistance to Turkey) is not reflected in the data. As before, the effects that intra-alliance rivalry have on defense spending must be included. Greece and Turkey are allies in relation to the common threat but are military rivals in relation to each other. For this reason, in estimating Turkey's (Greece's) defense expenditures we include Greece's (Turkey's) expenditures separately on the right-hand side of the equation. From the above, the equation to be estimated is

$$D^i = B_o^i \, \theta^i + B_1^i \, Q^i + B_2^i \, \overline{D}^{ik} + B_3^i \, T_N + B_4^i \, AID + B_5^i T_L^i \qquad (6'')$$

which is simply (6') augmented by $T_L^i$ (i.e., military expenditures by $i$'s local, non-Pact rival – specifically, Greece and Turkey) and by $AID$ (the amount of military and economic aid received). Equation (6") was estimated using maximum likelihood methods as part of a system of four equations.[18]

Table 4.15 presents the values of the estimated parameters. Many of the coefficients such as $a_1$, $\delta_N$, $B_4$, $\alpha_4$ are in most cases insignificant. This is perhaps due to the relatively small sample size and large number of parameters to be estimated. It is worth noting that the parameter $\lambda^i$ is significant in all four cases. For PGT taken together, $\lambda^i$ is found to be positive and statistically significant. Thus, we can reject the hypothesis that PGT taken together exhibit Cournot behavior in its interactions with the rest of NATO. It appears that PGT interact with the rest of NATO along the lines of a collaborative, Lindahl-type process.

Table 4.15. Tests to Distinguish Cooperative from Competitive Allocation Behavior Between PGT and the Rest of NATO

|  | PGT | Portugal | Greece | Turkey |
|---|---|---|---|---|
| $\lambda$: Coefficient of Conjectural Variation | 49.76* | −63.75** | 651.4* | 48.3* |
| $a_1$: Marginal Propensity to Allocate Resources to Defense | .0235 | .0017 | .0329 | .1815 |
| $\delta_N$: Responsiveness to Warsaw Pact Defense | 8.89 | 9.24 | 2287.21 | .471 |
| $B_4$: Effect of AID on Defense Outlay | −16.2 | 75.81 | 2026 | 13.2 |
| $B_5$: Effect of Local Adversary's Defense Outlay | – | – | 3242* | 74.81** |
| $\alpha_4$: Rest of NATO Marginal Propensity to Allocate Resources to Defense | .09* | .039 | −.222 | .069 |
| $\alpha_5$: Responsiveness of the Rest of NATO to Warsaw Pact Defense Outlays | 1.14 | 2.66* | 2.66 | 4.44* |

* significant at 90% level.
** significant at 95% level.

Note: The above values can be used to identify $B_0^i$, $B_1^i$, $B_2^i$, and $B_3^i$. For instance $B_3^{PGT}$, which indicates the effect of Warsaw Pact spending on spending by PGT, can be shown to equal $4.00. (The estimate, however, is not statistically significant).

The same cannot be said with regard to Portugal. The parameter $\lambda^P$ statistically differs from zero allowing us to rule out Cournot behavior. But $\lambda^P$ is also negative indicating that Portugal's level of defense expenditures is less than that associated with the Nash-Cournot resource allocation process. Apparently, Portugal believes its allies will decrease their defense expenditures following an increase in its expenditures.[19]

For Greece and Turkey individually, we find that $\lambda^G$ and $\lambda^T$ are both positive and significant. Therefore, we can again reject the Cournot hypothesis. This time, however, the evidence indicates that the two countries interact with the rest of NATO in a cooperative, e.g., Lindahl, manner. The analysis also indicates the presence of an arms race between Greece and Turkey. This can be inferred from the fact that $B_6^G$ and $B_6^T$ are both positive (disturbingly so) and significant.

How are these results to be explained? One possible explanation was touched on earlier. NATO defense expenditures may be less of a public good than we have assumed. It may be the case that the arms race between Greece and Turkey creates the appearance that these two countries interact in a cooperative fashion with the rest of NATO. The result that Portugal is a free-rider may possibly be attributed to its reduced need for forces independent of the common defense. An alternative explanation is that the proximity of Greece and Turkey to the Warsaw Pact induces their cooperative behavior. Portugal, being far removed from the Warsaw Pact, has less incentive to provide for the common defense and thus acts as a free-rider.

## ECONOMIC – DEFENSE PROJECTIONS

### Projected Defense Expenditures

The empirical results of the previous section suggest that a model of cooperative allocation among PGT and the rest of NATO better explains the behavior of PGT in the provision of defense than does a model of individual free-riders. The implication of these findings for burden sharing in the future can be partly illustrated by a simulation which relies on a linear approximation of the Lindahl model specified in equation 8.

In preparing the projections which follow, three fundamental assumptions were invoked to limit the range of possible scenarios. Given the relatively small (1 – 2 percent) contribution of PGT to total NATO member defense spending, it was decided to treat NATO outlays as an exogenous variable in PGT's own determinations of defense expenditures. It was further assumed that the NATO – Warsaw Pact arms race would remain stable throughout the rest of the decade so that the ratio of total defense expenditures by the two alliances would remain constant throughout the relevant period. Analogously, it was also assumed that the estimated parameters which characterized the local Greece – Turkey arms race over the sample period of the study could be extended to represent behavior to the end of the decade, also implying no radical change in the interaction of the two countries.

The first and second assumptions, taken together, mean that the major determinants of PGT defense expenditures are their respective future GDPs. For Greece and Turkey, there is additionally a small but positive impact from each country's reaction to the other's defense spending. The coefficients for these linear relations were calculated from the estimates listed in Table 4.14 for the GPT, U.S., and Warsaw Pact version of the Lindahl model. The GDP series were constructed from 1979 base year figures and exogenous forecasts of GDP growth rates.

Table 4.16 reports the projected defense expenditures of PGT for the period 1985 – 1990 as well as three series for total NATO defense expenditures given assumptions of annual growth rates in spending of 1 percent, 2 percent, and 3 percent. Also reported under each NATO growth assumption is one common measure of burden sharing, the percentage contribution of PGT as a group to NATO defense outlays.

Total GPT defense spending is projected to grow at an average rate of 4 percent annually with Greece exhibiting the lowest rate at 2.7 percent and Turkey the highest at 4.9 percent. Part, but not all, of this difference is attributable to Turkey's higher estimated reaction to Greek defense spending. The primary explanation for this variance, however, is the differences in projected GDP growth rates. The model's emphasis on the effect of this variable is evidenced by these projections since the ordering of the defense spending growth rates reflects exactly the ordering of the exogenous GDP growth rate forecasts. Turkey shows annual GDP growth rate forecasts between 3.6 and 4.9 percent while Greece's forecast rates are between 1.4 and 2.1 percent; Portugal lies in the middle with forecast rates ranging from 2.7 percent to 3.4 percent.

These GDP projections are consistent with the descriptions of the economies contained in the second section of this chapter. Portugal will succeed in meeting its expected 3 percent growth rate if it fully implements its IMF austerity package. The relatively low growth rates anticipated for Greece result from an increase in an already negative trade balance, declining private capital formation, and the application of substantial public investment funds to unproductive and noncompetitive industries. Turkey, on the other hand, can expect relatively high growth rates for precisely the opposite reason. It is anticipated that exports and private consumption and investment will increase while the government is encouraging privatization of the existing State Economic Enterprises.

A comparison of the projected burden sharing indices of Table 4.16 with their historical counterparts from the study sample period (Table 4.1) shows the projections to be significantly higher under any of the three NATO scenarios. Two plausible explanations are available to address this discrepancy. The first recognizes that the projected defense expenditures of Portugal are likely to be inflated since the sample used in estimating the coefficients was heavily weighted toward the country's colonialist period. The second explanation is an artifact of the model's explicit recognition of the local arms race. Given that only the Greece and Turkey defense

Table 4.16. Projected Defense Expenditures (1972 U.S.$, billions)

|  | 1985 | 1986 | 1987 | 1988 | 1989 | 1990 | Average Growth Rate 1985–1990 |
|---|---|---|---|---|---|---|---|
| Greece | 1.082 | 1.109 | 1.137 | 1.164 | 1.196 | 1.227 | 2.7% |
| Portugal | .645 | .671 | .697 | .722 | .745 | .771 | 3.9% |
| Turkey | 1.800 | 1.898 | 1.970 | 2.039 | 2.137 | 2.239 | 4.9% |
| GPT | 3.527 | 3.678 | 3.804 | 3.925 | 4.078 | 4.237 | 4.0% |
| NATO (1%) | 124.64 | 125.89 | 127.15 | 128.42 | 129.70 | 131.00 | 1.0% |
| GPT % | 2.8% | 2.9% | 3.0% | 3.1% | 3.1% | 3.2% | |
| NATO (2%) | 132.23 | 134.88 | 137.58 | 140.33 | 143.13 | 146.00 | 2.1% |
| GPT % | 2.7% | 2.7% | 2.8% | 2.8% | 2.8% | 2.9% | |
| NATO (3%) | 140.21 | 144.41 | 148.74 | 153.21 | 157.80 | 162.54 | 3.2% |
| GPT % | 2.5% | 2.5% | 2.6% | 2.6% | 2.6% | 2.6% | |

expenditure equations contain an additional term (with a positive coefficient) for each other's defense spending, their contributions as a percentage of total contributions are bound to increase, *ceteris paribus*. The trends from 1960 to 1979 support this contention.

It appears that, though somewhat overstated in these projections, PGT as a group will continue to increase their relative contributions to NATO defense spending. The magnitude of this increase also depends, of course, on the behavior of the other allies. If, for instance, the northern members uphold their commitments to a 3 percent increase and the United States maintains its own elevated rate of increase, PGT's relative contributions will be only marginally higher than in the past. If, however, the northern allies do not meet their pledges, then a 2-3 percent average increase for NATO seems more likely and PGT's share will be substantially larger, perhaps even twice that of previous levels.

A second, often used measure of burden sharing is the ratio defense expenditures to GDP; Table 4.2 presents historical data for this index for 1960 – 1979. In contrast, the projected values for the period 1985 – 1990 center around 6.3 percent for Greece, 5.1 percent for Portugal, and 6.9 percent for Turkey. The value for Portugal is high when compared to the data for the post-colonial period; this is further evidence that estimated defense spending levels for Portugal are inflated because of the structural change in the country's defense obligations after 1975. The values for Greece and Turkey are plausible and reinforce the notion that the relative contributions of these two members are increasing.

## Summary and Implications for U.S. Policy

This chapter has examined the resource allocation behavior of the four least developed members of NATO. The projected GNP of these four nations in total for the year 1992 is about $243.6 billion 1975 $U.S. or about $477 billion 1984 $U.S. An aggregate change in defense spending of 2 percent – which would be a dramatic change by historical standards (see Tables 4.1, 4.3, 4.5, 4.7) – would amount to $9.5 billion 1984 $U.S. or less than 3 percent of expected U.S. defense outlays. While $9.5 billion is not trivial to the United States, it represents vastly more to the poor countries of the southern tier of NATO. Thus, an assessment of the internal opportunity cost of increasing defense spending in PSGT would seem paramount in deciding whether the United States ought to press these countries for higher defense commitments. In none of them do we expect a robust recovery from the slump of recent years. In all four, unemployment will continue at unacceptable rates (9.6 to 17.7 percent) and inflation will be high (11.4 to 21.3 percent).

Obviously, in this environment, the actual effect of defense spending on other sectors of the economy is crucial. Although much greater detailed empirical research is necessary to answer this question, this study has at least shown that the "guns versus butter" view of the cost of defense spending is somewhat simplistic. Defense spending in our sample of countries could divert resources away *from in-*

*vestment as well as consumption.* Given that capital formation is one of the principal sources of economic growth, the result will be a lower rate of economic growth. Accordingly, future levels of consumption and possibly defense as well, could be lower than otherwise. However, this effect should be attenuated when unemployment is high. We have been unable to test out this idea, but it surely deserves further empirical research.

Not only can defense be neutral in its impact on investment/consumption if resources are underemployed, it could be positively stimulative. Investment may be stimulated by defense-induced improvements in infrastructure. If this were true, an increase in defense outlays would actually increase economic growth and thus permit higher levels of future expenditures on consumption and defense. Thus, the effect of defense on investment and hence on the growth rate is an important empirical question. Our limited results indicate that defense has an adverse effect on investment in the case of Spain and Turkey. *Ceteris paribus,* if either of these countries were to increase its level of defense expenditures, the result would be a lower level of investment and economic growth. A 1 percent increase in defense spending relative to GDP can be expected to reduce the growth *rate* by 0.11 percent in the case of Spain and 0.313 percent in the case of Turkey. These defense-induced reductions in growth take on note especially because of the already poor economic performance of these two countries.

It should be pointed out that the defense-induced reductions in growth need not occur if decision-makers were to implement policies that financed defense increases out of consumption rather than investment. This would not be costless even in robust and well-developed economies since such policies imply an eventual reduction in private consumption as resulting revenue shortfalls are eliminated. Given the relatively low per capita consumption levels of these countries, it is perhaps unrealistic to suppose that decision-makers will finance additional defense spending out of consumption so as to avoid defense's adverse effect on growth, and given the fragile nature of the capital markets in these countries, it is not clear that such an option even exists.

In consequence, to the extent that the statistical tests in this study accurately reflect the pattern of economic development in Spain and Turkey, significantly higher defense levels by these countries would seem undesirable because of defense's long-run impact on economic growth. More moderate spending levels may encourage economic development, increasing the amount that these countries are able to allocate to defense in the future.

With reference to Portugal and Greece, a different empirical result was obtained. Military spending in the case of Portugal was found to have no effect on the level of capital formation. There defense spending neither retards nor reinforces economic development. Whether it would be desirable for Portugal to increase its defense expenditure appears to be independent of development and growth objectives. For Greece, defense was found to stimulate investment. There it appears that defense may have fostered economic development. The case against further defense outlays by Greece cannot rest on the argument that military outlay retards growth.

*The Free-Rider Problem.* Just how the United States might, if it so wished, influence allocations within our four southern tier countries has not been explicitly addressed in this study. But whatever the policy instrument, it should only be exercised in the knowledge that the countries of NATO already form an interdependent resource allocation system. Our study has shed significant new light on the nature of this security and budgetary interdependence.

It has become typical to presume the existence of a free-rider problem especially with respect to smaller countries within an alliance such as NATO. Our research, however, shows that the free-rider problem may not be serious after all. In two out of the three countries tested, the analysis indicates ongoing cooperative Lindahl resource allocation processes as compared to noncooperative Cournot-Nash resource allocation processes. Evidence on free-riding was found only in the case of Portugal.

While Greece and Turkey were found to interact cooperatively with the rest of NATO, the data also revealed that these countries were engaged in their own local arms race. Increased defense spending by Greece and Turkey contributes to the common defense of NATO as well as possibly exacerbating tensions between these two countries. Accordingly, defense increases by Greece and Turkey are probably not desirable from the point of view of NATO to the extent that these increases simply fuel their arms race rather than provide for the common defense.

While defense increases by these countries may not be warranted in their own right, the finding of a cooperative interaction between PGT and the rest of the alliance enhances any argument for defense increases by the United States and other NATO allies. In a typical Cournot analysis of a defense increase by, say, the United States, the other allies are presumed to respond by decreasing their own expenditures – which would weaken the case for the initial defense increase. Our empirical analysis, however, indicates that this scenario may have little applicability (at least with reference to PGT). On the contrary, it appears that an increase in expenditures by the United States or another NATO ally will evoke a *cooperative* response from PGT (taken as a whole).

## Appendix A: Predicted vs. Actual Growth Rates

Table A.1 reports average historical values of $k$ and average values of $I/Q$, plus the predicted as well as actual growth rates for the period 1975 – 1977. Column 3 is obtained by dividing column 1 by column 2 and multiplying by 100. Comparison of column 3 with 4, i.e., the predicted growth rates with the actual, indicates that predicted growth rates are only reasonably close to the actual growth rates in the case of Greece and Spain. There was an extraordinary discrepancy between what historical relationships would predict and realized outcomes in the case of Portugal.

Table A.1.

|  | (1) I/Q | (2) k | (3) Predicted growth | (4) Actual growth |
|---|---|---|---|---|
| Greece | .217 | 4.38 | 4.95 | 5.2 |
| Portugal | .183 | 7.68 | 2.38 | 5.7 |
| Spain | .220 | 9.06 | 2.43 | 2.1 |
| Turkey | .213 | 3.18 | 6.69 | 5.5 |

Source: *World Tables* from the World Bank, 1981.

The dramatic differential is due primarily to excessive unsustainable expansion in domestic demand which in turn was fueled by over-rapid growth of public expenditures following the 1974 revolution. This outcome is not surprising given statistical error plus the numerous factors other than investment growth (e.g., oil prices, wages, exchange rates, capital labor substitution, technical change, etc.). To accommodate all these other factors would require a much more complicated and data-demanding model, beyond the scope of this exercise.[20]

# APPENDIX B: THE EFFECT OF DEFENSE ON INVESTMENT

## The Effect of Defense on Investment: No Resource Diversion

In order to model the possibly positive effect of military spending on human capital or infrastructure formation via spin-offs (i.e., the Benoit effect), we will assume that capital formation as a proportion of GDP is a function of infrastructure quality/human capital which, in turn, is a function of military spending in proportion to GDP. Expressing this in mathematical terms, we have

$$I/Q = f(D/Q) \qquad (B.1)$$

where $I/Q$ represents investment as a ratio of GDP and $D/Q$ represents defense expenditures in relation to GDP. In the absence of resource diversion the effect of military spending on investment via its impact on infrastructure/human capital is simply $d(I/Q)/d(D/Q)$ which, in accord with Benoit, is tentatively assumed to be non-negative and constant. More specifically, we assume that in the absence of resource diversion the relationship between $I/Q$ and $D/Q$ can be represented by

$$I/Q = a + b\,D/Q \qquad (B.2)$$

where $a$ represents the level of investment as a proportion of GDP that would be realized in the absence of any military spending at all. The parameter $b$ represents the marginal effect of $D/Q$ on $I/Q$.

## The Effect of Defense on Investment: No Infrastructure Effect

In the absence of an infrastructure effect, higher levels of defense can be expected to divert resources away from investment. To see this point consider the national income identity:

$$Q = C + I + D \tag{B.3}$$

where
$Q$ represents GDP
$I$ represents investment
$C$ represents consumption plus other public non-defense expenditures
$D$ represents national defense expenditures

Next let us assume a consumption function where consumption depends on both national output and on defense as follows:

$$C = cQ - \gamma D \tag{B.4}$$

where $c$ is the marginal propensity to consume, $0 < c < 1$. The parameter $\gamma$ is assumed to be greater than or equal to zero but less than or equal to one.

The parameter $\gamma$ indicates the extent to which there is a trade-off between guns and butter (i.e., military spending and consumption). If $\gamma$ equals 1, then an increase in defense spending of one dollar reduces consumption by one dollar. As a result, defense spending does not affect investment. The other polar case occurs when $\gamma$ equals zero. Higher levels of military spending leave consumption unaffected in this case; therefore, defense spending is financed out of investment. In this case, the trade-off is not between defense and consumption, but is rather between the present level of defense and future levels of consumption and defense. A value of $\gamma$ between 0 and 1 indicates that higher levels of defense spending influence both consumption and investment. Rearranging the national income identity and then substituting equation (B.4) gives

$$\begin{aligned} I &= Q - cQ - D + \gamma D, \\ &= (1-c)Q - (1-\gamma)D. \end{aligned} \tag{B.5}$$

Hence,

$$I/Q = (1-c) - (1-\gamma)D/Q \tag{B.6}$$

Here again we see that if $\gamma$ equals 1, defense does not affect investment. If, however, $\gamma$ is less than one, then increases in defense spending adversely affect investment via a resource diversion effect.

## The Effect of Defense on Investment: Synthesis

The combined effect of defense outlays on investment now becomes a sum of the two effects described by equations (B.2) and (B.6). Combining these two equations gives an overall relationship between the investment – GDP ratio and the defense – GDP ratio as follows:

$$I/Q = B_1 + B_2 (D/Q) \tag{B.7}$$

where

$$B_1 = a + (1-c),$$
$$B_2 = b - (1-\gamma).$$

## APPENDIX C: THE ARMS RACE INTERACTION BETWEEN NATO AND THE WARSAW PACT

In order to discuss the determinants of spending on defense in our sample of countries and to discriminate between alternative hypotheses as to the nature of the allocation process, several versions of equations (6) and (8) have been fitted to the data (estimated). Preliminary to this statistical work, however, we have examined the aggregate interaction between NATO and the Warsaw Pact with a view of determining whether each alliance's military outlays stimulate a response from the other. Equations (C.1) and (C.2) treat each alliance as a monolithic entity, assuming Nash-Cournot interaction between the two. This results in simplified versions of equation (6), since $\overline{D} = 0$ if $i$ includes *all* members of the NATO alliance, and in the aggregate $T_L = 0$ for NATO.

$$D^N = g_0 + g_1 Q^N + g_2 D^W \tag{C.1}$$
$$D^W = h_0 + h_1 Q_W + h_2 D^N \tag{C.2}$$

where

$D^N$ is the aggregate level of defense spending by NATO
$D^W$ is the aggregate level of defense spending by the Warsaw Pact
$Q^i$ $(i = N, W)$ is GNP of NATO and the Pact.

The statistical results from fitting the two equations simultaneously using maximum likelihood methods are presented in the following table. Two versions of (C.1) and (C.2) were run.

The noteworthy results to emerge from the table are (a) the high degree of interaction shown by coefficients $g_2$ and $h_2$ which in general are positive, less than unity, and very, very unlikely to differ from zero only due to random chance; (b) the stability of the implied NATO – PACT arms race to be inferred from the fact that both $g_2$ and $h_h$ are less than unity, and (c) the strong momentum in the arms race implied by the persistence each bloc has in under- or overshooting its desired expenditures.

(This latter effect follows from the highly significant year-to-year correlation of each alliance's expenditures). Due to variability in the estimates it is not possible to say which alliance, NATO or the Pact, is more reactive and which less, although it seems clear that NATO has a lower marginal propensity to spend GNP on defense.[21]

Table C.1. Arms Race Competition Between NATO and The Warsaw Pact 1960–1980

|  | NATO Equation | | | Pact Equation | | |
| --- | --- | --- | --- | --- | --- | --- |
|  | $g_0$ | $g_1$ | $g_2$ | $h_0$ | $h_1$ | $h_2$ |
| Case I[a] No independent allocation to defense allowed i.e., $g_0=0, h_0=0$ | 0 | .02* | .77*** | 0 | .04*** | .25*** |
| Case II[a] Independent requirements for defense allowed $g_0 \neq 0, h_0 \neq 0$ | −25Bil | .01 | -.03 | +26Bil | .04* | .79*** |

[a] In all equations the expenditure functions for each side showed tremendous momentum. The most important determinant of the fit (of equation to data) in any one year was the fit of the previous year.

\* significant at 90 percent level.
\*\* significant at 95 percent level.
\*\*\* significant at 99 percent level.

# NOTES

1. The seven industry groups selected were: aluminum, iron and steel, fertilizers, lignite, petroleum, coke, and chemicals. Source: Chase Econometrics, *Europe Service*.
2. Over the years, the SEEs, with some exceptions, have tended to become overgrown, inefficiently managed, and excessively investment-intensive. The new Ozal administration, however, has made reform of the SEEs a priority goal and has begun a move to decentralize the enterprises by turning control over to the respective ministries. Further decentralization plans being considered include the selling of shares in selected enterprises to the general public. For a more detailed discussion of the role of the SEEs in the Turkish economy, see *OECD Economic Surveys, 1983 – 84: Turkey*, Organization for Economic Cooperation and Development, Paris, May 1984.
3. After these sales, the government held some U.S. $9 billion worth of gold at market prices while outstanding foreign debt that year totaled U.S. $13.5 billion.
4. We are indebted to David Epstein of the Office of the Secretary of Defense for these insights.
5. E. Benoit, *Defense and Economic Growth in Developing Countries* (Lexington, Mass.: D.C. Heath and Co., 1973); Benoit, "Growth and Defense in Developing Countries," *Economic Development and Cultural Change* 26, No. 2 (January 1978): 271-280.

6. R. Faini, P. Annez, and L. Taylor, "Defense Spending, Economic Structure, and Growth: Evidence Among Countries and Overtime," *Economic Development and Cultural Change* 32, No. 3 (1984): 487–498; S. Deger, "Economic Development and Defense Expenditures," paper presented at S.S.R.C. Development Economics Study Group, London, 1979; S. Deger, "Investment, Defense, and Growth in Less Developed Countries," 1980; D. Lim, "Another Look at Growth and Defense in Less Developed Countries," *Economic Development and Cultural Change, 31* (1983): 378–384.
7. D. Lim, "Another Look at Growth and Defense in Less Developed Countries," 1983.
8. Robert J. Gordon, *Macroeconomics*, 2nd ed. (New York: Little-Brown, 1983), p. 568.
9. See Benoit, *Defense and Economic Growth in Developing Countries*, 1973; "Growth and Defense in Developing Countries," 1978. For a critique of Benoit, see Faini et al., "Defense Spending, Economic Structure, and Growth: Evidence Among Countries and Over Time," 1984.
10. An interesting question for conjecture concerns how the B-coefficients might vary over a typical business cycle. $B_1$ should vary according to the Keynesian accelerator principle. $B_3$ should be positive or negative depending on a very complicated set of relations – including the direction of causation between I/Q and AID. $B_2$ should have a tendency to be closer to zero (whether positive or negative) during a recession and farther from zero (whether positive or negative) during a cyclical expansion.
11. This anomaly in our result was called to our attention by Walter Galenson.
12. The caveats highlighted on p. 27 should be kept in mind.
13. C. Groth, and M. McGuire, "A Method for Identifying the Public Good Allocation Process Within a Group," *Quarterly Journal of Economics* (1985): 915–934.
14. T. Sandler and J. Forbes, "Burden Sharing, Strategy, and the Design of NATO," *Economic Inquiry 18* (1980): 425–444.
15. G. Marwell and R. Ames, "Economists Free Ride, Does Anyone Else?" *Journal of Public Economics* 15 (1981): 295–310; Peter Bohm, "Estimating Demand for Public Goods: An Experiment," *European Economic Review* 3, No. 2 (1972): 111–130.
16. L. Dudley and C. Montmarquette, "The Demand for Military Expenditures: An International Comparison," *Public Choice* 37, No. 1 (1981): 5–31.
17. R. Cornes and T. Sandler, "The Theory of Public Goods: Non-Nash Behavior," *Journal of Public Economics* 23 (1984): 381–390; T. E. Borcherding, "Comment: The Demand for Military Expenditures: An International Comparison," *Public Choice* 37, No. 1 (1981): 33–39.
18. The other three equations are

$$D_N = g_0 + g_1 GDP_N + g_2 D_W \tag{10}$$
$$T_N = h_0 + h_1 GDP_W + h_2 D_N \tag{11}$$
$$\overline{D}^i = \alpha_3^i + \alpha_4^i GDP_N^i + \alpha_5^i T_N + \alpha_6^i D^i \tag{12}$$

For estimating this complex system of four equations, the coefficients for equations (10) and (11) are drawn from Appendix C. The coefficient $\alpha_6^i$ is assumed to equal $\lambda^i$, i.e., the conjectures are assumed to be consistent. Thus $\lambda^i$ appears throughout the system as a component in $B_0^i...B_3^i$ and as $\alpha_6^i$.
19. An attempt was made to see what effect, if any, Portugal's decolonization had on its level of military expenditures. A dummy variable representing decolonization was included as an explanatory variable. Somewhat surprisingly, the coefficient turned out to be insignificant when Portugal's defense spending was estimated as part of a system. However, in a single equation model, decolonization was found to result in a lower level of defense expenditures.
20. The differential between "projected growth rates" and "actual growth rates" is due to the fact that ICOR has been calculated over some period of time, rather than for the precise years being modeled. If ICOR had been derived from the same 1975–1977 period actual

and predicted growth would have been necessarily identical. To have called such an exercise in tautology a "model" would be misleading at best (i.e., dividing GNP growth by investment, then multiplying it by investment, and getting the GNP growth you started with). The economic model proposed, however, is not tautological in this fashion. Our hypothesis is that the ICOR is a structural parameter of the economy, roughly constant over long periods. The test of the hypothesis is how good a predictor it is of growth. The answer we suggest is that as the *exclusive* predictor of growth a long-range ICOR model is insufficient; but with additional elaborations it may be quite useful.

21. It should be emphasized that our "arms race" estimates are twenty-year averages, merging various diverse patterns among nations and trends over time. For example, if we had used data just for the U.S.S.R. and the United States for the 1970s, the coefficient $g_2$ would be less than zero as the United States actually cut expenditures (in real terms) while the Soviet Union expanded.

# Chapter 5
# Japan and South Korea

Walter Galenson and David W. Galenson

## INTRODUCTION

Two major allies of the United States in East Asia, Japan and South Korea, share at least one characteristic: they have had very rapid rates of economic growth during the past two decades. From 1960 to 1970, Japan's gross domestic product rose by an average of 10.4 percent per annum, and by the lower but still respectable figure of 4.5 percent from 1970 to 1980. The corresponding increases for South Korea are 8.6 percent and 9.1 percent. A great deal has been written about these records, and there is no need to go into any detail here.[1] Suffice it to say that among the stimulative factors were heavy reliance on exports, high levels of saving and investment, relative freedom of private entrepreneurial action, and the maintenance of incentives to work.

In many other respects, however, there are great differences between the two countries. Japan entered the postwar era as a nation with a well-developed industrial base, although a good deal of it had been damaged or destroyed by wartime bombing. Rapid recovery and subsequent growth have raised Japan to the status of the world's second largest economic power. Its per capita income increased apace because of slow population growth – about one percent per annum from 1960 to 1980 – but living standards lagged because of high investment in heavy industry and infrastructure. The contrast between the great industrial expansion and the more modest rise in private consumption and social services is an important datum in explaining the attitude of the Japanese people toward defense expenditures.

South Korea, on the other hand, was a typically poor Asian country at the close of World War II. Even as late as 1960, its per capita GNP was well under $100. Recovery was impeded by civil war and partition, but once the country got started, it made up for lost time. By 1981, its per capita income exceeded that of many Latin American countries, to say nothing of virtually every African country and most of those in the Middle East, with the exception of the oil producers. It had graduated from the ranks of the less developed countries to become a member of a new international elite – the newly industrialized countries.

One of the sharpest differences between Japan and South Korea lies in the realm of national defense. Japan has followed a policy of self-imposed austerity in this sphere and is at the bottom of the list of U.S. allies in the proportion of GNP devoted to defense expenditures. South Korea, on the other hand, is near the top of the list. This difference emerges clearly from the data in Table 5.1.

One caveat in interpreting these data: the Japanese definition of defense expenditures is less inclusive than that used by the NATO countries, primarily in excluding military pensions from this budget category. Under the NATO definition, approximately 0.4 percent would be added to the ratios for the later years. For example, the figure for 1982 would be about 1.4 percent. Under either definition, however, Japanese defense expenditures are relatively low. The Korean figures reflect full costs in line with the NATO definition.

## THE ECONOMIC BACKGROUND

### Japan

Japan's record of economic growth since World War II is unmatched by that of any large nation. For the period 1960 to 1981, the GDP grew by an average of 7.5 percent a year, compared with 3.7 percent for the entire OECD group of countries. U.S. growth for the same period was 3.3 percent.

Table 5.1. Defense Expenditures as a Percentage of GNP, Japan and South Korea, 1971 – 1983

| Year | Japan[a] | South Korea |
|---|---|---|
| 1971 | 0.86 | 4.1 |
| 1972 | 0.88 | 4.3 |
| 1973 | 0.85 | 3.5 |
| 1974 | 0.92 | 4.1 |
| 1975 | 0.94 | 4.5 |
| 1976 | 0.92 | 5.3 |
| 1977 | 0.93 | 5.6 |
| 1978 | 0.93 | 5.6 |
| 1979 | 0.95 | 5.2 |
| 1980 | 0.96 | 6.6 |
| 1981 | 0.98 | 6.0 |
| 1982 | 0.99 | 5.8 |
| 1983 | 1.00 | n.a. |

*Sources:* Japan: Bank of Japan, *Economic Statistics Annual*, 1983. South Korea: Korean Development Institute, "National Defense and the National Defense Budget," *The National Budget and Policy Objectives*, 1982, p. 161.

[a] Defense expenditures are for the fiscal year beginning April 1; GNP is for the calendar year. The ratios would be slightly lower if GNP calendar year data were used because of GNP growth from January 1 to April 1. The expenditure data represent actual outlays rather than the budget figures often used by other sources in calculating the ratio.

The Japanese GDP growth data for the years 1970 – 1983 are shown in Table 5.2. Japan, like the rest of the developed industrial nations, was adversely affected by the recession of 1974 – 1975 following the first oil shock. However, the Japanese economy rebounded more rapidly than the others, and performed well into 1980. Growth was sustained in 1980 by domestic demand, but the decline in foreign demand attendant upon the second oil shock began to take its toll in 1981, and there was a marked deceleration in growth in 1982 and 1983.

Japan's high investment rate has been one of the most important factors behind growth (see Table 5.2). The average OECD rate for the years 1974 – 1982 was 21.6 percent of GDP; for Japan, 31.7 percent. Table 5.3 shows how Japan, the United States, and Germany spent their national products over the years 1974 – 1982. The contrast between Japan and the other two is striking.

A high level of investment implies a low level of consumption. In fact, the level of private consumption in Japan was close to that of Germany, but the government share was much higher in Germany than in Japan. In part, this is a reflection of Japan's lower defense expenditures, but it also indicates higher German government expenditures for social purposes. The Japanese made their investment level possible by a rate of household saving almost three times greater than that of the United States.

The high investment rate, plus Japanese fiscal policy, has placed some serious obstacles in the way of greater defense expenditures. Taxes claim a relatively small

Table. 5.2. Economic Growth and Investment in Japan, 1970 – 1983

| Year | Annual increases in real GDP (%) | Gross fixed capital formation (% of GDP) |
| --- | --- | --- |
| 1970 | 9.8 | 35.5 |
| 1971 | 4.6 | 34.3 |
| 1972 | 8.8 | 34.2 |
| 1973 | 8.8 | 36.4 |
| 1974 | −1.0 | 34.8 |
| 1975 | 2.3 | 32.4 |
| 1976 | 5.3 | 31.3 |
| 1977 | 5.3 | 31.3 |
| 1978 | 5.0 | 30.8 |
| 1979 | 5.1 | 32.1 |
| 1980 | 4.9 | 32.0 |
| 1981 | 4.0 | 31.0 |
| 1982 | 3.3[a] | 29.9[a] |
| 1983 | 3.0[a] | 28.4[a] |

Sources: OECD, *Historical Statistics, 1960 – 1982*, p. 44, OECD; *Economic Surveys, Japan*, 1984, p. 84.

[a]GNP.

Table 5.3. The Structure of National Expenditures: Japan, the United States, and Germany, 1974 – 1982 (Percent of Gross Domestic Product)

|  | Japan | U.S. | Germany |
|---|---|---|---|
| Total GDP | 100 | 100 | 100 |
| Private fixed consumption | 57.4 | 63.8 | 56.3 |
| Government fixed consumption | 9.8 | 18.2 | 19.9 |
| Gross fixed capital formation | 31.7 | 18.1 | 21.1 |
| Other | 1.1 | 0 | 2.7 |
| Net household saving as a percentage of disposable household income | 21.0 | 7.4 | 12.3 |

*Source:* OECD, *Historical Statistics, 1960 – 1982*, pp. 62 – 70.

proportion of GDP; from 1974 to 1982, government receipts were 26.1 percent of GDP for Japan, 32.1 percent for the United States, and 44.2 percent for Germany. Japan's government revenue has been insufficient to cover even the relatively low level of government expenditure, with the result that budget deficits have been mounting steadily.

Budget data for the years 1970 – 1983 are shown in Table 5.4. Deficits began to mount rapidly in 1975, reaching a peak of 6 percent of GNP in 1979, but remaining

Table 5.4. Japan, Central Government Budget Expenditures, 1970 – 1983

| Fiscal year | Deficit as percent of GNP | Expenditures as percent of government budget | | |
|---|---|---|---|---|
| | | Defense | Pensions and social security | Debt servicing |
| 1970 | 0.4 | 7.2 | 19.5 | 3.5 |
| 1971 | 1.3 | 7.3 | 19.1 | 3.3 |
| 1972 | 1.6 | 6.8 | 18.8 | 3.8 |
| 1973 | 0.6 | 6.5 | 20.1 | 4.6 |
| 1974 | 2.1 | 6.5 | 21.6 | 4.4 |
| 1975 | 3.9 | 6.7 | 25.8 | 5.3 |
| 1976 | 4.2 | 6.3 | 25.9 | 7.5 |
| 1977 | 5.2 | 5.8 | 25.9 | 7.9 |
| 1978 | 5.0 | 5.4 | 26.1 | 9.4 |
| 1979 | 6.0 | 5.3 | 25.5 | 11.0 |
| 1980 | 6.0 | 5.2 | 25.1 | 12.6 |
| 1981 | 5.1 | 5.2 | 25.0 | 14.1 |
| 1982 | 5.0 | 5.2 | 24.2 | 15.8 |
| 1983 | 4.9 | 5.4 | 25.3 | 16.0 |

*Sources:* OECD, *Economic Surveys, Japan,* 1984, p. 32; Bank of Japan, *Economic Statistics Annual,* 1983, pp. 217 – 218, 337 – 338.

relatively high thereafter. By way of comparison, the U.S. fiscal year 1983 budget deficit consumed 6.1 percent of GNP. If the deficit were measured against total budget expenditures, the Japanese deficit ratio would substantially exceed that of the United States because of the fact that the U.S. budget claims a larger share of the GNP than does that of Japan. Take 1982 as an example: the ratio of the Japanese budget deficit to total governmental outlays was 21.8 percent compared with 15.2 percent for the United States.[2]

One result of the rising Japanese deficit has been the higher cost of debt servicing.[3] But as Table 5.4 indicates, defense expenditures have absorbed a diminishing proportion of the national budget, down from 7.2 percent in 1970 to an estimated 5.4 percent in 1983.

The government has issued special deficit-financing bonds to cover the budgetary deficit. It announced in 1981 that it planned to stop the issuance of such bonds by fiscal year 1984. This proved to be impossible for several reasons that are likely to hold true for the rest of the decade. As the OECD put it: "There is still a large unsatisfied demand for social capital investment, though the pace of investment may slacken somewhat. More importantly, the rapid aging of the Japanese population will impose heavy burdens on future pension provision."[4] Additional defense costs would only add to the burden.

All of this reflects the fact that Japan is a low-tax country. The Japanese depend rather heavily on direct taxes; only the United States among major countries has a higher share. On the other hand, Japan has a narrow indirect tax base, deriving half its indirect revenues from taxes on liquor, tobacco, and gasoline. Nevertheless, despite reliance on direct taxes, the Japanese people cannot complain about inordinately high income taxes. A married couple with two children earning $27,000 in 1983 would have paid 14.7 percent of it to the tax collector in Japan compared with 17.7 percent in New York State – and 25.6 percent in the United Kingdom.[5] By international standards, Japan has plenty of room to raise both direct and indirect taxes. Whether the government is prepared to do so, particularly to help finance higher defense expenditures, is another matter.

In appraising the future potential of the Japanese economy, as well as nondefense relationships with the United States, foreign trade is an important variable. Japanese growth has been export-led; its exports have increased even more rapidly than its national product (Table 5.5). The country managed to run a trade surplus throughout the 1970s despite the oil price increases of 1974 and 1979, although for several years the surplus was very small.

Trade relations have been a major source of friction between the two countries. Apart from 1975, Japan has consistently had a favorable balance of trade with the United States, running very high for some years. The United States provided a market for 26 percent of Japanese exports in 1982, more than twice as much as the entire common market. In return, Japan provided the United States a market for 10 percent of its exports, compared with the 22 percent that it exported to the common market. This imbalance has been the cause of the problems, particularly because

Table 5.5. Japanese Foreign Trade, 1972 – 1983 (Current prices)

| Year | Exports of goods and services as % of GNP | Balance of trade surplus as percent of goods exports | Trade with the U.S., percent by which exports exceeded imports |
|---|---|---|---|
| 1972 | 11.2 | 32.0 | 51.2 |
| 1973 | 10.8 | 10.2 | 1.9 |
| 1974 | 14.5 | 2.6 | 1.0 |
| 1975 | 13.7 | 9.2 | −0.4 |
| 1976 | 14.4 | 15.0 | 32.9 |
| 1977 | 13.9 | 21.8 | 59.1 |
| 1978 | 11.9 | 25.7 | 68.5 |
| 1979 | 12.7 | 1.8 | 29.2 |
| 1980 | 15.1 | 1.7 | 28.5 |
| 1981 | 16.6 | 13.4 | 52.6 |
| 1982 | 16.9 | 13.1 | 50.3 |
| 1983 | 15.8 | 21.6 | 52.2 |

*Sources:* OECD, *Economic Surveys, Japan,* July, 1984, p. 93: Bank of Japan, *Economic Statistics Annual,* 1983, p. 229.

the principal Japanese exports to the United States are directly competitive with U.S. produced goods – automobiles, steel, electronic equipment – whereas a good portion of U.S. exports to Japan does not impinge upon Japanese producers – foodstuffs, lumber, raw materials.

Japan's foreign trade is critical to its economic well-being. Growing protectionist sentiment in the United States and Western Europe, particularly in the former, threatens continuation at present levels, let alone expansion. Early in 1985, a storm blew up in the U.S. Congress over what were regarded as strenuous efforts by the Japanese to increase their penetration of American markets combined with Japanese barriers to imports from the United States. The action of the Japanese government in raising projected 1985 automobile exports to the United States after the Reagan administration had terminated the de facto quota that had been in effect, added fuel to the fire. Prime Minister Nakasone attempted to cool the controversy by urging every Japanese citizen to spend $100 on imported goods, and promised that the various restrictions on imports would be reviewed. The dispute was still raging at the present writing, with no settlement in sight.

It is important, nevertheless, that the United States realize that there is a conflict between its two objectives vis-à-vis Japan. Curbing imports from Japan will make it more difficult to persuade the Japanese to raise their defense expenditures. On the other hand, the importance of the American market to Japan gives the United States considerable leverage in defense discussions with Japan, and it might not be unreasonable to require a quid pro quo from Japan in return for the maintenance of relatively free trade between the two countries.[6]

Finally, a word about Japanese living standards, which are not unimportant in assessing the willingness of the Japanese people to shoulder a heavier defense burden. International comparisons of living standards are notoriously tricky, not least because of varying consumption structures. However, some appreciation of the Japanese situation can be gained from the data in Table 5.6. Japan is well off in education and health; indeed, its infant mortality rates (not shown) are among the lowest in the world. Its educational system is legendary, particularly at the lower levels. Where Japan lags behind its peers is in social security and social capital, particularly housing.

Social security transfers in Japan have been rising rapidly in recent years, from 4.6 percent of GDP in 1970 to 10.8 percent in 1981, but they are still considerably below most OECD countries. (The United States is also among the laggard countries in this respect, although if private pensions were added, its social security level would rise considerably, whereas private pensions are not widespread in Japan.[7]) Where the Japanese are furthest behind is in the provision of what might be called social capital (parks, sewerage, housing, water supply) which is very costly and competes with industry and industrial infrastructure for the investment yen. The Japanese Economic Planning Agency had this to say on the subject:

> The buildup in social capital has made steady progress from the standpoint of dissolving bottlenecks in economic growth and enhancing Japanese national life. The level of buildup has therefore been raised considerably with the stock increasing by about seven times in the past 20 years. However, the buildup in social capital has not fully coped with the rapid progress in urbanization. As a result, the quality of Japa-

Table 5.6. Indicators of Living Standards, Japan and Selected Countries

|  | Japan | U.S. | Germany | U.K. | France | Italy |
|---|---|---|---|---|---|---|
| GNP per capita, 1981 (U.S. dollars) | 9,684 | 12,783 | 11,072 | 9,032 | 10,612 | 6,134 |
| Social security transfers as percent of GDP, 1981 | 10.8 | 11.5 | 17.4 | 13.3 | 24.4 | 17.4 |
| Doctors per 1000 inhabitants, 1977 | 1.2 | 1.7 | 2.0 | 1.5 | 1.6 | 2.3 |
| Number of hospital beds per 10,000 persons, 1975 – 1978 | 107.1 | 65.6 | 118.0 | 89.9 | n.a. | 105.8 |
| Full-time secondary school enrollment, percent of age group, 1979 | 71.4 | 75.0 | 45.4 | 46.2 | 55.9 | 43.9 |
| Availability of sewerage, percent of population, 1975 – 1977 | 26 | 71[a] | 88 | 97 | 65 | n.a. |
| Average number of persons per room | 0.8 (1978) | 0.6 (1970) | 0.6 (1976) | 0.6 (1971) | 0.8 (1973) | 0.9 (1971) |

Sources: OECD *Economic Surveys, Japan*, July, 1983, appendix table; Japan, Economic Planning Agency, *Japan in the Year 2000*, 1983, p. 168; Japan Institute for Social and Economic Affairs, *Japan 1983*, p. 5.

[a]1968

nese living space has remained at a low level. In terms of the standard of buildup of social capital, Japan is generally lower than America and the advanced countries of Western Europe.[8]

It is not only the quality, but also the quantity of living space that is at issue. Japanese houses and apartments are very small by Western standards. It will require a good deal of investment to raise Japanese housing to a level consonant with its per capita national product. On the other hand, when it comes to goods produced by their rapidly growing industries, particularly those that they export, Japanese consumers are well off. Refrigerators, television sets, washing machines, vacuum cleaners, and cameras are to be found in virtually all Japanese households, although automobiles are not as widely diffused, in part because of urban congestion.

The upshot of this is that a combination of lower growth rates in the future (see below) and the desire of the Japanese people for a larger portion of the national product to be allocated to individual and social consumption, will add to the political difficulty of raising defense expenditures. Facing the pressure of consumers for an improvement in the quality of life, on the one hand, and of industry for greater capital resources in order to maintain its international competitive position on the other, the government will be able to augment the national defense effort only if it can convince the Japanese people that their security demands it, something that it has not yet done.

## South Korea

There are few developing countries that have managed at the same time to sustain a large military establishment and to achieve a high rate of economic growth. South Korea is one of the best examples, with 6.7 percent of its GNP devoted to military expenditures in 1980. Among the other less developed countries with somewhat comparable military levels are Tanzania (9.0), Pakistan (5.0), Mauritania (12.6), Morocco (6.1), Syria (17.3), and Jordan (13.1), none of them noted for its growth record.[9] Taiwan may be Korea's only competitor in this respect.

Data relevant to South Korean economic growth since 1970 are contained in Table 5.7. The record is a truly remarkable one. Apart from 1980, when a combination of unfortunate events – the oil shock, the assassination of President Park, and a poor harvest due to bad weather – resulted in a temporary setback, the annual rise in GNP was never less than 5 percent for the past twelve years, and reached the double digit level during four years.

A good deal of the credit for the particularly rapid growth that South Korea experienced from 1976 to 1978 must go to the foreign trade policies of the government during this period. Import protection was reduced by the lowering of tariffs and the liberalization of import restrictions, while export credits and other subsidies were established. As a result of these policies, as well as of the growth of industry, the volume of exports rose by 85 percent from 1975 to 1978. The initial reaction to the first oil shock and the consequent slowdown of the world economy had been to go the opposite way – to promote import substitution in order to protect domestic manufacturing. Fortunately, the South Korean government was dissuaded from doing so.

High levels of investment were maintained consistently, matching those of Japan during much of the period. A great deal of this was directed to industry, with the results that also appear in Table 5.7. One looks in vain (except in South Korea's East Asian neighbors) for comparable increases in manufacturing output over the decade – 15.6 percent a year from 1970 to 1981.

As the data indicate, South Korea was adversely affected by the worldwide recession that began in 1979, but it managed to speed up the recovery by a series of measures that included devaluation of the currency, an increase in interest rates, wage restraint, the merging of companies in six key industries, and reform of the tax system.

Prior to 1982, the South Korean government provided "guidance" to the economy by a series of five-year plans which established specific quantitative targets for key variables such as exports, investment, and growth. The private sector retained considerable freedom of action, but the government did attempt to steer the economy through the use of financial and fiscal instruments, and occasionally by direct

Table 5.7. South Korea: Economic Growth and Investment, 1970 – 1984

| Year | Annual increase in real GNP (%) | Gross capital formation (% of GNP) | Annual increase in manufacturing output (%) |
|---|---|---|---|
| 1970 | 7.6 | 26.8 | 11.7 |
| 1971 | 9.4 | 25.2 | 16.4 |
| 1972 | 5.8 | 21.7 | 16.3 |
| 1973 | 14.9 | 25.6 | 35.6 |
| 1974 | 8.0 | 31.0 | 29.2 |
| 1975 | 7.1 | 29.4 | 19.5 |
| 1976 | 15.1 | 25.5 | 31.8 |
| 1977 | 10.3 | 27.3 | 20.4 |
| 1978 | 11.6 | 31.1 | 23.8 |
| 1979 | 6.4 | 35.4 | 12.1 |
| 1980 | −6.2 | 31.5 | −1.9 |
| 1981 | 6.4 | 28.4 | 13.5 |
| 1982 | 5.3 | 26.2 | 5.0 |
| 1983 | 4.3 | 27.6 | 15.9 |
| 1984 | 7.5[a] | n.a. | n.a. |

Sources: Economic Planning Board, *Major Statistics of the Korean Economy,* 1982, pp. 25, 28; Bank of Korea, *Principal Economic Indicators,* September 1983, p. 3; Economist Intelligence Unit, *Quarterly Review of South Korea,* Annual Supplement, 1984; No. 3, 1984, p. 2; No. 2, 1984, p. 13; *New York Times,* April 22, 1985, p. D12.

[a]Gross Domestic Product.

intervention. The philosophy of the fifth five-year plan, covering the period 1982 – 1986, is less interventionist:

> For private economic activities the indicative function of the Plan is brought into play. Aside from a limited number of large-scale projects, investment choices will be left to private initiative, and the government will do no more than indicate the general framework and direction in which such choices should be made. The government will further reduce its intervention in the market mechanism through regulation and protection and will gear various new incentive systems in order to foster greater endeavors in the private sector.
> However, the government will intervene directly in the area of basic needs such as education, housing, and health care, and thus complement the market mechanism. With respect to social development, technology and manpower development, and social overhead capital, the government will design concrete investment programs in order to maintain consistent and synthetic policy implementation within the limits of overall financial resources.[10]

The importance of defense spending throughout the last decade is indicated by the data in Table 5.8. Comparison with Table 5.4 shows once again the magnitude of the difference in defense expenditures between the two countries. Throughout the 1970s, South Korea devoted from one-third to one-fourth of its national budget to defense, whereas Japan allocated only between 5 and 6 percent.

To make the comparison even more striking, South Korea managed to do so without incurring large budget deficits. In recent years, there has generally been a surplus in the current revenue/expenditure balance, and the deficits that were incurred were due to government investment in and loans to the private sector. In

Table 5.8. South Korea: Public Sector and Defense Expenditures, 1970 – 1982

| Year | Central government expenditures as a % of GNP | Defense expenditures as a % of the central government budget |
|---|---|---|
| 1970 | 22.3 | 23.2 |
| 1971 | 22.3 | 26.0 |
| 1972 | 24.0 | 25.9 |
| 1973 | 18.3 | 28.0 |
| 1974 | 19.5 | 29.3 |
| 1975 | 21.7 | 28.8 |
| 1976 | 21.8 | 32.9 |
| 1977 | 21.8 | 34.7 |
| 1978 | 20.7 | 37.0 |
| 1979 | 22.2 | 30.8 |
| 1980 | 25.2 | 35.6 |
| 1981 | 26.2 | 33.8 |
| 1982 | 24.9 | 34.8 |

*Source:* Economic Planning Board, *Major Statistics of Korean Economy,* 1982, p. 177; *Korea Annual,* p. 116.

1980, for example, when the deficit was higher than it had been during the previous decade, current revenue exceeded current expenditures by 50 percent. Capital expenditures and net lending produced an overall deficit of 15 percent of revenue. Moreover, this was a depression year; the comparable figure for 1979 was only 6 percent.[11]

The answer is, of course, that South Korea has been prepared to levy sufficient taxes to avoid accumulation of a large national debt. The principal reliance has been on indirect taxes, which yielded 47 percent of the total revenue in 1981. Direct taxes accounted for only 22 percent of the total in the same year, while a defense surtax contributed 16 percent.[12] A special educational tax was introduced in 1982, expected to yield from 2 to 2.5 percent of revenue during the fifth plan, in order "to solve the problem of overcrowded classrooms, to extend compulsory education to middle school, and to raise teachers' salaries."[13]

There still appears to be room for additional taxation if it were necessary to raise defense expenditures. Property tax rates and assessments are low by international standards. Various exemptions from direct taxes are estimated to have cost one-third of the receipts from this source in 1980, while exemptions from the value-added tax reduced its yield by 13 percent. Currently, 30 percent of all households pay income taxes; it is planned to raise this to 50 percent.

Of perhaps greater significance as potential constraints to defense spending are foreign trade problems and the revolution of rising expectations. South Korean growth has been heavily dependent on foreign trade, but as can be seen from Table 5.9, there has been a consistent trade deficit during the past decade, to which oil prices contributed in significant measure.

To finance this deficit, South Korea has been a heavy international borrower, with the result that its debt service ratio (the ratio of external interest payments to exports) was 20 percent in 1981. Its "mandatory" external payments – debt service, fuel imports, imports essential to the production of exports – came to more than 80 percent of earnings from exports. Without further borrowing, its import capacity is severely limited, a fact that is important when it comes to the purchase of more sophisticated defense equipment from abroad.

With respect to the direction of its foreign trade, almost half of its exports went to the United States in 1971, but this fell to one-quarter and one-third a decade later (Table 5.9). Exports were directed increasingly to other developing countries. An interesting fact is that South Korea has been doing an increasing volume of overseas contract construction, mainly in the Middle East. By 1981, almost 170,000 South Koreans were engaged in such work.

Apart from oil, South Korean imports were derived largely from the United States and Japan. South Korean imports consist primarily of raw materials and high technology capital goods, as well as military equipment. Unfortunately, some of its major exports to the United States and Western Europe – textiles, electronic products, footwear, iron, and steel – are threatened by the rising tide of protectionism.

Table 5.9. Foreign Trade of South Korea, 1970 – 1983

| Year | Trade deficit as a percentage of exports | Percentage of foreign trade with the U.S. | |
|---|---|---|---|
| | | Exports | Imports |
| 1970 | 104.5 | 47.3 | 29.5 |
| 1971 | 92.4 | 49.8 | 27.5 |
| 1972 | 34.2 | 47.1 | 25.7 |
| 1973 | 17.3 | 29.9 | 28.3 |
| 1974 | 42.9 | 33.5 | 24.8 |
| 1975 | 33.4 | 30.2 | 25.9 |
| 1976 | 7.6 | 32.3 | 22.4 |
| 1977 | 4.7 | 31.0 | 22.6 |
| 1978 | 14.0 | 31.9 | 20.3 |
| 1979 | 29.9 | 29.1 | 22.6 |
| 1980 | 25.5 | 26.3 | 21.9 |
| 1981 | 14.3 | 26.7 | 23.1 |
| 1982 | 11.0 | 28.6 | 24.9 |
| 1983 | 7.1 | 33.7 | 23.9 |

Source: Economic Planning Board, *Major Statistics of Korean Economy, 1982*, pp. 213 – 214. Economist Intelligence Unit, *Quarterly Review of South Korea*, 1984, No. 4, Appendix 2.

South Korea is closely tied to the United States economically as well as politically. Without access to the American market, South Korea would be hard put to maintain its present level of defense, let alone increase it. In 1984, South Korea sold the United States some $9.9 billion worth of goods and imported $6.5 billion. This commodity trade surplus was reduced to $2.2 billion by net export of U.S. services to South Korea, but it was still large enough to raise protectionist sentiment. South Korea reduced steel shipments to the United States, and has adopted measures designed to facilitate imports, but pressure is likely to continue, particularly with respect to shoes and textiles. Here again the United States faces a clash of objectives: the desire to protect its industries and at the same time to reduce the burden of helping defend South Korea.

The heavy industrial investment that sparked South Korea's economic growth limited consumption, particularly in the earlier years. But as development proceeded, a greater volume of goods and services became available to meet consumer needs. South Korea provides a good example of the shortest road to economic development, but one that requires initial sacrifice on the part of its citizens.

As the data in Table 5.10 demonstrate, there has been a considerable improvement in living standards over the last two decades, particularly in health and education. Primary school enrollment is universal and secondary school enrollment widespread. South Korea's progress relative to countries that started at much the same economic level after World War II is illustrated by Table 5.11; a similar pattern prevails in other aspects of living conditions.

Table 5.10. South Korea: Social Indicators, 1960 and 1980

|  | 1960 | 1980 |
|---|---|---|
| Life expectancy at birth, years | 54.2 | 63.4 |
| Infant mortality rate, per 1000 births | 62 | 32 |
| Hospital beds per 1000 persons | 36.7[a] | 99.7 |
| Access to piped water, percent of population | 13.2[a] | 54.6 |
| Number of persons per room in dwellings | 2.5 | 2.0 |
| Access to electricity, rural dwellings, percent | 12.4 | 64.9 |
| Average protein intake per day, adults, grams | 53.2[a] | 69.6[b] |
| Secondary school enrollment, percent of relevant age group | 27 | 74 |
| Telephones per 100 persons | 0.5[a] | 8.9 |

*Sources:* Economic Planning Board, *Major Statistics of Korean Economy,* 1982; Korea Development Institute, *The Fifth Five-Year Plan,* 1982.

[a] 1962.

[b] 1979.

Yet South Korea still has a long way to go until it enters the ranks of even the less affluent of developed industrial nations. Housing is in short supply despite the fact that 5 percent of its GNP was devoted to the construction of new homes during the fourth plan (1977 – 1981). There is no national pension scheme; medical and health insurance covered only 36 percent of the population in 1981.

In the context of social development, defense has placed a heavy burden on South Korea. Expenditures for education, housing, social welfare, and water supply absorbed 24 percent of the central government budget during the fourth plan period, while 35 percent went for defense. If the Japanese level of defense expenditure had prevailed in South Korea, social expenditures could have more than doubled.[14]

## DEFENSE POLICIES

### Japan

Japanese defense policy has been based on a passage that appeared in the 1946 Constitution, resolutions of the Diet, and a constant, careful sounding of public opinion by the Liberal Democratic administration. It has changed a good deal over the past forty years, and is in the process of a fairly rapid evolution at the present time.

Table 5.11. Social Indicators for South Korea and Selected Less Developed Countries[a]

|  | South Korea | Thailand | Colombia | Nigeria |
|---|---|---|---|---|
| GNP per capita, 1981 (dollars) | 1,700 | 770 | 1,380 | 870 |
| GNP growth rate, average per annum, 1960 – 1981 (percent) | 6.9 | 4.6 | 3.2 | 3.5 |
| Infant mortality rate, 1981 (per 1000 births) | 33 | 53 | 55 | 133 |
| Population per physician, 1980 | 1,690 | 7,180 | 1,920 | 12,550 |
| Daily per capita calorie supply, 1980 | 2,957 | 2,308 | 2,529 | 2,595 |
| Number enrolled in secondary school, percent of relevant age group, 1980 | 85 | 86 | 46 | 34 |

*Source:* World Bank, *World Development Report*, 1983.

[a]Data for South Korea are derived from a different source than those in Table 5.10. The reasons for the inconsistency in the school enrollment figures are not clear from the data sources.

A number of factors have contributed to the altered perception of Japan's security requirements, particularly among the leadership of the Liberal Democrats. Among them were the establishment of diplomatic relations between the United States and the People's Republic of China; the rapid deployment of Soviet SS-20 nuclear missiles; and the destruction of a South Korean airliner by Soviet fighter planes close to the shores of Japan.[15]

A major barrier to the expansion of Japan's military efforts was a 1976 resolution of the Diet approving a government statement to the effect that "defense buildup should be carried out to the extent that, for the time being, annual defense-related expenditures do not exceed an amount equivalent to one percent of the gross national product for each particular fiscal year." This self-imposed maximum has thus far inhibited military expenditures. The Liberal Democratic Party has shown signs of a desire to exceed it; one of its committees recommended in July 1984 that the ceiling be increased to 1.4 percent. But thus far, the political situation (discussed below) has prevented movement in this direction.

The relevant language of the 1946 Constitution, which has been subject to a good deal of interpretation and reinterpretation, reads as follows:

> Aspiring sincerely to an international peace based on justice and order, the Japanese people forever renounce war as a sovereign right of the nation and the threat or use of force as a means of settling international disputes.
> In order to accomplish the aim of the preceding paragraph, land, sea, and air forces, as well as other war potential, will never be maintained. The right of belligerency of the state will not be recognized.

At first glance, this provision appears to bar the maintenance of any armed forces at all. However, its apparent commitment to complete disarmament, reflecting the impact of the country's disastrous wartime experience at the time it was adopted, was subsequently modified by governmental interpretation. A cabinet resolution issued in May 1957 stated that it was within the meaning of Article 9 that Japan could "develop progressively the effective defense capabilities necessary for self-defense, with due regard to the nation's resources and the prevailing domestic situation." But in 1967, the government declared that it would not produce nuclear weapons, permit them to be stationed in Japan, or transshipped through its territory.[16] U.S. warships suspected of carrying nuclear weapons are still liable to face hostile demonstrations when they enter Japanese ports.

A second cornerstone of Japanese defense policy is the Treaty of Mutual Cooperation and Security between Japan and the United States entered into in 1952, revised in 1960, and extended subsequently, and still in effect. *Inter alia,* it granted the United States access to facilities for land, naval, and air forces in Japan. It stipulated that "each party recognizes that an armed attack against either party in the territories under the administration of Japan would be dangerous to its own peace and safety and declares that it would act to meet the common danger in accordance with its constitutional provisions and processes."

This treaty stops a considerable distance short of providing for a full military alliance. It commits the United States to defend Japanese territories that may come under attack, but there is no corresponding obligation for Japan to defend the United States unless there were an attack against U.S. forces on Japanese territory.

Beginning in 1958, Japan instituted a series of three- and five-year plans designed to build up its self-defense forces (SDF), as Japan's military establishment is called. In general these plans were implemented. Faced in 1976 with economic problems stemming from the oil crisis and the ensuing recession, as well as mounting political opposition to the expansion of the SDF, specific targets were abandoned and replaced by a National Defense Program Outline, which provides the basic guidelines for defense policy.

Very briefly, the Outline makes the following declarations:

- Japan's policy is to possess a defense capability adequate to prevent armed invasion, while relying upon the United States to defend it against nuclear threat.

- Direct aggression against Japan will be met with immediate responsive action. Limited and small-scale aggression will be repelled without external assistance. Where this is not feasible, "Japan will continue an unyielding resistance by mobilizing all available forces until such time as cooperation from the United States is introduced, thus rebuffing such aggression."

- There must be sufficient capability to conduct warning and surveillance missions within Japan "and neighboring sea and air space," and to repel invading aircraft.

The Outline has been interpreted and supplemented by subsequent parliamentary declarations. Defense of the sea-lanes includes protection of ports and straits as well as antisubmarine operations. The geographical limit of sea-lane defense is 1,000 nautical miles beyond Japanese shores, including Guam and the ocean area north of the Philippines. It is expected that the United States will provide protection beyond these limits. Foreign ships carrying cargoes bound for Japan are *not* in principle accorded Japanese protection against attack, except that if Japan were attacked, and the cargoes were vital to its defense, "the SDF action to repel such attacks as part of the defense operations for Japan could be considered as the necessary minimum for the defense of the country."[17] Thus a blockade of Japanese ports would presumably be the kind of aggressive action to which Japan would respond.

As of March 31, 1983, the authorized strength of the SDF was 180,000, although the actual number was 155, 938. The ground forces comprised 12 infantry divisions, an armored division, and 6 specialized brigades, supported by 366 aircraft. The maritime force had 166 ships, including 48 destroyers, 40 mine layers, and 14 submarines, supported by 200 aircraft. The air force had 417 planes, only 23 of which were the advanced F-15s. In some respects, these totals did not even meet the planned levels for 1976.[18]

The chief concern of Japanese and U.S. military planners has been the rapid buildup of Soviet forces in the Far East. Since 1978, a Soviet division has been deployed in Kunashiri, Etorofu, and Shikoton, islands off its northern coast over which Japan claims sovereignty. Ten advanced MIG-21 fighters were placed on Etorofu in 1982, replacing older models. The Soviet Pacific fleet numbers about 820 ships, including 85 major surface vessels and 135 submarines, 65 of them nuclear-powered. Some of the most advanced Soviet aircraft carriers, missile cruisers, and destroyers are in the Pacific. The Soviet Union maintains on the order of 370,000 troops along the Sino-Soviet border east of Lake Baikal and in areas near Japan, as well as 2,100 combat aircraft, 108 SS-20 missiles, and 70 Backfire bombers.[19]

To back up Japan, as well as to protect its other interests in the Pacific, the United States maintains sizable forces in the Pacific. There are 29,000 U.S. Army combat troops in South Korea and 2,400 in Japan. The Marine Corps has some 30,000 members stationed in Japan, the Philippines, and Guam; the Navy deploys 47,000 personnel; the Air Force, 38,000. There are 65 ships in the U.S. Seventh Fleet, including three aircraft carriers plus 280 combat aircraft, while the Air Force maintains a similar number.[20] However, the U.S. Pacific Command covers a huge geographical area, including the Indian Ocean, as does the Soviet Pacific fleet.

Where the regional balance of power lies is a debatable question to which there is no conclusive answer. Soviet numerical strength is offset by its long lines of communication. None of this, moreover, takes into account Chinese military power, which pins down Soviet troops along the Sino-Soviet border. A great deal more is involved than the defense of Japan, and it might not be prudent for the Japanese to assume that they will continue to be sheltered safely under the American umbrella.

The SDF have been criticized as inadequate even to fulfill the limited mission assigned to them by Japanese defense doctrine. Among the deficiencies that have been cited are the following:

- The ground forces rely heavily on armor as a mobile strike force. About 70 percent of their 900 tanks date from the early 1960s and are outmoded, as are many of their artillery and anti-tank weapons.

- The maritime force is relatively modern and emphasizes anti-submarine warfare capability because of Japan's reliance on fuel and other imports. However, it is vulnerable to air attack because of insufficient air support, and is not strong enough to control and blockade the major straits that border on Japan.

- The air defense force requires extensive modernization. Some 90 F-104Js are to be replaced by F-15s, and additional early warning planes will be obtained to supplement the present inventory of two.[21]

Some aggregate data on the cost of defense appear in Tables 5.1 and 5.4. A more detailed breakdown of the composition of defense expenditures appears in Table 5.12. The sharp increase in personnel costs after 1974 was due to rising wages following the oil-induced inflation, but it declined thereafter when the wage push was modified. In general, military salaries have followed the civilian trend. The rise in the equipment share since 1979 reflects the replacement of older planes, ships, and tanks by more modern ones.

At about one percent of the military budget, research and development costs have been very low, reflecting Japanese reliance on U.S. military technology. Comparable figures for the United States, Britain, and France are about 10 percent, while that for West Germany is about 5 percent.[22] The share allocated to improvement of base environment, termed by the Japanese "base countermeasures," reflects an attempt to prevent environmentalists from impeding defense efforts. Among the programs that come under this rubric are:

- Nuisance prevention, such as maintenance of roads damaged by heavy equipment, and reclaiming of land used for firing practice.

- Measures against air base noises. Noise suppression devices are used at the bases themselves, and grants are given for noise abatement in nearby schools and hospitals.

- Subsidies for public welfare facilities in communities impacted by defense activities.

- Compensation for business and other losses caused by heavy air and vehicular traffic.

Japan also spends substantial amounts to help maintain facilities occupied by

Table 5.12. Structure of Japanese Defense Expenditures, 1972–1983 (Percent of Total Expenditures)

| Fiscal year | Salaries and provisions | Maintenance and training of personnel | Equipment | Maintenance of facilities | Research and development | Improvement of base environment | Other |
|---|---|---|---|---|---|---|---|
| 1972 | 46.6 | 14.7 | 24.9 | 2.9 | 1.4 | 7.6 | 1.9 |
| 1973 | 46.5 | 14.2 | 25.4 | 3.1 | 1.3 | 7.5 | 2.0 |
| 1974 | 48.5 | 14.2 | 22.9 | 2.6 | 1.1 | 8.8 | 1.9 |
| 1975 | 52.9 | 14.5 | 19.0 | 2.3 | 0.9 | 8.6 | 1.8 |
| 1976 | 56.0 | 14.5 | 16.4 | 2.3 | 0.9 | 8.2 | 1.7 |
| 1977 | 55.0 | 14.5 | 17.4 | 2.4 | 0.9 | 8.0 | 1.6 |
| 1978 | 54.4 | 14.5 | 17.1 | 2.4 | 0.9 | 8.7 | 2.0 |
| 1979 | 51.4 | 13.9 | 18.7 | 2.9 | 1.0 | 10.2 | 1.8 |
| 1980 | 49.3 | 14.1 | 20.7 | 2.8 | 1.0 | 10.4 | 1.8 |
| 1981 | 47.7 | 14.7 | 22.5 | 2.2 | 1.0 | 10.5 | 1.5 |
| 1982 | 46.6 | 15.8 | 22.4 | 2.3 | 1.1 | 10.4 | 1.4 |
| 1983 | 44.5 | 16.3 | 24.9 | 1.9 | 1.1 | 10.0 | 1.3 |

Source: Defense of Japan, 1983, p. 198.

U.S. forces. Approximately 21,000 Japanese are employed on U.S. bases, and since 1978, Japan has shared the cost of their wages and fringe benefits. It has also improved housing for American personnel and reconstructed such equipment as oil tanks for American use.[23] The current annual cost of these subsidies is on the order of $750 million, which is considerably more per serviceman than the NATO allies provide for U.S. forces in Europe.

The military procurement policy of Japan has been subject to conflicting pressures. On the one hand, there is a desire to patronize domestic industry, particularly during periods of economic recession. Domestic production may guarantee a steady supply in times of crisis. On the other hand, advanced imported equipment is likely to be cheaper than Japanese-produced equipment, particularly because Japan is precluded by its constitution from exporting any war material, so that it cannot match the U.S. scale of production. Purchase of weapons from the United States also helps alleviate a source of friction between the two countries by reducing the Japanese trade surplus.

The results of the policy appear in Table 5.13. Obviously much of the material needed for maintenance of personnel will come from local sources. However, in 1981 about 20 percent of procurement (less in earlier years) represented U.S. sales to Japan in one form or another. Commercial imports are purchased by the Defense Agency through trading companies, while foreign military purchases represent direct government-to-government transactions.

Japan also produces some items under license, among them fighter planes, antisubmarine aircraft, and self-propelled howitzers. There has been a consistent policy of coproduction, involving domestic production of portions of U.S. systems by agreement with the United States.

Military procurement from the United States during the 1970 – 1981 period constituted about 4 percent of total imports from the United States, or 7.5 percent of Japan's trade surplus with the United States. If instead of producing big ticket items like F-15 planes under license – these planes can cost up to $50 million each – Japan were to buy them, this would not even out the trade imbalance, but it would help.

To assure the Japanese public that defense expenditures do not place too great a

Table 5.13. Japan: Sources of Military Procurement, 1977 – 1981 (Percent of Total)

| Fiscal Year | Domestic procurement | Commercial imports | Foreign military purchases |
|---|---|---|---|
| 1977 | 93.4 | 3.5 | 3.1 |
| 1978 | 85.4 | 2.5 | 12.1 |
| 1979 | 85.2 | 4.6 | 10.2 |
| 1980 | 88.5 | 4.8 | 6.7 |
| 1981 | 80.5 | 6.0 | 13.5 |

*Source: Defense of Japan,* 1983, p. 27.

burden on the economy, the Defense Agency publishes data that place in perspective the relationship between defense procurement and industrial output. From 1972 to 1981, the procurement/output ratio was only 0.4 percent. As the Agency put it, "the ratio of defense production to total industrial output of the nation in yen terms, in fiscal 1981, approximately equalled that of the bread industry or the tires and tubes for automobiles industry."[24] Opponents of defense might argue that total defense expenditures equaled 12 percent of the value added by the iron and steel, machinery and equipment, and transportation equipment industries. But they would have a hard time convincing the citizens of other major nations that they were making too great a sacrifice.

## South Korea

It is not difficult to appreciate why attitudes toward defense are so different in South Korea and Japan. The huge hostile army of North Korea is only 25 miles away from Seoul, the South Korean capital. South Korea faces not a potential enemy, but a real self-proclaimed one which has even resorted to assassination of some of its cabinet members. Of course, there are also differences in political structure. South Korean opponents of defense are not in a position to do much about it.

Some comparisons of the North and South Korean economies are shown in Table 5.14. The North Korean figures should be regarded with more than the usual measure of caution, since apart from the demographic data they represent very rough estimates by outside agencies. The most striking difference is in population. South Korea has more than twice as many inhabitants as the North, although this advantage is being eroded by more rapid population growth in the North.

Table 5.14. Comparisons of the Economies of North and South Korea

|  | South Korea | North Korea |
|---|---|---|
| Population, mid-1981 (millions) | 38.9 | 18.7 |
| Estimated annual current growth of population (percent per annum) | 1.6 | 2.3 |
| GNP per capita, 1979 (U.S. dollars) |  |  |
| World Bank estimate | 1480 | 1130 |
| CIA estimate | 1550 | 806 |
| Average annual growth of GNP, 1970–1979 (percent) | 10.3 | 6.2 |
| Defense expenditures as a share of GNP, 1980 (percent) | 6.7 | 10 |
| Percent of labor force in agriculture, 1980 | 34 | 49 |

*Sources:* World Bank, *World Development Report,* 1981, 1982, 1983; U.S. Central Intelligence Agency, *Handbook of Economic Statistics,* 1980; RAND Corporation, Document R-2894-NA.

Two estimates for GNP per capita are shown. Those for South Korea are not too far apart as these things go; the differences may be due to the exchange rate used in converting Korean currency into U.S. dollars or to other adjustments. The estimates for North Korea differ substantially, and to reconcile them one would have to have access to the respective estimating procedures. In judging which is more likely to be nearer the truth, however, it might be noted that the World Bank ceased publishing national product data for most communist countries, including North Korea, after 1981, because of doubts about their meaningfulness.

Regardless of which estimate is accepted, South Korea was a wealthier country than North Korea in 1979, and there is every reason to believe that this disparity prevails at the present time. When it comes to defense expenditures out of total GNP, however, the relationship is reversed. Even the comparative data in Table 5.14 do not measure the true relative burdens imposed by military expenditures on the two economies. As a recent RAND study points out:

> In a society (like that of North Korea) whose overriding national objective is military in character – namely, to unify the peninsula by military force – it is often extremely difficult, and to some extent misleading, to distinguish between military and nonmilitary use of resources. On the one hand, the military engages extensively in civil "nation building" activities in agriculture, industrial construction, and civil engineering. On the other hand, the "civil" economy is pervaded by North Korea's overriding military objective; in education and manpower policies, in the planning and use of civil investment and infrastructure, and in industrial priorities, investment, and production....In the North Korean context, it is hardly more accurate to refer to the burden imposed by the military on the civil economy than to refer to the burden that strictly civil pursuits impose on the military.[25]

While the South Korean GNP share devoted to military expenditures increased through the 1970s from about 4 percent to the current 6 percent plus, the North Korean military share has probably exceeded 10 percent throughout the decade, and may have been as high as 15 percent in 1982.

The relative military strength of the two countries is shown in Table 5.15. According to a Japanese estimate, the North Korean ground forces are superior to those of the South not only in numbers, but in mobility and firepower as well. The core of the South Korean fleet is its destroyers, and it is currently building up its flotilla of high-speed missile boats. This advantage is countered by North Korean submarines and its preponderant strength in landing craft. South Korea is outnumbered in the air, but many of the North Korean planes are outmoded. The United States has recently agreed to help upgrade the South Korean air force by delivering a fleet of F-16 fighters to it.

Critical to the defense of South Korea is the presence there of about 40,000 U.S. combat and support units plus about 100 U.S. planes. South Korea relies heavily on the "trip-wire effect" of having U.S. troops stationed along the armistice line, so that an attack by the North would immediately involve the United States. The announcement in 1977 by the Carter administration that U.S. troops would be with-

Table 5.15. Military Strength of South and North Korea, 1982 – 1983

|  | South Korea | North Korea |
|---|---|---|
| *Armies* | | |
| Personnel | 520,000 | 700,000 |
| Major units | | |
| Infantry divisions | 20 | 35 |
| Motorized infantry divisions | 1 | 3 |
| Main battle tanks | 1,000 | 2,675 |
| Armored personnel carriers | 850 | 1,000 |
| Guns/howitzers | 2,104 | 4,100 |
| SSM missiles | 12 | 54 |
| SAM missiles | 180 | ? |
| *Navies* | | |
| Personnel (including marines) | 49,000 | 33,000 |
| Major vessels | | |
| Submarines | 0 | 19 |
| Destroyers and escort ships | 20 | 4 |
| Missile patrol boats | 11 | 18 |
| Amphibious warfare craft | 28 | 99 |
| *Air Forces* | | |
| Bombers | 0 | 70 |
| Fighters and fighter-bombers | 434 | 622 |
| Helicopters | 36 | 40 |
| Transports | 48 | 230 |

Sources: *Defense of Japan*, 1983, pp. 253 – 254; William L. Scully, *The Korean Peninsula Military Balance*, Heritage Foundation, July 11, 1983.

drawn over a period of four or five years understandably sent a shock through South Korea, but a subsequent upward reevaluation of North Korean strength by U.S. intelligence agencies, as well as strong congressional resistance, led to an abandonment of this plan. The Reagan administration, when it came into office, quickly affirmed its intention to continue the policy of support contained in the Mutual Security Treaty of 1954.

The Japanese Defense Agency summed up the present situation in the following terms:

> The Republic of Korea's efforts to build up its defense capabilities as well as the U.S. commitment to the defense of the South seem to be greatly contributing to successful deterrence against an outbreak of armed conflicts, minimizing the possibility of a full-scale clash for the moment. But in view of a massive military buildup in the North, the situation in the Peninsula warrants no optimism.[26]

Up to 1971, South Korea relied primarily on the United States for its defense. The withdrawal of the U.S. Seventh Division in that year led to a rapid expansion of its own defense industry through subsidies and tax advantages. A special defense tax was imposed in 1975 to finance an armed forces improvement plan; by 1981, this provided almost 16 percent of the total revenue of the national government. A second plan of military modernization was adopted in 1982 to cover the period 1982–1986.

A more detailed picture of how South Korea has financed its remarkable defense buildup is presented in Table 5.16. Prior to 1970, U.S. assistance in one form or another was very significant. Counterpart funds, which were phased out after 1970, consisted of local currency payments for P.L. 480 grain shipped by the United States to South Korea; the government could spend this money in agreement with the U.S. All military aid from the United States ended a few years later. By 1976, South Korea was financing almost all its military expenditures internally.[27]

The manner in which defense funds were used is shown in Table 5.17. There are some interesting differences between the pattern of South Korean expenditures and those of Japan, as shown in Table 5.12. Personnel costs took a higher proportion of the South Korean military budget at the beginning of the 1970s, but fell sharply thereafter. Japanese personnel expenditures started low, rose, and then fell again. The South Korean pattern does not appear to be related, as the Japanese was, to civilian labor costs, since they were rising rapidly throughout the period. Real wages in manufacturing increased by 224 percent between 1970 and 1980. The answer may lie in the swift rise of equipment expenditures as U.S. assistance was phased out, as well as in the fact that South Korea has a military draft, whereas the Japanese SDF must compete in the civilian labor market for voluntary recruits. Neither country invested much in research and development, however. South Korea, like Japan, has relied heavily on the United States for advanced equipment, although its own industry is now capable of producing such sophisticated weapons as F-5 fighter aircraft.

## THE PROSPECTS FOR FUTURE ECONOMIC GROWTH

### Japan

Though the Nakasone government has been exploring various means of circumventing the one percent GNP limit on defense expenditures, unless there is a change in the 1976 Diet resolution or a political agreement to vitiate it, the expected rate of economic growth becomes a critical constraint in assessing the outlook for defense. The Japanese argue that this formula resulted in an average annual increase in defense spending of 7 percent during the 1970s, while U.S. defense spending remained flat and that of NATO rose by only 3 percent a year. They point out that the Japanese defense budget is the eighth largest in the world; that compared with the 15 NATO allies of the United States, Japan is fourth in naval tonnage, fifth in submarines, and sixth in combat aircraft; and that its ground forces are about the size

Table 5.16. South Korea: Financing of Defense Expenditures, 1966–1982

| Year | Counterpart funds as a share of defense expenditures (%) | Ratio of U.S. aid to total defense expenditures (%) | Ratio of military loans from U.S. to total defense expenditures (%) | Ratio of defense tax revenues to total defense expenditures (%) | Proportion of defense expenditures provided internally (%) | Defense expenditures as a percentage of GNP | Defense expenditures plus U.S. aid funds spent on defense as a percentage of GNP |
|---|---|---|---|---|---|---|---|
| 1966 | 63.7 | 119.7 | — | — | 16.4 | 3.9 | 8.6 |
| 1967 | 49.1 | 103.2 | — | — | 24.8 | 3.9 | 7.9 |
| 1968 | 29.7 | 128.4 | — | — | 30.6 | 3.6 | 8.9 |
| 1969 | 18.4 | 56.2 | — | — | 52.2 | 3.9 | 6.1 |
| 1970 | 12.5 | 52.0 | — | — | 57.6 | 3.8 | 5.8 |
| 1971 | 5.7 | 92.4 | 4.0 | — | 50.0 | 4.1 | 8.0 |
| 1972 | 0.8 | 49.3 | 3.8 | — | 67.3 | 4.3 | 6.6 |
| 1973 | — | 35.8 | 5.2 | — | 74.3 | 3.5 | 4.9 |
| 1974 | — | 14.3 | 4.5 | — | 87.9 | 4.1 | 4.8 |
| 1975 | — | 9.4 | 6.3 | 14.1 | 91.7 | 4.5 | 5.1 |
| 1976 | — | 4.4 | 10.1 | 38.2 | 96.1 | 5.3 | 5.9 |
| 1977 | — | 0.3 | 8.3 | 36.0 | 99.8 | 5.6 | 5.9 |
| 1978 | — | 0.1 | 15.3 | 36.7 | 99.9 | 5.6 | 6.3 |
| 1979 | — | — | 9.1 | 41.4 | 100.0 | 5.2 | 5.5 |
| 1980 | — | — | n.a. | 37.9 | 100.0 | 6.6 | n.a. |
| 1981[a] | — | — | n.a. | 38.1 | 100.0 | 6.0 | n.a. |
| 1982[a] | — | — | — | 42.6 | 100.0 | 5.8 | n.a. |

*Source:* Korean Development Institute, *The National Budget and Policy Objectives*, 1982, p. 161 (in Korean).

[a]Planned.

Table 5.17. South Korea: Allocation of Defense Expenditures, by Use, 1970 – 1980
(Percent of Total)

| Year | Wages, salaries payments in kind | System maintenance | Maintenance of equipment | Research and development | Purchase of military equipment[a] |
|---|---|---|---|---|---|
| 1970 | 67.5 | 21.9 | 0.6 | –    | 10.1 |
| 1971 | 60.7 | 27.2 | 1.1  | 0.2  | 10.7 |
| 1972 | 55.9 | 17.4 | 14.6 | 1.1  | 11.0 |
| 1973 | 58.9 | 14.5 | 18.4 | 1.1  | 7.1  |
| 1974 | 48.6 | 9.7  | 31.8 | 2.8  | 7.2  |
| 1975 | 47.2 | 10.0 | 21.9 | 2.9  | 18.0 |
| 1976 | 42.5 | 8.5  | 15.8 | 5.1  | 28.1 |
| 1977 | 41.4 | 9.3  | 15.4 | 3.8  | 30.0 |
| 1978 | 37.5 | 9.0  | 17.1 | 2.4  | 34.0 |
| 1979 | 38.8 | 12.7 | 16.9 | 3.1  | 28.6 |
| 1980 | 35.1 | 13.1 | 21.2 | 3.1  | 28.5 |

*Source:* Korean Development Institute, *The National Budget and Policy Objectives,* 1982, pp. 168 – 169 (in Korean).
[a]Includes redemption of loans from the United States.
[b]Planned.

of Britain's.[28] What this fails to point out is that the three largest NATO allies of the United States, Germany, France, and Britain, are considerably smaller than Japan in population and national product, and that Italy, the only other NATO country of substantial size, and with a much lower per capita income, spends almost as much as Japan for defense. Still, if it were true that Japan's future economic growth were to be considerably higher than that of the NATO countries in the years to come, the one percent formula would allow Japan to catch up with the others.

There are a number of projections of Japanese growth for the current decade; they appear in Table 5.18. The most optimistic is the forecast by the Economic Council, and has been adopted by the government for policy guideline purposes. In any event, the differences among the forecasts are not great.

The Nomura forecast emphasized several factors that are expected to be more favorable during the next five years than in the recent past. Private demand, benefiting from stable prices, is expected to be greater. The rate of saving may fall, but leisure time expenditures may increase as the five-day week spreads and longer summer vacations become common. Investment in housing may rise to make up for past deficits. Investment in plant and equipment in the electronics and biotechnical industries is expected to be particularly high. Possible negative factors cited, all exogenous, are the possibility of an oil price rise, of a dampening of the U.S. economy, and of outside pressures on the Japanese government to follow a more stimulative policy, which might entail inflation.

The structural components of the GNP on which the forecasts are based are

Table 5.18. Protections of Japanese Economic Growth

| Source | GNP growth per annum (%) |
|---|---|
| Economic Council (governmental), FY 1983 – 1990 | 4.0 |
| Nomura Research Institute (private) | |
|   FY 1983 – 1988 | 3.7 |
|   FY 1989 – 1992 | 4.0 |
| Asahi Life Insurance Co. FY 1983 – 1987 | 3.8 |
| Research Institute of the National Economy, private | |
|   FY 1982 – 1987 | 3.6 |
|   FY 1987 – 1992 | 3.7 |

Sources: *Japan Economic Journal*, August 16, 1983; Press summaries, U.S. Embassy, Tokyo.

shown in Table 5.19. All the data are consistent with the notion that Japan is headed for a slower rate of growth than it has enjoyed in the past.

Reduction of the budget deficit and retirement of the deficit-financing bonds that have been issued since 1975 are priority objectives of the Japanese government. What may be in store during the next few years is exemplified by the fiscal year 1984 budget process. The budget increase of 0.5 percent is the smallest since 1955. Income taxes were reduced and the loss of revenue compensated for by raising commodity and corporate taxes. Even with this austere budget, it will be necessary to borrow a quarter of the total. The only item to escape the axe was defense expenditures, which were to increase by 4.8 percent after adjustment for projected inflation. Even these figures represent one of the smallest defense cost increases of the last two decades.[29]

Table 5.19. Structural Components of Japanese Economic Forecasts
(Average Annual Percent Increase)

| | 1975 – 1982 (actual) | 1983 – 1987 (Nomura) | 1988 – 1992 (Nomura) | 1983 – 1987 (Asahi) |
|---|---|---|---|---|
| GNP | 4.6 | 3.7 | 4.0 | 3.8 |
| Private consumption | 3.5 | 3.9 | 4.3 | 3.9 |
| Housing | −0.2 | 3.4 | 2.0 | 2.8 |
| Plant/equipment investment | 5.3 | 4.6 | 5.0 | 4.6 |
| Public consumption | 4.0 | 2.3 | 2.4 | 1.7 |
| Public investment | 4.1 | 0.5 | 1.7 | 1.9 |
| Exports | 9.8 | 3.7 | 4.0 | 5.2 |
| Imports | 4.6 | 3.9 | 4.1 | 4.1 |
| Consumer prices | 5.5 | 3.0 | 3.5 | 3.4 |
| Unemployment (rate) | 2.5 | 2.9 | 3.2 | 2.6 |
| | (1982) | (1987) | (1992) | (1987) |

Sources: Press summaries, U.S. Embassy, Tokyo.

These figures suggest that if the government is to maintain the level of defense expenditures, let alone raise it, there is no alternative to raising taxes. A defense surtax à la South Korea would be the most straightforward solution, but that has not even been suggested. Cutting other budget items does not seem feasible. The proportion that now goes for social welfare will be under increasing pressure because of the country's aging population and the maturation of the pension system. While Japan has spent 13 percent of its GNP on public infrastructure over the past decade, economic growth and urban overcrowding will require still more. As the OECD put it:

> Containing the growth of public spending and limiting subsidies is clearly an essential element in any medium-term strategy to restore a more balanced fiscal position. But relying *entirely* on expenditure cuts may not be desirable from the resource allocation point of view. Important public expenditure cuts would risk reducing necessary investment in social infrastructure. Furthermore, social transfers are certain to rise considerably because of demographic factors and past decisions. If benefits had to be reduced welfare standards could be jeopardized. These conflicting policy aims, both in the short and medium term, may be hard to resolve without increasing taxes.[30]

With respect to the manpower outlook, Japan has had some difficulty mobilizing the 180,000 military personnel currently authorized. As of March 31, 1983, total military strength was 156,000. From 16 to 18 thousand fixed-term people resign or retire annually from the SDF, plus 4 to 6 thousand who are not on fixed terms, which means an annual recruitment of 20,000 or more. The eligible age population (18 to 25 years) has been declining, and applicants are also harder to find because of the spread of higher education and the desire of young people to enter Japan's system of "permanent employment." The low social status accorded to military occupations is another negative factor.

Those who retire young have difficulty finding favorable civilian employment because large firms recruit only directly from schools. The Defense Agency provides vocational training for its personnel and maintains employment offices, but it concedes that the post-military employment situation remains an obstacle to recruitment.[31] The low level of unemployment also militates against meeting manpower targets. The rate of unemployment has not exceeded 2.4 percent since 1970. This may be somewhat misleading in the sense that many large firms carry surplus workers on their payrolls; it does mean that relatively few people must turn to the military as an alternative to unemployment.

The military have also been very selective in their recruitment policy, perhaps exceedingly so. In FY 1982, out of 40,000 applicants for positions as army privates, apprentice seamen, and air trainees, only 16,000 were accepted. The ratio for officers accepted was much lower, varying from one in nine to one in twenty-three.[32]

The basic manpower situation for the rest of the 1980s is not unambiguously favorable to ease of recruitment. As the data in Table 5.20 indicate, there will be a substantial increase in the younger age group from which 80 percent of the lowest

Table 5.20. Japan: Population Change Estimates, 1980 – 1990 (Percent Annual Increase)

|  | 1970 – 1980 | 1980 – 1990 |
|---|---|---|
| Total population | 1.1 | 0.5 |
| Age 15 – 64, of which | 1.0 | 0.9 |
| 15 – 19 | – 0.1 | 2.0 |
| 20 – 54 | 1.1 | 0.2 |
| 55 – 64 | 2.2 | 3.6 |
| 65 + | 3.7 | 3.1 |

Source: OECD Economic Surveys, Japan, July, 1983, p. 41.

grades were recruited in 1982. On the other hand, civilian employment opportunities may provide stiffer competition. The female labor force participation rate in 1982 was higher than in any Western country except the United States, so additions to this source of labor will probably not be very large. The population of prime working age, 20 to 54 years, will scarcely increase, so that young entrants to the labor force will be at a premium. Another drain on labor supply will probably come from a reduction in working hours. Most Japanese still work more than a five-day week and take short vacations. Annual hours worked in Japanese manufacturing in 1981 exceeded those in the United States by 8.2 percent, and in Germany by 11.1 percent.[33]

None of this is to suggest that there are insurmountable economic or manpower barriers to the maintenance of armed forces of 180,000 out of a population of 120 million. Germany has twice that number with half the population, France has 315,000 with 54 million people. The U.S. Army is more than four times as great as that of Japan with a population less than double the Japanese. If Japan were to double the size of its armed forces, it would still be well below the NATO countries in terms of the net loss of civilian working time. It is true that most NATO countries rely on conscription, and might be hard put to meet their military quotas if they did not. But the United States, like Japan, has a volunteer army. The manpower constraints on Japan are clearly political, not economic.

## South Korea

The revised fifth five-year plan forecasts a 7.5 percent annual rate of GNP growth for South Korea during the period 1984 – 1988 inclusive. The original plan was for 1982 – 1986, but the projected growth was raised because the economy performed above expectations in 1983. Some of the key plan indicators, as well as actual data for 1981 – 1983, are shown in Table 5.21.

The plan is optimistic in predicting a buoyant and well-ordered economy. Inflation is to fall to very low levels and will, together with improvements in productiv-

Table 5.21. South Korea: Key Indicators of Economic Performance During 1981 – 1983 and Estimates of the Fifth Five-Year Plan, 1984 – 1988

|  | Actual 1981 – 1983 | Planned 1984 – 1988 |
|---|---|---|
| GNP, average annual growth (percent) | 7.0 | 7.5 |
| Employment, average annual growth (percent) | 2.2 | 2.9 |
| GNP deflator, average annual increase (percent) | 8.5 | 1.8 |
| Merchandise exports, average annual increase (percent) | 10.5 | 14.3 |
| Investment, percent of GNP | 27.6 | 29.3 |
| Savings, percent of GNP | 22.8 | 28.6 |

*Source: Business Korea,* February, 1984, p. 25.

ity, result in a substantial increase in exports. This, it is hoped, will lead to a surplus in the foreign trade balance, since imports are to be reduced by the substitution of domestically produced machinery and chemical products.

Investment is planned to continue at about the previous level. The forecast of a drop in the incremental capital/output ratio, which usually rises in the course of economic development, is based upon the expectation that South Korea will move away from heavy industry, which was overexpanded because of erroneous estimates of foreign demand for products of such industry, toward less capital-intensive sectors.

The fifth plan is also optimistic about government revenues, relying in part on a restructuring of the tax system from one with high tax rates and generous exemptions to lower rates and tighter deduction schedules. Past surpluses in the current account balance of the central government are projected to rise, and a cutback in government capital transfers and loans to the private sector would reduce the deficit in the capital account balance. Expenditures for social welfare will rise only modestly.

The manpower situation during the plan period is favorable to the maintenance of the armed forces at their present level. Population growth slowed from 2.2 percent in 1970 to 1.6 percent in 1980, but employment is expected to grow by 2.9 percent during the plan period. The labor force participation rate is still relatively low (about 40 percent), particularly for women, and should be rising. The one negative factor is the projected decline in the population share of the 15- to 24-year-age groups from which military manpower is drawn, from 23 percent in 1982 to 21.3 percent in 1988. However, the absolute number in this pool will increase slightly, from 4.589 million in 1982 to 4.599 million in 1988.[34]

The opportunity cost of mobilizing a larger military force was reduced, in the past, by the existence of unemployment and employment in low productivity jobs. The labor market may be tighter in the years ahead if manufacturing expands in a more labor-intensive direction, and also because service employment is likely to rise, although not as rapidly as in manufacturing. However, the recruitment problem that faces Japan is not likely to constitute an obstacle in South Korea. Conscripting military manpower may be more expensive economically, but there is no indication that the government is not prepared to pay the price.

## An Estimate of Future Defense Costs

At least two basic types of cost can be identified; these are referred to as the static and dynamic costs. Following a discussion of the nature of each of these, estimates of both for Japan and South Korea will be provided, and the implications of these estimates considered.

In any given year, military spending reduces the resources available to a country's economy for private consumption and saving. The amount of this reduction can be considered to be the static cost of current defense spending. For the purposes of this analysis, military wages and salaries will be included in these static costs, in recognition of the diversion of manpower resources away from use in the private sector. It should be noted that published statements of defense spending may not always accord with the relevant economic definition of static costs, for in a country that relies on military conscription, wages paid to those in the armed forces will not necessarily reflect the full opportunity cost of that labor.

Part of the static cost of defense spending will fall on private saving. In consequence, the total resources available to the private sector in future years may be reduced due to a reduction in private capital accumulation. This can in turn lower both the level and the rate of growth of total private income.[35] These effects can logically be called the dynamic costs of current defense spending.

Both of these types of cost are frequently considered in public discussion of the defense burden, and their magnitudes are key variables in many debates over the appropriate level of defense spending. In attempting to estimate the relevant magnitudes, relatively simple approaches are adopted, intended to produce reliable although rough estimates of the costs involved. The measurement of static costs will simply be based on published estimates of defense spending undertaken by the governments of Japan and South Korea, with an adjustment for South Korea intended to capture at least approximately the effect of the underestimate of the social cost of their conscripted military labor.

Estimating dynamic costs is more complicated. The first step is to estimate the reduction in private savings in each year that is attributable to military spending; this can be done by multiplying the military budget by the private sector's estimated marginal propensity to save.[36] Together with an estimate of the rate of depreciation of the capital stock, this allows calculation of the hypothetical size of a country's capital stock in each year in the absence of defense spending. The problem then is to determine what total private income would have been with this hypothetically larger capital stock, and thus the loss in income that resulted from military spending.[37]

An approach sometimes used to estimate the output foregone from a hypothetical reduction in the capital stock has been to multiply the lost investment by the multiplicative inverse of a country's incremental capital-output ratio. Yet because capital accumulation is not the only source of economic growth, this procedure will tend to overestimate the gain in private income that could be obtained by diverting military spending to the use of the private sector.[38] The gain in income due to an increment of capital should instead be measured by the marginal productivity of capital. Our formulation of the decline in income resulting from decreased capital accumulation due to military spending is therefore:

$$\Delta Y_t = r (K_t^* - K_t), \qquad (1)$$

where

$\Delta Y_t$ = change in current income,
$r$ = real rate of return on capital,
$K_t$ = actual current capital stock, and
$K_t^*$ = hypothetical current capital stock.

As described above, (2)

$$K_t^* = K_t + \sum_{i=0}^{t} (1-d)^{t-i} \Delta I_i$$

where

$\Delta I^i$ reduction in investment attributable to military spending, i.e., the military budget in year $i$ multiplied by the private marginal propensity to save, and

$d$ = annual rate of depreciation of capital stock.

Consider first the case of South Korea, which is somewhat more complicated than that of Japan. In devising the estimates of the defense burden, only those defense expenditures actually financed by that country will be considered, thus excluding funds for military expenditures provided by aid from abroad. As Table 5.22 shows, the gap between internally financed and total military spending declined sharply in South Korea after the mid-1960s, and by the mid-1970s virtually all defense spending was financed domestically. As noted above, calculation of the static cost of defense spending for South Korea requires an adjustment to domestically financed expenditures because of the use of conscription by the armed forces. Evidence from the period after 1969 indicates that conscripts have been paid roughly 60 percent of the average industrial wage in South Korea.[39] Accordingly expenditures on military wages and salaries have been adjusted upward to make some allowance for the higher social opportunity cost of military labor.[40] The adjusted estimates of the total static costs of defense spending during 1965–1982 are given in Column 3 of Table 5.22. The figures for the late 1970s and early 1980s are large, ranging from 6 to nearly 8 percent of GNP annually.[41]

Some additional perspective on these estimates of static costs can be gained from Table 5.23, which compares them to some other types of expenditure. These show

Table 5.22. Defense Spending by South Korea, 1965 – 1982

| Year | Total defense spending as % of GNP[a] | Internally financed defense expenditures as % of GNP[a] | Total national cost of defense spending as % of GNP[b] |
|---|---|---|---|
| 1965 | 3.7 | 0.7 | 2.2 |
| 1966 | 3.9 | 0.6 | 2.2 |
| 1967 | 3.9 | 1.0 | 2.4 |
| 1968 | 3.6 | 1.1 | 2.4 |
| 1969 | 3.9 | 2.0 | 3.3 |
| 1970 | 3.8 | 2.2 | 3.5 |
| 1971 | 4.1 | 2.1 | 3.3 |
| 1972 | 4.3 | 2.9 | 4.1 |
| 1973 | 3.5 | 2.6 | 3.6 |
| 1974 | 4.1 | 3.6 | 4.6 |
| 1975 | 4.5 | 4.1 | 5.2 |
| 1976 | 5.3 | 5.1 | 6.2 |
| 1977 | 5.6 | 5.6 | 6.8 |
| 1978 | 5.6 | 5.6 | 6.6 |
| 1979 | 5.2 | 5.2 | 6.2 |
| 1980 | 6.6 | 6.6 | 7.8 |
| 1981 | 6.0 | 6.0 | 7.1 |
| 1982 | 5.8 | 5.8 | 6.8 |

[a]Data in columns 1 and 2 from "National Defense and the National Defense Budget," in Korean Development Institute, *The National Budget and Policy Objectives*, Seoul, 1982, Table 5-5, p. 161.
[b]Data in column 3 derived from column 2; see text for procedure.

that in recent years, the static cost of defense has been of a size equivalent to as much as 11 percent of total private consumption in South Korea. They further reveal that throughout the period 1969 – 1977, South Korean taxpayers financed annual defense expenditures greater in size than total expenditures on private medical care; during 1976 – 1977 annual defense expenditures were nearly two and a half times the size of medical expenditures. Similarly, during the 1960s and 1970s, the defense burden was consistently greater than total private outlays for residential construction.

During the period 1965 – 1982, aggregate saving in the South Korean economy ranged from a low of 8.6 percent to a high of 20.1 percent of GNP annually. Two measures of dynamic cost have been calculated, intended to provide lower- and upper-bound estimates. For the low case, a marginal propensity to save of 15 percent is used, and a real rate of return to capital of 10 percent; for the high case, the marginal propensity to save is set equal to 25 percent, and the return on capital at 15 percent. In both cases it is assumed that the real annual rate of depreciation of capital is 10 percent. Then by the procedure described earlier, the estimates of Table 5.24 are derived. They show the annual reduction in South Korea's GNP attributable to past defense spending.

Table 5.23. Static Cost of South Korean Defense Spending as Percentage of Selected Private Outlays, 1965 – 1977

| | Defense spending as % of | | |
|---|---|---|---|
| Year | Private consumption | Private medical care | Residential building |
| 1965 | 2.6 | 95.0 | 127.0 |
| 1966 | 2.8 | 94.1 | 105.7 |
| 1967 | 3.0 | 93.7 | 114.3 |
| 1968 | 3.6 | 87.3 | 80.1 |
| 1969 | 4.5 | 131.1 | 122.9 |
| 1970 | 4.8 | 154.5 | 103.3 |
| 1971 | 4.5 | 144.5 | 102.1 |
| 1972 | 5.6 | 155.3 | 150.2 |
| 1973 | 5.5 | 141.1 | 110.3 |
| 1974 | 6.8 | 160.1 | 103.7 |
| 1975 | 7.6 | 189.3 | 116.1 |
| 1976 | 9.4 | 242.9 | 183.2 |
| 1977 | 11.1 | 243.6 | 159.8 |

*Source:* Derived from Table 5.1, Column 3; and United Nations, *Yearbook of National Accounts Statistics,* Vol. 1, Individual Country Data, various years.

Table 5.24. Dynamic Cost of South Korean Defense Spending, 1965 – 1982

| Year | Low case (% of GNP) | High case (% of GNP) |
|---|---|---|
| 1965 | 0.02 | 0.04 |
| 1966 | 0.04 | 0.11 |
| 1967 | 0.07 | 0.17 |
| 1968 | 0.09 | 0.22 |
| 1969 | 0.11 | 0.28 |
| 1970 | 0.14 | 0.35 |
| 1971 | 0.16 | 0.40 |
| 1972 | 0.21 | 0.53 |
| 1973 | 0.21 | 0.53 |
| 1974 | 0.24 | 0.60 |
| 1975 | 0.27 | 0.67 |
| 1976 | 0.30 | 0.74 |
| 1977 | 0.33 | 0.84 |
| 1978 | 0.36 | 0.89 |
| 1979 | 0.39 | 0.97 |
| 1980 | 0.48 | 1.19 |
| 1981 | 0.50 | 1.24 |
| 1982 | 0.52 | 1.29 |

*Source:* See p. 182 for the specification of the model used for these estimates.

Table 5.25. Projections of Dynamic Cost of Defense Spending for South Korea, 1983 – 1994

| Year | Defense spending annually 5% of GNP | | Defense spending annually 8 % of GNP | |
|---|---|---|---|---|
| | Low (% of GNP) | High (% of GNP) | Low (% of GNP) | High (% of GNP) |
| 1983 | 0.49 | 1.13 | 0.53 | 1.33 |
| 1984 | 0.48 | 1.12 | 0.55 | 1.34 |
| 1985 | 0.45 | 1.12 | 0.57 | 1.43 |
| 1986 | 0.45 | 1.13 | 0.59 | 1.46 |
| 1987 | 0.45 | 1.13 | 0.60 | 1.50 |
| 1988 | 0.45 | 1.12 | 0.61 | 1.52 |
| 1989 | 0.44 | 1.10 | 0.62 | 1.54 |
| 1990 | 0.44 | 1.09 | 0.62 | 1.56 |
| 1991 | 0.43 | 1.08 | 0.63 | 1.57 |
| 1992 | 0.43 | 1.07 | 0.63 | 1.59 |
| 1993 | 0.43 | 1.07 | 0.64 | 1.60 |
| 1994 | 0.42 | 1.06 | 0.64 | 1.61 |

*Source:* See p. 182 for the specification of the model used for these estimates.

*Note:* These calculations were done assuming an annual rate of growth of GNP of 7.6 percent after 1983.

What these figures suggest is that the dynamic costs of military spending have been low; the effect of military spending on the growth of South Korean output is relatively small. Even under the extreme assumptions of the high case, which probably significantly overstates the true effect, the largest estimated impact of military spending was to lower GNP in 1982 by 1.3 percent. Projections of these dynamic costs for the next decade are shown in Table 5.25.[42] Again, low and high estimates are calculated with the same assumptions used above; furthermore, an annual rate of growth of GNP of 7.6 percent is assumed. Two possible rates of military spending are used; in one case, defense expenditures are assumed to be 5 percent of GNP annually, in the other, 8 percent. The basic import of the resultant estimates obtained does not appear to change; even under relatively extreme pessimistic assumptions, the maximum estimated dynamic cost of defense spending would be to reduce South Korea's GNP by about 1.6 percent in 1990.

Turning to Japan, the much lower share of GNP accounted for by military spending clearly makes the defense burden much smaller. Table 5.26 shows that the static costs of Japanese military spending are low, since during the 1970s, total defense spending was equivalent to only 1.5 percent of annual aggregate private consumption. Defense expenditures were consistently less than 20 percent of total private expenditures on medical care, and less than 13 percent of expenditures on residential construction.

Table 5.26. Static Cost of Japanese Defense Spending as Percentage
of Selected Private Outlays, 1965 – 1982

| Year | Japanese defense spending as % of GNP[a] | Defense spending as percent of [b] | | |
| --- | --- | --- | --- | --- |
| | | Private consumption | Private medical care | Residential building |
| 1965 | 0.9 | – | – | – |
| 1966 | 0.9 | – | – | – |
| 1967 | 0.8 | – | – | – |
| 1968 | 0.8 | – | – | – |
| 1969 | 0.8 | – | – | – |
| 1970 | 0.8 | 1.5 | 18.8 | 11.0 |
| 1971 | 0.9 | 1.5 | 19.6 | 12.5 |
| 1972 | 0.9 | 1.5 | 19.0 | 10.9 |
| 1973 | 0.9 | 1.5 | 19.2 | 9.1 |
| 1974 | 0.9 | 1.6 | 18.9 | 10.6 |
| 1975 | 0.9 | 1.5 | 17.1 | 11.4 |
| 1976 | 0.9 | 1.5 | 16.6 | 10.9 |
| 1977 | 0.9 | 1.5 | 16.3 | 11.5 |
| 1978 | 0.9 | 1.5 | 15.5 | 11.7 |
| 1979 | 0.9 | 1.5 | 15.3 | 11.7 |
| 1980 | 1.0 | – | – | – |
| 1981 | 1.0 | – | – | – |
| 1982 | 1.0 | – | – | – |

[a]Data from Bank of Japan, *Economic Statistics Annual*, 1983. Data are rounded to the nearest one-tenth of one percent.
[b]Data from OECD, *National Accounts of OECD Countries, 1962 – 1979*, Vol. II, 1981.

Estimates of the dynamic costs of Japanese military spending during 1965 – 1982 are presented in Table 5.27. Aggregate annual saving in Japan during this period ranged from 17 to 27 percent of GNP. Again, lower-and upper-bound estimates of dynamic costs are computed, using a marginal propensity to save of 20 percent and a real rate of return on capital of 10 percent for the first, and a savings rate of 30 percent and an interest rate of 15 percent for the second. A 10 percent rate of depreciation of capital is assumed. The estimates of Table 5.27 suggest that the impact of military spending on Japanese economic growth has been very small, since in no year through 1982 do even the upper-bound estimates yield a decline of more than one-quarter of one percent of GNP attributable to the reduction of private saving due to military spending.

Projections for the coming decade do not suggest a change in this result. Table 5.28 shows projections of the dynamic costs of Japanese defense spending under two hypothetical regimes.[43] For both, GNP is assumed to grow at a rate of 4 percent per year. In one, defense spending remains constant at its current level of 1 percent of GNP annually. The estimates show that even for the upper-bound case, the loss

Table 5.27. Dynamic Cost of Japanese Defense Spending, 1965 – 1982

| Year | Low case (% of GNP) | High case (% of GNP) |
|---|---|---|
| 1965 | .02 | .05 |
| 1966 | .04 | .08 |
| 1967 | .05 | .10 |
| 1968 | .05 | .11 |
| 1969 | .06 | .13 |
| 1970 | .06 | .14 |
| 1971 | .07 | .15 |
| 1972 | .07 | .15 |
| 1973 | .07 | .16 |
| 1974 | .08 | .18 |
| 1975 | .09 | .20 |
| 1976 | .09 | .20 |
| 1977 | .09 | .20 |
| 1978 | .09 | .20 |
| 1979 | .09 | .21 |
| 1980 | .10 | .22 |
| 1981 | .10 | .23 |
| 1982 | .11 | .24 |

*Source:* See p. 182 for the specification of the model used for these estimates.


Table 5.28. Projections of Dynamic Cost of Defense Spending for Japan, 1983 – 1994

| | Defense spending annually 1% of GNP | | Defense spending annually 2% of GNP | |
|---|---|---|---|---|
| | Low (% of GNP) | High (% of GNP) | Low (% of GNP) | High (% of GNP) |
| 1983 | 0.11 | 0.25 | 0.13 | 0.29 |
| 1984 | 0.11 | 0.26 | 0.15 | 0.33 |
| 1985 | 0.12 | 0.26 | 0.16 | 0.37 |
| 1986 | 0.12 | 0.27 | 0.17 | 0.40 |
| 1987 | 0.12 | 0.27 | 0.19 | 0.43 |
| 1988 | 0.12 | 0.28 | 0.20 | 0.45 |
| 1989 | 0.12 | 0.28 | 0.21 | 0.47 |
| 1990 | 0.13 | 0.28 | 0.22 | 0.49 |
| 1991 | 0.13 | 0.28 | 0.22 | 0.50 |
| 1992 | 0.13 | 0.29 | 0.23 | 0.52 |
| 1993 | 0.13 | 0.29 | 0.24 | 0.53 |
| 1994 | 0.13 | 0.29 | 0.24 | 0.54 |

*Source:* See p. 182 for the specification of the model used for these estimates.

*Note:* These calculations were done assuming an annual rate of growth of GNP of 4% after 1983.

in GNP would be only one-quarter of one percent in each year through 1990. In a second case, defense spending is assumed to double, rising to a level of 2 percent of GNP annually from 1983. Even in this case, the impact on economic growth appears relatively small, as the upper-bound case never indicates an annual reduction of as much as one-half of one percent in GNP through 1990.

The conclusions of this exercise in assessing the economic burden of defense spending can be stated quite simply. For South Korea, the estimates suggest that military expenditures impose a major burden on current private consumption. The cost of defense to the rate of growth of total output over time is rather small by contrast. For Japan, both the static and the dynamic costs of its limited defense spending appear minor.

It should be stressed once more that these conclusions are based on approximate calculations derived from particular theoretical formulations. Yet the theoretical approaches appear reasonable, and the conclusions appear robust to a wide range of empirical calculations. Nor are the conclusions very surprising for either country. Certainly the low level of military spending in Japan could not be expected to impose a great burden on the economy. Perhaps the most significant result obtained is that the cost of military spending in South Korea is borne primarily by current consumers. Yet this is also probably not surprising, in view of the fact that the political situation that forces the high level of South Korean defense spending cannot reasonably be expected to improve dramatically in the foreseeable future.

## THE PROSPECTS FOR FUTURE MILITARY EXPENDITURES

### Japan

The Japanese Defense Agency formulated in 1982 a Medium-Term Defense Program Estimate (the Japanese nomenclature is 56 Chugyo) for the fiscal years 1983 – 1987. It is to serve as a guideline for annual defense appropriation requests, subject to annual revision as well as a three-year review. No increase in the current manpower authorization is planned, although the recruitment system is to be strengthened.

The cost of the *major projects* envisioned by the program for the fiscal years 1983 – 1987 was estimated at between 4,400 and 4,600 billion yen at 1982 prices. Total defense-related expenditures for the period were estimated at between 15,600 and 16,400 billion yen.[44]

Japan's GNP for 1982 was 263,939 billion yen, while defense expenditures were 2,586 billion yen. On the assumption that GNP grows at 4 percent per annum from 1983 to 1987, and that defense expenditures are held to the limit of one percent of GNP, the projected defense costs for the period are as follows (billions of yen):

| | |
|---|---|
| FY 1983 | 2,745.0 |
| FY 1984 | 2,854.8 |
| FY 1985 | 2,969.0 |
| FY 1986 | 3,087.7 |
| FY 1987 | 3,211.1 |
| TOTAL | 14,867.7 |

The total for the five years is 5 percent less than the lower of the Medium-Term Estimate figures, and 10 percent less than the higher figure. The Defense Agency undoubtedly made the same calculation, but noted that "the gross national product changes with economic conditions. Therefore, both defense-related expenditures and the GNP have uncertain factors and are fluid."[45]

There is a much more difficult question: What would it cost Japan to establish the military capacity to fulfill its self-proclaimed goal of protecting itself against invasion and "having the ability to provide protection of sea lines of communication in sea waters extending to about 1,000 nautical miles or so from its shores?" A program developed by a group of experts that might begin to answer this question is set forth in Table 5.29. The cost estimates are based on U.S. 1982 prices. For example, the first item, which calls for an additional 90 F-15 fighter planes to be supplied over the period, will cost $48 million per plane, plus $1 million to cover aircraft shelter and base expansion costs, plus $1.4 million for pilot training costs.

Table 5.29. Additional Defense Equipment Required to Meet Japan's Defense Goals, 1983 – 1990 (Millions of 1982 Dollars, Fiscal Years)

| Equipment | 1983 | 1984 | 1985 | 1986 | 1987 | 1988 | 1989 | 1990 |
|---|---|---|---|---|---|---|---|---|
| 90 fighter interceptors | 236 | 464 | 500 | 563 | 628 | 653 | 677 | 689 |
| 180 fighters for air defense | 306 | 777 | 1,129 | 1,392 | 1,462 | 1,412 | 1,468 | 1,520 |
| 12 air tankers and 8 early warning planes | 100 | 206 | 280 | 498 | 496 | 604 | 634 | 422 |
| 44 transport planes | – | 37 | 89 | 204 | 295 | 319 | 343 | 343 |
| 45 technical aircraft | 13 | 28 | 41 | 53 | 101 | 128 | 146 | 157 |
| Various naval vessels | 63 | 146 | 260 | 324 | 401 | 491 | 585 | 635 |
| 80 naval aircraft | 135 | 297 | 444 | 618 | 642 | 654 | 815 | 989 |
| Mine layers, mine sweepers, helicopters | 29 | 65 | 118 | 144 | 166 | 208 | 268 | 383 |
| Additional personnel[a] | 76 | 152 | 228 | 304 | 381 | 457 | 533 | 609 |
| Ammunition and small arms[b] | 355 | 605 | 855 | 1,105 | 1,355 | 1,605 | 1,855 | 2,105 |
| Total | 1,313 | 2,777 | 4,044 | 5,205 | 5,927 | 6,531 | 7,324 | 7,852 |

[a]Required to bring strength up to 180,000 authorized.

[b]Required to increase stocks to 60- to 90-day supply level.

Table 5.30. Projected Defense Expenditures for Japan,
Including Additional Buildup, 1982 – 1990

| Fiscal year | GNP, billions 1982 dollars[a] | Defense costs at 1% of GNP, billions 1982 dollars[b] | Additional cost expanded program, billions 1982 dollars | Total defense costs, billions 1982 dollars | Ratio of defense costs to GNP, % |
|---|---|---|---|---|---|
| 1982 | 1,060.0 | 10.60 | – | 10.60 | 1.0 |
| 1983 | 1,102.4 | 11.02 | 1.31 | 12.33 | 1.12 |
| 1984 | 1,146.5 | 11.46 | 2.78 | 14.24 | 1.24 |
| 1985 | 1,192.4 | 11.92 | 4.04 | 15.96 | 1.34 |
| 1986 | 1,240.1 | 12.40 | 5.21 | 17.61 | 1.42 |
| 1987 | 1,289.7 | 12.90 | 5.92 | 18.82 | 1.46 |
| 1988 | 1,341.3 | 13.41 | 6.53 | 19.94 | 1.49 |
| 1989 | 1,395.0 | 13.95 | 7.32 | 21.27 | 1.52 |
| 1990 | 1,450.8 | 14.51 | 7.85 | 22.36 | 1.54 |

*Source:* OECD *Economic Surveys, Japan,* July, 1983, p. 76; Table 23.

[a]1982, actual; 1983-1990, based on 4% annual increase of GNP.

[b]1% of GNP.

The impact of an additional program of this size on Japanese defense expenditures is shown in Table 5.30. Assuming that the GNP will increase at 4 percent per annum, it is clear that the effectuation of this program would require that the one percent of the GNP barrier be breached. By fiscal year 1990, defense costs might be up to 1.54 percent of GNP, and if the NATO definition of defense expenditures were employed, up to around 2 percent.

Whether a program of this order can be realized depends on the political outlook. Japan's governing party, the Liberal Democrats, has been generally pro-defense, although this is not true of all the factions within the party. It was anticipated that the one percent limit would be discarded if the party did well in the December 1983 elections. It suffered a major setback in its representation in the Diet, dropping from 286 to 258 seats and was deprived of its majority. A new government was formed in coalition with a small conservative party, but any new defense initiative was postponed.

The largest opposition party is the Socialist Party, which increased its Diet contingent from 101 to 112 seats. Its 1982 program included the pledge that it would work "to create a peaceful international environment and to reduce and eventually disband the SDF, and for a program of achieving abolition of the Security Treaty (with the United States)." However, a party convention held in February 1984 moved away from this position, which many members believed was an important factor behind its drop in the share of the popular vote from 35.5 percent in 1958 to 19.3 percent in 1983. The new policy, while stating that the armed services were still unconstitutional, conceded that nonetheless, they "exist according to law." The party chairman told the convention that he still believed that the SDF should be disbanded in the future, but that it was important for the party to take a pragmatic stand.[46]

Komeito, the third largest party, has as its long-term goal "abolition of the Japan–U.S. security treaty and the reorganization of the SDF into a national police reserve." However, it pledged that if it were to become a member of a coalition government, it would support continuation of the treaty for the time being, and of the SDF in its present form. The small Democratic Socialist Party is the only opposition group that not only supports the current level of defense, but is even prepared to countenance a buildup. The Communist Party would abrogate the security treaty, and proposes to "conduct [the SDF's] democratic reeducation and to reduce and dissolve it."[47]

There appears to be substantial political support for the status quo in defense, but not for any additional effort. In the meantime, achievement of the 1976 guidelines and subsequent government commitments have not been secured. By 1984, some 40 percent of the weapons purchases were to have been consummated, but only 27 percent had been made. Only four of the eleven or twelve sets of short-range surface-to-air missiles that were to have been installed by 1984 were actually in place. What in fact has happened is that the defense timetable has fallen two or three years behind.[48] The Japanese commitment to defend up to the 1,000-mile limit is more an aspiration than a likely capability.

As can be appreciated from the cost estimates shown above, breaking the one percent of GDP barrier would not seriously impinge upon either consumption or growth in Japan. The country can easily afford to raise military expenditures. It may take some serious shock, such as aggressive Soviet moves in the Far East, to remove the current taboos.

As for South Korea, the fifth five-year plan provides that "the share of defense expenditures will be maintained at 6 percent of GNP," which is roughly the present level. In 1982, defense costs came to almost $4 billion. If the planned GNP growth rate is realized, the defense budget for 1986 should be on the order of $5.4 billion (in 1982 prices).

President Chun of Korea is a career military officer, and is undoubtedly aware of the precarious balance of military power on the Korean peninsula. He is not likely to receive any pressure from the United States to raise military expenditures. Given the sacrifices that the South Korean people are called upon to make to finance their defense, economic rather than political factors are likely to determine what South Korea will spend on defense during the rest of the present decade.[49]

## NOTES

1. See, e.g., Hugh Patrick and Henry Rosovsky, editors, *Asia's New Giant,* Brookings Institution, 1976; Edward S. Mason et. al., *The Economic and Social Modernization of the Republic of Korea,* Harvard University Press, 1980.

2. For both countries, only direct government budget expenditures are included. It would be difficult to compare such off-budget items as guarantees, conditional subsidies, and the cost of government-owned enterprises for the two countries.
3. The debt service burden would have been even higher were it not for the Japanese policy of maintaining interest rates at an artificially low level.
4. OECD *Economic Surveys, Japan,* July, 1983, p. 55. The state pension systems for employees and for the self-employed cover about 90 percent of the labor force. Apart from aging of the population, increases in pension costs are due to the fact that Japanese pension schemes were developed relatively recently, and since benefits are related to length of service, the average pensions are rising rapidly.
5. Japan Institute for Social and Economic Affairs, *Japan 1983*, p.73.
6. Beef and citrus are good examples of the problem. Japanese consumers are obliged to pay high prices for these products in order to protect domestic producers who have considerable political clout.
7. Only 11 percent of all large firms in Japan (employing 1,000 or more) had pension plans in 1981. The normal custom is to provide a retiring employee with a lump sum payment; 25 percent of the large firms did that. Japan Institute of Labor, *Japanese Work Life Profile*, 1984, p.65.
8. Economic Planning Agency, *Japan in the Year 2000*, 1983, p. 167.
9. Data are from World Bank, *World Development Report*, 1983, pp. 198 – 199.
10. Korea Development Institute, *The Fifth Five-Year Economic and Social Development Plan*, 1982, pp. 14 – 15.
11. Economic Planning Board, *Major Statistics of Korean Economy*, 1982.
12. Ibid., pp. 192 – 193.
13. Korea Development Institute, *The Fifth Five-Year Plan*, p. 22.
14. See below for more precise estimates of the trade-off.
15. For further discussion of these recent events, see David B. H. Denoon, "Japan and the U.S. – The Security Agenda,"*Current History,* November 1983, p. 353.
16. It should be emphasized that this was not a constitutional provision and can be modified by Diet resolution.
17. Japanese Defense Agency, *Defense of Japan,* 1983, pp. 75 – 77.
18. *Defense of Japan,* pp. 190, 276 – 277.
19. Ibid., pp. 28 – 35.
20. The three aircraft carriers are not always in the Pacific, particularly after the Soviet invasion of Afghanistan.
21. For a discussion of these deficiencies, see Yukio Satoh, *The Evolution of Japanese Security Policy,* Adelphi Papers No. 178, London, 1982; William L. Scully and Guy M. Hicks, *Japanese Defense Policy,* Heritage Foundation, 1981; and William L. Scully, *Why Japan Needs More Defense Muscle,* Heritage Foundation, 1983.
22. Yukio Satoh, op. cit., p. 23.
23. *Defense of Japan,* 1983, pp. 217 – 218.
24. Ibid., pp. 105 – 106.
25. Rand Corporation, Report No. R-2894-NA, p. 33 (no date, based on data from 1977 to 1981).
26. *Defense of Japan,* 1983, p. 43.
27. It is not clear from the context of Table 5.17 why the figures in the final column fail to agree with those in Table 5.1 above. However, the differences are not great, averaging less than 0.2 percent per annum.
28. See, for example, an article by the Japanese consul general in New York in the *New York Times, February 29, 1984.* Apart from the NATO countries, the other countries whose defense budget exceeds that of Japan are the Soviet Union, China, and Saudi Arabia.

29. *New York Times*, January 22, 1984, p. 3; January 26,1984, p. A3; February 5, 1984, p. 15; *The Wall Street Journal*, January 23, 1984.
30. OECD Economic Surveys, *Japan*, July 1983, pp. 64–65.
31. *Defense of Japan*, 1983, pp. 168–174.
32. Ibid., p. 284.
33. OECD Economic Surveys, *Japan*, July 1983, p. 41.
34. These projections are the most recent ones made by the Korean Institute for Population and Health.
35. A recent study provides empirical support for this effect; see Riccardo Faini, Patricia Annez, and Lance Taylor, "Defense Spending, Economic Structure, and Growth: Evidence About Countries and Over Time," *Economic Development and Cultural Change* 32 (1984): 487–498.
36. The basic assumption underlying the analysis is that the government expenditures in question are financed by taxation.
37. The calculation of dynamic costs is obviously based on a general formulation that need not be applied solely to the actual costs of defense spending, for the procedure can equally be applied to any hypothetical level of defense spending, whether lower or higher than the current one. Thus, for example, in the projection of dynamic costs into the future, several possible hypothetical levels of defense spending for both South Korea and Japan will be considered, and it is similarly possible to calculate the current dynamic costs that would have been due to any hypothetical past levels of defense spending.
38. The calculation of the ICOR from past years summarizes the relationship between changes in the capital stock and changes in output without holding constant the amounts of other productive inputs and the state of technology. Use of the ICOR is therefore not appropriate in the present case, for the question of interest here is how current output would change if the private capital stock alone were changed by an amount equivalent to current military spending, without changes in the quantities of other inputs or in technology. The marginal productivity of capital is the appropriate measure of this effect.
39. The average military wage in South Korea was obtained by dividing annual total military wages and salaries (as given in "National Defense and the National Defense Budget," in Korean Development Institute, *The National Budget and Policy Objectives*, Seoul: 1982, Tables 5–6, pp. 168-169) by annual total military employment (from London Institute for Strategic Studies, *The Military Balance*, various years). This was compared with average annual earnings of employees in mining and manufacturing, available since 1969 in the *Monthly Statistical Bulletin of the Bank of Korea*, various issues.
40. The adjustments were done under the assumption that the conscripts' true average marginal product was 90 percent of that of industrial workers. The use of a ratio of less than unity is due to the conscripts' younger ages.
41. In principle, these figures should be reduced to indicate the reduction in private consumption, for if the funds devoted to military spending were shifted to the private sector, some would be saved. Thus the effect on current consumption would be approximated by multiplying the figures in Column 3 of Table 5.22 by the marginal propensity to consume. But this adjustment would not be a major one, for the marginal propensity to consume would be on the order of .80 to .85. The resulting figure would also ignore the utility people derive from saving, including the security this provides. This adjustment has thus not been made; however, making it, for either South Korea or Japan, would not significantly affect the magnitudes of the estimates, or the basic conclusions.
42. In calculating these costs, the past effects of military spending on the capital stock were included, beginning in 1965.
43. As in the case of South Korea, the calculations include the past effects of military spending on the capital stock from 1965 on.

44. *Defense of Japan*, 1973, p. 182.
45. Ibid.
46. *New York Times*, March 1, 1984, p. A12.
47. *Defense of Japan*, 1982, pp. 132 – 135.
48. *New York Times*, May 13, 1984, p. 15; August 1, 1984, p. A7.
49. The authors would like to acknowledge the assistance of John Devereux in making some of the calculations in this chapter.

# Chapter 6

# Conclusions: Economic Constraints and U.S. Defense Policy in the 1980s

David B. H. Denoon

### PRINCIPAL FINDINGS

*"Strategy and cost are interdependent."*
C. Hitch and R. McKean, 1961

The purpose of this book has been to answer three questions: (a) What will the economic performance of the United States and its major allies be in the next 3 – 5 years? (b) What is the relationship between defense spending and economic performance in these countries? and (c) How should the United States respond given the anticipated performance of its allies?

Obviously these questions lead to a host of interrelated political and military issues as well as the economic topics here receiving principal attention. The intent of this chapter is to tie together these economic, political, and military factors. What we cannot do is address all these issues on an equal basis. For example, in choosing U.S. policy options, we need to be sensitive to future behavior by the Soviet Union and other Warsaw Pact countries. Should the growing closeness between East and West Germany begin to threaten the basic Soviet dominance over Eastern Europe, the whole character of the East-West military balance would change. Similarly, there could be growing disarray in the NATO alliance affecting cohesion in the West.

Nevertheless, it is both prudent and important to assess the various implications if the basic trends of the past two decades continue. We have thus assumed that the Warsaw Pact will persist with a steady increase (2 – 4 percent per year of real growth) in defense expenditures and that the Pact will maintain its basic cohesiveness. We have also assumed that, although there are likely to be changes in the political orientation of several U.S. allies, the new governments will be essentially moderate and pro-Western. This latter assumption may prove overly optimistic, given the strength of the neutralism in West Germany and the recurring rancor between the United States and Greece over American air and naval base agreements. Yet, it is worthwhile to highlight those changes in U.S. policy which will be necessary even if there are no dramatic world political realignments. To base U.S. policy on significantly more favorable assumptions is clearly unwise.

There are seven basic conclusions from this research:

- Europe is the key to the most fundamental decisions that need to be made about U.S. defense policy.
- As Britain, France, and West Germany each contribute about 10 percent of NATO's total defense expenditures and all the other Western European members of NATO combined contribute about 10 percent, these three Northern European countries are the cornerstones of Western European defense.
- It is highly unlikely that the Western European members of NATO will not meet their 1978 pledge to increase real defense spending 3 percent per year during the remainder of the 1980s.
- The basic character of military burden-sharing among U.S. allies has not changed significantly since 1975.
- The current NATO/Warsaw Pact military balance and the trends in that balance are such that a broad range of Western military analysts are convinced that major changes in NATO strategy and tactics are necessary.
- If the United States and its principal allies do not reach a new understanding on burden-sharing and strategy, the Western European nations, and the U.S. troops stationed there, will be increasingly vulnerable to political and military pressure from the Soviet Union and the Warsaw Pact.
- There are strategies which provide reasonable confidence in dealing with the growing Warsaw Pact and Soviet conventional threat, but they all require increased defense expenditures and changes in force structure to be effective.

If we are entering a period when U.S. defense expenditure increases are slowing down, and the Gramm – Rudman legislation virtually ensures that, then the allies will no longer be able to count on the United States accepting an expanded percentage of the joint defense burden.

Why are developments in Europe so critical for U.S. national security? Europe is crucial because, at present, the United States and its allies can handle the Soviet conventional threat outside the European landmass. Although a conflict in the Persian Gulf poses particular difficulties, in East Asia, Africa, Latin America, and the Mediterranean, the United States and cooperating nations have distinct strategic advantages.

Europe is also a geopolitical prize. Its skilled population, income-generating capacity, advanced armaments industry, and location (limiting Soviet naval access to the Atlantic, Baltic, and Mediterranean) are all vital attributes. Europe's future will also have an important psychological effect on non-Marxist countries around the globe. In addition, the ancestral ties that most Americans have to Europe create a political bond that cannot be evaluated in purely military terms. It is here that Western Europe's special relationship with the United States comes into play.

Nevertheless, both structural and political factors may limit the extent of Western Europe's commitment to developing a credible conventional deterrent to the Warsaw Pact. The structural factors are the most predictable: The demographic profile limits the number of young men available for military service and creates a growing budgetary obligation to support an aging population. The two recessions in the past decade (1974 – 1975 and 1980 – 1982) and the proliferation of various types of state support (welfare, unemployment compensation, and trade adjustment assistance) have created a large number of Western European young people who have never worked consistently and who do not have the high motivation and job skills of their parents. This problem is accentuated by militant unions in Britain and a growing preference for short workweeks in West Germany. Unless these trends are reversed, labor productivity and future economic growth will be sharply limited. The declining competitiveness of Western European industry makes selling to the Warsaw Pact countries an attractive market. This, in turn, makes it difficult to develop a political consensus in the West for an expanded military capability because of fears that this will antagonize potential clients.

The political factors are much more difficult to forecast. NATO is now benefiting from conservative leadership in Britain and West Germany as well as the strongly anti-Soviet views of the socialist Mitterrand government in France. It is unclear, however, how long this constellation will hold. The parties on the Left, should they come to power, would pursue significantly different policies.

It is thus essential to monitor domestic political trends within the principal allied countries if one wishes to predict overall alliance behavior. In Britain, the Conservative party received a major setback in local and municipal elections in May 1985 and lost its considerable lead over the Labour party in national polls.[1] In France, the Socialist party suffered badly in the 1984 elections for the European Parliament and in the March 1985 local elections. If the 1986 French parliamentary elections go poorly for the Socialists, France faces the possibility of a legislature controlled by opponents of President Mitterrand whose term in office expires in 1988.[2]

In West Germany, the Kohl government has been jolted by a militant leftist, Oscar La Fontaine, winning the mayoral race in Stuttgart, and the Social Democratic party winning control of local government in North Rhine-Westphalia which is a large constituency, broadly representative of the West German electorate.[3] Although these midterm results do not mean that all the incumbent governments will be replaced in upcoming general elections, it does mean that each of the governments is in a less secure position and therefore less likely to take on new and unpopular burdens in the defense arena.

In the smaller NATO countries, there are disturbing patterns as well. The Norwegian Labor party has endorsed a nuclear-free zone in the northern region of NATO; the Danish Social Democratic party is so far to the left that in 1984 its leader returned from a trip to Asia lauding the Kim Il Sung regime in North Korea (however, neither of these two Labor parties is in power); the Dutch conservative coalition government faced such internal opposition that it was unable to marshall a majority for meeting an earlier commitment for deployment of the Pershing II and Ground Launched Cruise Missiles (GLCMs); and the socialist government in Spain is pressing the United States to reduce American personnel at key air bases in Spain.

While it is unlikely that the Left would come to power simultaneously in all these NATO countries, the internal pressure that the present governments face is tangible. Moreover, even if the Left were to gain office in only one or two major NATO countries, it could stall plans for integrated defense efforts.

Recent budgetary debates in Western Europe are indicative of these problems.[4] The British Liberal and Social Democratic parties have taken positions similar to the Labour party favoring the cancellation of the Tridents. Although the West German government is committed to maintaining its current military manpower levels of 456,000 men and has proposed increases in the length of draft service from 15 to 18 months to start in 1989, military funding is not increasing as a percentage of government budgetary allocations. In France, despite the Gaullist party favoring an annual 4 percent real increase in defense expenditures and Giscard d'Estaing's Union for French Democracy being publicly committed to the current Five-Year Defense Plan, the Mitterrand government submitted a military budget for 1985 which is substantially below the targets stated in its own Defense Plan.

If the Western European members of NATO prove unwilling to develop an adequate conventional defense, the 326,000 American troops stationed in Europe will face increasingly grave risks. Although the timing would vary depending upon the pace of Warsaw Pact increases in capability, at some point a U.S. president would face pressures to choose between those risks and withdrawal. Moreover, if an adequate deterrent is not maintained, the United States could well be risking its homeland should escalation be inadequately controlled.

At the other extreme, if the Western Europeans prove particularly serious about redressing the conventional force imbalance and make major commitments of new resources, then NATO planners will have something of an ideal situation where they could pick the optimal force structure for the 1990s and the early part of the twenty-first century. In this situation, there would almost certainly be an emphasis on mobility (mechanized infantry and armor, airlift, and sealift) and a new apportionment of roles between Europe and the United States. This would probably lead to different deployments of American troops and a new mix of responsibilities for

Europe in either Africa or the Middle East. Again, the extent of European commitments would affect the range of U.S. options.

The most probable outcome, however, is for the West Europeans to make modest efforts, below their official pledges but neither so little as to outrage the American public nor enough to provide a credible conventional defense.

What role will economic performance play in this? There are two key constraints: (a) parliamentary budget decisions about the percentage of expenditures to be devoted to defense, and (b) how fast the economies are growing and thus what tax revenues are available for spending.[5] In Chapter 3, Todd Sandler and James Murdoch estimate that, unless the parliaments allocate larger shares for defense, the West German, French, and British economies would have to grow respectively at annual rates of 11 percent, 7.5 percent, and 10 percent to make it likely that they will meet their pledge of 3 percent real growth in defense spending. As the principal forecasts for France, Germany, and Britain anticipate GNP growth in the range of 1 – 2.5 percent, it is highly improbable that 3 percent growth target for defense will be achieved unless there is a significant change in budget allocations.

To put these alliance decisions in context, let us first turn to the forecasts for economic performance and the findings on the relationship between economic performance and defense spending.

## ECONOMIC PERFORMANCE AND DEFENSE SPENDING

### The United States

The recent macroeconomic performance in the United States has been dramatic. Unemployment has dropped from 10.4 percent in 1982 to 7.0 percent in 1985; real GNP grew 6.0 percent in 1983 and 6.3 percent in 1984. Not only has the recovery from the 1980 – 1982 recession been vigorous, but it shows signs of continuing, at a moderating rate. None of the prominent, quantitative economic forecasters in 1982 predicted this type of resilient economic growth; we may thus want to look at their forecasts for the 1985 – 1989 period with caution. Nevertheless, there is now considerable optimism about future U.S. economic trends. Most of the current forecasts anticipate that the United States economy will grow in the range of 2.5 – 4.0 percent annually for the remainder of the decade.

The danger of such "surprise-free" forecasts is that there can and almost certainly will be unanticipated factors which affect performance. Yet, there are some very basic reasons to be optimistic about the U.S. economy: improved savings rates, high rates of investment, steady growth in labor productivity, and, since 1982, rapid expansion with low inflation (down from 12 percent in 1980 to approximately 4 – 5 percent at mid-decade).

The two principal causes of concern about the U.S. economy are: the size of the federal budget deficit and the large trade deficit. Both have complex effects on

American economic performance. The federal budget deficit (which totaled $167 billion for Fiscal Year 1984) clearly had a useful stimulative effect in the 1981 – 1983 period, but, as the economy approaches full employment, there is a growing possibility that the deficit will inhibit private investment and accelerate inflationary pressures. The trade deficit (which was running at over $12 billion per month in mid-1985) was caused by the high price of the U.S. dollar and the rapid economic recovery from the 1980 – 1982 recession which stimulated import demand. With the sharp increase in capital flows into the United States from Western Europe and Japan (helping to finance both the trade and budget deficits), the United States faces the additional problem of becoming a major debtor nation. None of these problems seems insurmountable: the price of the dollar fell significantly in 1985, the Congress finally seemed willing to take some unpopular steps to significantly constrain the federal budget deficit, and the trade deficit should wane as the European and Japanese recoveries proceed.

Future prospects for the U.S. economy are bright. Though 1985 and 1986 may well be years of slower growth than the 1982 – 1984 period, the high rates of investment, innovation, and increases in labor productivity should all contribute to continued growth. Additionally, with further deregulation of business and tax simplification likely, current capital stock can be used more efficiently, creating the possibility for further long-run increases in GNP growth.

How has the buoyant economic picture affected defense spending in the United States? Despite widely publicized warnings from Lester Thurow and others,[6] the rapid increase in defense outlays between 1981 and 1985 has not wrecked the American economy, nor has it been a devious plan to "save capitalism."[7] The consensus among a wide variety of analysts, using different quantitative models,[8] is that the recent increases in defense spending have been part of a generally stimulative fiscal policy and have been accommodated by the U.S. economy with few identifiable adverse effects. There appear to be four principal reasons why the American economy was able to adapt with minimal dislocation:

- The most rapid increases in expenditures came in 1981 – 1982 when the economy was in deep recession, so there was excess industrial capacity and unemployed labor to draw upon.

- The U.S. economy is so large and diversified, producing such a broad range of high-technology items that the defense buildup could be accommodated without major dislocation.

- Although there have been very rapid increases in the equipment and research and development parts of the U.S. defense budget, more than 50 percent still goes to salaries, pensions, and supplies; thus much of defense spending is similar to civilian government expenditures.

- The 1981 changes in the tax code have significantly reduced the overall cost of capital which has led to sizable increases in investment and productive capacity;

these supply-side changes have made it more likely that the United States can maintain non-inflationary growth.

Although there are certain idiosyncracies in the case of the United States, it seems clear that the larger and more diversified the economy and the greater the number of potential suppliers of defense goods, the more one can view defense spending as comparable to other fiscal policy measures. To the extent that defense purchases are made from nationalized or protected defense firms, that military design or production draws skilled labor from other growing sectors, and that procurement accentuates rather than smooths business cycles, defense spending can have negative effects and warrants special attention.

The future course of defense spending in the United States is likely to be constrained more by political than economic factors. The Reagan administration has made a sustained effort to shift the mix of federal spending, limiting the rate of growth of social programs and using up considerable political capital to continue expanding defense outlays. Although it is not clear whether President Reagan's decision to accept a "freeze" on defense appropriations for Fiscal Year 1986[9] implies further freezes for Fiscal Years 1987 – 1989, there is a definite indication that both the Senate and the House are unwilling to continue with defense funding expansion at the rates seen in the early 1980s. Also, with growing public resentment at the extent of malfeasance by defense contractors,[10] budget reviews will be increasingly contentious.

The greatest uncertainty regarding the direction and composition of defense spending, however, comes from the administration's proposal to establish a Strategic Defense Initiative (SDI). At present, this is a $26 billion research program designed to accelerate the development of sensors, communication equipment, computers, software, and munitions to defend against offensive missiles and aircraft. Should the research and development and testing stages of the SDI go well and the Congress ultimately authorize the actual deployment of a defensive system, the capital costs could dwarf current procurement for strategic systems.

It is not likely that a substantial part of the SDI system will be deployed in the 1980s, but if it appears that the United States is shifting an increasing part of its effort to defensive capabilities, procurement for offensive systems and conventional power projection may well be limited. Moreover, the massive increase in research and development funds will, almost certainly, cause bidding for scarce talent and facilities in this area.

In sum, the United States is in an excellent position to maintain annual GDP growth rates of 2.5 – 4.0 percent for the remainder of the 1980s. With the Reagan administration's major defense buildup coming to an end, budgetary allocations for national security could begin to decline as a percentage of GDP after 1986. The overall defense burden is thus easily sustainable. The major uncertainties about the economic effects of defense spending come not from the aggregate levels but from potential changes in the composition of defense procurement.

## Britain, France and West Germany

The initial post-World War II economic performance of France and West Germany (hereafter referred to as Germany) was impressive. In the 1945 – 1973 period, French GDP grew at an average of 6.5 percent per year, and labor productivity almost kept pace, expanding at 5.5 percent annually. The German recovery was even more dramatic, with GNP rising at a rate of 8 percent yearly in the 1950s and then slowing to a sprightly 4.7 percent rate in the 1960s.

British economic performance was sluggish, however. From being the world's preeminent financial center and leading exporter of manufactured goods, Britain has declined precipitously. A variety of factors have caused this slide: high tax rates, low savings rates, the emigration of skilled professionals, an adversarial labor – management environment, and a setting where wages have grown at twice the rate of labor productivity. This has meant that British capital and skills have become somewhat antiquated and the country has been unable to maintain its trade competitiveness.

Fundamental problems in all three of these economies became obvious in the 1970s. In the 1973 – 1982 period, French GDP grew at 2.4 percent, Germany's at 2.9 percent and Britain's at 0.6 percent. The United Kingdom and France faced especially serious inflationary problems, and all three countries had to deal with aging capital stock, slowing productivity growth, and high unemployment. France and Germany had high savings rates in the 1970s (26 – 27 percent of GDP) but these dropped to less than 11 percent in 1979 – 1981. Although the Thatcher government in Britain has successfully lowered the inflation rate, other desired structural changes (in labor productivity and rapid development of new industries) have not occurred.

Some analysts have attributed much of this poor performance to the oil price shocks and subsequent adjustments,[11] while others see the slowing of growth between the 1950s and 1970s as a reflection of inefficient labor practice, generous unemployment and welfare benefits, and numerous policies which do not provide adequate incentives for entrepreneurial activity and investment.[12] Despite the differing diagnoses, there is a consensus among the quantitative forecasters that growth in Britain, France, and Germany is unlikely to average more than 1.5 percent to 3.0 percent annually for the remainder of the 1980s.

The United States thus faces a situation where the principal contributors to Western European defense will all have basic internal problems to solve for themselves. Each of the three countries has been making major investments to revitalize its capital stock,[13] but there are doubts about whether these investments are in industries that will maximize growth and employment generation for the future. Specifically, Western Europe seems to be falling farther and farther behind the United States and Japan in such critical areas as computers, information processing, and electronics while new investments in steel and chemicals may yield only modest returns.[14] Some Europeans see this as a result of a U.S.-Japanese cabal to exclude them from the latest high-technology developments,[15] but the lack of dynamism and innovation is so obvious in a broad range of sectors that the problems cannot be attributed to external causes alone.

Germany has the most promising prospects of the three. Its economic growth rate is the highest, corporate profits have risen 25 percent between 1983 and 1985, and about 170,000 businesses were founded in 1984 (which is 30 percent more than in 1983).[16] In addition, the Kohl government has promised to reduce taxes, lower the share of GDP devoted to the public sector, and reduce regulation in the financial markets which could lead to substantial inflows of foreign capital and provide incentives for higher domestic savings rates.[17]

These are the positive signs but they need to be weighed against record high unemployment rates and the German labor movement's goal of a 35-hour week, foreboding difficulties with labor productivity.

The British picture is the most distressing. Despite vigorous efforts by Prime Minister Thatcher to modernize industry and stimulate entrepreneurship, the United Kingdom has shown few signs that it can compete effectively in areas of higher technology and new product development. Also with 5 percent inflation and 13 percent unemployment in 1984, the British public has been suffering. Though 1985 results are encouraging in terms of GDP growth (estimated to be about 2.5 percent), the British tax structure and incentives schemes appear to be encouraging growth in capital-intensive industries but not necessarily generating the innovation or employment creation that will be needed as Britain tries to adjust to the economic future.[18]

Moreover, though the United Kingdom's balance of payments position has been helped during the past two decades by North Sea oil proceeds, in the 1990s those revenues will decline and the country will face further stringency. However, it could well be that the most important questions for Britain are attitudinal: Can conditions and viewpoints in the workplace be changed to encourage increases in labor productivity? And can sufficient risk-taking and innovation be developed so that new industries can replace the ones where Britain has lost its competitiveness?

France's prospects are somewhere between those of Britain and Germany. Although its current economic growth rate is the slowest of the three and the Mitterrand government caused many of its own problems by running large budget deficits and raising wages much faster than productivity increased in 1981 – 1982, the selection of L. Fabius as prime minister in 1984 and decisions to limit subsidies to nationalized industries are signs of greater pragmatism. Also, the French have a demonstrated commitment to modernization of industry and the development of higher technological capabilities.[19] The prime concerns are whether political stalemate between now and the next general election in 1988 will be a serious disincentive to investment and whether long-standing protectionist measures for French farmers and business will inhibit the transformation to a more modern industrial structure.

As T. Sandler and J. Murdoch point out in Chapter 3, in Britain, France, and Germany there is a very direct relationship between macroeconomic performance and willingness to fund defense. None of these three countries appears likely to grow fast enough to meet its official pledge of 3 percent real increases in defense expenditures. In addition, it is clear that political decision-makers in all three countries see a direct trade-off between U.S. defense spending and their own. In the 1955 – 1981 period, every time the United States spent a dollar more, Britain, France, and Germany spent 18 cents less. The United States also has put itself in the position of making up for European sluggishness: everytime U.S. allies spend a dollar less on defense, the U.S. spends 87 cents more.[20]

There are some interesting patterns in the European defense choices as well. As nuclear nations, France and the U.K. spend considerably more on research and development than does Germany and they have carried significantly higher overall burdens. This gap has closed in the last decade, however. Today it is striking to see how similar the overall contributions of the three countries are in terms of defense expenditures per capita and percent of total NATO spending. Because German incomes are higher, the German percent of GDP devoted to defense is lower than the percentages of Britain and France.

The internal effects of defense spending vary noticeably among the three. The French, for example, have been willing to pay very high premiums to develop their own weapon systems and minimize dependence on external suppliers. This has often affected the quality of French equipment but it does generate domestic investment and employment and limits the balance of payment effects that would come from foreign purchases. All three countries, however, suffer because their domestic defense industries are small in scale and often inefficient.

Thus, there is a sharp contrast between the likely prospects of the four countries that contribute 90 percent of NATO's funding. The United States, the principal contributor, should have no problems in maintaining its present level of defense expenditures (which have increased by more than 50 percent in real terms in five years) and continuing its expansion and modernization of military capabilities. But Britain, France, and Germany, each of which is critical to NATO's future, face fundamental structural problems with economies that are likely to seriously constrain public willingness to fund military improvements necessary to deal with growing Warsaw Pact capabilities.

## Portugal, Spain, Greece, and Turkey

These four countries have a number of similarities from an economic perspective. They have modest per capita incomes, industry represents a small percentage of their GNPs, and savings rates are low. They have also followed relatively similar paths in the 1970s. All four were adversely affected by the OPEC oil price increases, chose to try to maintain growth through external borrowing, allowed their public sectors to expand considerably, and were forced to retrench by the time of the 1980 – 1982 recession. All four are currently growing slowly and face serious unemployment, inflation, and balance of payments problems.

Interestingly, all are critical from a strategic perspective as well. The Lajes air force base in the Azores, controlled by Portugal, is a vital link for air traffic in the mid-Atlantic; Spain's position on the northwest salient of the Mediterranean is important for assuring access to the Straits of Gibraltar; while Greece and Turkey can play an essential role in limiting access of the Soviet Black Sea fleet to the Mediterranean. In addition, the Turkish army is formidable, and, should there be a conflict in the Persian Gulf region, Turkish air force bases could prove critical. Thus, even though Portugal, Spain, Greece, and Turkey combined provide less than 10 percent of NATO's defense expenditures, they are essential for Western defense.

Of the four countries, Turkey faced its financial crises first. By 1978 it was clear that Turkey could not meet its international debt obligations. The military intervened to oust Prime Minister Encevit, stop the growing internal guerrilla movement, and impose an economic austerity program. Turkey's international creditors have agreed to a series of debt reschedulings, the exponential growth of the public sector has been stopped, and the stabilization program has jolted the economy. In 1979, a sharp recession started with GDP actually dropping 8.9 percent. Yet, five years after the initiation of the austerity measures, Turkey has had consistently high inflation rates, and slow growth has meant that unemployment persists in the 15 percent range. In 1984, the military supervised elections of its civilian successors, and, as growth resumes at a steadier pace, it is possible that Turkey could have GDP growth in the range of 3 – 4 percent in the 1985 – 1989 period.

The situation in Greece is far less optimistic. The Papandreou government has followed a classic socialist course of nationalizing industry, expanding the regulatory functions of government, and adding employees to the public sector. Balance of payments problems have become increasingly serious, unemployment is in the 8 – 10 percent range, and none of the principal forecasters sees GDP growth above 2 percent for the remainder of the decade. This picture poses problems in both the economic and defense areas. The European Economic Community will need to decide about whether to continue subsidies, and the economic malaise will almost certainly provide a setting where the Papandreou government will try to extract greater concessions for NATO use of its air and naval bases. The pervasive Greek-Turkish enmity also limits the certainty of cooperation on NATO's southern flank. Still other complicating factors are the frequent anti-Western and anti-U.S. statements by Papandreou himself.

Spain and Portugal provide slightly more optimistic circumstances. Spain's principal public agenda has been to make a transition to liberal democratic government after the Franco era. Income redistribution has been achieved by raising wages faster than labor productivity for the past decade, but this has slowed GDP growth (which averaged only 1.5 percent in the 1970s) and limited new job creation making unemployment extremely high (18 percent in 1983). Portugal followed very stimulative policies in the 1970s, nationalizing industry, expropriating land, and rapidly increasing public sector wages. This splurge has now led to balance of payment problems and the Portuguese government has agreed to an IMF stabilization package. As adjustments are being made by both governments, long-run performance may be better than that in the immediate future and the main forecasts anticipate economic growth in the 2 – 3 percent bracket during 1985 – 1989.

The overall picture for the European countries we are analyzing is, therefore, uninspiring. Of the seven countries, only Turkey appears likely to grow faster than the 2 – 3 percent average. NATO thus faces a very fundamental problem: the member governments can no longer count on rapid economic growth to ease the political cost of financing defense expenditures.

In Chapter 4, K. Forbes, G. Korsun, and M. McGuire have developed a sophisticated series of econometric tests to explore the effects of defense spending in Portugal, Spain, Greece, and Turkey. There are four principal factors which explain the respective levels of defense budgets: domestic GDP, size of the Warsaw Pact defense funding, expenditures by other Western allies, and the quantity of foreign economic and military assistance.

All four of these countries receive significant amounts of aid. Some of this is in the form of payments for military base access, some from European Economic Community subsidies, while other support is indirect through soft terms on debt reschedulings. It is interesting to note that for Portugal, Spain, Greece, and Turkey, military spending is positively correlated with aid which means that these governments do not substitute foreign resources for domestic defense expenditures. Also, unlike their Northern European neighbors, these Southern Tier countries are not "free riders"; when the other members of NATO increase defense spending, they do so as well.

Forbes, Korsun, and McGuire have also tested what effects defense spending has had on economic performance in these countries. By measuring whether defense displaced consumption or investment in 1960 – 1979 and then estimating the subsequent effects, the results show considerable variation: Spain and Turkey are adversely affected by defense spending, while in Portugal there is no measurable effect, and in Greece defense budgets actually stimulate growth.[21] To know if these patterns would continue in the future, we would need to know more about the likely composition of future defense spending and how this would reinforce or detract from other economic developments. Nevertheless, it is fair to say that, on expenditure questions, the Southern Tier countries play a cooperative role within the Western alliance even though two of the four nations reduce their growth rates in the process.

## Japan and South Korea

There is a striking contrast between European economic performance and the exceptionally rapid growth of Japan and South Korea (hereafter referred to as Korea). In the 1960 – 1981 period, Japan grew at twice the average rate for all the

OECD countries. Korea grew at modest rates in the 1950s[22] but then accelerated in the 1960s. In the 1970s, there were five years in which Korean GDP grew more than 9.0 percent in real terms. Even given the two oil price shocks, Korean income rose at an average of over 7 percent for the 1974 – 1982 period. What is most stunning about the Korean performance is that these growth rates were achieved while spending 4 – 6 percent of GNP on defense and without building up national budget deficits.

Future prospects for both Japan and Korea are excellent. For the remainder of the 1980s, Korea is expected to grow at approximately 7 percent in real terms and Japan at 4 percent. The formula that both countries have followed is to have: high savings rates, high investment rates, continuous increases in labor productivity, and rapid expansion of exports. These fundamental goals have been supplemented with low tax rates, constraining government to a small percentage of GNP, and an industrial strategy of aggressively upgrading the quality of manufactured goods and services provided. The principal internal constraints on this strategy seem to be: (a) the likelihood that wage rates will continue to rise sharply given labor shortages, and (b) the problem that Japan faces with rising budget deficits. The key external constraints are: the reliance on imported raw material and energy supplies, and the possibility of protectionism in Europe and the United States limiting the future growth of exports.

Nevertheless, from the U.S. perspective both Japan and Korea are attractive potential allies, not only because of their strategic location, GNP, and human capital levels, but because both are clearly capable of shouldering increased defense burdens in the future. Also, given that neither is likely to become a nuclear power, they show signs of willingness to purchase and develop the conventional military systems necessary to respond to the growing Soviet naval and air capability in the region.

In Chapter 5, Walter and David Galenson have estimated the costs of defense spending to the Japanese and Korean economies by first dividing the burden into its static and dynamic elements. The static costs are the direct outlays in any given year that the military uses (and which cannot therefore be available for civilian purposes). The dynamic costs are the subsequent income which is foregone because involvement is reduced by current military spending.[23]

For Korea the static burdens of defense have been significant. After adjusting for foreign assistance that was available in the 1960s and the fact that conscription leads to an understatement of the costs for labor, we see that defense has risen from 2.2 percent of GNP in 1965 to 7.1 percent in 1981. This compares with a move from .9 percent to 1.0 percent of GNP in Japan during the same period. By taking high and low estimates for savings rates and the return on capital, the Galensons have estimated that dynamic costs for Japan from 1965 to 1981 were never more that .11 to .24 percent of GNP while in Korea the largest impact was between .52 and 1.29 percent of GNP.[24] What these calculations show is that countries with very high savings and investment rates and efficient utilization of capital can easily afford defense expenditures in the range of 2 – 6 percent of GNP. For example, in looking forward to 1990, the Galensons estimate that the dynamic costs to Korea will be no more than 1.6 percent of GNP and to Japan no more that .49 percent of GNP. We can thus conclude for Korea and Japan that, within anticipated ranges, limitations on defense spending are political and not due to economic constraints.

Here are some interesting implications for Western Europe. Where savings and investment rates are low and the utilization of capital is inefficient, increasing defense expenditures could very well reduce growth rates that are already small. This could have both severe economic and political costs. Conversely, taking measures to stimulate growth could dramatically reduce the percentage of incremental future income allocated to defense.

In sum, we see that that the United States, Japan, and Korea are each in a strong position to fund present and anticipated future levels of defense expenditures. The Northern and Southern European members of NATO face more difficult choices, however. With slow growth and low savings and investment rates, increasing defense spending will have a more noticeable impact on either consumption or investment. Clearly, the more desirable circumstance from the standpoint of Western European political leaders would be to first increase economic growth rates and then expand defense budgets.

## WHY HAVE THE MAJOR U.S. ALLIANCES STAYED INTACT?

Unlike the Warsaw Pact, which is held together by coercion, the relationships that the United States has with Japan, South Korea, Canada, and the European members of NATO are voluntary ones and they have remained remarkably stable over the past three decades. What have been the key factors in preserving these alliances? The bonds have been maintained because of four basic reasons:

*Military credibility* has been vital in making links with the United States increase in a tangible way a country's security. During the 1950s and 1960s when the United States had a clear preponderance in nuclear weaponry and sea and air power, a U.S. military guarantee was tantamount to protection (at least from external aggression). At the time, it was frequently referred to as the "U.S. nuclear umbrella." It is precisely because U.S. strategic superiority has waned that military ties to the United States have begun to entail tangible risks.

Part of the problem in judging the credibility of U.S. military guarantees arises from the uncertainty as to whether NATO conventional forces would be able to stop a Warsaw Pact advance without giving up major areas of West Germany. If NATO were successful at slowing and eventually stopping the Warsaw Pact while avoiding the use of nuclear weapons, then the conflict could develop into a long, a conventional war. Under these specific circumstances, the West would have distinct advantages given its level of income, skilled manpower, and technology. However, the scenario that haunts the European members of NATO is one where the Warsaw Pact is advancing rapidly and the alliance must decide if it should escalate to nuclear weapons. What is not known is whether the Western European goverments would actually request the use of nuclear weapons and whether the United States would comply (then putting U.S. territory and population at risk).

*Economic pragmatism* has also reinforced ties. In the early post-World War II period, the United States was not only a key market but a large supplier of aid as well.[25] The size and vitality of the American economy will remain a critical inducement, particularly for countries interested in obtaining high-technology items and in promoting their exports.

The long and successful history of post-World War II economic interchange between the United States and Western Europe has created commercial links which generally serve as ballast when political or military differences place strains on the alliance. Protectionist pressures in the steel, auto, chemical, and agricultural sectors have been a cause of recent friction. Yet, the steady growth of trans-Atlantic trade and enactment of both the Kennedy and Tokyo Rounds of tariff reductions (as well as planning for new trade negotiations) are signs of basic resilience and strength in the economic relationships.

*Political, cultural, and ethnic bonds* have also been significant. For the descendants of European immigrants, an important part of the foreign policy relationship with Europe has consisted of ties to the "former homeland." For Japan and South Korea, immigration has been a less important link, but the homelands' sense of vulnerability and closeness to the Soviet Union has added an emotional component to the alliances. Moreover, although there have been major periods in the post-1945 era when Spain, Portugal, Greece, Turkey, and South Korea have not had democratic governments, the major U.S. alliance relationships have been with democracies. Even more importantly, the leadership in all the alliance countries has been anxious to limit communist influence inside their countries and to thwart the expansion of communist spheres of influence. This amalgam of factors cements the relationships and makes it possible to refer to the composite as the "Western Alliance."

*Lack of attractive alternative alliances* may be an involuted feature also helping to sustain current arrangements. During the height of the détente period (1972 – 1975) there was a great deal of optimism, especially in Europe, that U.S.-Soviet competition would decline. In the late 1970s, however, as events in Angola, Ethiopia, Nicaragua, El Salvador, Cambodia, Laos, and Afghanistan unfolded, it became obvious that a global competition with the Soviet Union for influence was still very much a part of the international scene. The Japanese and South Koreans wanted reassurances, and the European members of NATO made their 1978 pledge of a 3 percent real growth in defense spending and the 1979 "two-track" decision on deployment of Pershing II and Ground Launched Cruise Missiles (GLCMs).[26] Yet, there is still great unease about NATO strategy.

What issues cause the most friction between the United States and its European allies? The most persistent and fundamental debate is over what constitutes an effective deterrent, this being further complicated by the uncertainty over the implications of the Reagan administration's Strategic Defense Initiative (SDI). As discussed in Chapter 1, a widely held European view[27] holds that NATO serves predominantly as a political commitment to collective defense, and the main purpose of the alliance is to demonstrate that, if a conflict develops, group resources will be devoted to common goals. The prevailing view in the United States is that deterrence is not effective unless a potential opponent knows that, at each stage of escalation, he can be checked. This leads many American defense specialists to conclude that deterrence necessitates having a ready and effective war-fighting capacity.

A reasonable question to ask is: What is Soviet doctrine regarding deterrence? Unfortunately there is no definitive answer. Some analysts see the Soviet Union as cautious, intending to use its military buildup primarily for political advantage,[28] while others are convinced that Moscow is developing a strategy for winning either a conventional or nuclear conflict.[29] Given the uncertainty about Soviet intentions, however, there is an escapist element in the European view that NATO serves mainly a political function. It is widely acknowledged that most NATO forces have only ten days to one month of supplies. If a war did start, this would place an enormous strain on the NATO command to escalate quickly or surrender. Thus, once the NATO threat to escalate lost its certainty (after SALT I), it could become a distinct possibility that the outcome of a conventional conflict would determine the future political map of Europe.

The Strategic Defense Initiative adds to alliance problems from a number of perspectives. First, although the United States and its allies may ultimately develop space-based weapons that can defend against intercontinental ballistic missiles, the Europeans might still be vulnerable to Soviet missiles like the SS-21, SS-22, and SS-23 all of which stay within the atmosphere in their trajectories. This does not mean the space-based systems may be worthless, but it does mean that Europe may become relatively more vulnerable than the United States. In this case, future U.S. governments might be less committed to Europe's defense – which could exacerbate the precise "decoupling" problem that the Pershing II and GLCM deployments were intended to address. Second, if strategic defense systems are ever deployed on a large scale, they are almost certain to be extremely expensive and will doubtless claim some resources that would otherwise have been used for conventional forces. Third, many of the technologies needed for strategic defense are likely to have important commercial applications, leading to elaborate bargaining among the allies about which countries should handle which parts of the endeavor.

The resolution of these differences over strategy and economic matters, will require coherence among all the European members of NATO. Former Chancellor Helmut Schmidt succinctly summarized how these alliance fissures persist:

> The European Community is politically ill because all the member states are economically ill. England has only one foot in the EC. France has only one foot in the common defense efforts of the alliance. West Germany is fully committed to both associations but is aware of its potential reduction to the role of a battlefield and also longs for reunification with East Germany. More than most other Europeans, the West

Germans are afraid of the deterioration of the climate between the East and West. Americans like to overlook Europe's political diversity and therefore understandably show signs of impatience toward Europe....[30]

Therefore, NATO faces a situation where a growing number of U.S. observers believe that the Europeans should enhance their defense capabilities, particularly in the conventional forces area, while many Europeans are worried that they will be making their homeland a testing ground for the superpowers. If there were to be a war between the United States and the Soviet Union, Europe would be the most likely area for large troop engagements, yet few strategists think such a clash would start with a nuclear exchange and then spread to conventional weapons. If there is a conflict in Central Europe, it is far more likely to start as a conventional battle. In that case, the East is pushed back to the basic question: What will the West Germans and NATO decide to do if there is a conventional war in Germany and the NATO forces are about to exhaust their supplies or lose key cities? It is the uncertainty in any answer to this question that has created the repeated efforts to develop a more flexible and credible response.[31]

The link to economic performance must be considered because conventional weapons are high-cost means of defense. It is precisely because conventional systems are labor-intensive, requiring maintenance of elaborate hardware, and because they have lower levels of destructiveness per resource expended that the Europeans and the Japanese have preferred to rely on the U.S. nuclear guarantee. It is ironic that, just at the time the NATO member governments were recognizing the need for a change in military doctrine and capabilities, the OPEC oil price increase led to the two worst recessions (1975–1976 and 1980–1982) since the 1930s. Thus, the relationship between defense options and economic constraints came into full view.

## STRATEGIC OPTIONS FOR THE UNITED STATES

We should start by noting that this is not a book about military strategy and this part of the conclusion is, therefore, not meant to be detailed or definitive. Yet, it is worthwhile to see the connection between different strategies and the resources necessary to implement them.

In very simplified terms, U.S. military capabilities should maintain an effective strategic deterrent, and, at the conventional level, aim to achieve four prime objectives: to (a) preserve the current favorable balance in the Pacific, (b) avoid further erosion of the Western position in the Middle East, (c) reverse the unfavorable NATO-Warsaw Pact balance in Europe, and (d) prevent Soviet inroads in Central and South America.

In seeking to reach these goals, the United States faces a number of basic problems: the growing Warsaw Pact conventional capability,[32] loss of escalation dominance, the vulnerability of Western Europe and Japan to outside sources of energy and raw materials,[33] relatively low states of readiness for manpower,[34] limited supplies,[35] and a foreign policy decision-making apparatus that makes setting of priorities difficult and thus frequently leads to overcommitment of U.S. forces.

U.S. assets are, nonetheless, considerable: the size, scope, and growth rate of the economy, a basic political solidarity based on the openness and lack of coercion in the system, technological sophistication, geographic insularity with secure borders, and clear success in managing its main alliance relationships. With these objectives, assets, and liabilities in mind, let us now turn to a discussion of six different strategies that could possibly be used to deal with the challenges facing the United States and its allies.

The first three strategies are positive measures that, if implemented, would increase NATO's conventional compability; the last three strategies are second best alternatives that the U.S. might adopt if a coherent NATO revitalization program proves unattainable.

*Economics First.* Given that the United States, Japan, and South Korea are likely to do well economically and that the United States still has a conventional force dominance in the Pacific, the basic alliance problems concern Northern and Southern European weaknesses vis-à-vis the Warsaw Pact. As we have elaborately documented earlier in this volume, the savings, investment, and income growth rates in Western Europe are very low. Thus, increasing defense spending will have a noticeable effect on either consumption or investment.

Few democratically elected leaders are willing to ask their citizens to cut down on consumption during peacetime, and limits on investment will affect future growth rates. Because of this bind, the Western European members of NATO have chosen instead not to meet their commitments to steadily expand defense capabilities. One possible way to deal with this dilemma is for the United States and its Pacific allies to say that, because of their relatively favorable current economic circumstances, they will, in the short run, take on larger defense burdens if the Europeans do something tangible to improve their long-run economic growth (and thus defense) prospects.

Some might see this as a curious reversal of roles between such financial institutions as the International Monetary Fund and NATO; yet if the Western Europeans were willing to constrain social spending and increase savings and investment rates for the purpose of economic growth, the long-term potential for responding adequately to the Warsaw Pact would be dramatically improved. Presumably, one would not want the type of visible "conditionality" required for IMF support. But there could be explicit understandings among the NATO countries that the defense spending target of 3 percent real growth be set aside for a three-year period. If the member governments did not make serious efforts to accelerate economic growth rates, the United States could take that as explicit evidence that the European members of NATO were downgrading the importance of the alliance.

There is a clear danger in this strategy and that is the possibility that the West Europeans will limit their defense budgets and then claim, after several years, that the military situation is no longer as threatening as it was in the mid-1980s and that they are quite happy with the new allocation of burdens between the United States and Europe. There are several advantages, however. The approach is likely to be readily understood and accepted by the mainstream public especially in view of the fact that the current situation is clearly at an impasse, with Western Europe achieving neither adequate economic growth nor its defense targets. It is also possible that a freeze in European defense spending could be used as part of a negotiating strategy to facilitate the next global round of talks on reductions in tariffs and even on disarmament.

The French have taken an adamant position on preserving the imports protection and subsidies involved in the European Community's common agricultural policy, but there are other European non-tariff barriers to trade (like health, safety, and licensing standards) which limit economies of scale in the biotechnology and electronics fields. If a pause in defense spending was to be used by European leaders to justify major efforts at reducing trade barriers, improving efficiency, and encouraging innovation, the benefits in long-term economic growth performance could well outweigh the short-term disadvantages in freezing defense expenditures.

Moreover, this approach could result in some positive results vis-à-vis Japan. The Japanese are already increasing their aid to Pakistan and some Middle Eastern countries, and a program focused on the linkage between economic performance and national security could be a means of getting the Japanesse public to see defense planning in a broader context. Furthermore, an intense focus on economic issues might result in more serious efforts being made for the purpose of addressing European and Japanese resource vulnerabilities and a tightening of controls on technology flows to Warsaw Pact countries.[36]

*Closer Integration with the Allies.* The principal thrust of the Carter administration's defense efforts vis-à-vis Europe was based on the assumption that NATO should try for the efficiency, economies of scale, and inter-operability of equipment that already benefited the Warsaw Pact. As reviewed in Chapter 1, there was a blossoming of initiatives under Defense Secretary Harold Brown. These included the efforts for rationalization, standardization, and inter-operability (RSI), the long-term defense program (LTDP), and commitments on host nation support (HNS). All were designed to increase integration among the allies. Unfortunately, managing such complex, collaborative efforts is extremely difficult in a setting like NATO. Moreover, the protectionist sentiments both in the U.S. Congress and in the European parliaments make it hard to plan for the co-production and co-development projects necessary to achieve significant improvements in standardization and inter-operability.

There may in fact be some technological and economic aspects which make tighter integration among the allies more attractive. As the cost of developing the newest and most sophisticated precision-guided weapons increases and as the technological strength of the Europeans and Japanese grows, the actual cost savings from collaborative programs will be substantial. Also, there is an expanding number of areas where the Europeans and Japanese are demonstrably ahead of the United States in the development of technology with military applications. In these areas, it will clearly be vital for the United States to incorporate these foreign systems or components.[37]

Another factor making for closer integration will be the necessary evolution in NATO doctrine. The present deployment of NATO's various contingents in Germany has been compared to a layer cake,[38] and the difficulties involved in coordinating such a diverse, multinational fighting force are formidable. If NATO is to make effective use of such concepts as "deep interdiction" and "battlefield extension," not only will tactics need to be better coordinated, but NATO's own supplies and lines of communication will need to be harmonized. The difficulties inherent in this strategy should not be minimized, however. The budgetary and procurement cycles among the allies are quite different[39] and some allies will be slow in sharing their technology should they develop a lead that appears to have important commercial advantages.[40] Yet, if the Europeans devise an acceptable work-sharing arrangement for projects under the European Research Coordination Agency (Eureka) and there is an acceptable compromise on SDI programs, closer allied integration may be feasible. There are no measures which can compel this, however, so this is hardly an approach that the United States can count on with any certainty.

A *case-by-case approach,* which avoids any grand strategy, would encourage U.S. allies to pursue those military measures most acceptable to their domestic constituencies. There is an American tendency to want simplicity and predictability in dealing with allies. Yet, in any set of economic, political, cultural, and military relationships as complicated as the current U.S. alliances there are bound to be countries or circumstances that do not fit nicely into an overall strategy. For example, few observers of NATO would have thought that a decade after Charles De Gaulle's departure from office there would have been the close Franco-German collaboration that Giscard d'Estaing and Helmut Schmidt pursued. Thus, to have attempted a fundamental reconfiguation of NATO after De Gaulle's withdrawal of French forces might have created a break that would later have been hard to heal. Similarly, in today's environment, pressing for a systematic schema may cause more friction than is warranted.

In essence, pursuing a case-by-case approach would emphasize bilateral relations. It would avoid the political costs of mounting major alliance-wide initiatives, yet lose the advantages of group pressure to share common burdens. However, it would put the onus on the Europeans to begin taking a more assertive role themselves in deciding how to deal with the Warsaw Pact military buildup.

A key problem in Western strategy that can only be handled on a case-by-case approach is nuclear system development. The British and the French are both willing to pay very substantial sums to maintain their nuclear capabilities. The British are willing to buy Trident submarines from the United States, whereas the French spend large amounts to develop systems that are less capable than those based on British or American technology. Part of this is a reaction against previous American refusals to share nuclear information with the French, but part of it is also the French desire to maintain the intellectual and productive capacity to permit French autonomy. Although it would clearly be preferable to have France fully integrated into NATO and to have an explicit agreement on how the West will link conventional and nuclear weapons in Europe, there is a tacit understanding that there are limits to consistency.

The United States must also decide how to deal with what might be termed the "reluctant participants" in NATO. For instance, the Spanish socialist government of Felipe Gonzales appears to be doing a delicate balancing act in pleasing the Left and some nationalists by pressing for reductions in U.S. servicemen at certain air bases but proceeding with a referendum on whether to stay in NATO which could well end up pleasing the moderates and Right. The militant socialist government of Andreas Papandreou in Greece (reelected for a second four-year term in June 1985) is more blatant in its attempts to extract resources from its allies. Though, during his first term, Papandreou did not follow through on his initial campaign pledge to rid Greece of American bases, he has repeatedly criticized his allies, kept Greek forces from participating in various NATO exercises, and used NATO membership as a ploy in negotiating for subsidies from the European Common Market. Since both Spain and Greece are critical to NATO for geopolitical reasons, the United States must treat each of these situations separately and delicately. Although following a case-by-case approach does not provide a military strategy and is essentially a diplomatic tactic, it is a way to preserve vital relationships while inducing the key West European members of NATO to play a stronger leadership role themselves.

*A New Division of Labor.* There are essentially two broad groups advocating a new division of responsibilities within NATO: (a) those who would like to change the relative weights of the U.S. and European contributions to NATO, and (b) those who think it is politically unrealistic to expect the Europeans to spend substantially more but that it may be possible to use the current forces more efficiently.

Henry Kissinger, for example, favors relatively modest changes in strategy (increased European manpower and anti-tank weapons linked with greater U.S. air and sea lift),[41] but urges that the United States use leverage to get these changes. Those who agree with this approach think that the Western Europeans will never increase defense spending on their own accord because it is clearly rational to be "free riders" and the political support for strengthening defenses is limited. If this is the case, then only the ultimate threat of U.S. reductions in commitments can force the West Europeans to face up to the need to spend adequately to defend themselves.

The other variant of the "division of labor" school argues for changes in strategy and tactics that will create a more cost-effective deterrent within present budget constraints. Canby and Dörfer stress a new mix of responsibilities where the United States and the Europeans would each rely more on their comparative advantage.[42] The United States, having a large air force but requiring 4 – 6 weeks to deploy substantial numbers of new ground troops on the Continent, might thus further emphasize its air force contribution to NATO if the Europeans would build up their ground strength. A related idea, which is part of the "deep interdiction" strategy, is to have NATO make air attacks far into the rear of the Warsaw Pact forces and to actually reduce armor of NATO ground forces, stressing mobility and agility in finding vulnerable spots in the opponent's flank.

These two variants of the "division of labor" school are based on different philosophies about alliance relations. The Kissinger view is that NATO is in sufficient trouble to warrant the United States taking steps which ultimately risk the dissolution of the alliance; while those who favor readjusting force structure commitments are asking for greater integration and mutual trust among the allies than ever achieved in the past.

Interestingly, a strategy which emphasizes a conventional/non-nuclear deterrent limits the ability of any one Western nation to be a "free rider." Since it is hard to define what is an adequate nuclear deterrent, there is a tendency for non-nuclear nations to say that, as long as there is a credible retaliatory capability maintained by a nuclear ally, their own defense effort is not essential. In conventional defense planning, however, there are clear territorial borders, air space, and sea lanes to be defended and there is less ambiguity on what is needed to stop an opponent.

Clearly the United States cannot pursue both variants of the "division of labor" proposals simultaneously. It is not realistic to threaten to withdraw and, at the same time, urge the Europeans to scale back future investments in their air forces because the United States will be available during emergencies. However, there is one common advantage to both sets of proposals: they serve notice to the European members of NATO that the United States is unlikely to persist indefinitely with both the current strategy and the current level of contribution to allied defense.

*Pacific Tilt.* For those who believe that Europe's defense problems stem from an irreversible slowdown in economic growth and vitality, there is a clear logic to linking long-term U.S. defense plans to allies that appear more capable of defending themselves. Although no mainstream analysts are presently advocating that the United States completely disengage from Europe, many pragmatists are arguing that the United States must at least be ready for that possibility. Some observers already claim that the U.S. government has begun a gradual move toward heightening the profile of U.S.-Japanese relations[43] while others see the development of a tacit entente between China, Japan, South Korea, and the United States.

The obvious attraction of emphasizing U.S. ties in the Pacific is to keep military commitments in rough alignment with economic interests. With the high savings, investment, and growth rates in the Pacific, economic opportunities appear buoyant. If there is not a turn-around in Western European economic and defense performance, the United States faces the danger of allowing emotional and political ties with Europe to outweigh national-interest considerations.

However, for a Pacific alliance to become a reality, both the Chinese and the Japanese would need to see clear long-term benefits in a closer alliance with the United States. At present, this is unlikely as the People's Republic of China enhances its flexibility by keeping its distance from both the United States and Soviet Union. Also, with the Japanese public still showing a strong aversion to any military commitments other than self-defense and the Japanese government quite content to be a "free rider" on U.S. largesse, it appears that global military balance would need to shift before either the Japanese or Chinese would take the risks entailed in such an overtly anti-Soviet move. Nevertheless, should Western Europe actually reduce its defense capabilities and show signs of conceding to Soviet pressure, this would almost certainly heighten anxieties in China and Japan. If the United States was then able to develop a close working relationship on military matters with both the Chinese and the Japanese, this might well become the prime constellation of forces in the early twenty-first century.

It is also possible that the United States could strengthen its position in Southeast Asia by a closer working relationship with the ASEAN countries. The deteriorating political and economic circumstances in the Philippines should not be allowed to sour U.S. relations with the other nations in the ASEAN area. The United States might use a mix of expanded tariff preferences and less restrictive trade quotas as inducements for solidifying ties in Southeast Asia. A longer-term objective of a Pacific Treaty Organization could gradually be explored if a close working relationship between the United States, Japan, and China developed.

*Greater U.S. Autonomy.* Given the inherent difficulty of managing alliances, there has always been a sizable segment of American public opinion that has favored various forms of disengagement from foreign military and political commitments. The Monroe Doctrine was as much a statement that the United States would not be involved in Europe as it was a warning against European influence in the Americas.[44] Yet, few realists looking at the world scene think the United States would be safer if it fully disengaged from Europe and the Pacific. Those who argue in favor of greater U.S. autonomy generally advocate either a form of forward deployment through strengthening the Navy or a repositioning of U.S. forces (back to U.S. soil) with the development of an increased air and sea lift capability.

The maritime strategy[45] which places primary emphasis on U.S. dominance of air and sea lines of communications has strong supporters in the Reagan administration. Its basic rationale is to rely on the comparative advantage that the United States now possesses over the Soviet Union in air and naval forces, and to deploy those forces in a manner which maximizes deterrence and threatens the greatest damage to the Soviet homeland. Although the United States might, at some stage, choose this as an alternative to outright isolationism, it is still significantly more cost-effective to have air and ground forces stationed in Europe. Also, political analysts are concerned that emphasizing maritime superiority would signal that the United States was ceding dominance of the Eurasian landmass to the Soviet Union.

The other main method advocated for increasing U.S. autonomy is to limit forward deployments and enhance "mobility forces." Efforts on this tack have a long history. During the 1950s, General Maxwell Taylor favored this approach,[46] and part of the "flexible response" strategy developed in the Kennedy administration involved the reduction of overseas troop commitments and the expansion of air and sealift capabilities.[47] Yet, stressing mobility forces has usually run into three types of opposition: (a) the U.S. military leadership has worried that pulling troops back to the United States would create an appearance of excess troops on U.S. soil, possibly leading Congress to cut the entire force structure, (b) allies of the United States frequently see even discussion of troop reduction as a sign of decreased American commitment and have vociferously lobbied against it,[48] and (c) the Congress has never shown much enthusiasm for funding the air and sealift necessary to make greater autonomy a viable military strategy.

These factors do not mean that greater autonomy isn't possible, but, if it is not to be a strategy of anything other than isolationism, the United States would need credible means to reassure its allies that autonomy did not mean a withdrawal from world commitments.

In sum, there is a clear link between economic performance and defense policy. These relationships can be quantified and have shown consistent patterns in the post-World War II era. If the Western European members of NATO show no greater willingness to fund their own defense in the late 1980s than they did in the 1945–1985 period, the United States must face fundamental choices about its long-term strategy and alliance relationships. Several of the military strategies discussed previously could decidedly enhance U.S. and allied conventional capabilities, but they all require changes in force structure and planning in order to be implemented. Moreover, the political implications of a fundamental change in U.S. defense strategy are momentous. It would be unfortunate to allow poor economic performance by our allies to be the key constraining factor in U.S. defense policy.

## NOTES

1. B. Feder, "Britons Assess Poor Showing for Tories," *New York Times*, May 6, 1985, p. A3.
2. S. Hoffman, "Mitterrand versus France," *The New York Review of Books*, September 27, 1984; and J. Vinocur, "French Center and Right Make Gains, "*New York Times*, March 10, 1985, p. A1.
3. J. Markham, "NATO Critic Wins West German Vote," *New York Times*, March 11, 1985, p. A3; and J. Markham, "Kohl Loses Badly in Key State Vote," *New York Times*, May 13, 1985, p. A1.

4. For an overview of the current debates on defense budgets see "Defence: Is there an alternative?" *The Economist,* September 29, 1984, p. 58; G. Hoffman, "Vom Störfaktor zum Machtfaktor," *Die Zeit,* 5. Oktober 1984, p. 3; J. Isnard, "Budget Militaire: austérité en 1985," *Le Monde,* 19 Septembre 1984, pp. 1, 6; and P. Langereux, "Le RPR se pronounce pour un renforcement des moyens de defense," *Air et Cosmos,* 5 février 1984, p. 39.
5. Like the United States government, the British, French, and West German governments have all been running major deficits in the 1980s, so it is possible to argue that the European leaders of NATO could increase their defense spending by expanding deficits. Yet, all three governments have made explicit efforts to reduce the size of their respective deficits. Tax revenue growth is thus the easiest source of financing for increasing defense.
6. L. Thurow, "How to Wreck the Economy," *New York Review of Books,* May 14, 1981, pp. 3–8.
7. A. Cockburn and J. Ridgeway, "Can the Pentagon Still Save Capitalism?" *The Village Voice,* May 17, 1985, pp. 18–21, 102.
8. See Chapter 2 for an extended discussion of the micro and macro effects of defense spending on the United States. In addition to the three major commercial macroeconomic modeling services which have looked at this question (Data Resources, Inc., Chase Econometrics, and Wharton Econometric Forecasting Associates) there is detailed micro-sector analysis available from input-output modeling: see D. Blond, *The Domestic Economic Impact Model Simulator* (DEIMS) (Washington, DC: U.S. Department of Defense, 1983).
9. At the time of the final drafting of this chapter (June 1985), there was a sharp disagreement between the House and Senate version of the "freeze" for Fiscal Year 1986 defense funding. The Senate version was a freeze in "real terms" (i.e., adjusted for inflation) while the House version was a freeze without any inflation adjustment. President Reagan agreed only to the Senate version. The Gramm – Rudman legislation (December 1985) puts additional constraints on U.S. defense expenditure increases.
10. J. Gerth, "General Electric Admits Falsifying Billing on Missile," *New York Times,* May 14, 1985, p. A1.
11. S. Ostry, "The World Economy in 1983: Marking Time,"*Foreign Affairs – America and the World 1983* 62 (1984): 533–560.
12. M. Albert, *Un Pari Pour L'Europe* (Paris: Editions du Seuil, 1983), Chapter 1.
13. Organization for Economic Cooperation and Development, *OECD Economic Survey 1982–1983: France* (Paris: OECD, 1983).
14. *The Economist,* "Europe's Technology Gap," November 24, 1984, pp. 93–98.
15. This fear was expressed to me by Pierre Lellouche, of the French Institute for Foreign Relations (I.F.R.I.) in a personal interview on March 6, 1984. The November 1983 visit of President Reagan to Japan did produce a series of accords in which the Japanese agreed to export military technology to the United States (only) in exchange for military technology that the United States was providing Japan.
16. L. Richman, "Testing Time for Germany's Miracle," *Fortune,* May 12, 1985, pp. 114–120.
17. P. Norman, "Bonn, Bundesbank Promise Lower Taxes and Measures to Draw Foreign Investment," *European Wall Street Journal,* March 27, 1985, Section 2, p. 1.
18. "Why Doesn't My Boom Get Votes?" *The Economist,* May 18, 1985, p. 13.
19. R. Bernstein, "European Project Picks Up Support," *New York Times,* May 25, 1985, p. 4.
20. See the conclusion of Chapter 3 in this volume. These calculations assume all other factors are held constant.

21. For a full discussion of these growth-stimulating or inhibiting effects, see Chapter 4, "Defense, Growth, and Allocation Behavior in the Alliance: The Southern Tier of NATO."
22. For a discussion of the factors limiting Korean economic growth in the 1950s, see D. Cole and P. Lyman's *Korean Development* (Cambridge, MA: Harvard University Press, 1971).
23. These estimates focus only on the costs of the defense burden and do not make an attempt to estimate benefits that may come from training, infrastructure, or research and development.
24. See the last section of Chapter 5, "Japan and South Korea."
25. In addition to the Marshall Plan for Europe, the United States provided direct, bilateral aid for Japan and South Korea and support to multilateral institutions like the International Monetary Fund and the World Bank. It is worth noting that Japan's per capita income was so low in the early post-World War II period that Japan was the largest single borrower from the World Bank until 1960.
26. See Chapter 1 for a discussion of the two-track decision to link deployment of the Pershing IIs and the GLCMs to progress in the U.S.-Soviet intermediate nuclear force talks.
27. There are some Americans who share this view as well. See, for example, R. Barnet's *Real Security* (New York: Simon & Schuster, 1981).
28. L. Caldwell and R. Legvold, "Reagan Through Soviet Eyes," *Foreign Policy* 52 (Fall 1983): 3 – 21.
29. R. Pipes, "Why the Soviet Union Thinks It Can Fight and Win a Nuclear War," *Commentary* 64, No. 1 (July 1977): 21 – 34.
30. H. Schmidt, "A Direct Hit, Kissinger's Analysis Is Correct: The Western Countries Need to Finally Work Out Together a New Global Strategy" (In German), *Die Zeit*, Nr. 11, March 9, 1984.
31. See, for example, the discussion of the relationship between conventional and nuclear strategy in R. W. Tucker, "The Nuclear Debate," *Foreign Affairs* 63, No. 1 (Fall 1984): 1 – 32.
32. W. Mako, *U.S. Ground Forces and the Defense of Central Europe* (Washington, D C: The Brookings Institution, 1983).
33. R. Morse, *The Politics of Japan's Energy Strategy* (Berkeley, CA: University of California Press, 1981).
34. For an interesting discussion of American beliefs about the professional military and maintaining high states of readiness, see B. Tuchman's "American People and Military Power," *Adelphi Paper #173* (London: IISS, Spring 1982).
35. In the *New York Times*, see the series titled "Billions for Defense/The Spending Debate," The second feature (May 15, 1985, p. B10) notes the tendency of the Congress to fund major weapons systems but stretch out or cut requests for supplies and readiness.
36. See L. Walinsky, "Coherent Defense Strategy: The Case for Economic Denial," *Foreign Affairs* 61 (1982 – 1983): 272 – 291, for an analysis of the technology control debate.
37. D. Denoon, "Report on Enhancing Technology Flow from Our Allies" (Washington, D.C.: U.S. Department of Defense, September 15, 1984). Mimeo.
38. J. Dean, "Reply to Conventional Deterrence and Conventional Retaliation into Eastern Europe," *International Security* 9, No. 1 (1984): 206.
39. For an interesting comparison of the British versus U.S. systems for management and defense budgeting, see M. Hobkirk, *The Politics of Defense* (Washington, DC: National Defense University Press, 1982).
40. "Rearming Japan," *Business Week*, March 14, 1983, pp. 106 – 116.
41. H. Kissinger, "A Plan to Reshape NATO," *Time*, March 5, 1984, pp. 20 – 24.

42. S. Canby and I. Dörfer, "More Troops, Fewer Missiles," *Foreign Policy*, No. 57 (1983 – 1984): 3 – 17.
43. R. Nations, "A Tilt Toward Tokyo," *Far Eastern Economic Review*, April 21, 1983, pp. 36 – 40.
44. G. Smith, "The Legacy of Monroe's Doctrine," *New York Times Magazine*, September 9, 1984, pp. 46 – 55.
45. See K. Dunn and W. Staudenmaier, "Strategy for Survival," *Foreign Policy*, No. 52 (1983): 22 – 41.
46. M. Taylor, *The Uncertain Trumpet* (New York: Harper, 1960).
47. W. Kaufman, *Planning Conventional Forces 1950 – 1980* (Washington, DC: Brookings Institution, 1982).
48. During the 1976 presidential election campaign, Governor Jimmy Carter promised to withdraw troops from South Korea. Once he became president, both the Korean government and the U.S. Congress were so strongly opposed to his campaign pledge that Carter dropped the proposal.

# BIBLIOGRAPHY

## DEFENSE ECONOMICS

### In English

Albert, M., and R. J. Ball. *Towards European Economic Recovery in the 1980s: Report Presented to the European Parliament.* European Parliament: Working Documents, August 31, 1983

American Enterprise Institute for Public Policy Research. *Military Base Closings: Benefits for Community Adjustment.* Washington, DC, 1977.

Anderson, James R. *The Pentagon Tax: The Impact of the Military Budget on Major American Cities* (Lansing, MI: Employment Research Associates, 1972).

Anderson, Marion. *The Empty Pork Barrel: Unemployment and the Pentagon Budget* (Lansing, MI: Employment Research Associates, 1978).

Antonio, R. J., and D. Braa. "Military Spending and the Contemporary American Crisis: A Marxist Analysis." *Economic Forum* 13, No. 1 (1982): 111 – 134.

Ash, J., B. Udis, and R. McNown. "Enlistments in the All-Volunteer Force: A Military Personnel Supply Model and its Forecasts." *American Economic Review* 73, No. 17 (1983): 145 – 155.

Ball, Nicole. "Defense and Development: A Critique of the Benoit Study." *Economic Development and Cultural Change* 31 (1983): 507 – 524.

Barro, Robert J. "Output Effects of Government Purchases." *Journal of Political Economy* 89 (1981): 1086 – 1121.

Benoit, E. *Defense and Economic Growth in Developing Countries* (Lexington, MA: Lexington Books, 1973).

Benoit, E. "Growth and Defense in Developing Countries." *Economic Development and Cultural Change* 26, No. 2 (1978): 271 – 280.

Benoit, E. "The Monetary and Real Costs of National Defense." *American Economic Review* 58 (1968): 398 – 445.

Benoit, E., and K. Boulding, eds. *Disarmament and the Economy* (New York: Harper and Row, 1963).

Binkin, Martin, and Irene Kyriakopolous. *Paying the Modern Military* (Washington, DC: Brookings Institution, 1981).

Blanchard, J. "Current and Anticipated Deficits, Interest Rates and Economic Activity." NBER Working Paper No. 1265, January 1984.

Blond, D. *The Defense Economic Impact Model Simulator* (DEIMS) (Washington, DC: U.S. Department of Defense, 1983).

Blond, D. "The Industrial and Labor Composition of Defense Demand." Office of the Secretary of Defense, 1983, mimeo.

Blond, D. "On the Adequacy and Inherent Strength of the U.S. Industrial Technological Base: Guns versus Butter in Today's Economy." Data Resources, Inc., *Defense Economics Research Report*, 1983.

Bohm, Peter. "Estimating Demand for Public Goods: An Experiment." *European Economic Review* 3, No. 2 (1972): 111 – 130.

Bolton, Roger E., ed. *Defense and Disarmament: The Economics of Transition* (Englewood Cliffs, NJ: Prentice-Hall, 1966).

Borcherding, T. E. "Comment: The Demand for Military Expenditures: And International Comparison." *Public Choice* 37, No. 1 (1981): 33 – 39.

Bordewich, Fergus. "Turkey: From Anarchy to Modernity." *The Atlantic Monthly*, December 1984, pp. 44 – 52.

Brzoska, Michael. "The Reporting of Military Expenditures." *Journal of Peace Research* 18 (1981): 261 – 275.

Burt, Richard. *New Weapons Technologies: Debate and Directions* (London: International Institute for Strategic Studies [IISS] 1976).

Clark, Peter K. "Investment in the 1970s: Theory, Performance and Prediction." *Brookings Papers on Economic Activity*, No. 1 (1979), pp. 73 – 113.

Clayton, James L., ed. *The Economic Impact of the Cold War: Sources and Readings* (New York: Harcourt, Brace and World, 1970).

Cockburn, A., and J. Ridgeway. "Can the Pentagon Still Save Capitalism?" *The Village Voice*, May 17, 1983, pp. 18 – 21, 102.

Congressional Budget Office. *Budgetary Cost Savings to the Department of Defense Resulting from Foreign Military Sales*. Washington, DC, 1976.

Congressional Budget Office. *Defense Spending and the Economy*. Washington, DC, February 1983.

Congressional Budget Office. *The Effect of Foreign Military Sales on the U.S. Economy*. Washington, DC, July 1976.

Congressional Budget Office. *Foreign Military Sales and U.S. Weapons Costs*. Washington, DC, 1976.

Cornes, and T. Sandler. "The Theory of Public Goods: Non-Nash Behaviour." *Journal of Public Economics* 23 (1984): 381 – 390.

Council on Economic Priorities. *Military Expansion, Economic Decline: The Impact of Military Spending on U.S. Economic Performance* (New York: M.E. Sharpe, 1983).

Cusack, Thomas R., and Michael D. Ward. "Military Spending in the United States, the Soviet Union, and the People's Republic of China." *Journal of Conflict Resolution* 25 (1981): 429 – 469.

Daly, G., and J. Schuttinga. "Price Competition and the Acquisition of Weapons Systems." *Journal of Policy Analysis and Management* 2, No. 1 (1982): 55 – 65.

Data Resources, Inc. *An Approach to Evaluating Industry Bottleneck Potential: The Industrial Capacity Monitoring System*. March 1984, mimeo.

Data Resource, Inc. "Defense Inflation Prospects." *Defense Economics Research Report*, May 1983.

Data Resources, Inc. "Industry/Occupational Outlook." *Defense Economics Research Report,* December 1982.

Davis, O., M. Dempster, and A. Wildavsky. *On the Process of Budgeting.* Reprint No. 252 (Pittsburgh: Carnegie-Mellon University, 1966).

"Defence: Is There an Alternative?" *The Economist,* Sept. 29, 1984, pp. 58.

Deger, S. "Economic Development and Defense Expenditures." Paper presented at S.S.R.C. Development Economics Study Group, London, 1979.

Deger, S., and S. Sen. "Military Expenditure, Spin-Off and Economic Development." *Journal of Development Economics* 13, Nos. 1 – 2 (1983): 67 – 83.

Deger, Saadet, and Ron Smith. "Military Expenditure and Growth in Less Developed Countries." *Journal of Conflict Resolution* 27 (1983): 335 – 353.

Delauer, R. "Remarks on Arms Collaboration and the Emerging Technologies." Conference Sponsored by *The Economist* (London: February 9, 1984).

Denison, E. *Accounting for Slower Economic Growth* (Washington, DC: Brookings Institution, 1979).

Dempsey, R., and D. Schmude. "Occupational Impact of Defense Expenditures." *Monthly Labor Review* 94, No. 12 (1971): 12 – 15.

Denoon, D. "Report on Enhancing Technology Flow from Our Allies." Washington, DC: U.S. Department of Defense (mimeo), September 15, 1984.

Desai, M., and D. Blake. "Modelling the Ultimate Absurdity: A Comment on 'A Quantitative Study of the Strategic Arms Race in the Missile Age'." *Review of Economics and Statistics* 58 (1981): 629 – 632.

Domke, William K., Richard C. Eichenberg, and Catherine M. Kelleher. "The Illusion of Choice: Defense and Welfare in the Advanced Industrial Democracies, 1948 – 1978." *American Political Science Review* 77, No. 1 (1983): 19 – 35.

Dreash, S. P. *Disarmament: Economic Consequences and Development Potential* (New Haven, CT: Yale University Press, 1972).

Dudley, Leonard. "Foreign Aid and the Theory of Alliances." *Review of Economics and Statistics* 61 (1979): 564 – 571.

Dudley Leonard and Claude Montmarquette. "The Demand for Military Expenditures: An International Comparison." *Public Choice* 37, No. 1 (1981): 5 – 31.

Dumas, L. J. "The Impact of the Military Budget on the Domestic Economy." *Economic Forum* 13, No. 1 (1982): 71 – 86.

Eckstein, Otto. "Measuring the Impact of the Defense Budget 1983 – 1988." Prepared Statement before the U.S. Joint Economic Committee of Congress on the Impact of Defense on the U.S. Economy, 1983.

Economic Planning Agency. *Japan in the Year 2000* (Tokyo: EPA, 1983).

Economic Planning Board. *Major Statistics of Korean Economy* (Seoul, Korea: EPB, 1982).

Edmonds, Martin, ed. *International Arms Procurement* (New York: Praeger, 1981).

Eisner, Robert, and M. I. Nadiri. "Investment Behavior and the Neoclassical Theory." *Review of Economic Statistics* 50 (1968): 369 – 381.

"Europe, defend thyself." *The Economist,* May 19 – 25, 1984, p. 55.

"European Elections: A Double Snub." *The Economist,* June 23 – 29, 1984, pp. 31 – 32.

Faini, Riccardo, Patricia Annez, and Lance Taylor. "Defense Spending, Economic Structure, and Growth: Evidence among Countries and over Time." *Economic Development and Cultural Change* 32 (1984): 487 – 498.

Feldstein, Martin. "Can an Increased Budget Deficit Be Contractionary?" NBER Working Paper No. 1434, August 1984.

Feldstein, Martin. "Depressing the Dollar, Gently." *The Wall Street Journal,* November 9, 1984, p. 30.

Fergusson, Adam. *Report Drawn up on behalf of the Political Affairs Committee on Arms Procurement within a Common Industrial Policy and Arms Sales.* European Parliament: Doc 1-455/83, June 27, 1983.

Fox, J. *Arming America* (Cambridge, MA: Harvard University Press, 1974).

"France Sets 1983 – 88 Defense Funding." *Aviation Week and Space Technology.* April 25, 1983, pp. 22 – 23.

Gansler, J. *The Defense Industry* (Cambridge, MA: MIT Press, 1982).

Garrison, C. B., and A. Mayhew. "The Alleged Vietnam Origins of the Current Inflation: A Comment." *Journal of Economic Issues* 17, No. 1 (1983): 175 – 186.

*The Geographic Distribution of Potential Defense Expenditure,* Department of Defense, July 1984.

Gordon, G. *A Study to Measure the Direct and Indirect Impact of Defense on an Economy.* (Seattle, WA: Arms Control and Disarmament Agency, 1966).

Gordon, R. J. "Do Economists Deserve a Failing Grade?" *The Gordon Update,* Fall 1984.

Gordon, R. J. *Macroeconomics.* 2nd ed. (New York: Little, Brown, 1983).

Greenwood, David. *Budgeting for Defence* (London: Royal United Services Institute for Defence Studies, 1972).

Greenwood, David. *A Policy for Promoting Defence and Technological Cooperation among West European Countries* (Aberdeen: Center for Defence Studies, at the request of the Commission of the European Communities [Brussels, 1980]).

Griffin, L. J., M. Wallace, and J. Devine. "The Political Economy of Military Spending: Evidence from the United States." *Cambridge Journal of Economics* 6 (1982): 1 – 14.

Groth, C., and M. McGuire. "A Method for Identifying the Public Good Allocation Process within a Group." *Quarterly Journal of Economics,* forthcoming.

Haberman, Clyde. "Japan Limits Rise in Military Spending to 7%." *New York Times,* August 1, 1984, p. A7.

Hartley, Keith. "Choices in Defence Expenditure." *The Journal of Economic Affairs* 1, No. 1 (1980): 31 – 35.

Hartley, Keith. "Estimating Military Aircraft Production Outlays: The British Experience." *Economic Journal* 79 (1969): 861 – 881.

Hartley, Keith, and Pat McLean. "Military Expenditure and Capitalism: A Comment." *Cambridge Journal of Economics* 2 (1978): 287 – 292.

Hartley, Keith, and Pat McLean. "U.K. Defence Expenditure." *Public Finance* 36 (1981): 172 – 192.

Hartley, K., and A. Peacock. "Combined Defence and International Economic Cooperation." *World Economy* 1 (1978): 327 – 339.

Hoag, Malcolm. "Economic Problems of Alliance." *Journal of Political Economy* 65 (1957): 522 – 534.

Hobkirk, M. *The Politics of Defense* (Washington, DC: National Defense University Press, 1982).

Holzman, F. D. "Are the Soviets Really Outspending the U.S. on Defense?" *International Security* 4, No. 4 (1980): 86 – 104.

Hough, J. R. *The French Economy* (New York: Holmes and Meier, 1982).

Hunter, L. "The Economic Effects of Military Expenditure in the Third World." *Economic Forum* 13, No. 1 (1982): 137 – 147.

IMF. *IMF World Economic Outlook* (Washington, DC: IMF, 1983).

Japanese Defense Agency. *Defense of Japan* (Tokyo: JDA, 1983).

Jorgenson, Dale. "Capital Theory and Investment Behavior." *American Economic Review* 53 (1963): 247 – 259.

Kanabayashi, Masayoshi. "Japan's Draft Budget Calls for 5.1% Rise in Defense Spending, Cuts in Other Areas." *The Wall Street Journal,* January 23, 1984, p. 27.

Kaufman, R. F. "Soviet Defense Trends." A Staff Study, Subcommittee on International Trade, Finance and Security Economics, Joint Economic Committee, Congress of the U.S., September 1983.

Kaufman, W. W. *The 1985 Defense Budget* (Washington, DC: The Brookings Institution, 1984).

Keel, Alton G., Jr. "The FY 1984 Defense Budget. The View from OMB." Presented to the Southern Economics Association, November 21, 1983.

Kennedy, Gavin. *Defense Economics* (New York: St. Martin's Press, 1983).

Kindleberger, Charles P. "Germany and the Economic Recovery of Europe." *Proceedings of the Academy of Political Science* 23 (1949): 288–301.

Knight, F. "Some Fallacies in Interpretation of Social Cost." *Quarterly Journal of Economics* 38 (1924): 582–606.

Korea Development Institute. *The Fifth Five-Year Economic and Social Development Plan* (Seoul: KDI, 1982).

Korea Development Institute. *The National Budget and Policy Objectives* (Seoul: KDI, 1982).

Kurth, James R. "Why We Buy the Weapons We Do." *Foreign Policy* 11 (Summer 1973): 33–56.

Lee, William T. *The Estimation of Soviet Defense Expenditures, 1955–75: An Unconventional Approach* (New York: Praeger Publishers, 1977).

Leontief, W., and F. Duchin. *Military Spending: Facts and Figures, Worldwide Implications, and Future Outlook* (New York: Oxford University Press, 1983).

Leontief, W., and M. Hoffenberg. "The Economic Effects of Disarmament." *Scientific American* 204, No. 4 (1961): 47–55.

Lim, D. "Another Look at Growth and Defense in Less Developed Countries." *Economic Development and Cultural Change* 31 (1983): 378–384.

Mansfield, Edwin, ed. *Defense, Science and Public Policy* (New York: W. W. Norton, 1968).

Marwell, G., and R. Ames. "Economists Free Ride, Does Anyone Else?" *Journal of Public Economics* 15 (1981): 295–310.

Matthews, Kent, and Patrick Minford. "Recent Developments and Forecasts." *Quarterly Economic Bulletin: Liverpool Research Group in Macroeconomics* 4, No. 4 (1983): 10–18.

McGuire, M. "Group Size, Group Homogeneity, and the Aggregate Provision of a Pure Public Good under Cournot Behavior." *Public Choice* 18 (1974): 107–126.

McGuire, M. "The Structure of Choice between Deterrence and Defense." in Roland McKean (ed.), *Issues in Defense Economics*. New York: National Bureau of Economic Research, 1967, pp. 129–149.

McGuire, M. "U.S. Foreign Assistance, Israeli Resource Allocation and the Arms Race in the Middle East: An Analysis of Three Interdependent Resource Allocation Processes." *Journal of Conflict Resolution* 26 (1982): 199–235.

McKean, R. N. *Issues in Defense Economics* (New York: Columbia University Press, 1967).

Mehrling, Perry. "Has Mrs. Thatcher Exorcised the Demons?" *Challenge* 25, No. 6 (1983): 57–70.

Melman, S. *Pentagon Capitalism: The Political Economy of War* (New York: McGraw-Hill, 1970).

Melman, S., ed., *The War Economy of the U.S.: Readings on Military Industry and Economy* (New York: St. Martin's Press, 1971).

Minford, Patrick. "Only a Holding Operation." *Quarterly Economic Bulletin: Liverpool Research Group in Macroeconomics* 4, No. 4 (1983): 3–9.

Minford, Patrick. "Public Expenditure: A Review of the Issues." *Quarterly Economic Bulletin: Liverpool Research Group in Macroeconomics* 4, No. 4 (1983): 23 – 31.

Moll, Kendall D., and Gregory M. Luebbert. "Arms Race and Military Expenditure Models." *Journal of Conflict Resolution* 24, No. 1 (1980): 153 - 185.

Morse, R. *The Politics of Japan's Energy Strategy* (Berkeley, CA: University of California Press, 1981).

Murdoch, James C., and Todd Sandler. "Australian Demand for Military Expenditures: 1961 – 1979." *Australian Economic Papers,* forthcoming (June 1985).

Nadiri, Ishaq. "An Alternative Model of Investment Spending." *Brookings Economic Paper,* 1971, pp. 547 – 578.

Nations, R. "A Tilt Toward Tokyo." *Far Eastern Economic Review,* April 21, 1983, pp. 36 – 40.

Nawaz, S. "Economic Impact of Defense Expenditures." *Finance Development* 20, No. 1 (1983): 34 – 35.

Nincic, M. "Fluctuations in Soviet Defense Spending: A Research Note." *Journal of Conflict Resolution* 27 (1983): 648 – 660.

Nincic, M., and T. R. Cusack. "The Political Economy of U.S. Military Spending." *Journal of Peace Research* 16, No. 2 (1979): 101 – 115.

Norman, Peter, and Roger Thurow. "Bonn's Recovery." *The Wall Street Journal,* January 9, 1984, pp. 1, 2.

"The North Sea's Second Wind." *The Economist,* May 12 – 18, 1984, pp. 88 – 89.

OECD. *OECD Economic Outlook* (Paris: OECD, 1983).

OECD. *OECD Economic Surveys 1982 – 1983: United Kingdom* (Paris: OECD, February 1983).

OECD. *OECD Economic Surveys 1982 – 1983: France* (Paris: OECD, March 1983).

OECD. *OECD Economic Surveys 1982 – 1983: Germany* (Paris: OECD, June 1983).

OECD. *National Accounts of OECD Countries, 1962 – 1979* (Paris: 1981).

OECD. *OECD Economic Surveys 1983 – 84: Greece* (Paris: OECD, November 1983).

OECD. *OECD Economic Surveys 1983 – 84: Portugal* (Paris: OECD, June 1984).

OECD. *OECD Economic Surveys 1983 – 84: Spain* (Paris: OECD, May 1984).

OECD. *OECD Economic Surveys 1983 – 84: Turkey* (Paris: OECD, May 1984).

Office of Management and Budget. *Federal Government Finances* (Washington, DC: U.S. Government Printing Office, March 1981).

Oliver, R. "Employment Effects of Reduced Defense Spending." *Monthly Labor Review* 94, No. 12 (1971): 3 – 11.

Olson, M., and R. Zeckhauser. "Collective Goods, Comparative Advantage, and Alliance Efficiency." In Roland McKean, ed., *Issues in Defense Economics* (New York: National Bureau of Economic Research, 1967), pp. 25 – 48.

Olson, M., and R. Zeckhauser. "An Economic Theory of Alliances." *Review of Economics and Statistics* 48 (1966): 266 – 279.

Olvey, Lee D., Henry A. Leonard, and Bruce Arlinghaus, eds. *Industrial Capacity and Defense Planning: Sustained Conflict and Surge Capability in the 1980s* (Lexington, MA: Toronto: Lexington/Heath, 1983).

Oppenheimer, Joe. "Collective Goods and Alliances: A Reassessment." *Journal of Conflict Resolution* 23 (1979): 387 – 407.

Ostry, S. "The World Economy in 1983: Marking Time." *Foreign Affairs* 62 (1984): 533 – 560.

Palme, Olof, et al. "Military Spending: The Economic and Social Consequences." *Challenge* 25, No. 4 (1982): 4 – 21.

Peroff, Kathleen, and Margaret Podolak-Warren. "Does Spending on Defense Cut Spending on Health? A Time Series Analysis of the U.S. Economy 1929 – 1974." *British Journal of Political Science* 9, No. 1 (1979): 21 – 39.

Rattinger, Hans. "Armaments, Detente and Bureaucracy: The Case of the Arms in Europe." *Journal of Conflict Resolution* 19 (1975): 571 – 595.

Reich, M. "Military Spending and Production for Profit." In R. Edwards et al. eds., *The Capitalist System*, 2nd ed. (Englewood-Cliffs, NJ: Prentice-Hall, 1978), pp. 409 – 418.

Reich, R. *The Next American Frontier* (New York: Times Books, 1983).

Richman, L. "Testing Time for Germany's Miracle." *Fortune*, May 12, 1985, pp. 114 – 120.

Ricklefs, Roger. "The Arms Business: France, a Big Exporter of Weapons, Is Hurt by Decline in Volume." *The Wall Street Journal*, July 20, 1984, p. 1.

Riddell, T., "Militarism: The Other Side of Supply." *Economic Forum* 13, No. 1 (1982): 49 – 70.

Riker, W. *The Theory of Political Coalitions* (New Haven: Yale University Press, 1970).

Rivlan, Alice, ed. *Economic Choices 1984* (Washington, DC: The Brookings Institution, 1984).

Rothschild, Kurt W. "Military Expenditures, Exports and Growth." *Kyklos* 26 (1973): 804 – 814.

Russett, Bruce. *What Price Vigilance: The Burdens of National Defense* (New Haven: Yale University Press, 1970).

Russett, Bruce. "Defense Expenditures and National Well-Being." *American Political Science Review* 76 (1982): 767 – 777.

Samuelson, Paul. "The Pure Theory of Public Expenditure." *Review of Economics and Statistics* 36 (1954): 387 – 389.

Sandler, Todd. "The Economic Theory of Alliances: Realigned." In C. Liske et al. eds., *Comparative Public Policy: Issues, Theories and Methods* (New York: John Wiley & Sons, 1975), pp. 223 – 239.

Sandler, Todd. "Impurity of Defense: An Application to the Economics of Alliances." *Kyklos* 30 (1977): 443 – 460.

Sandler, Todd, and Jon Cauley. "On the Economic Theory of Alliances." *Journal of Conflict Resolution* 19 (1975): 330 – 348.

Sandler, Todd, Jon Cauley, and John F. Forbes. "In Defense of a Collective Goods Theory of Alliances." *Journal of Conflict Resolution* 24 (1980): 537 – 547.

Sandler, Todd, and John Forbes. "Burden Sharing, Strategy, and the Design of NATO." *Economic Inquiry* 18 (1980): 425 – 444.

Schelling, T. C. "Arms Control Will Not Cut Defense Costs." *Harvard Business Review* 39 (April 1961): 6 – 14.

Schultze, C. L. "Do More Dollars Mean Better Defense?" *Challenge* 24, No. 6 (1982): 30 – 35.

Scott, B. "Can Industry Survive the Welfare State?" *Harvard Business Review* 60 (September-October 1982): 70 – 84.

Sinai, Allen. "Aftemath of the First Four Years." Shearson Lehman Bulletin Series, September 28, 1984.

Sinai, Allen, Andrew List, and Russell Robbins. "Taxes, Saving and Investment: Some Empirical Evidence." *National Tax Journal* 36 (1983): 321 – 345.

Sivard, R. L. *World Military and Social Expenditures* (Leesburg, VA: WMSE Publications, 1977).

Smith, Eric Owen. *The West German Economy* (New York: St. Martin's Press, 1983).

Smith, R. P., "The Demand for Military Expenditures." *The Economic Journal* 90 (1980): 811 – 820.

Smith, R. P., "Military Expenditure and Capitalism." *Cambridge Journal of Economics* 1 (1977): 61 – 76.

Smith, R. P., "Military Expenditure and Capitalism: A Reply." *Cambridge Journal of Economics* 2 (1978): 229 – 304.

Smith, R. P., "Military Expenditure and Investment In OECD Countries." *Journal of Comparative Economics* 4, No. 1 (1980): 19 – 32.

Smith, V. L. "Experiments with a Decentralized Mechanism for Public Good Decisions." *American Economic Review* 70 (1980): 584 – 599.

Solow, R. "Technological Change and the Aggregate Production Function." *The Review of Economics and Statistics* 39 (1957): 312 – 320.

Stein, H. "The Economics of American Defense: Q & A." *The Wall Street Journal*, July 7, 1981, p. 28.

Stockholm International Peace Research Institute (SIPRI). *World Armaments and Disarmament: SIPRI Yearbook* (New York: Crane, Russak & Co., 1983).

Thurow, Lester. "How to Wreck the Economy." *New York Review of Books*, May 14, 1981, pp. 3 – 8.

Udis, B., ed. *The Economic Consequences of Military Spending* (Lexington, MA: Lexington Books, 1973).

United States Arms Control and Disarmament Agency. *World Military Expenditures and Arms Transfers 1971 – 1980* (Washington, DC: March 1983).

United States Department of Commerce. *Sectoral Implications of Defense Expenditures* (mimeo) (Washington, DC: Bureau of Industrial Economics, 1982).

Väyrynen, Raimo. "The Theory of Collective Goods, Military Alliances and International Security." *International Social Science Journal* 38 (1976): 288 – 305.

Wakefield, J. C., and R. C. Ziemer. "National Defense Purchases: Detailed Quarterly Estimates, 1977 – 1982." *Survey of Current Business* 62, No. 11 (1982): 13 – 17.

Walinsky, Louis J. "Coherent Defense Strategy: The Case for Economic Denial." *Foreign Affairs* 61 (1982/83): 272 – 291.

Ward, Michael D. "Differential Paths to Parity: A Study of the Contemporary Arms Race." *American Political Science Review* 78 (1984): 297 – 317.

Wasserman, U. "World Trade in Armaments." *Journal of World Trade Law* 16 (1982): 362 – 366.

Wayne, Leslie. "Astounding American Job Machine." *New York Times*, June 17, 1984, pp. F1, F25.

Weidenbaum, M. L. *The Economics of Peacetime Defense* (New York: Praeger Publishers, 1974).

Weidenbaum, M. L. "Let's Examine National Defense Spending." *Challenge* 25, No. 6 (1983): 50 – 53.

Weinberger, C. *Annual Report to the Congress – FY 1985*. Washington, DC: U.S. Government Printing Office, February 1, 1984.

Wharton Econometrics. *World Economic Outlook,* 1983.

Whynes, D. K. *The Economics of Third World Military Expenditure* (Austin, TX: University of Texas Press, 1979).

World Bank. *World Development Report* (Washington, DC: World Bank, 1983).

Zimmerman, William, and Glenn Palmer. "Words and Deeds in Soviet Foreign Policy: The Case of Soviet Military Expenditures." *American Political Science Review* 77 (1983): 358 – 367.

## In French

Albert, Michel. *Un Pari pour l'Europe* [A Challenge for the European Community.] (Paris: Seuil, 1983).

Audigier, Pierre. "Les implications stratégiques du commerce Est-Ouest" [The Strategic Implications of East-West Trade]. *Défense Nationale* 40 (février 1984): 9 – 24.

Audigier, Pierre. "Le poids des dépenses de défense sur l'économie soviétique" (The Burden of Defense Spending on the Soviet Economy.) *Défense Nationale* 39 (février 1983): 65 – 81.

Audoux, Jean-Pierre, and Francis Pichet. "L'impact économique des dépenses militaires: des doctrines aux réalités" [The Economic Impact of Military Expenditures: from Doctrines to Reality.] *Stratégique* No. 13 (1er trimestre 1982): 93 – 104.

Boulin, Robert. "Le poids de la défense dans l'économie" [The Impact of Defense Spending on the Economy.] *Défense Nationale* 33 (juillet 1977): 7 – 22.

Chatillon, Georges. "La France et le Tiers Monde: Problèmes d'armements" [France and the Third World: Problems in Armaments]. *Défense Nationale* 39 (juillet 1983): 73 – 96.

Fontanel, Jacques. "La comparaison des dépenses militaires" [Comparison of Military Expenditures]. *Défense Nationale* 38 (novembre 1982): 107 – 121.

Fontanel, Jacques. *L'Economie des Armes* [Armaments Economics] (Paris: La Découverte/Maspero, 1983).

Fontanel, Jacques, Daniel Colard, and Jean-François Guilhaudis. *Le Désarmement pour le Développement: Dossier d'un Pari Difficile* [Disarmament for Development: The Dossier of a Difficult Challenge] (Paris: Fondation pour les Etudes de Défense Nationale, 1981).

Institut des Hautes Etudes de Défense Nationale. "Les dépenses militaires et l'économie de la Nation" [Military Spending and the Nation's Economy]. *Stratégique*, No. 11 (3ème trimestre 1981): 7 – 40.

Institut des Hautes Etudes de Défense Nationale. "Les défenses militaires et l'économie de la Nation. Fin" [Military Spending and the Nation's Economy. End]. *Stratégique*, No. 12 (4ème trimestre 1981): 53 – 111.

Isnard, J. "Budget militaire: austérité en 1985." *Le Monde*, 19 septembre 1984, pp. 1, 6.

La Gorce, Paul Marie de. *L'Effort de Défense de Quelques Grandes Puissances* [The Defense Effort of a Few Great Powers]. (Veneux-les-Sablons: J. Lopez, 1976).

Langereux, P. "Le RPR se prononce pour un renforcement des moyens de défense." *Air et Cosmos*, 5 février 1984, p. 39.

Laulan, Yves. "Le réarmement américain et la conjoncture aux Etats-Unis." [The American Rearmament and the U.S. Economy]. *Défense Nationale* 36 (juillet 1980): 81 – 95.

Ministère de la Défense. *Programme de la Défense, 1984 – 88* (Paris: Service d'Information et de Relations Publiques des Armées, 1983).

Percebois, Jacques. "Budget militaire, finances publiques et redéploiement industriel" [Military Budget, Public Finances and Industrial Redeployment]. *Arès, Défense et Sécurité*, II (1978 – 79): 195 – 208.

Percebois, Jacques. "Quelques considérations économiques à propos du budget militaire 1978" [A few Economic Considerations Concerning the 1978 Military Budget]. *Arès, Défense et Sécurité* I (1977): 271 – 281.

Perget, Jacques. "Pour une intégration des dépenses militaires dans la stratégie économique et financière de la Nation: 'recherche d'un optimum' [For an Integration of Military Spending into the Economic and Financial Strategy of the Nation: Pursuit of the Optimum Solution]. *Défense Nationale* 32 (novembre 1976): 29 – 46.

Pinatel, J.B. "Sécurité et développement économique: deux impératifs conciliables" [Security and Economic Development: Two Reconcilable Imperatives]. *Défense Nationale* 34 (août/septembre 1978): 73 – 88.

Rainaud, Jean-Marie, and Jacques Spindler. "Les exportations de matériels militaires: aspects juridiques et économiques" [Exports of Military Equipment: Legal and Economic Aspects]. *Arès, Défense et Sécurité* I (1977): 153 – 191.

Schmidt, Christian. "Economie et défense: un domaine aux multiples intersections" [Economics and Defense: an Area with Multiple Cross-sections]. *Défense Nationale* 38 (novembre 1982): 95 – 105.

Schmidt, Christian. "L'économie de la défense en France" [French Defense Economics]. *Revue d'Economie Politique*, No. 6 (1980): 33 – 49.

Sokoloff, Georges. *L'Economie de la Détente: l'U.R.S.S. et le Capital Occidental* [The Economics of Detente: The USSR and Western Capital]. (Paris: Presses de la Fondation Nationale des Sciences Politiques, 1983).

Tezenas du Montcel, Henri. "Economie et défense" [Economics and Defense]. *Défense Nationale* 37 (février 1981): 95 – 105.

## In German

Albrecht, Ulrich, *Rüstungskonversionsforschung: eine Literaturstudie mit Forschungsempfehlungen* [Arms Conversion Research: a Literature Study with Recommendations for Research]. (Baden-Baden: Nomos-Verlag, 1979).

Albrecht, Ulrich, Peter Lock, and Herbert Wulf. *Arbeitsplätze durch Rüstung? Warnung vor falschen Hoffnungen* [Jobs via Armaments? Warning against False Hopes]. (Reinbeck bei Hamburg; Rowohlt Verlag, 1978).

Baring, Arnulf, and Masamorie Sase, eds. *Zwei zaghafte Riesen? Deutschland und Japan seit 1945* [Two Faint-hearted Giants? Germany and Japan since 1945]. (Stuttgart, Zurich: Belser Verlag, 1977).

Bielfeldt, Carola. *Rüstungsausgaben und Staatsinterventionismus: Das Beispiel der Bundesrepublik Deutschland 1950 – 1971* [Armament Spending and Government Intervention: The Example of the Federal Republic of Germany 1950 – 1971]. (Frankfurt a.M.: Campus Verlag, 1977).

Bielfeldt, Carola. "Zum Verhältnis von Entspannungspolitik, militärischer Sicherheit und Rüstungskontrolle in der Bundesrepublik Deutschland" [On the Relationship between Detente, Military Security and Arms Control in the Federal Republic of Germany]. In *Europäische Sicherheit und Rüstungswettlauf*, HSFK ed. (Frankfurt a.M., New York: Campus Verlag, 1979), pp. 157 – 164.

Engelhardt, Klaus. "Umstellung von Rüstungsproduktion auf friedlichen Bedarf. Möglichkeiten und Hindernisse" [Converting Armaments Production into Peaceful Uses. Possibilities and Obstacles] In *Von den Kriegs-zur Friedensproduktion*, Eric Burhop and Jörg Huffschmid, eds. (Köln: Pahl-Rugenstein Verlag, 1980), pp. 64 – 72.

Grünewald, Guido. "Abrüstung und Arbeitsplatzsicherung. Zur Diskussion über Rüstungskonversion und Arbeitslosigkeit" [Disarmament and Job Security. Contribution to the Debate over Arms Conversion and Unemployment]. *Blätter für deutsche und internationale Politik*, No. 6 (1978): 657 – 680.

Huffschmid, Jörg. "Ökonomie der Abrüstung" [Economics of Disarmament]. *Blätter für deutsche und internationale Politik*, No. 5 (1977): 532 – 552.

Köllner, Lutz. "Zur Finanzierung der Militärausgaben" [On the Financing of Military Spending]. *Liberal*, No. 12 (1980): 913 – 920.

Mehrens, Klaus. "Arbeitsplätze und Rüstungsindustrie" [Jobs and the Arms Industry]. *Neue Gesellschaft*, No. 4 (1979): 328 – 330.

Reichelstein, Hans-Egon. "Das Wechselverhältnis von Rüstung und Wirtschaft" [The Correlation between Armaments and the Economy]. In *Militär und Ökonomie: Beiträge zu einem Symposium,* Karl-Ernst Schulz, ed. (Göttingen: Vandenhoeck und Ruprecht, 1977), pp. 23 – 32.

Senger, Jürgen. *Rüstungswirtschaft und Rüstungstechnologie. Zur gesamtwirtschaftlichen Bedeutung der rüstungstechnologischen Forschung und Entwicklung* [Armament Industry and Armament Technology. On the Macroeconomic Importance of Technological Armament Research and Development]. (Würzburg: Königshausen und Neumann Verlag, 1980).

Sonntag, Philipp, ed. *Rüstung und Ökonomie* [Arms Production and the Economy]. (Frankfurt a.M.: Haag und Herchen Verlag, 1982).

Thiel, Elke. *Dollar-Dominanz, Lastenteilung und amerikanische Truppenpräsenz in Europa. Zur Frage kritischer Verknüpfungen währungs und stationierungspolitischer Zielsetzung in den deutsch-amerikanischen Beziehungen* [Dollar Dominance, Burden-sharing and the Presence of American Troops in Europe. On the Question of Critical Interlinking of Monetary and Stationing Policy Objectives in German-American Relations]. (Baden-Baden: Nomos Verlag, 1979).

Walter, Franz. "Zum Problem der Belastung der Sowjetwirtschaft durch die Militäraufwendungen" [On the Burden of Military Expenditures on the Soviet Economy]. In *Politik, Strategie und Rüstung in der Sowijetunion,* Weltforschung aktuell, Band 7 (Stuttgart, München: Arbeitskreis für Weltforschung, 1977). pp. 90 – 111.

Wulf, Herbert. "Arbrüstung – eine politische und wirtschaftliche Notwendigkeit" [Disarmament – a Political and Economic Necessity]. *Druck und Papier,* No. 18 (1979): 4 – 7.

Wulf, Herbert. *Rüstungsimport als Technologietransfer, die negativen Auswirkungen von Rüstungsimporten auf die Industrialisierung in Peripherieländern* [Imports of Armaments as Technology Transfer: the Negative Impact of Arms Imports on the Industrialization of Peripheral Countries]. Weltwirtschaft und Internationale Beziehungen, Studien 20 (München, London: Weltforum Verlag, 1979)

Wulf, Herbert. "Zum Zusammenhang von Aussen-, Militär- und Wirtschaftspolitik der Reagan-Administration" [On the Relationship between the Foreign, Military and Economic Policies of the Reagan Administration] *Blätter für Deutsche und Internationale Politik,* No. 5 (1982): pp. 544 – 571.

Wulf, Herbert, and Ralph Peter. *Sicherheitspolitik, Rüstung und Abrüstung* [Security Policy, Armament and Disarmament]. (Frankfurt a.M.: Diesterweg, 1982).

# STRATEGY AND ALLIANCE ISSUES

## In English

Aldridge, Robert C. *The Counterforce Syndrome: A Guide to U.S. Nuclear Weapons and Strategic Doctrine.* 2nd ed. n.p. (Published by the Institute for Policy Studies, 1979).

Alford, Jonathan. "NATO's Conventional Forces and the Soviet Mobilization Potential." *NATO Review* 28, No. 3 (1980): 18 – 22.

Alford, Jonathan. *The Impact of New Military Technology.* Adelphi Library 4 (Farnborough, England: Gower; Montclair, NJ: Allanheld, Osmun; published for the International Institute for Strategic Studies, 1981).

Allen, A. F., and Ian Bellamy, eds. *The Future of the British Nuclear Deterrent* (Lancaster, England: University of Lancaster Center for the Study of Arms Control and International Security, 1980).

Allison, G. *Essence of Decision* (Boston: Little, Brown, 1971).

Andelman, David A. "Over Western Europe." *Foreign Policy*, No. 49 (Winter 1982 – 1983): 37 – 51.

"A Question of Confidence." *The Economist*, February 19, 1949, pp. 313 – 314.

Ball, Desmond. "Déjà Vu: The Return to Counterforce in the Nixon Administration." *California Seminar on Arms Control and Foreign Policy* (Los Angeles: UCLA, 1975).

Barnet, R. *Real Security* (New York: Simon & Schuster, 1981).

Baylis, John, ed. *British Defence Policy in a Changing World* (London: Croom Helm, 1977).

Beer, Francis. "The Political Economy of Alliances: Benefits, Costs and Institutions in NATO." *Sage Professional Papers in International Studies* (Beverly Hills, CA: Sage Publications, 1972).

Bellamy, Ian, and C. D. Blacker. *Antiballistic Missile Defence in the 1980s* (London: Frank Cass, 1983).

Bertram, Christoph. "Europe and America in 1983." *Foreign Affairs* 62 (1984): 616 – 631).

Bertram, Christoph, ed. *The Future of Strategic Deterrence* (Hamden, CT: Archon Books, 1981).

Bertram, Christoph, ed. *Strategic Deterrence in a Changing Environment*. Adelphi Library 6 (Farnborough, England: Gower; Montclair, NJ: Allanheld, Osmun; published for the International Institute for Strategic Studies, 1981).

Betts, Richard K. "Conventional Forces: What Price Readiness?" *Survival* 25, No. 1 (1983): 24 – 34.

Blaker, J., and A. Hamilton. *Assessing the NATO – Warsaw Pact Military Balance* (Washington, DC: Congressional Budget Office, December 1977).

Blechman, Barry. "Is There a Conventional Defense Option?" *The Washington Quarterly* 5, No. 3 (1982): 59 – 66.

Brayton, Abbott A. "Confidence-Building Measures in European Security." *The World Today*, October 1980, pp. 382 – 391.

Brodie, B. "Strategic Implications of the North Atlantic Pact." *Yale Review* 39 (1950): 193 – 208.

Brown, H. *Annual Report to the Congress, Fiscal Year 1982* (Washington, DC: US GPO, 1981).

Brown, H. *Seventh Report to the U.S. Congress on Rationalization, Standardization within NATO* (Washington, DC: U.S. Department of Defense, January 1981).

Brown, H., and L. Davis. "Nuclear Arms Control: Where Do We Stand?" *Foreign Affairs* 62 (1984): 1145 – 1160.

Bundy, McGeorge, George F. Kennan, Robert S. McNamara, and Gerard Smith. "Nuclear Weapons and the Atlantic Alliance." *Foreign Affairs* 60 (1982): 753 – 768.

Bundy, McGeorge, and François de Rose. "Nuclear Forces and Alliance Relations." *Survival* 24, No. 1 (1982): 19 – 23.

Burke, Kelly H. "Electronic Combat: Warfare of the Future." *Armed Forces Journal International* 120, No. 4 (1982): 52 – 54.

Burrows, B., and C. Edwards. *The Defence of Western Europe* (London: Butterworth, 1982).

Caldwell, L., and R. Legvold. "Regan through Soviet Eyes." *Foreign Policy*, No. 52 (Fall 1983): 3 – 21.

Canby, S., and I. Dörfer. "More Troops, Fewer Missiles." *Foreign Policy*, No. 53 (Winter 1983 – 84): 3 – 17.

Carlton, D. *Great Britain and NATO: A Parting of the Ways?* (London: International Institute for Strategic Studies [IISS] [Occasional Paper No.2], 1982).

Carver, Field Marshal Lord. "Conventional Defence of Europe" *RUSI* 128 (June 1983): 7 – 11.

Chichester, Michael. "Britain and NATO: the Case for Revision." *The World Today,* November 1982, pp. 415 – 421.

Chichester, Michael, and John Wilkinson. *The Uncertain Ally: British Defence Policy 1960 – 90* (Aldershot: Gower, 1982).

Close, Robert. *Time for Action* (Oxford: Pergamon Press, 1983).

Crozier, Brian. *Strategy for Survival* (London: Temple Smith, 1978).

Danwitz, Thomas von. "Medium-Range Nuclear Weapons and European Security." *Aussenpolitik,* 33 (1982): 203 – 212.

Dean, Jonathan. "Beyond First Use." *Foreign Policy,* No. 48 (Fall 1982): 37 – 53.

Dean, Jonathan. "Reply to 'Conventional Deterrence and Conventional Retaliation into Eastern Europe.'" *International Security* 9, No 1 (1984) 203 – 210.

*Defence without the Bomb: the Report of the Alternative Defence Commission* (London, New York: Taylor and Francis, 1983).

Denoon, David B. H. "Japan and the U.S. – The Security Agenda." *Current History* 82, No. 487 (November 1983): 353 – 356, 393 – 394.

Denoon, David B. H. "Report on Obtaining Military Technology from our Allies." Washington, DC: U.S. Department of Defense, September 15, 1984.

Deutsche Gesellschaft für Auswärtige Politik. *Nuclear Policy in Europe* (Bonn: Europe Union Verlag, 1980).

Dinter, Elmar, and Paddy Griffith. *Not over by Christmas: NATO's Central Front in World War III* (London: Anthony Bird; New York: Hippocrene, 1983).

Dunn, K., and W. Staudenmaier. "Strategy for Survival." *Foreign Policy,* No. 52 (Fall 1983): 22 – 41.

Eagleburger, L. "The Transatlantic Relationship – A Long-Term Perspective." *NATO Review* 32, No. 2 (1984): 8 – 14.

Eichenberg, R. "The Myth of Hollanditis." *International Security* 8, No. 2 (1983): 143 – 159.

Eliot, G. "Organizing the Atlantic Community: The Strategic Problem." *Proceedings of the Academy of Political Science* 23 (1949): 302 – 309.

Enthoven, A., and W. Smith. *How Much Is Enough?* (New York: Harper & Row, 1969).

Fischer, D. "Nonmilitary Defense Strategies." *C.V. Starr Center for Applied Economics Paper No. 32* (New York: New York University, March 1984).

Flynn, Gregory, ed. *The Internal Fabric of Western Security* (Totowa, NJ: Allenheld, Osmun; London: Croom Helm; for the Atlantic Institute for International Affairs, 1981).

Fox, W. T. R., and W. R. Schelling. *European Security and the Atlantic System* (New York: Columbia University Press, 1973).

Freedman, Lawrence. *Arms Control in Europe* (London: Royal Institute of International Affairs, 1981).

Freedman, Lawrence. *Britain and Nuclear Weapons* (London: Macmillan; for the Royal Institute of International Affairs, 1980).

Freedman, Lawrence. "Britain's Contribution to NATO." *International Affairs* 54 (1978): 30 – 47.

Freedman, Lawrence. "SALT II and the Strategic Balance."*The World Today* (August 1979): 315 – 323.

Freedman, Lawrence. "The Atlantic Crisis." *International Affairs* 58 (1982): 395 – 412.

Freedman, Lawrence. "The Dilemma of Theater Nuclear Arms Control." *Survival* 23, No. 1 (1981): 2 – 10.

Freedman, Lawrence. *The Evolution of Nuclear Strategy* (London: Macmillan, 1981).

Frost, Ellen L., and Angela E. Stent. "NATO's Troubles with East-West Trade." *International Security* 8, No. 1 (1983): 179 – 200.

Frye, Alton. "Nuclear Weapons in Europe: No Exit from Ambivalence." *Survival* 22, No. 3 (1980): 98 – 106.

Frye, Alton. "Strategic Build Down: A Context for Restraint." *Foreign Affairs* 62 (1983 – 84), 293 – 317.

Gallois, Pierre. "Soviet Military Doctrine and European Defence: NATO's Obsolete Concepts." *Conflict Studies*, No. 96, June 1978.

Garvey, Deborah, and Gail Picard. "Airland Battle 2000." *Military Intelligence* 9, No. 4 (1983): 6 – 10.

Golden, J. *NATO Burden-Sharing: Risks and Opportunities* (New York: Praeger Press, 1983).

Gompert, D., et al. *Nuclear Weapons and World Politics*. 1980s Project/Council on Foreign Relations (McGraw-Hill, 1978).

Gray, Colin S. "A New Debate on Ballistic Missile Defence." *Survival* 23, No. 2 (1981): 60 – 71.

Gray, Colin S. "Nuclear Strategy: A Case for a Theory of Victory." *International Security* 4, No. 1 (1979): 54 – 87.

Gray, Colin S. "Nuclear Weapons in NATO Strategy." *NATO's Fifteen Nations* 23, No. 1 (1978): 82 – 92.

Gray, Colin S. *Strategic Studies: A Critical Assessment*. Westport, CT: Greenwood Press, 1982.

Gray, Colin S. *The MX ICBM and National Security* (New York: Praeger, 1981).

Greenwood, David. "Paying for Defense: Will NATO's Strength Decline?" *NATO Review* 30, No. 2 (1982): 29 – 33.

Gregory, W. "NATO's Newest Crisis." *Aviation Week and Space Technology*, May 21, 1984, p. 13.

Gutteridge, William, ed. *European Security, Nuclear Weapons and Public Confidence* (London: Macmillan, 1982).

Gutteridge, William, and Trevor Taylor. *The Dangers of New Weapon Systems* (London: Macmillan, 1983).

Haberman, Clyde. "Japan Is Delaying Military Buildup." *New York Times*, May 13, 1984, p. 15.

Haberman, Clyde. "Japan Responds to U.S. Defense Critics." *New York Times*, January 22, 1984, p. 3.

Hagen, Lawrence S., ed. *The Crisis in Western Security* (New York: St. Martin's Press, 1982).

Hagen, Lawrence S., ed. *Twisting Arms: Political, Military and Economic Aspects of Arms Co-operation in the Atlantic Alliance* (Kingston, Ontario: Center for International Relations, 1980).

Hahn, Walter F., and Robert L. Pfaltzgraff, eds. *Atlantic Community in Crisis: A Redefinition of the Transatlantic Relationship* (New York: Pergamon Press, 1979).

Haig, Alexander M. "A Strategic American Foreign Policy." *NATO Review* 29, No. 6 (1981): 1 – 7.

Hampson, Fen L. "Groping for Technical Panaceas: The European Conventional Balance and Nuclear Stability." *International Security* 8, No. 3 (1983 – 84): 57 – 82.

Heldring, Jerome L. "Rhetoric and Reality in Dutch Foreign Policy." *The World Today*, October 1978, pp. 409 – 416.

Hoffman, S. *Gulliver's Troubles or the Setting of American Foreign Policy* (New York: McGraw-Hill, 1968).

Holst, Johan Jørgen. "Confidence-Building Measures: A Conceptual Framework." *Survival* 25, No. 1 (1983): 2 – 15.

Holst, Johan Jørgen, and Uwe Nerlich. *Beyond Nuclear Deterrence: New Aims, New Arms* (New York: Crane, Russak & Co., 1977).

Houllez, Marcel. "The Atlantic: A Broadening Ocean. General and Specific Causes of Divergences between the United States and Western Europe in the Field of East – West Relations and European Security." *Studia Diplomatica* 36 (1983): 337 – 413.

Hunter, Robert E. "What Crisis." *The Washington Quarterly* 5, No. 3 (1982): 53 – 57.

Huntington, Samuel. "Conventional Deterrence and Conventional Retaliation in Europe." *International Security* 8, No. 3 (1983 – 84): 32 – 56.

International Institute for Strategic Studies (IISS). *The Military Balance: 1983 – 84* (London: IISS, 1983).

Kaplan, Lawrence S. "NATO in the 2nd Generation." *NATO Review* 28, No. 5 (1980): 1 – 7.

Kaufman, W. *Planning Conventional Forces 1950 – 1980* (Washington, DC: Brookings Institution, 1982).

Kelley, James. "New Challenges to NATO Strategy." *Time*, April 19, 1982, p. 18.

Kennan, George. *American Diplomacy* (Chicago: University of Chicago Press, 1951).

Kennedy, G. *Burden-sharing in NATO* (New York: Holmes and Meier, 1979).

Killick, Sir John. "Is NATO Relevant to the 1980s?" *The World Today*, January 1980, pp. 4 – 10.

King-Harman, Anthony L. "NATO Strategy – A New Look." *RUSI* 129, No. 1 (1984): 26 – 29.

Kirk, G. "The Atlantic Pact and International Security." *International Organization* 3 (1949): 239 – 251.

Kissinger, H. *Nuclear Weapons and Foreign Policy* (New York: Harper, 1957).

Kissinger, H. "A Plan to Reshape NATO." *Time*, March 5, 1984, pp. 20 – 24.

Kissinger, H. *The Troubled Partnership* (New York: McGraw-Hill, 1965).

Komer, Robert W. "Looking Ahead." *The Atlantic Community Quarterly*, 17 (1979 – 80): 445 – 453.

Komer, Robert W. "The Trick Is How to Get It." *Armed Forces Journal International* 119, No. 2 (1981): 70 – 74.

Krippendorff, Ekkehart, and Volker Rittberger, eds. *The Foreign Policy of West Germany: Formation and Contents* (Beverly Hills, London: Sage Publications, 1980).

Kugler, R. L. Warsaw Pact Forces and the Conventional Military Balance in Central Europe, MS. George Washington University, May 1983.

Kyle, Deborah M. "Electronic Defense: At the Crossroads, But Gaining Momentum." *Armed Forces Journal International* 119, No. 6 (1982): 50 – 56.

Laird, M., and L. Korb. *The Problem of Military Readiness* (Washington, DC: American Enterprise Institute, 1980).

Leebart, Derek. *European Security: Prospects for the 1980s* (Toronto: Lexington Books, 1979).

Leitenberg, Milton. "The Neutron Bomb. Enhanced Radiation Warheads." *Journal of Strategic Studies* 5 (1982): 341 – 369.

Lellouche, Pierre. "Does NATO Have a Future? A European View." *The Washington Quarterly* 5, No. 3 (1982): 40 – 52.

Lellouche, Pierre. "SALT and European Security: The French Dilemma." *Survival* 22, No. 1 (1980): 2 – 6.

Lerner, D., and Raymond Aron, eds. *France Defeats EDC* (New York: Praeger, 1957).

Luck, Edward C. "The Reagan Administration's Nuclear Strategy." *Current History* 82, No. 484 (May 1983): 193, 232 – 233.

Lunn, S. *Burden-Sharing in NATO* (London: Routledge and Kegan Paul, 1983).

Luttwak, E. "How to Think about Nuclear War." *Commentary* 74, No. 2 (1982): 21 – 28.

Mahan, A. T. *The Influence of Sea Power upon History, 1660 – 1783.* 17th ed. (Boston: Little, Brown & Co., 1890).

Mako, W. *U.S. Ground Forces and the Defense of Central Europe* (Washington, DC: The Brookings Institution, 1983).

Mandelbaum, Michael. *The Nuclear Revolution: International Politics Before and After Hiroshima* (Cambridge: Cambridge University Press, 1981).

Martin, Lawrence W., ed. *Strategic Thought in the Nuclear Age* (Baltimore: Johns Hopkins University Press, 1979).

Martin, Michael L. *Warriors to Managers: The French Military Establishment since 1945* (Chapel Hill: The University of North Carolina Press, 1981).

McGeehan, Robert. "The Atlantic Alliance and the Reagan Administration." *The World Today,* July – August 1981, pp. 254 – 262.

McMahan, Jeff. *British Nuclear Weapons: For and Against* (London: Junction Books, 1981).

Mearsheimer, John J. "Maneuver, Mobile Defense and the NATO Central Front." *International Security* 6, No. 3 (1981 – 82): 104 – 122.

Mearsheimer, John J. "Precision-Guided Munitions and Conventional Deterrence." *Survival* 21, No. 2 (1979): 68 – 76.

Menaul, Stewart. "Changing Concept of Nuclear War." *Conflict Studies,* No. 125, December 1980.

Menaul, Stewart. *Countdown: Britain's Strategic Nuclear Forces* (London: Robert Hale, 1980).

Menaul, Stewart. "NATO in the Eighties: A War-Winning Strategy." *Conflict Studies,* No. 117, April 1980.

Menaul, Stewart. "SALT II: The Eurostrategic Imbalance." *Conflict Studies,* No. 104, February 1979.

Middleton, Drew. "Crisis Brings to the Fore Problems Facing NATO." *New York Times,* May 1, 1982, p. 7.

Middleton, Drew. "French Army's New Look Draws Praise." *New York Times,* July 31, 1984, p. A3.

Midleton, Drew. "NATO Strategy: Major Debate Developing." *New York Times,* March 4, 1982, p. A6.

Millar, Thomas Bruce. *The East-West Strategic Balance* (Boston: Allen & Unwin, 1981).

Mitchell, D. "Strategy and the Atlantic Pact." *Current History* 17, No. 98 (October 1949): 213 – 215.

Miyoshi, Osamu. "Toward a New U.S. – Japan Alliance: The Crucial Choices of the Eighties." *Comparative Strategy* 2 (1980): 279 – 301.

Murdoch, James C., and Todd Sandler. "Complementarity, Free Riding and the Military Expenditure of NATO Allies." *Journal of Public Economics* 25 (1984): 83 – 101.

Murdoch, James C., and Todd Sandler. "A Theoretical and Empirical Analysis of NATO." *Journal of Conflict Resolution* 26 (1982): 237 – 263.

Murray, Douglas J., and Paul R. Viotti. *The Defense Policies of Nations: A Comparative Study* (Baltimore: Johns Hopkins University Press, 1982).

Myers, A. K., ed. *NATO: The Next Thirty Years* (Boulder, CO: Westview; London: Croom Helm, for the Centre for Strategic and International Studies, 1980).

*NATO and the Warsaw Pact: Force Comparisons* (Brussels: NATO, 1982).

NATO Information Service. *NATO: Facts and Figures* (Brussels: NATO Publications, 1976).

NATO Press Service. *Financial and Economic Data Relating to NATO Defence* (Brussels: NATO [Press Release M-DPC-2(B2)24]), December 1, 1982.

Nailor, Peter, and Jonathan Alford. *The Future of Britain's Deterrent Force*. Adelphi Paper 156 (London: International Institute for Strategic Studies, 1980).

Nairn, Ronald C. "Why NATO Doesn't Work." *The Wall Street Journal*, March 26, 1982, p. 26.

Neidle, A., ed. *Nuclear Negotiations: Reassessing Arms Control Goals in U.S-Soviet Relations* (Austin: University of Texas Press, 1982).

Nott, John. "Decisions to Modernize U.K.'s Nuclear Contribution to NATO Strengthen Deterrence." *NATO Review* 29, No. 2 (1981): 1 – 5.

Okazaki, H. "Japanese Security Policy: A Time for Strategy." *International Security* 7, No. 2 (1982): 188 – 197.

Osgood, R. *Limited War: The Challenge to American Strategy* (Chicago: University of Chicago Press, 1957).

Patijn, Schelto. *General Report on the Economics of Atlantic Security* (Brussels: North Atlantic Assembly, Economic Committee, International Secretariat, [Doc. AA 172 - EC (83) 8]), November 1983.

Perlmutter, Amos, and Valerie Plave Bennet. *The Political Influence of the Military: A Comparative Reader* (New Haven, London: Yale University Press, 1980).

Pipes, R. "Why the Soviet Union Thinks It Can Fight and Win a Nuclear War." *Commentary* 64, No. 1 (1977): 21 – 34.

*RUSI & Brassey's Defence Yearbook 1984*. Ed. by RUSI (London: Brassey's Defence Publishers, 1984).

Raj, Christopher S. *American Military in Europe: Controversy over NATO Burden Sharing* (New Dehli: ABC Publishing House, 1983).

Ravenal, Earl C. "Counterforce and Alliance: The Ultimate Connection." *International Security* 6, No. 4 (1982): 26 – 43.

Raymond, George A. *Conflict Resolution and the Structure of the State System: An Analysis of Arbitrative Settlements* (Alphen aan der Rijn: Sijthoff and Noordhoff, 1981).

Reuters. "NATO Cuts Soviet Bloc Estimate." *New York Times*, June 22, 1984, p. A4.

Robinson, C. "NATO: Reshaping the Alliance – Economics, Politics Portend Shifts." *Aviation Week and Space Technology*, May 21, 1984, pp. 50 – 63.

Rogers, Bernard W. "The Atlantic Alliance: Prescriptions for a Difficult Decade." *Foreign Affairs* 60 (1982): 1145 – 1156.

Rogers, Bernard W. "Greater Flexibility for NATO's Flexible Response." *Atlantic Community Quarterly* 21 (1983): 233 – 243.

Rogers, Bernard W. "Increasing Threats to NATO's Security Call for Sustained Response." *NATO Review* 129, No. 3 (1981): 1 – 6.

Rose, François de. "Alternative Strategy for the West." *NATO's Fifteen Nations* (August/September 1982): 56 ff.

Rose, François de. "Updating Deterrence in Europe: Inflexible Response?" *Survival* 24, No. 1 (1982): 19 - 23.

Rossiter, C., and J. Lare, eds. *The Essential Lippman* (New York: Random House, 1963).

Ruehl, Lothar. "INF: Threat or Protection." *NATO's Sixteen Nations* 8, No. 8 (1983 – 84): 18 – 24.

Rupp, Rainer W. "Sharing the Defense Burden." *NATO Review* 30, No. 5 (1982): 24 – 28.

Rush, Kenneth, Brent Scowcroft, and Joseph J. Wolf. "The Credibility of the NATO Deterrent: Bringing the Deterrent up to Date – Part 1." *NATO Review* 29, No. 5 (1981): 7 – 13.

Rush, Kenneth, Brent Scowcroft, and Joseph J. Wolf. "Part 2." *NATO Review* 29, No. 6 (1981): 23 – 27.

Sandler, Todd, and John F. Forbes. "Burden Sharing, Strategy and the Design of NATO." *Economic Inquiry* 18 (1980): 425 – 444.

Satoh, Yukio. *The Evolution of Japanese Security Policy.* Adelphi Papers 178 (London: International Institute for Strategic Studies, 1982).

Schemmer, Benjamin F. "NATO's New Strategy: Defend Forward, But Strike Deep." *Armed Forces Journal International* 120, No. 3 (1982): 50 – 68.

Schmidt, Helmut. "Saving the Western Alliance." *New York Review of Books*, May 31, 1984, pp. 25 – 27.

Schultze-Rhonhof, Gerd. "Men and Machines: The Automation of the Battlefield." *NATO's Fifteen Nations* 26, No. 6 (1981 – 82): 28 – 34.

Scully, William L. *Why Japan Needs More Defense Muscle* (Washington, DC: Heritage Foundation, 1983).

Scully, William L. *The Korean Peninsula Military Balance* (Washington, DC: Heritage Foundation), July 11, 1983.

Scully, William L., and Guy M. Hicks. *Japanese Defense Policy* (Washington, DC: Heritage Foundation, 1981).

Segal, Gerald, Edwina Morton, Lawrence Freedman, and John Baylis. *Nuclear War and Nuclear Peace* (London: Macmillan, 1983).

Serfaty, Simon. "The United States and Europe." *The Washington Quarterly* 4, No. 1 (1981): 70 – 86.

Shaffer, Stephen M. "The Influence of Threat and Alliance Setting on National Defense Expenditures: NATO, 1950 – 1969." Ph.D. Diss. University of Michigan, 1975.

Shuttleworth, T. M. "NATO's Forward Defence: New Strategy." *Armed Forces*, July 1983, pp. 254 – 255.

Simpson, John. *The Independent Nuclear State: The United States, Britain and the Military Atom* (London: Macmillan, 1983).

Sloan, Stanley R. "Major Issues Facing NATO." *National Defense* 66, No. 376 (1982): 20 – 22, 47.

Smart, Ian. *The Future of the British Nuclear Deterrent: Technical, Economic, and Strategic Issues* (London: Royal Institute of International Affairs, 1977).

Smith, G. "The Legacy of Monroe's Doctrine." *New York Times Magazine*, September 9, 1984, pp. 46 ff.

Smyser, William R. *German-American Relations.* The Washington Papers, Vol. 8, No. 74 (Beverly Hills, London: Sage Publications, 1980).

Snow, Donald M. "Current Nuclear Deterrence Thinking: An Overview and Review." *International Studies Quarterly* 23 (1979): 445 – 486.

Speed, Roger D. *Strategic Deterrence in the 1980's* (Stanford: Hoover Institution Press, 1979).

Steel, R. *Pax Americana* (New York: Viking Press, 1967).

Stockholm International Peace Research Institute (SIPRI). *Tactical Nuclear Weapons: European Perspectives* (London: Taylor and Francis, 1978).

*Strengthening Conventional Deterrence in Europe: Proposals for the 1980s.* Report of the European Security Study (ESECS) (London: Macmillan, 1983).

Taylor, A. J. P. *The Origins of the Second World War* (New York: Premier Books, 1961).

Taylor, M. *The Uncertain Trumpet* (New York: Harper, 1960).

Taylor, P. "Weapons Standardization in NATO." *International Organization* 36, No. 1 (1982): 95 – 112.

Thomson, James A. "Nuclear Weapons in Europe: Planning for NATO's Nuclear Deterrent in the 1980s and 1990s." *Survival* 25, No. 3 (1983): 98 – 109.

Tornetta, Vincenzo. "The Nuclear Strategy of the Atlantic Alliance and the 'No-First-Use' Debate." *NATO Review* 30, No. 5 (1982): 1 – 7.

Traverton, Gregory F. *The Dollar Drain and American Forces in Germany: Managing the Political Economics of Alliance* (Athens, OH: Ohio University Press, 1978).

Tuchman, B. "American People and Military Power" (London: IISS, Adelphi Paper 173, Spring 1982).
Tucker, R. W. "The Nuclear Debate." *Foreign Affairs* 63 (1984): 1 – 32.
Tugendhat, Christopher. "Europe's Need for Self-Confidence." *International Affairs* 58 (1981 – 82): 7 – 12.
Turner, S., and G. Thibault. "Preparing for the Unexpected: The Need for a New Military Strategy." *Foreign Affairs* 61 (1982): 122 – 135.
United Kingdom. Parliament. Sixth Report from the Expenditure Committee. Session 1978 – 1979. *The Future of the United Kingdom's Nuclear Weapons Policy.* House of Commons Paper 348. (London: Her Majesty's Stationery Office, 1979).
Vaernø, Grethe. "The Atlantic Alliance and European Integration." *NATO Review* 26, No. 2 (1978): 23 – 39.
Van Cleave, William R., and Samuel T. Cohen. *Tactical Nuclear Weapons: An Examination of the Issues* (New York: Crane, Russak, 1978).
Wall, Sir Patrick. "What Lies Ahead for NATO." *Defense and Foreign Affairs* 10, No. 4 (1982): 60 – 61.
Weede, Erich, Dietmar Schössler, and Matthias Jung. "West German Elite Views on National Security Issues: Evidence from a 1980/1 Survey of Experts." *The Journal of Strategic Studies* 6, No. 1 (1983): 82 – 95.
Western European Union. *Burden-Sharing in the Alliance* (Document 947) (Paris: Assembly of Western European Union, 1983).
Wettig, Gerhard. "The Problem of Military Balance of Power." *Aussenpolitik* 33 (1982): 348 – 369.
Wettig, Gerhard. "The Soviet INF Data Critically Reviewed." *Aussenpolitik* 34 (1983): 30 – 42.
Wörner, Manfred. "Current Prospects for European Security." *Atlantic Community Quarterly* 21 (1983): 226 - 232.
Yost, David S. "NATO's Political Military Strategies." *Current History* 81, No. 479 (December 1982): 401 – 404, 435 – 438.
Yost, David S., ed. *NATO's Strategic Options: Arms Control and Defense* (New York, Oxford: Pergamon Press, 1981).
Yost, David S. "The French Defence Debate." *Survival* 23, No. 1 (1981), 19 – 28.
Yost, David S. "START, INF and European Security." *The World Today,* November 1983, pp. 417 – 428.
Ypersele de Strihou, Jacques van. "Sharing the Defense Burden Among Western Allies." *Review of Economics and Statistics* 49 (1967): 527 – 536.

# In French

Agnelli, Giovanni. "Le rôle du milieu des affaires dans la stratégie occidentale" [The Role Played by the Business World in Western Strategy]. *Politique Etrangère* 44 (1979): 321 – 330.
Andréani, Jacques. "L'Europe, l'OTAN et la France: les problèmes non résolus de la défense européenne" [Europe, NATO, and France: The Unsolved Problems of European Defense]. *Politique Etrangère* 48 (1983): 341 – 356.
Aurillac, Michel. "Une garantie nucléaire française pour l'Europe est-elle possible?" [Is a French Nuclear Guarantee Possible for Europe?] *Politique Etrangère* 48 (1983): 371 – 380.
Ausseur, Philippe. "La stratégie des moyens" [A Strategy of the Means] *Défense Nationale* 38 (octobre 1982): 13 – 28.

Boyer, Yves. *La politique de défense nationale en France et la nouvelle majorité* [The French National Defense Policy and the New Majority] (Geneve: Institute of International Studies, 1981).

Brigot, André. "L'Allemagne et ses différences" [Germany and its Differences] *Stratégique*, 3ème trimestre 1983, pp. 93 – 114.

Brigot, A., and Dominique David. *Le désir d'Europe: l'introuvable défense commune* [The Longing for Europe: the Elusive Common Defense] (Paris: Fondation pour les Etudes de Défense Nationale, 1980).

Close, Robert. *Encore un effort et nous aurons définitivement perdu la troisième guerre mondiale.* [One More Effort and We Certainly Will Have Lost WW III] (Paris: Belfond, 1981).

Comité Permanent des Armements (Union de l'Europe Occidentale). *L'industrie d'armement des pays membres de l'UEO* [The Armaments Industries of the Western European Union Member States]. Document SAC (82)IA-D/27, avril 1982.

David, Dominique. "La FAR en Europe: le dire des armes" [The French Rapid Strike Force in Europe: When Weapons Do the Talking] *Défense Nationale* 40 (juin 1984): 27 – 49.

Delmas, Claude. *L'OTAN* [NATO] (Paris: Presses Universitaires de France, 1981).

Denis, Jacques-Marie. "L'après-Brejnev: aspects stratégiques et diplomatiques" [The Post-Brezhnev Era: Strategic and Diplomatic Aspects]. *Défense Nationale* 39 (février 1983): 49 – 54.

Ecole Nationale d'Administration. *La défense nucléaire de la France: recherche et développement à fins militaires* [The French Nuclear Defense: R & D for Military Uses]. Cahier No. 11. (Paris: Fondation pour les Etudes de Défense Nationale, 1978).

Eylau-Wagram, Pierre. "Propositions pour une stratégie française de 1980 à 1990." [Proposals for a French Strategy in the 1980s]. *Politique Etrangère* 46 (1981): 121 – 135.

Hautefeuille, Pierre. "Etude sur défense et dissuasion nucléaires. (1ère partie)" [Study of Nuclear Defense and Deterrence. (Part 1)]. *Stratégique,* 1er trimestre 1980, pp. 81 – 113.

Hautefeuille, Pierre. "(2ème partie)" [(Part 2)], 2ème trimestre 1980, pp. 23 – 44.

Howard, Michael. "La défense occidentale dans les années 80: les conditions du consensus" [Western Defense in the 1980s: Conditions for a Consensus]. *Politique Etrangère* 48 (1983): 949 – 965.

Huntzinger, Jacques. "Défense de la France, sécurité de l'Europe" [French Defense, European Security]. *Politique Etrangère* 48 (1983): 39 – 402.

Kaiser, Karl, Lord Wiston, Thierry de Montbrial, and David Watt. *La sécurité de l'Europe: bilan et orientations* [European Security: Results and Directions]. (Paris: Economica, 1981).

Klein, Jean. "La France, l'arme nucléaire et la défense de l'Europe" [France, the Nuclear Weapon and European Defense]. *Politique Etrangère* 44 (1979): 461 – 479.

Klein, Jean. "Stratégie de non-guerre et hypothèses de conflit nucléaire" [Non-war Strategy and Hypotheses of Nuclear Conflict]. *Défense Nationale* 35 (mai 1979): 17 – 46.

Le Borgne, Claude. "Le général Rogers, l'Amérique et l'Europe" [General Rogers, the US, and Europe]. *Défense Nationale* 39 (février 1983): 25 – 32.

Lellouche, Pierre. "La France dans l'après-Pershing" [France in the Post-Pershing Period]. *Politique Etrangère* 48 (1983): 859 – 878.

Lellouche, Pierre. "La France et la politique américaine à l'égard de la sécurité de l'Europe" [France and American Policies vis-à-vis European Security]. *Politique Etrangère* 44 (1979): 481 – 497.

Lellouche, Pierre. "La France, les SALT et la sécurité de l'Europe" [France, SALT and European Security]. *Politique Etrangère* 44 (1979): 249 – 271.

Lellouche, Pierre, ed. *La Sécurité de l'Europe dans les années 80* [European Security in the 1980s] (Paris: IFRI, 1981).

Lellouche, Pierre. *Pacifisme et Dissuasion* [Pacifism and Deterrence] (Paris: IFRI, 1983).

Leman, Maurice. "Les neutrons: l'arme anti-invasion pour une défense européenne" [The Neutron Bomb: The anti-invasion Weapon for a European Defense]. *Politique Etrangère* 46 (1981): 409–425.

Lutz, Dieter S. *La guerre mondiale malgré nous? La controverse des euromissiles* [A World War in spite of ourselves? The Euromissiles Controversy] (Paris: La Découverte/Maspero, 1983).

Manel, Michel. *L'Europe sans défense* [Defenseless Europe] (Paris: Berger-Levrault, 1982).

Massigli, René. *Une comédie des erreurs, 1943 – 1956* [A Comedy of Errors: 1943 – 1956] (Paris: Plon, 1978).

Mattei, André. "Le facteur nucléaire" [The Nuclear Factor] *Politique Etrangère* 43 (1978): 675–690.

Melandri, Pierre. "L'Alliance atlantique: incertitudes stratégiques, incertitudes diplomatiques" [The Atlantic Alliance: Strategic and Diplomatic Uncertainties]. *Relations Internationales* 36 (1983): 395–413.

Monnet, Jean. *Mémoires* (Paris: Arthème Fayard, 1976).

Pigasse, Jean-Paul. *Le bouclier d'Europe* [Europe's Shield] (Paris: Seghers, 1982).

Pigasse, Jean-Paul. *Le deuxième pilier* [The Second Pillar] (Paris: Fondation pour les Etudes de Défense Nationale, 1980).

Poirier, Lucien. *Essais de stratégie théorique* [Essays in Strategy Theory] Les Sept Epées, Cahier No. 22 de la Fondation pour les Etudes de Défense Nationale, 2ème trimestre 1982, Paris.

Poirier, Lucien. "Quelques problèmes actuels de la stratégie nucléaire française" [Some Problems Presently Confronting French Nuclear Strategy] *Défense Nationale* 35 (décembre 1979): 43–62.

Robin, Gabriel. "Aux origines des désaccords transatlantiques" [At the Origin of Transatlantic Disagreements] *Politique Etrangère* 48 (1983): 933–948.

Rose, François de. *La France et l'OTAN* [France and NATO] (Paris: Seuil, 1976).

Ruehl, Lothar. "La Défense de l'Europe" [Europe's Defense]. *Politique Etrangère* 48 (1983): 27–38.

Ruehl, Lothar. *La politique militaire de la Vème République* [Military Policies of the Fifth Republic] (Paris: Presses de la Fondation Nationale des Sciences Politiques, 1976).

Ruehl, Lothar. "L'Europe sacrifiée aux accords SALT?" [Did SALT Sacrifice Europe?] *Défense Nationale* 35 (1979): 41–58.

Schmidt, Helmut. "Une stratégie pour l'Alliance" [A Strategy for the Alliance]. *Politique Etrangère* 48 (1983): 283–296.

Schutze, Walter. "Les Options" [The Options]. *Politique Etrangère* 43 (1978): 693–732.

Tatu, Michel. *La bataille des Euromissiles* [The Euromissile controversy]. Les Sept Epées, Cahier No. 29 de la Fondation pour les Etudes de Défense Nationales (Paris: Seuil, 1983).

Yochelson, John. "Nouvelles réalités de l'OTAN et politique américaine" [New NATO Realities and American Policies]. *Politique Etrangère* 44 (1979): 445–460.

# In German

Afheldt, Horst. *Defensive Verteidigung* [Defensive Defense] (Reinbeck: Rowholt, 1983).

Birnstiel, Fritz. "Die Vorneverteidigung – Kern der konventionellen NATO-Abwehr" [The Forward Defense – Core of the Conventional NATO Defense]. *Europäische Wehrkunde* 29, No. 5 (1980): 213–221.

Brady, Linda P., and Dieter Fleck. "Transatlantische militärische Zusammenarbeit in Krisenzeiten. Das deutsch-amerikanische Abkommen über die Unterstützung von US-Streitkräften in der Bundesrepublik Deutschland" [Military Transatlantic Cooperation in Times of Crisis. The German-American Agreement on the Support of U.S. Forces Stationed in West Germany]. *Europa-Archiv* 38, No. 19 (1983): 581 – 588.

Carstens, Karl, and Dieter Mahncke, eds. *Westeuropäische Verteidigungskooperation* [Western European Defense Cooperation] (Bonn: Deutsche Gesellschaft für Auswärtige Politik, 1972).

Coker, Christopher, and Heinz Schulte. "Strategiekritik und Pazifismus. Zwei Haupttendenzen in den westeuropäischen Friedensbewegungen" [Strategy Criticism and Pacifism. Two Crucial Tendencies in the West European Peace Movements]. *Europa-Archiv* 38, No.14 (1983), 413 – 420.

Ege, Konrad. "Schlachtfeld Europa. Die neue Heeresdoktrin der USA" [Battlefield Europe. The New Army Doctrine of the USA.] *Blätter für deutsche und internationale Politik*, No. 12 (1982): 1438 – 1447.

Forndran, Erhard, and Paul J. Friedrich, eds. *Rüstungskontrolle und Sicherheit in Europa* [Arms Control and Security in Europe] (Bonn: Europa Union Verlag GmbH, 1979).

Genscher, Hans-Dietrich. "Deutsche Sicherheitspolitik im nuklearen Zeitalter" [German Security in the Nuclear Age] *Europäische Wehrkunde* 33, No.2 (1984): 64 – 70.

Haftendorne, Helga. *Sicherheit und Entspannung. Zur Aussenpolitik der Bundesrepublik Deutschland, 1955 – 1982* [Security and Detente. On the Foreign Policy of West Germany, 1955-1982] (Baden-Baden: Nomos Verlagsgesellschaft, 1983).

Hoffman, G. "Vom Störfaktor zum Machtfaktor" [From Element of Trouble to Element of Power]. *Die Zeit* 5. Oktober 1984, p. 3.

Holst, Johan Jørgen. "Nukleare Mittelstreckenwaffen und das politische Gleichgewicht in Europa" [Nuclear Medium-range Weapons and the Political Balance in Europe]. *Europa-Archiv* 38, No. 17 (1983): 507 – 516.

Holst, Johan Jørgen. "Verteidigungsplanung und europäische Sicherheitspolitik. Das Spektrum potentieller Konflikte" [Defense Planning and European Security. The Specter of Potential Conflicts]. *Europa-Archiv* 33, No. 10 (1978): 281 – 289.

Hubatschek, Gerhard. "Die 'deutsche Frage' als ein Kernproblem der Friedensordnung in Europa" [The 'German Question' as Crucial to Maintaining Peace in Europe] *Europäische Wehrkunde* 33, No. 4 (1984): 209 – 215.

Kaiser, Karl. "Keine Alternative zur nuklearen Abschreckung" [No Alternative to Nuclear Deterrence]. *Europäische Wehrkunde* 33, No. 5 (1984): 273 – 278.

Krell, Gert, and Hans-Joachim Schmidt. *Der Rüstungswettlauf in Europa: Mittelstreckensysteme, konventionelle Waffen, Rüstungskontrolle* [The Arms Race in Europe: Medium-Range Systems, Conventional Weapons, Arms Control] (Frankfurt, New York: Campus Verlag, 1982).

Lauk, Kurt J. *Die nuklearen Optionen der Bundesrepublik Deutschland* [The Nuclear Options of the Federal Republic of Germany] (Berlin: Duncker und Humboldt, 1979).

Pasti, Nino. "Politisch-militärische und biologisch-medizinische Gefahren der Neutronbombe" [Political/Military and Biological/Medical Dangers of the Neutron Bomb] *Blätter für deutsche und internationale Politik*, No. 1 (1979): 27 – 36.

Rodejohann, Jo. "Militärische Aspekte der Auseinandersetzung um die Neutronwaffen (ERW): eine Zwischenbilanz" [Military Aspects of the ERW Agreement: A Provisional Evaluation]. *Blätter für deutsche und internationale Politik*, No. 8 (1978): 926 – 937.

Ruehl, Lothar. "Das Salt-II-Abkommen und die europäischen Interessen" [Salt II and European Interests]. *Europa-Archiv* 34, No. 15 (1979): 461 – 472.

Ruehl, Lothar. "Die Auswirkungen von Salt-2 auf Europa" [The Impact of Salt-II on Europe]. *Europäische Wehrkunde* 27, No. 12 (1978): 618 – 623.

Ruehl, Lothar. "Die Nichtentscheidung über die 'Neutronwaffen.' Ein Beispiel verfehlter Bündnispolitik" [The Non-Decision Concerning the Neutron Bomb; An Instance of Failed Alliance Policy]. *Europa-Archiv* 34, No. 5 (1979): 137 – 150.

Schwarz, Klaus-Dieter, ed. *Sicherheitspolitik. Analysen zur politischen und militärischen Sicherheit* [The Politics of Security: Political and Military Aspects] 3rd ed. (Bad Honnef-Erpel: Osang Verlag, 1978).

Uhle-Wetter, Franz. *Gefechtsfeld Mitteleuropa: Gefahr der Übertechnisierung von Streitkräften* [Battlefield Central Europe: Dangers of Excessive Reliance on Technology for the Armed Forces] (Munich: Bernard & Graefe, 1980).

Voigt, Karsten D. "Das Risiko eines begrenzten Nuklearkrieges in Europa. Zur Diskussion über die westliche Militärdoktrin und den NATO-Doppelbeschluss vom Dezember 1979." [The Risk of a Limited Nuclear War in Europe. The Western Military Doctrine and the Coupling Decision of December 1979]. *Europa-Archiv* 37, No. 6 (1982): 151 – 160.

Williams, Phil. "Grossbritannien am Scheideweg. Grenzen der Finanzbarkeit der Verteidigung und die ungesicherte Zukunft der NATO" [Great Britain at the Crossroads. Limits to the Ability to Finance Defense, and the Uncertainty of NATO's Future]. In *Sicherheit – zu Welchem Preis?*, Wolf Dieter Eberwein and Catherine M. Kelleher, eds. (München: Olzog Verlag, 1983), pp. 177 – 198.

Wörner, Manfred. "Das wertlose Ja zur Nato" [The Worthless Yes to NATO]. *Der Spiegel* 4. Juni 1984, pp. 42 – 43.

# Index

Alliance cohesion, 2, 9-10, 208-211, 213-214
Arms control, 4
Atlantic Alliance, 114

Battlefield extension, 214
"Benoit effect," 130-132, 146
Benoit, Emile, 127, 130
Brown, Harold, 213
Burden sharing
　analytical analyses, 87-105
　behaviors, 59-63
　descriptive analysis of, 87-90
　military, 8-10, 13-14, 59-113, 141-143, 196
Business cycles, 37-38

Campaign for Nuclear Disarmament (CND), 85
Capacity utilization rates, 43-44, 46-47
Carter, James Earl, 7
CENTO, 8
China
　relations with Japan, 165
　relations with U.S., 3, 165, 216-217
Civilian industries, 30
CND. *See* Campaign for Nuclear Disarmament
Consumer Price Index, U.S., 47
Crowding out effect, 38, 43-45, 52-54, 84
Culver/Nunn Amendment, 7

Deep interdiction, 6, 214, 216
Defense expenditures
　Japan, 164-171
　Northern European allies
　　analytical analyses, 90-108
　　demand equation for, 90-91, 94-95
　　employment effects, 48-51
　　growth forecasts, 105-108
　South Korea, 159, 171-174
　　estimates, 181-188
　　projections, 181-191
　Southern Tier countries
　　and capital formation, 130-132, 144-145
　　determinants, 125-127, 132-140
　　diversionary *vs.* stimulative effects of, 130-132
　　effects on economic growth, 127-140
　　effects on investment, 128-129, 146-148
　　projections, 140-143
　United States, 196
　　on aggregate demand, 38
　　alternative programs, 27-28, 36-38
　　controversies, 28-31, 201
　　deflator, 47-48
　　demand effects of, 41-43
　　determinants, 31-33
　　and the federal deficit, 38-41
　　increases, 27-58
　　and investment accounts, 34
　　macroeconomic factors, viii, 14-15, 28, 38-45
　　microeconomic effects of, 15-16
　　sectoral and regional effects, 28, 45-52
　　spin-off effects, viii
　　and taxation, 41
Defense industry studies, 15-16

Defense policy, U.S., 4
  and economic constraints, 195–221
  strategic options, 211–218
Defense-sensitive industries, 45–46, 47–52
Defense–welfare trade-off, 84–87
Deficit
  Japan, 153–159, 177
  South Korean, 159–164
  U.S., 36–38, 43, 199–201
    and aggregate demand, 44, 52
    and defense spending, 38–41, 52
    impact of budget, 82–83
    and imports, 41
    projections, 39–40
    trade, 199–200
DeGaulle, Charles, 214
DEIMS. *See* Domestic Economic Impact Model Simulator
Deindustrialization process
  in the United Kingdom, 81–82
Demand for military expenditures
  cross-sectional analysis, 95–99
  equation, 94–95
  time-series analysis, 99–105
Deregulation, 38, 200
d'Estaing, Giscard, 198, 214
Détente, 4–5, 209
Deterrence, 198, 209–211, 216
Domestic Economic Impact Model Simulator (DEIMS), 15
Dynamic costs, 181–188, 207

Economic performance definitions, 68
Economic pragmatism, 209
EEC. *See* European Economic Community
Employment, U.S., 13, 15, 27
  and defense expenditures, 48–51
Energy costs, 7, 47–48, 63
Eureka. *See* European Research Coordination Agency
Europe
  geopolitical advantages, 197
  political factors, 197
  strategic advantages, 197–198
  and U.S. defense policy, 196

European Common Market, 215
European Economic Community (EEC), 117–118, 122, 125, 205–206
European Research Coordination Agency (Eureka), 214

Fabius, Laurent, 77, 203
Fixed-percent target rate, 63
Flexible response, doctrine of, 93–94, 100, 104, 106, 108, 218
France
  analytical analyses, 87–108
  arms industries, 64–65
    austerity program, 78
  burden-sharing, 64–65, 87–108
  defense growth forecasts, 105–108
  demand equation for, 90–91, 94–95
  economic analysis, 59, 67–70, 199
  economic policies, 65, 75–79, 202–204
  employment, 48–51
  energy requirements, 78
  gross domestic product, 77, 202
  gross national product, 202
  growth predictions, 62, 82, 83, 104–105
  inflation, 78
  military expenditures, 60–62, 65, 86–87, 198, 202–204
  Ninth Plan, 77
  response to spillins, 104–105
  strategic forces, 64
  unemployment, 67, 78–79
Free rider hypothesis, 13–14, 62, 91–94, 99–100, 106, 114, 115, 127, 137, 140, 145, 206, 215–216, 217
Frontal aviation, 3

GDP. *See* Gross domestic product
General Purpose forces, U.S., 32
General System of Preferences (GSP), 19
GLCM. *See* Ground Launched Cruise Missiles
GNP. *See* Gross national product

# INDEX

Gonzales, Felip, 122, 215
Greece
  as free rider, 115, 127, 145, 206
  burden sharing, 141–143
  defense projections, 140–143
  defense spending, 204–206
  defense spending determinants, 132–140
  defense spending effects, 128–132
  economic outlook, 117–118
  economic performance, 204–206
  geographic importance of, 115, 140, 205
  gross domestic product, 206
  growth rates, 145–146
  historic trends, 117–118
  investment effects, 128–132, 146–148
  resource allocation behavior, 115, 135, 140
Greens, the, 84
Gross domestic product (GDP), 59–60, 62, 64, 67–77, 87–89, 90–92
  in France, 77, 202
  in NATO's fringe, 116, 126
  in United States, 201
Gross national product (GNP), 11, 13, 29, 32–33, 39, 43, 54, 199
  in France, 202
  U.S. forecasts, 36–37, 42
  West German, 79–80
Ground Launched Cruise Missiles (GLCM), 5, 198, 210
GSP. *See* General System of Preferences
"Guns versus butter," 12–13, 14, 64, 143–144

HNS. *See* Host nation support
Host nation support (HNS), 213

IMF. *See* International Monetary Fund
Income elasticity measures, 63, 101–105, 108–109
Index of threat, 31–32
INF. *See* Intermediate-range Nuclear Force

Inflation, 13, 15, 30–31, 33
  and defense spending, 51–52
  in France, 78
  in the United Kingdom, 81–82
  and the U.S. deficit, 39, 40
  U.S. projections, 37, 42–43
Information-based technology, 37–38
Interest rates, 37, 41, 43, 44, 53
  U.S. projections, 42–43
  West German, 79–81
Intermediate-range Nuclear Force (INF), 1–6
International Monetary Fund (IMF), 9, 212
  and Portugal, 125, 141, 206
Investment/consumption, 143–144
Iran, American hostages in, 1, 17

Japan
  as free rider, 217
  Defense Agency, 173, 188
  defense estimates, 181–191
  defense expenditures, 164–171, 178, 206–208
  defense policies, 164–171
  deficit, 153–156, 177
  economic background, 153–159, 206–208
  economic growth prospects, 174–179
  foreign trade, 156–157, 170
  gross domestic product, 152, 154, 191
  gross national product, 165, 174, 176–177, 186–191, 207
  investment rate, 154
  Komeito, 191
  Liberal Democrats, 17, 190
  manpower levels, 178–179
  Medium-Term Defense Program Estimate, 188–191
  National Defense Program Outline, 4
  relations with China, 165
  Socialist Party, 190–191
  taxation, 162, 178
  unemployment, 178
  U.S. relations, 3

Kennan, George, 8
Kissinger, Henry, 7, 215

Labor costs
  Northern European allies', 67-75
  in United Kingdom, 71
  in United States, 47-48
  in West Germany, 79
LaFontaine, Oscar, 197
Lend-Lease bill, 7
Limited war, 88
Lindahl process, 134, 136-138, 140, 145
Lippmann, Walter, 8
Long-term defense program (LTDP), 5, 213
LTDP. *See* Long-term defense program

Macroeconomics, 38-45, 199, 204
MAD. *See* Mutual Assured Destruction
Manpower levels, 30, 32, 50, 211-212
  in West Germany, 198
Maritime strategy, U.S., 217-218
Marshall Plan, 8, 11
Military credibility, 208-209
Military tactics, problems of, 2
Monroe Doctrine, 7, 217
Mutual Assured Destruction (MAD), 93, 99-100
Mutual Security Treaty, 173

Nash-Cournot process, 134-140, 145
Nationalization
  French, 75-76
  Greek, 205
  Portuguese, 124, 205
NATO. *See* North Atlantic Treaty Organization
Net investment rates, 66-83
North Atlantic Treaty Organization (NATO), viii, 2, 18
  burden sharing behavior, 59-62
  changes in strategy, 6
  defense outlays, vii, 29, 32, 143, 196, 212
  division of labor, 7, 215-216
  expansion of forces, 5
  military goals, 8
  Mutual Assured Destruction, 93, 99-100
  Nuclear Planning Group, 88
  Warsaw Pact balance, 3, 6, 101, 140, 148-149, 195-196, 211-212
Nunn Amendment, 7

Occupational distribution, and U.S. defense spending, 48-51
Oil prices, 77, 95, 100-101, 108, 202, 204-205, 211
Ozal, Turgut, 120

Pacific Treaty Organization, 217
Papandreou, Andreas, 205, 215
Peace movement, 84-85
Pershing II, 5, 84, 88, 198, 210
Polaris submarine, 64
Portugal
  burden sharing, 141-143
  defense projections, 140-143
  defense spending, 204-206
  defense spending determinants, 132-140
  defense spending effects, 129-132
  economic outlook, 125-127
  economic performance, 204-206
  as free rider, 116, 127, 140, 145, 206
  geographic importance of, 115, 205
  gross domestic product, 205-206
  growth rates, 145-146
  historic trends, 116, 123-125
  International Monetary Fund, 125, 141, 206
  resource allocation behavior, 115, 135, 140
"Program for Economic Recovery," U.S., 33-36
Public goods theory, 12, 91-92, 136, 140

Rationalization, stabilization, and interoperability (RSI), 6, 213
Reagan, President Ronald, 6-7, 201
Real-time target identification, 6

INDEX 249

Recession, United Kingdom, 81-82, 83
Regional impacts, of U.S. defense spending, 51-52
Remote sensing technology, 6, 16
Resource allocation behavior, 115, 127, 143
  analytical models of, 128-129
  cooperative processes, 137-140
  Greece, 115, 135, 140
  Lindahl process, 134, 136-138, 140, 145
  Nash-Cournot process, 134-140, 145
  Portugal, 115, 135, 140
  Spain, 115
Rogers, Bernard, 3, 5
RSI. *See* Rationalization, stabilization, and interoperability

SALT I Accords, 2-3, 4-5, 210
Schmidt, Helmut, 5, 210-211, 214
SDI. *See* Strategic Defense Initiative
SEATO, 8
Sectoral output growth, U.S., 45-46, 53
Security threat, to Southern Tier nations, 126-127, 137
SEE. *See* State Economic Enterprises
Signal processing, 6, 16
SIPRI. *See* Stockholm International Peace Research Institute
Social Democratic Party (West German), 5
South Korea
  defense estimates, 175-185
  defense policies, 171-174
  defense spending, 161, 175-185, 206-208
  deficit, 162-163
  economic background, 159-164, 171, 206-208
  economic growth prospects, 179-181
  foreign trade, 159-160, 163, 180
  gross domestic product, 152, 207
  gross national product, 172, 179-180, 207
  investment levels, 160, 180
  labor costs, 175
  and North Korea, 171-174
  manpower levels, 180
  taxation, 162, 180
Soviet Union (U.S.S.R.)
  defense spending, 35, 63
  invasion of Afghanistan, 1, 17
Space weapons, 4, 6
Spain
  burden sharing, 141-143
  defense spending, 204-206
  defense spending determinants, 132-140
  defense spending effects, 129-132
  economic outlook, 123
  economic performance, 204-206
  energy costs, 122
  as free rider, 115, 127, 145, 206
  geographic importance of, 115, 205
  gross domestic product, 205-206
  growth rates, 145-146
  historic trends, 116-117, 121-123
  labor costs, 121
  resource allocation behavior, 115
Spillin elasticity measures, 62, 93, 99-108
Star Wars. *See* Strategic Defense Initiative (SDI)
START. *See* Strategic Arms Reduction Talks
State Economic Enterprises (SEEs), 119, 120-121
Static costs, 181-188, 207
Stevens Amendment, 7
Stockholm International Peace Research Institute (SIPRI), 64, 99
Strategic arms, 1, 4, 5
  and NATO allies, 64
Strategic Arms Reduction Talks (START), 4
Strategic bombing, 8
Strategic Defense Initiative (SDI), 6-7, 201, 209-210, 214

Taxation, U.S., 43-45, 54, 200
Taylor, Maxwell, 218
Thatcher, Margaret, 203

Thinning, 92, 108
Thurow, Lester, 15
Trade balances
　French, 78
　Northern European allies', 66–75
　United States, 13, 15
Transfer mechanism, U.S., 30, 52
Treaty of Mutual Cooperation and
　　Security, 166, 190–191
Treaty of Versailles, 7
Trident submarines, 64, 87, 198, 215
Turkey
　burden sharing, 141–143
　defense projections, 140–143
　defense spending, 204–206
　defense spending determinants,
　　132–140
　defense spending effects, 129–132
　economic outlook, 120–121
　economic performance, 204–206
　as free rider, 115, 127, 145, 206
　geographic importance of, 115, 140,
　　205
　gross domestic product, 204–206
　growth rates, 145–146
　historic trends, 116, 119–121
　resource allocation behavior, 115,
　　135, 140
Turkey-Greece relations, 126

Unemployment, 41–43
　in France, 67, 78–79
　in Japan, 178
　in the United Kingdom, 74–75, 81,
　　203
　in West Germany, 70–74, 79
　U.S. forecasts, 36–37, 199
United Kingdom
　arms industries, 64–65
　burden sharing, 65, 87–108
　defense growth forecasts, 105–108
　economic analysis, 59, 74–75, 76,
　　199
　economic policies, 65, 81–82,
　　202–204
　gross domestic product, 203

growth predictions, 62, 81–82
inflation, 81, 203
labor costs, 74
military expenditures, 60, 61, 63, 65,
　86–87, 202–204
recession, 80
response to spillins, 104–105
strategic forces, 64
unemployment, 74–75, 81, 203
United States
　alliance cohesion, 208–211, 213–214
　alliance problems, 7–10, 13,
　　143–145, 208–211
　alliances and key events, 20–21
　autonomy, 217–218
　China relations, 3, 165, 216–217
　Consumer Price Index, 47
　defense spending, 1, 199–201
　economic issues, 10
　economic outlook, 36–38, 52
　economic performance, 199–201
　labor costs, 47–48
　maritime strategy, 217–218
　military capabilities, 1
　Pacific alliances, 216–217
　sectoral output growth, 45–46, 53
　strategic options, 211–218
　taxation, 43–45, 54, 200
　unemployment, 36–37, 199
U.S.-Japan Security Treaty, 11
U.S.S.R. *See* Soviet Union

Warsaw Pact, 3, 6, 9, 18, 92, 114, 140,
　195–196
　and NATO, 148–149, 208, 211–212
　military advances, 11
　military expenditures, 31–32, 101,
　　126, 136, 206
Welfare-defense trade-off. *See*
　Defense-welfare trade-off
West Germany
　arms industries, 64–65
　burden sharing, 65, 87–105
　defense growth forecasts, 105–108
　deficit, 72–74

economic analysis, 59, 71-74, 199
economic policies, 65, 79-81, 202-204
gross domestic product, 202-204
gross national product, 79-80
growth predictions, 62, 79-81
interest rates, 80
labor costs, 80
manpower levels, 198
military expenditures, 59-62, 64, 65, 86-87, 202-204
response to spillins, 104-105
unemployment, 70-74, 79
Western alliance. *See* United States alliances
World Bank, 9, 172

# About the Editor and Contributors

*David Denoon* received his B.A. from Harvard University, his M.P.A. from Princeton University, and his Ph.D. from the Massachusetts Institute of Technology. He is the editor of *The New International Economic Order: A U.S. Response,* author of *Devaluation Under Pressure: India, Indonesia, and Ghana,* and has authored articles dealing with economic development and national security. He is Associate Professor of Politics and Economics at New York University. He was vice president of the U.S. Export – Import Bank (1978 – 1979) and Deputy Assistant Secretary of Defense (1981 – 1982).

## THE CONTRIBUTORS

*Kevin Forbes* received his Ph.D. from the University of Maryland and is currently an Assistant Professor of Economics at the Catholic University of America. His research interests include defense economics, budget deficits and growth, and models of oligopoly.

*David Galenson* received his B.A. and his Ph.D. from Harvard University. He is Associate Professor of Economics at the University of Chicago, a Research Associate at the National Bureau of Economic Research, and an Alfred Sloan Research Fellow. He is the author of the following books: *White Servitude in Colonial America: An Economic Analysis,* Cambridge University Press, 1981; *Traders, Planters, and Slaves: Market Behavior in Early English America,* Cambridge University Press, 1985.

*Walter Galenson* received his B.A. and his Ph.D. from Columbia University. He is Jacob Gould Schurman Professor Emeritus, Cornell University. He is the author of the following books: *Labor Productivity in Soviet and American Industry,* Columbia University Press, 1955; *The Chinese Economy Under Communism,* Aldine Press, 1969. He is editor of *Economic Growth and Structural Change in Taiwan,*

Cornell University Press, 1979; *Foreign Trade and Investment: The Newly Industrializing Asian countries,* University of Wisconsin Press, 1985.

*George Korsun* is completing his Ph.D. at the University of Maryland. His major research interests include strategic behavior in economic clubs and dynamic models of public goods allocation.

*Martin McGuire* received his undergraduate degrees from the United States Military Academy and Oxford University, and his Ph.D. from Harvard University. He is the author of *Secrecy and the Arms Race* and articles in the area of defense economics, public-good resource allocation processes, and intra-governmental grants.

*James Murdoch* received his Ph.D. from the University of Wyoming and is currently Chairman of the Department of Economics and Finance at Northeast Louisiana University. His articles have been in such fields as strategic behavior, public policy, and conflict resolution.

*M.I. Nadiri* received his Ph.D. from the University of California, Berkeley and has taught at Berkeley, Northwestern University, and Columbia University in addition to his present position as Jay Gould Professor of Economics at New York University. His articles and books have been in such fields as technological change, productivity growth, investment theory, and applied econometrics.

*Todd Sandler* received his Ph.D. from the State University of New York at Binghamton, and has taught at The University of York, the University of Wyoming, and the University of South Carolina prior to his present position as Professor of Economics at Iowa State University. He has published in such areas as strategic behavior, public choice theory and economic factors influencing defense policy. In addition to previous books, he has a co-authored, forthcoming book, *The Theory of Externalities, Public Goods and Club Goods.*

RAYMOND H. FOGLER LIBRARY
**DATE DUE**